THE MANAGEMENT OF STRUGGLE

Elements of Dispute Resolution Through Negotiation, Mediation, and Arbitration

SCA Applied Communication Publication Program

Gary L. Kreps, Editor
Northern Illinois University

The SCA Program in Applied Communication supports the Speech Communication Association mission of promoting the study, criticism, research, teaching, and application of artistic, humanistic, and scientific principles of communication. Specifically, the goal of this publication program is to develop an innovative, theoretically informed, and socially relevant body of scholarly works that examine a wide range of applied communication topics. Each publication clearly demonstrates the value of human communication in addressing serious social issues and challenges.

THE MANAGEMENT OF STRUGGLE

Elements of Dispute Resolution Through Negotiation, Mediation, and Arbitration

John W. (Sam) Keltner
Consulting Associates

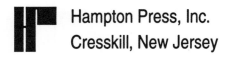
Hampton Press, Inc.
Cresskill, New Jersey

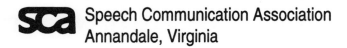
Speech Communication Association
Annandale, Virginia

Printed in the United States of America

Second printing 1997

Library of Congress Cataloging-in-Publication Data

Keltner, John W.
        The management of struggle : elements of dispute resolution
through negotiation, mediation, and arbitration / John W. (Sam)
Keltner.
                p.   cm. – (The Speech Communication Association/Hampton Press
applied communication program)
        Includes bibliographical references and index.
        ISBN 1-881303-43-8
        1. Conflict management. 2. Mediation. 3. Arbitration and award.
        I. Title. II. Series.
HD42.K45   1992
658.4–dc20   92-39491
                                                                                                                        CIP

Hampton Press, Inc.
23 Broadway
Cresskill, NJ 07626

To Maria

Contents

//

Preface

Since I was in secondary school I have been concerned about peace, what it is, and the methods whereby it can be achieved. My early efforts in peace oratory gave way to more sophisticated processes as I demonstrated, attended teach-ins and workshops, and sought means to blunt the destruction of uncontrolled struggle. Although negotiation was a basic process it was not until 1957 that I came face to face with the practical process of mediation.

That year I contracted with the Federal Mediation and Conciliation Service to provide some training to federal labor-management mediators in communication, problem solving and group processes. During those training projects I became acquainted with most of the mediators in the FMCS as well as many of the administrative personnel. A whole new concept of dispute management emerged for me from these contacts and from the incredibly realistic demonstrations that the mediators provided. I became very excited about the process as a significant tool in managing the struggle between people and groups.

I was so intrigued with the process that in 1958 I left the academic world and became a full-time mediator-in-training with the FMCS. What followed was an intense and exciting year of training that changed my life. I discovered that mediators are not measured by academic degrees, titles, certificates, or other superficial tags. They are judged for what they can do. Some of my most helpful tutors were seasoned mediators who had not graduated from secondary school but who had exquisite mediation skills.

After that year of training I became a journeyman mediator with humility and an intense desire to learn more about the process by doing it. Later I became the training officer for FMCS and worked with all the mediators in exploring their processes and developing their skills. This was a significant period of training and development for me. As a trainer of professional mediators I sought the advice and knowledge of those experienced practitioners whose daily lives were filled with facilitating the resolution of disputes. I sought information and experience that was nontheoretical and dealt with the realities of the processes. I collected from the mediators in the FMCS a large array of the procedures they used in handling disputes, many of which helped me in functioning as a journeyman mediator.

When I returned to academic life it was with a strong desire to put to use some of the practical learning that I had acquired with the FMCS. I began to include ideas on conflict management in my work and writing on interpersonal communication and eventually designed and provided course work in conflict management and mediation.

After leaving the FMCS it was natural for me to add the work of arbitration in labor-management disputes to my skills in mediation. It was an entirely different process, but many of its roots are found in mediation. I have continued both functions in my professional practice and have branched out beyond the labor-management arena to many other areas of struggle, such as family mediation, divorce and child custody, commercial, neighborhood dispute resolution programs, interpersonal disputes, intra- and interagency struggles, and so forth. The negotiation process has been part of my life since the beginning. It has been a basic tool in the everyday process of growing up, department administration, teaching and training, conducting a consulting business, and dealing with the affairs of living.

Throughout all these years I have sought greater understanding of and skill in the processes of dispute prevention and resolution. I have discovered that it is a complicated and delicate process. Skill in it requires a great deal of preparation and training. My most valuable training was "on the job" under the guidance of seasoned mediators who had many years of experience. As I develop courses and training projects in dispute resolution this information, plus my own experience as a mediator, arbitrator, and negotiator, has a profound influence on the design of those courses and training projects.

The core of this book, therefore, is based on actual experiences and is backed up with some of the research and writing that confirms these experiences. The book is not designed as a theoretical essay. It is designed to provide information and opportunities for all persons who want to know more about the process of managing struggle and particularly those who are willing to engage in the experiences necessary to learn how to do it.

There is no age prerequisite for becoming skilled in negotiation, mediation, and/or arbitration. The more people who learn about the processes and who are willing to go through the discipline of learning how to perform them the greater the possibility that the destructive phases of struggle in our society can be prevented or de-escalated.

This book is an expansion of a quite successful book published by the Speech Communication Association in 1987 titled *Mediation: Toward a Civilized System of Dispute Resolution.* It is my hope that this book will be used as a manual, a text, and a reference. Most of all I hope that this book may facilitate more effective use of the peacemaking skills that it explores. From the single dispute between wife and husband to the struggles between nations I believe the dispute resolution skills explored in this book are vital to a world that seeks peace.

John (Sam) Keltner,
December 1993

Acknowledgments

I owe a great debt of gratitude to the many professionals in the Federal Mediation & Conciliation Service who shared their experience and patiently guided me as I sought to become a mediator. Many students have contributed to my understanding of the ways to facilitate their grasp of the dispute resolution processes.

The Speech Communication Association and its executive director and publications staff encouraged me to pursue this expansion of the basic work published in 1987. I am also indebted to Gary Kreps, the Editor of the Applied Communication Publications Program, and to Barbara Bernstein of Hampton Press, for their editorial assistance and support.

Most of all I wish to recognized the many clients who, in their way, contribute significantly to my understanding and skill in mediation, arbitration, and the management of struggle.

CHAPTER 1

//

The Struggle Spectrum

INTRODUCTION

Look around you and notice the number of people involved in what are called "fights," "conflicts," "disputes," "arguments," or "disagreements." You will discover, if you look close, that all of us are involved in some kind of struggle a good part of the time. Struggle exists in all of our worlds as an inherent process. It is ubiquitous, that is, it is everywhere.

For many years people talked about the necessity to eliminate "conflict" as a means of making decisions. The principal effort seems based on the idea that if we could eliminate conflict we could save the world. But that doesn't seem at all realistic.

In the first place, there are such wide variations in our perception of conflict that we hardly know what we really wish to eliminate. In a recent workshop with a mixed audience of educators, business executives, church officers, and government officials, I began by asking each to define what conflict means. The resulting collection of definitions ranged all the way from mild disagreements to a shooting war. I believe this is characteristic of the general population. Conflict has become an ambiguous word, referring to mild disagreement as well as to more violent forms of fighting. To some conflict is a desirable and natural state of affairs, to others it is a violent and destructive process that should be eliminated.

Therefore, in this book instead of the term conflict I want to use, as much as possible, the term "struggle." Conflict seems much too restrictive and negative in its general implications, and it has many contradictory implications and referents in our society. Because of these wide variances in perception and usage, *I intend to use the term "struggle" to apply to all those situations in which people alone or in groups are in disagreement with each other or operating in opposition to each other.*

These situations and conditions range from mild forms of disagreement, as I shall demonstrate shortly, to violent and destructive forms of interaction between people and their social-political entities. I shall, for the most part, use the term conflict to *refer only to those struggle behaviors that are destructive of people, resources, and so on.* I intend to use the term struggle to *refer to the whole spectrum of behaviors and situations in which people find themselves differing with each other, including violent behaviors.* (Although this may seem to be substituting one abstract word for another, the purpose is to use a term which is deliberately more abstract and which will allow us to define the subspecies of struggle more explicitly.)

Struggle is a term which represents the act of striving against some form of resistance much like pushing against a door that is sticking, as well as trying to overcome social or political patterns that inhibit us, as in trying to breach a police line or trying to push the military enemy back. It represents the fundamental effort to move away from or change the status quo or to sustain one's immediate position against efforts to alter it.

The precursors to violent and destructive struggle (conflict) are found within us and in the interactions with others as we seek to cope with conditions that resist and oppose our immediate and long term goals, direction, or status quo. For the sake of clarity, we will view conflict as only that advanced form of struggle in which the threads of the relationship between the parties take on a more polarized state of being and forms of physical and psychological violence become characteristic of the process.

Struggle is ubiquitous. It is natural and unavoidable in human affairs. We are all engaged in various phases and forms of struggle most of the time. Our struggles range from intrapersonal struggles as in cognitive dissonance; to interpersonal struggles with others; to intergroup struggles between our reference groups; to struggles among societies, cultures, and nations.

Thus, rather than eliminate struggle, we should manage it so that it does not become destructive. In recent years many have abandoned their efforts to develop methods and theories of conflict elimination. In place of this, research and speculation now aim at developing theories and practical methods of controlling and managing conflict and struggle in creative ways. We must make a place in our society for forms of managed struggle.

Resolving struggle at any phase requires problem solving of one kind or another. Solving struggle problems demands viable (capable of growth) and versatile skills in the management and use of problem-solving strategies. Among these skills is the development and use of strategies that lead to optimal results or just "good enough" results (see Janis & Mann, 1977). These strategies are closely related to the goals we seek in resolving differences.

There are many values that arise from the process of struggle. Among the positive values are such things as increased cohesion within groups, stimulation of creative activity by individuals, increased perceptions of self and others, strengthening the tools of interaction, positive change, and so forth. Managing struggle should retain the positive values, while protecting us from negative values such as bigotry, selfishness, and the destructive results of violence from struggles gone rampant.

Danger comes from our inability to confront struggle realistically and cope with it practically and creatively. Too many of us run and hide when we see a struggle brewing and escalating into its more destructive form. Many of us are unable to recognize the significance and possible danger of a minor struggle left unresolved. Not enough of us seek an integrative style of behavior which would allow us to cope with the struggle and control it so that it doesn't become harmful or destructive. Not many of us know about or are able to apply *preventive* and *interventive* processes in the management of struggle.

Resorting to overpowering force is one way to terminate a struggle. But when we come to this resort we have failed in our attempts to manage a struggle peacefully.

Peace, by the way, does not mean the absence of struggle! It means the management of affairs, including the whole range of struggle, in such a way that there is not destruction of the human condition and potential.

The failure to manage the struggles in Viet Nam, the Middle East, Africa, India, Europe, and Central America short of destructive force are painful examples of our attempts, nationally and internationally, at handling dangerous levels of struggle constructively and peacefully. Our failure to cope constructively with intrapersonal, interpersonal, intergroup, economic, social, political, and organizational struggle is further evidence of our extensive incapacity.

Struggle management is possible for skilled and sensitive people who do not avoid struggle and who are able to live with the realities of human existence. Managed struggle is not available to people who avoid confrontation with the issues or who refuse to de-escalate the destructive trends of some struggles.

> *The violence in many distressed neighborhoods in large cities of the U.S. has escalated into more violent levels from disagreements over space, noise, cleanliness, resources, recognition, and a host of other issues that have been avoided and ignored by political, private, and social agencies, and leaders who refused to confront the problems.*

Managed struggle is also unavailable to people who are preoccupied with everybody "winning" in a society in which win-lose is a fundamental characteristic of the system. We need much work on learning how to lose well and how to "win" nondestructively.

THE STRUGGLE SPECTRUM

> *Jack and Jane were just returning home from work and as they entered the kitchen of their apartment, Jane threw her jacket over the back of one of the chairs and with a big sigh said, " I know it's my turn but I don't feel like cooking tonight, Jack. Could we go out to dinner?" Jack went into the living room, plopped down with some*
> *(continued)*

> *exhaustion into an easy chair and said with approval, "That's a good idea. You deserve a break and I'm tired too. Where shall we go?"*
>
> *"Hmmm, I think I'd like some seafood tonight." replied Jane as she came into the living room and sat opposite Jack. "We haven't had good seafood for a long time."*
>
> *Jack closed his eyes for a minute and scratched his head. "Well, the best place I know for seafood is only four blocks away . . . Captain Kidd's . . . you know."*
>
> *Jane brightened and started to answer, then sighed." Darn, it's Monday and they're not open on Monday. Depend on me to want something I can't get. Let's see . . . maybe some oriental type. I know," she said leaning forward in her chair, "Chinese! There's that wonderful little Chinese place down on 4th street. And some good Chinese food would go just right tonight. Don't you agree?"*
>
> *"I don't think so, Jane," Jack said with a pat on his stomach. "The last time I ate there I was miserable for two days. But how about that Thai place over on 5th? I've always wanted to try that out, and people say its very good. Whaddya say?"*
>
> *"Negative!" snapped Jane. She leaned back in her chair and with a frown said slowly, "I guess I really don't want Chinese after all."*
>
> *"But all reports are that it's very good food. And what's wrong with Chinese food? You've always liked it," answered Jack with some irritation.*
>
> *Jane seemed confused, tired, and was beginning to get frustrated. "Maybe we could just go to Bennies Hamburger Haven," she said. "After all, it's cheaper and we can save our money for one of your more fancy dinners over the weekend or something like that."*
>
> *"For God's sake, Jane," Jack blurted as his patience seemed to give way. "Make up your mind. First you want fish, then you want Chinese, and now you want nobody knows what."*
>
> *Jane looked at him with irritation. "Well, whatever I suggest you seem to veto." She turned away from him and picked up a newspaper.*
>
> *Jack sat upright in his chair, put his hand on his head and stared at Jane. "I veto! You just vetoed the Thai place and Chinese food and that was your suggestion! You can't make up your mind and you blame it on me. Just like your mother, always avoiding the . . ."*

Is this a violent struggle? Not yet. It is a struggle and it could well become a more violent one shortly. At this point it is a difference of opinion, a disagreement about perceptions, and perhaps a surface expression of some deeper struggle that may be going on between the two people.

We have long realized that many violent struggles have their beginnings in differences of opinions, goals, perceptions, and disagreements. There is a difference between disagreements that we call disputes and those that have escalated to the violent level. (What most people identify as conflict.) Disagreements and disputes usually arise when we have to make decisions and find ourselves at odds with ourselves and/or each other over the nature of the decision. The issues may arise from such things as distribution of scarce resources, different perceptions of the world, variations in values, cultural contradictions, failures in communication, and so on. Most of their roots are in goals that are incompatible. We discuss that in more detail in Chapter 2.

Let's continue the story of Jack and Jane:

> *Jane slammed the paper down and leaned forward in her chair, her face red and angry, "My Mother!" she shouted, "What's my mother got to do with this. Here we were simply discussing where to go to dinner and you make nasty remarks about my mother!" She jumped up and took a step toward Jack. "You miss no opportunity to make snide references to my mother! Damn you!"*
>
> *"I did not make a nasty remark about your mother," Jack shouted back. "Anyway, the fact is you do have a number of your mother's dumb habits and . . ."*
>
> *"You keep my mother out of this, you bully," shouted Jane. "I'm really getting tired of your constant nasty remarks about my mother and my family . . ."*
>
> *Jack jumped out of his chair and stood close to Jane, facing her with an angry look.*
>
> *"And I'm getting completely disgusted with your holding your mother and your family high on a pedestal that they could never reach no matter what. You are so unrealistic about them," he countered. "If you'll let go of your obscene preoccupation with your family I'll quit reminding you of it. "*
>
> *"You never have liked my family, you bastard!" screeched Jane, almost in tears. "And you keep battering*
>
> *(continued)*

> *me with your shit about them! I'm getting real tired of this."*
>
> *"You're getting tired, well so am I getting tired of your bitchiness and always carrying a chip around on your shoulder about your God-awful family!"*
>
> *Jane stared at Jack in violent anger, rushed toward him, and with a wide swinging right arm slapped him on the left side of his head so hard that it knocked his glasses off. He recoiled from the blow. With one hand he grabbed his glasses and with the other hand he speared her arm and held it in a tight grip as she started to swing the other fist.*
>
> *"I've had it with you," Jane snarled. "We'll never get this settled. I'm going to a lawyer. I want a divorce."*
>
> *"If that's what you want, that's what you'll get," snapped Jack as he pushed her violently so that she fell back on the sofa. " And when I get through with you everybody in town will know what a cheat and sleazy trick you really are."*
>
> *Jane jumped up, screaming, "You lousy bastard! I always knew you were a bum. I've had enough!" And with that she rushed to the kitchen, grabbed her coat and charged out the back door slamming it after her. She got into her car and drove wildly to her parents home, some five miles across town.*
>
> *Within the next few days Jack moved out of the apartment, took most of his things with him and refused to pay the back rent due. Jane spent much of her time with her parents, family, and friends discussing details of the struggle with Jack, painting him not only as an undesirable partner but also as a criminal type and woman chaser. She seemed determined to destroy any reputation that he might have had. Jack, on the other hand, went to friends of both of theirs and told them his story, with the result that the friends became quite cold toward Jane.*
>
> *Their struggle seemed to get worse. Jane gathered up all Jack's things that he left in the apartment, put them into a box and put it in the apartment trash dumpster. When Jack came back to get these things and found them gone, he wrote a violent note and left it on the kitchen table. The note threatened legal action if she didn't return his belongings.*
>
> *There was no effort to get back together. Jack and Jane went to separate lawyers, and shortly thereafter their divorce case was filed. When they eventually came to court the dispute was bitter. Each was determined to make the other person lose and to smear the other's reputation. The court granted the divorce but refused Jane any alimony, support, or legal fees. Jack was ordered to pay the rent on the apartment up to the time he left.*
>
> *Jane was violently angry with the decision, as was her family who gathered in her defense. Following the court decision Jane made considerable effort to find occasions to make things uncomfortable for Jack. She wrote letters to his employer complaining of his behavior, called the police to accuse him of harassing her, and called all his friends and represented him as really not their friend.*
>
> *Jack, on the other hand, was busy trying to counter the negative gossip that she created, while at the same time telling many of her friends of her unfaithfulness in the past, of her "unhealthy" preoccupation with her family, and of their generally bad marriage.*
>
> *Jane's family picked up her cry of woe and conducted its own campaign. Jack found his tires slashed one morning. On another occasion, the windows on his car were broken. Two of his old friends refused to talk to him. His employer told him that if he couldn't keep his personal affairs away from the job he would be fired.*
>
> *Finally, in desperation, Jack resigned from his job and prepared to move out of town and seek another job. On the night before he planned to leave he arrived at his apartment around midnight to find the lights on. As he walked into the living room there stood Jane with a gun in her hand aimed directly at him . .*
>
> *(adapted from Keltner, "Mild Disagreement to War: The Struggle Spectrum" in J. Stewart,* Bridges Not Walls, *5th ed. McGraw-Hill, 1990, p. 317 ff.). Reprinted with permission.*

This has now become a violent struggle. Let's take a closer look at the stages through which this event developed.

Our basic assumption here is that disputes and conflict are part of the larger struggle process which is a basic function of living and involves all of us either alone and/or in interaction with each other. Notice "The Struggle Spectrum" chart on page 5. This model was developed after many years of study and experience in dealing with struggle and conflict. The spectrum contains six stages and reflects the manner in which mild differences may escalate to disagreement, to dispute, to campaign, to litigation, and finally to fight or war (see headings across the top of the chart). The distinguishing characteristic of the Struggle Spectrum is that it demonstrates that what is usually identified as conflict has its origins in less violent conditions. A number of factors affect this spectrum: the processes we use with each other, our behaviors, our relationships, our goals, our orientation to each other, our communication, our decision making, possible outcomes, and our intractability potential.

THE STRUGGLE SPECTRUM

John (Sam) Keltner. 1992

good for mediation discussion

CONDITIONS	STAGE 1 *Mild Difference*	STAGE 2 *Disagreement*	STAGE 3 *Dispute*	STAGE 4 *Campaign*	STAGE 5 *Litigation*	STAGE 6 *Fight or War*
Processes Leading to Resolution	Discussion	Discussion Negotiation	Argument Bargaining	Persuasion Pressure	Advocacy Debate	Violent Conflict
Problem-Solving Behavior	Joint Problem solving	Contentions over Choices	Rational Proof & Game Playing By Rules	Emotional and Logical Strategies	Selective Proofs before Judges or Juries	Psychological or Physical Violence
Relationship Between Parties	Partners, Friends & Acquaintances	Rivals	Opponents	Competitors	Antagonists	Enemies
Goals	Includes Other	Includes Other	Excludes Other	Excludes Other	Excludes Other	Eliminates Other
Orientation to Each Other	Cooperative & Amicable	Disputative Conciliatory	Win-Lose 1 Hostile	Win-Lose 2 Estranged	Win-Lose 3 Alienated	Irreconcilable
Communication	Open-Friendly	Open but strained	Limited Tense	Restricted & Planned	Blocked & Controlled	Closed Except for Violent Acts
Decision Making	Mutual Decisions	Joint Decisions and Agreements	Joint Decision in Mediation-Third Party Decisions in Arbitration	Vote by Constituents or Third Party Decisions	Third Party Courtroom Decisions by Judge or Jury	Each Side Seeks Control by Forcing the Other
Intervention Possibilities	None Needed	Mediation by Neutral Party	Mediation or Arbitration by Neutral Party	Arbitration by Neutral Party or Election-Vote	Arbitration or Judge or Jury	Force of Police or Other Military or Power Intervention
Possible Outcomes	Integrated Agreement: Mutual Satisfaction	Accommodated Agreement with Both Satisfied	Compromise Agreement or One Wins But One or Both Dissatisfied	A Win or Draw. Winner Pleased with Loser Accepting but Dissatisfied	One Wins and Winner Celebrates. Loser Frustrated, etc.	One Prevails. Other or Both Destroyed or Harmed. High Fear in Both
Intractability Potential	Very Low	Low	Medium	High	High	Very High

NOTES
A. Mediation is relatively useless in Stages 1,4,5, and 6., but may be used in 4 under special arrangement.
B. Win-Lose escalates from Level 1 to Level 3. The longer it exists, the more intense it becomes.
C. Neutral third parties have no stake in the outcome of the struggle. They include mediators, arbitrators, judges, and juries.
D. Parties lose their joint decision-making power when mediation is no longer applicable.
E. When issues are not resolved at one stage, the tendency is to move to the right on the continuum.
F. De-escalation from right to left is possible under special circumstances (See chapter on de-escalation).
G. Disputes may become intractable (stalemated) at any stage in the process and may thus require special efforts to "unfreeze" them.

The Sequencing of Struggle

Many people have tried to explore the development of struggle through process phases. Rapaport (1960) writes of struggle as "a theme that has occupied the thinking of man more than any other, save only God and love" (p. 11). He takes this theme and describes three modes of interaction: fights, games, and debates. They represent a basic continuum ranging from the least to the most cooperative means of settling differences. Moore (1986), in discussing approaches to managing and resolving struggle, provides a continuum of conflict management and resolution approaches in which he scales the system from struggle avoidance and problem solving through informal discussion to violence. Hocker and Wilmot (1985) describe destructive conflicts in terms of "conflict spirals" in which a relationship beginning with a misunderstanding escalates to a destructive level. Folger and Poole (1984) discuss several phase theories that attempt to identify phases and the behaviors characteristic of each phase of the struggle. Kelley (1987) describes three phases that include the beginning one, in which agenda building takes place, the middle phase, in which arguing takes place, and the last phase, in which negotiation takes place. There seems to be general agreement that struggle emerges and passes through sequences ranging from mild to violent forms. The identification of the phases, however, appears to have less agreement.

Working from the assumption that violent struggles such as war and fighting have prerequisite and antecedent conditions that bring the destructive level into being, we may discover a more extensive continuum than those conceived by Rapaport, Moore, Hocker and Wilmot, Folger and Poole, Kelley, and others. I shall explore such a continuum. I have discovered a different continuum over the past 30 years through study of the nature of conflict and through practice in methods of managing the process.

The reasons for exploring this continuum are based on my belief that a better knowledge and understanding of the conditions whereby we experience escalation of disagreement to violence and destruction may give us better insight into the points at which the several tools of dispute management and/or resolution may be appropriately and successfully applied. My experience in dispute resolution during more than one-third of a century as a mediator, arbitrator, advocate, and student has taught me that there are many situations and conditions in which certain dispute resolution tools are not effective. By looking at the Struggle Spectrum I can see, somewhat more clearly, when and why the various systems have practical value and when they may be useless.

The Spectrum is Not Linear: De-escalation is Possible

Although we usually think of a continuum as a linear figure set in two-dimensional space with unidirectional thrust, the Struggle Spectrum is, in fact, more like a helical system that flows upward and downward and back. Approaching violence or real violence itself, for example, can be de-escalated to less violent processes of negotiation under certain conditions and with particular efforts (see Chapter 7). In addition, the spectrum seems to have many threads to its structure that interact and interweave to produce the observable behaviors and the corresponding stages or phases. All of these can be interrupted and changed under certain conditions which we will suggest.

These stages may have interim phases but the selection of these particular identifiers for the conditions seems a practical and parsimonious direction to take.

Each of these stages is identifiable in terms of common *threads* that weave together in particular ways within the various stages. These threads involve *processes and outcomes*. Each stage has a number of these threads. The ones this Spectrum examines are:

- characteristic **processes** leading to resolution
- kinds of problem-solving **behaviors** used to resolve the issue(s)
- **relationships** between the parties to the dispute
- general character of the **goals** each party holds
- parties' basic **orientation** to each other
- **communication** between the parties
- **decision-making** processes commonly used at that stage
- **intervention** possibilities for third parties to assist in the resolution of the situation

- possible **outcomes** at that stage
- **potential for de-escalation** to a less intense stage.

There are many other threads that can be examined in this context. The identification and exploration of these threads is a continuing and viable subject for future research and investigation. My main purpose here is to outline the broad dimensions of the spectrum. It remains for subsequent experience, research, and investigation to expand it, adjust it, and fill in the gaps.

Individuals and Groups

It should be noted that the struggle spectrum appears to apply to individuals as well as groups. That is, we are looking at interpersonal as well as intergroup struggle. This is somewhat contrary to the position taken by Blake and Mouton (1984) who argue that "intergroup conflict cannot be understood by presuming it to be more or less the same as conflict between individuals" (pp. 5-6). They point to the freedom of an individual to act independently of other people in contrast to the restrictions that control the behavior of a group member. The Struggle Spectrum does not distinguish between individual and groups per se in terms of the flow of behaviors. It does recognize, however, that the processes at each stage that involve groups will involve many more dimensions and aspects of interpersonal behavior than those involving a dyad. However, the depth and significance of those group processes does not seem to effect the flow along the spectrum (except perhaps on a time dimension) in either the interpersonal or intergroup context. It appears that we can plot the path of a struggle between nations along the same kind of spectrum as we plot the path of a struggle between husband and wife. The internal processes may be significantly different but the larger flow of conditions appear to follow the spectrum. Two individuals may come to blows for many of the same reasons that two nations go to war, that is, they may both want a resource that they perceive only one can have. If we are to engage in effective study and practice in the management of struggle it is important that we understand it in both the interpersonal and intergroup contexts. (This is not to exclude the intrapersonal context in which struggles are also in process within us.)

Group decision making and individual decision making are cases in point. An individual deals with personal attitudes, history, personal goals, and customs surrounding the social conditions in which he or she operates as part of his or her decision making. A group, likewise, must deal with the attitudes, history, personal goals, and customs surrounding the existence of the group as it strives to bring its members in sufficient concert to make decisions representing the group. In each case the decisions have an effect on the outcomes of relationships. A group struggles for many goals similar to those individuals seek: territory, security, identity, integrity, control, and so on. As these come in collision with other groups or individuals, struggle emerges.

> *Certainly many of the struggles in Africa, the Middle East, the Balkan states, the former USSR, and other nations are between national groups that seek the same territory or resources—much as individuals fought over land in the westward movement in North America.*

Some contemporary personality theories suggest that each of us comprise a "group" of internal selves with different functions and awarenesses (Yarbrough, 1983). Thus, the expansion of the struggle concept from intrapersonal to interpersonal to intergroup does not seem unrealistic in a "wholistic" world. We are probably looking at a truly organic system in which unresolved intrapersonal struggles affect interpersonal and the intergroup behaviors. There are innumerable cases in which a person who is involved in a high intrapersonal struggle is unable to function effectively as a member of a team or work unit.

> *A highly skilled guard of a basketball team was having an intrapersonal struggle over what he felt was an unfair financial settlement on his contract and was considering leaving the team. He suddenly found himself in a struggle with one of the power forwards. The two were suddenly competing with each other for position and recognition. The guard would not pass off to the forward even though the forward was in a key position to score. It was apparent that they were not able to function as efficiently as team members as they would have if their prime attention was directed toward the team effort.*

> *The struggle between two members of the board of directors of a large corporation emerged from both persons' need to feel that they were in command. The struggle became so intense that the rest of the board was unable to do business. The corporation went into a decline, and the board suffered due to the battle between its members.*

TRACKING A STRUGGLE: THE STAGES AND CONDITIONS OF THE STRUGGLE SPECTRUM

Stage 1. Mild Difference

General Character of Stage 1

The struggle between people appears to begin with mild differences and relatively limited collision of interests. These differences emerge from many types of conditions.

- A *change in status quo* is involved when one partner, for instance, wants to move a desk in their office from where it had been for some time, and the other partner would rather it be left where it is.
- A *collision of time commitments* is involved when a wife wants her husband to pick up the children from school in order to allow her to visit a sick friend and he expects not to be free at that time.
- *Varying goals* are involved when an employer wants an employee to work extra hours, and the employee has already made plans for that period.
- *Changes in practice* are involved when one group wants some minor changes in a contract for services between them and the other group would prefer to keep the contract as it is.
- *Different preferences* were involved when Jane and Jack were trying to decide on where to go to dinner.

These are mild differences and do not represent, at this point, serious difficulties.

Conditions of Stage 1

Usually the behavior exhibited at this level, in the rare event other issues are not contaminating the situation, is a joint problem-solving activity in which the parties, in a friendly and collaborative manner, explore the problem and reach decisions together. Their goals are mutually inclusive. In general, their orientation to each other is cooperative and friendly. Their communication is open and reasonably clear and unobstructed—there are no blocks or interferences that prevent them from saying what they think and feel to each other, and they each respect the other's differing point of view. The decision making is predominantly by mutual agreement. The interests and needs of each party are openly shared. No firm positions are taken.

At this stage there are no reasons for intervention by third parties. In fact, well meaning meddling by others at this stage could create tension where tension did not exist before.

The outcomes of this stage can be integrated agreement and satisfaction by both parties.

> *Jane and Jack, as they were trying to decide on where to go for dinner could have agreed to go to a French restaurant by keeping control of their differences and engaging in more calm exploration of their interests, needs, and alternatives.*
>
> *Or, in another context, union representatives and management, after some open and careful discussion of scheduling problems, agree to change the shift schedules to improve efficiency and provide workers with better shift preferences.*

When satisfactory outcomes are not forthcoming and there is no resolution, the stage may shift to the next level.

Although we recognize that there are many hidden motives and conditions that exist within differences, mild differences represent a level in which those other factors are relatively insignificant in relation to the issue at hand or are quite openly recognized but not considered relevant to the points of discussion. The particular appetites of Jane and Jack were important to the selection of the place to eat but in Stage 1 they would not stand in the way of the decision. But this did not happen, and they escalated the difference. In the scheduling problem, some shift workers would be temporarily inconvenienced, but the larger effect was perceived as a benefit to everyone. There are many examples of this kind of mild disagreement and resolution in our daily lives as we interact with each other.

Sometimes we resolve differences at this level in respect to matters of high value and significance as when management and the union worked out rules for changing individual shift-time schedules. There were some mild differences as to how the schedules should be applied but after open discussion of the needs and interests by all the involved personnel, the differences were resolved and a new schedule devised and put into operation.

This stage is usually accompanied by a lot of good will and good faith between the parties. For example, neighbors deal with problems by willingly joining together and discussing needs, perceptions, interests and the like openly and forthrightly; issues at the bargaining table are resolved as problems that are faced by both parties; and husbands and wives talk over their differences and work out agreements on how to deal with the larger problem from which their differences may arise.

Stage 2. Disagreement

General Character of Stage 2

When mild differences are not resolved they may be laid aside and forgotten, stored in memory for future reference, avoided, or they may escalate into disagreements. When they escalate, the usual development is toward a more apparent level of disagreement. Here the parties begin to show signs of becoming polarized. Interests and needs become translated into positions. The mild differences become more explicit and focused differences. The intensity of the interaction increases. The agreement level diminishes, and each party begins to search for ways to support, defend, and justify positions taken and to gain concessions from the other.

Conditions of Stage 2

The initial *problem-solving* processes are *joint deliberation* between the parties but as the stage progresses and resolution of the differences does not occur the parties may begin *negotiating* with each other. They begin to seek ways of resolving their disagreement through presentation of their positions in order to gain concessions and at the same time attempt to find ways of cooperating or compromising in order to find some satisfactory settlement outcome (see Chapter 4, this volume; also, Lewicki & Litterer, 1985; Nierenberg, 1968; Pruitt, 1981; Rangarajan, 1985; Rule 1962; Schatzki, 1981).

Both parties to the situation begin to select positions, contend over their choice, and formulate and present persuasive statements in support of their choice. The *polarization* between them becomes increasingly apparent to them and to outside observers. These contentions are usually stated to each other. Soon they begin to see themselves as *rivals* or contrary advocates.

> So, when Jane and Jack cannot agree on where to go to dinner, each begins to support the favored position with some contentions and persuasive efforts. They each begin to assume that they must **change the other's** position in order to reach an agreement.
>
> When management's proposal to change the shift hours ran counter to some personal schedules of a number of workers, each side began to bring forward their reasons and justifications for their position, while at the same time the spokespersons realized that changes in both sides might have to occur.

Goals at this stage are still mutually inclusive and neither party seeks a solution that does not provide satisfaction for themselves as well as their rivals. Their *orientation to each other* is ambivalent. On the one hand, the parties are still conciliatory with each other. On the other hand, each side begins to dispute the other's position and presentation.

Decision making at this stage can still be achieved through joint decisions and agreements. By sharing their differences and making special efforts to cooperate and accommodate each other's goals, the parties can reach decisions together and have a possibility of consensus.

The *communication* at this stage is less open than it was in the preceding stage. Although it is still relatively open, more guarded statements and conditional statements begin to appear in the talk. Such statements as, "If you can't accept this then . . .," begin to appear. The openness is modified by a seeming strain in the communication exhibited by fewer complimentary phrases to each other, occasional accusatory or derogative remarks, and sometimes outright expressions of anger or frustration.

The *outcome* of this stage may be in the form of agreements that accommodate both parties. Here compromise plays an important role.

Because of the increasing difficulty in communicating and the modification of the openness, this stage often *results* in a stalemate in which the parties are unable to find a solution to their differences. At this point the situation may escalate to the dispute level or a neutral third party may be invited in to function as a mediator (see Keltner, 1987b; Chapter 5, this volume).

A mediator can serve effectively at this stage because the polarization has not become excessively intense, and there is still a mutual desire to find a solution that can satisfy both parties. The primary functions of a mediator at this point are to provide for some de-escalation of the areas of tension and to help shift the interaction to a more cooperative level. Under these conditions the mediator can be very helpful in facilitating the parties' efforts to communicate with each other, to look at alternatives, to find accommodation for each other, and to reach a solution that is satisfactory to them.

Not very many people know how to use mediators at this stage or even later. Also, there are not many skilled mediators available because it takes extensive and special training that is not readily accessible. Even so, the process is highly useful and important when used properly (see Chapter 5, this volume).

Stage 3. Dispute

General Character of Stage 3

Failure to resolve the disagreement usually escalates the matter to more intense interaction between the parties. Arguments become heated, and the polarization becomes quite powerful and controlling. The parties' perceptions of each other become increasingly negative. Many disputes break open or first appear at this stage when the previous stages have been relatively hidden or have been avoided or ignored as the issues developed.

At this point, the parties may move into at least two levels of interaction: formal rule-controlled and/or intense attack and defense behaviors. Rule-controlled interactions are those that are restrained in part by rules either set by the parties to the interaction or by others who supervise the interaction. Thus, a couple who agree not to sleep until their disagreements are resolved are operating under a rule they have set for themselves. A couple who decide to go to court will be controlled by the rules of the court. A game or contest is usually a struggle interaction controlled by a set of rules as in basketball, chess, and so on.

In the case of structured competitive situations, the overt interaction begins at this stage. In the labor-management field when a grievance has remained unresolved, after having been discussed at least on two levels of the organization, the dispute becomes more intense. The polarization of the parties around their point of view becomes firmer, positions become more intractable, the groups and the principals involved become more alienated toward each other, and the system seems increasingly unable to bring the matter to a resolution through joint deliberation means.

> *Here is where Jane and Jack find themselves shouting at each other, accusing each other of foul and heinous intents and behaviors, and of improper attempts to manipulate each other against their will. In the heat of the dispute, when Jane accuses Jack of maligning her mother, the direction and intensity of the dispute escalates rapidly. Emotions become aroused and the atmosphere is charged with feelings. Old unresolved issues get dragged into the dispute and become points of contention.*

Often at this stage other issues will be introduced into the dispute. Frequently these issues have nothing to do with the matter over which the disagreement began. (Some have called these "gunnysack" issues that have been stored away and are brought out under the conditions of this stage.)

Conditions of Stage 3

The characteristic processes at this stage of struggle are intense argument and *bargaining*, or "hard negotiating." I separate negotiation and bargaining in this spectrum for the purpose of showing degrees of intensity and also because there are some differences in mode that each engenders. This is much like what Fisher and Ury (1981) have suggested when they separate "soft" and "hard" bargaining. The process that they call "soft" bargaining I prefer to identify as negotiation and what they call "hard" bargaining I prefer to identify as bargaining (p. 9). The bargaining situation in this stage brings into play a much higher incidence of argument, persuasion, threat, and exclusiveness of needs-goals and positions than does the negotiation atmosphere. Negotiation, as I perceive it in this spectrum, involves much more joint interest and mutual goal sharing than does bargaining (see chapter 4, this volume).

Here the processes of bargaining involve argument, persuasion, threats, proposals, counter proposals, and "horse trading" on a significant scale. The interplay of power and tactics is an essential characteristic of such bargaining (Bacharach & Lawler, 1981). The attempts to reach resolution are usually suffused with a quid pro quo kind of interaction. What may have been more calm and thoughtful negotiations escalates into more acrid accusation and defense.

In many situations, such as the labor-management context, the parties become involved in game playing by a set of rules established by their contractual relationship, the structure of the situation, or other previously agreed upon restrictions. Each side takes its turn to present its arguments and rebuttals. There is an attempt to cloak dispute in logical or often legal terms, to find evidence to support the arguments, or to bring witnesses to testify in favor or against the participants. In less formal dispute situations there may be attempts by outsiders to control the dispute by insisting that the parties follow some rules of behavior in their attacks on each other.

Many sporting events have the character of disputes in that they are run by a set of firm rules which have been agreed to by the parties to the game. *There are also clearly identified winners and losers in these events.* These rules are administered by persons outside the dispute, and there are penalties for violation of the rules. These are clear cases of structured competition and dispute.

Perhaps the most significant difference between the dispute stage and those stages which precede it are the *goal and orientation* conditions. In the dispute stage the matter becomes a win-lose situation (Keltner, 1987; see also Chapter 6, this volume). Each party is convinced that it must overcome or supersede the other and gain its point of view or objective. The goals are perceived to have become mutually exclusive and the result is a highly competitive situation (Kohn, 1986). That is, what one wins the other cannot have. Although the actual fact may be that the goals are still mutually inclusive, the parties to the dispute have, in their intensity and polarization, come to perceive them as being exclusive and that *perception controls their behaviors toward each other.*

The *orientation* to each other is a hostile one. The friendliness of the prior stages seems to melt away and in its place appears an animosity and a fervent hostility that is highly emotional.

Communication between the parties is tense and limited. Each party restricts the information that it sends to the other. Each party is actually unable to perceive or hear what the other side may be saying. Emotional barriers to the understanding of each other are very strong. There is a high incidence of accusatory messages being sent to each other.

When Jack mentioned Jane's mother, a dispute began to grow.

The dispute emerged when the union accused management of wrongful acts toward the workers, when one neighbor accused the other of being a "land hungry liar," when a developer accused the county commissioners of petty politics and restraint of trade, or when one nation accused the other of violating treaties or agreements.

The *outcomes* of this stage are, of course, related to the perception of *who wins?* Because of the win-lose orientation, the common conception is that the winner takes the rewards and the game (dispute) is over. However, this may not always be the case for in many situations in which there is a winner and a loser, the loser goes "lean and hungry" and retreats for a while to plan future attacks in order to win back what was lost. Thus, the dispute is really not resolved.

In this stage it is still possible for the parties to find ways to cooperate and to work toward joint decision making and compromise. The most significant and useful way is through the intervention of a neutral mediator who facilitates the parties in their attempts to find resolution. The mediator does not make decisions nor direct the decision making toward one solution or another. The function is facilitative and in the process the parties must be led to de-escalate the dispute to its prior stages so that more open communication and consideration of alternatives can take place. The mediator actually helps the parties to overcome the barriers to joint decision making and helps them make their own decisions (see Chapter 5, this volume). However, mediation is not possible if the parties do not have a desire to work out a solution to the dispute. If the parties are simply frozen into a win-lose attitude it is very difficult for a mediator to defuse the situation so that other conditions can be considered.

When skilled intervention takes place it may be possible to de-escalate the situation and to modify the win-lose condition so that compromises can be designed that will allow for resolution of the dispute.

Compromises are important and valuable means when they allow for settlements that extend the values of an agreement to both sides of a dispute. *They do, however, require a modification of the win-lose orientation in the dispute.*

Sometimes when the parties have exhausted themselves without resolution and realize that they cannot find a solution themselves or through the good services of a mediator they may agree to bring in a neutral third party to make a decision for them. This is called arbitration (see Chapter 6, this volume).

Special Structural Conditions Appearing at this Stage

The entire spectrum is based on a natural process that occurs between people, groups, social entities, and nations as they seek to resolve differences. It is at this stage that the highly "intentional" competition as described by Kohn (1986) emerges or develops. "Intentional" competition, according to Kohn, is internal on the part of the person and involves the desire to be the best, number one, better than another, and so on. It's an "individual's competitiveness, his or her proclivity for besting others" (1986, pp. 4-5).

Another process is "structural competition." Structural competition has numerous faces. They are conditions of the society into which people are thrust without any internal or intentional desire to be competitive. The win-lose setting is characteristic. The structure of the labor-management relationship is often of such a nature that a win-lose orientation is inherent in the interaction. The Sherif studies (1966) on conflict support this analysis. They demonstrated that when the structure of the situation is competitive, then the behavior of the participants becomes competitive. The Zimbardo studies (1972) reaffirmed the same concept when they demonstrated that students placed in prestructured prison guard roles adopted aggressive behavior toward the "prisoners" without any instruction to perform in this manner.

Admission to a high-rated college as a result of being accepted over others is another form of structural competition. In that situation all others are not excluded because others may also be admitted, but the criteria for acceptance may include a mix of personal judgment and objective data. In a beauty contest someone wins on the basis of subjective criteria based on the personal bias of the judges.

In a basketball game the criteria are more or less objective. In such conditions, another factor becomes significant: one side must *make the other fail* in order to win (as is true in war, tennis, football, political office, etc.). Not only must the competitor be better than the opponent, but must also act to deny or destroy the opponent's effectiveness. There are sets of conditions that put in motion competitiveness and disputes at the *very beginning of an interaction.* These lead to structural competition. Thus, certain external conditions force people to begin their interactions at the dispute stage of competition and to abridge the earlier stages of dealing with differences and disagreements. *In other words, many differences and disagreements are built into the social, political, and economic structure.* They, in turn, affect the relations between people.

Stage 4. Campaign

If the parties fail to find a resolution of their differences at Stage 3, the escalation moves to Stages 4 or 5. Although I have identified these stages in a continuum relationship to each other, they are, in reality, interchangeable. Stage 4, Campaign, may not be encountered until after Litigation (Stage 5) has taken place or it may not take place at all. Similarly, failure to settle a dispute at Stage 3 may be followed by a fight or war when the other phases are not perceived as having potential for resolution.

General Character of Stage 4

With no resolution appearing in the previous stages the parties may begin to expand the struggle and to involve more and more participants in the situation. The dispute "goes public." The effort here is to get supporters, to gather power by the numbers and nature of people who "join up" with the parties involved. The efforts move toward the use of the media and group situations in which others can be drawn into the dispute.

> *Thus, Jane and Jack sought to gain the support of their neighbors, their relatives, and of others who might be able to bring some pressure to bear on the opposition.*

In this stage, the political arena is the most typical example as the decisions are made by the numbers of votes gathered. The disputants in a land-use dispute will organize a public meeting at which their point of view can be presented. The union and/or the employer will prepare press releases for the media that support their positions. Nations will seek to involve other nations in the support of their goals and positions and thereby build coalitions.

The thrust of the campaign stage is not directed at the opponent or competitor but at people surrounding the situation in order to ultimately influence the behavior of the opponent. The function is to mold constituencies that will provide power to the advocate.

Conditions of Stage 4

Psychological processes of persuasion become important tools in the campaign stage. In the disagreement and dispute stage persuasion is used also, but the primary emphasis is on forms of "logical" support and logical proof. In Stage 4, all of the persuasive tools are brought to bear to bring about changes in and to build constituencies, and there is a great emphasis on nonrational processes. Even so, both emotional and logical strategies are designed and employed by the parties in their process of going public with the dispute. The various media are drawn into the process including newspaper and radio-TV releases, pamphlets and books, mass meetings, small group sessions, brochures, signs, and so on. Skilled speakers and performers are enlisted in the campaign. House-to-house solicitation is often used. In some instances theater is even drawn into the scheme as plays are written and produced dramatizing the theme and directing the resolution to the side espoused by one of the parties to the dispute. *Uncle Tom's Cabin*, for example, played a very important role in the American Civil War.

The *goals*, by this time, are highly exclusive in nature. Signs of compromise or joint agreement are hardly admissible to the campaign positions and are viewed as undesirable. The win-lose context is paramount. Each side seeks to exclude the other and the other's position in any resolution. De-escalation, although possible, becomes increasingly difficult.

The *communication* systems between the parties themselves are almost totally blocked. The competitors or their representatives may appear together on a platform, but each speaks more to the audience than to the other. They listen to each other only to the degree that they can find faults and errors in what their opponent may be saying. The messages are highly planned and directed not at the adversary but at the audience in order to generate support. They are antagonistic messages that contradict each other in the essential elements and possible resolutions of the dispute. It is in this context that attempts to destroy the credibility of the opponent often occur. One way to defeat an opponent is to destroy or damage the perception of the ethics and honesty of that opponent.

The *decision-making* processes at this stage reach beyond that of the parties themselves. Having gone public or having brought others into the dispute, the decision may depend on the pressure of those others who have been drawn into the campaign. Here the voting and election procedures come into play in public policy and related types of disputes. The action by the constituents becomes the decision-making standard. The power of numbers becomes important.

In some cases in which there is a real stalemate all around, the parties may agree to neutral third party arbitration. But this act, in and of itself, requires an agreement to arbitrate. Sometimes even reaching that level of agreement is difficult.

The *outcomes* of the campaign stage are several. A winner can emerge. There can be an impasse from a tie vote. There can be a decision by an arbitrator that does not allow either side to actually prevail or win, yet both parties agree to accept the decision. An arbitrator can also rule so as to provide a winner and a loser.

There are situations in which no matter what the outcome of the campaign, its results are not accepted by the parties to the dispute. At this point there are several directions that the matter may take. There may be a de-escalation of the struggle to the point at which more negotiation and bargaining can take place. The parties may become so impassioned by their frustrations that they will engage in physical fighting or war. Or, the parties may go to litigation either by choice of one or both, or by law. Frequently, when there is a superior force lurking around the margins of the struggle, that force may intervene and take control and impose externally made decisions on the disputants.

> *Two neighboring landowners, for example, struggled over the identification and zoning classification of some lowland adjacent to a river. The dispute had escalated to the point where each had involved other neighbors and friends in the struggle. It seemed that the whole community was on one side or the other. Finally, the state land-use commission stepped in and issued the directive that controlled the situation.*

Stage 5. Litigation

General Characteristics of Stage 5

Disputes at this stage go before the court and judges and juries to determine the outcome. The parties usually hire specialists in advocacy (lawyers) to represent them. These "hired guns" appear before the court carrying the cause of their clients with as much skill and ability as they can bring to bear. The difference between this stage and those stages in which informal arbitration is used is that the parties have little or no choice in the selection of the court of jurisdiction which will hear the dispute. Therefore, they have no choice of the judge and limited choice of the jurors. In arbitration the parties mutually select the arbitrator who will hear their dispute and make a decision. Arbitration can be considered a milder form of litigation in which lawyers are brought into the dispute to represent the parties to the dispute. One of the significant differences between court litigation and arbitration is the condition that the court litigation most typically involves charges involving alleged violations of the law or equity (see Chapter 6, this volume).

Conditions of Stage 5

The principle processes at this stage are the use of *advocacy, formal argument, debate, and persuasion.* The process is proscribed by the rules of the court and the procedural constraints found therein. This means that legal rules of evidence must be followed, formal briefs are filed, and a prescribed order of events takes place.

The representatives of the parties present selected proofs before the judge and/or the jury. Witnesses are brought forth to testify in favor of or against each of the principals in the dispute. The *orientation* of the principals is antagonistic and each seeks to prevail over the other. The win-lose condition is probably at its next most intense level, and the parties are highly alienated toward each other.

Communication between the parties themselves is blocked and controlled. Usually any communication between the parties is conducted through the services of the hired guns. The parties themselves, at this stage, rarely talk or communicate to each other directly. If they do it is usually hostile and highly inflammatory. The control of the communication results in the presentation of the parties' positions in such a manner as to make them appear better than the other's. In this process, many actual facts of the situation are carefully covered up because they may jeopardize one or the other side. This is one of the more serious problems in litigation, namely, that litigants are not primarily interested in solving a problem but in getting their position accepted. The resulting strategy relies heavily on the restriction of information that may be damaging.

The *decision making* is done by the judge or jury and the parties to the dispute have no function in the making of that decision. It is entirely out of their hands.

In some situations the parties may choose to litigate the situation before an arbitrator that they choose rather than go to court. When a dispute does not involve a matter of legal judgment this process can be useful. However, many parties may have tried this process earlier in the history of the dispute and arrived at this stage because the decision did not satisfy one or both of the parties to the extent that they would abide by it. (Although, in most cases in which arbitration is selected by the parties, they have agreed to abide by the decision. In some cases, however, an agreement to abide by a decision may be defaulted because one or both of the parties refuse to honor their agreement or feel that there was a procedural error in the arbitrator's decision. This, in turn, can throw them into court on the matter in the form of an appeal.)

The *outcome* of the litigation stage is that one of the parties wins and the other loses unless wider jurisdiction is allowed by the court, such as dividing up the available resources as in a divorce proceeding. In that case there could be a division of the resources that would not represent a clear win by one or the other of the disputants.

When the court or arbitration decision does not satisfy the parties to the dispute the alternatives become very limited. They must abide by the decision handed down to them or violate the law and abandon the effort, de-escalate, or become engaged in the ultimate, destructive level of struggle through fighting or war.

Stage 6. Fight and/or War

General Characteristics of Stage 6

The critical characteristic of this stage is the presence of violence and behaviors that are aimed at damaging or destroying the "enemy." Fights involve forms of violence toward each other as when two neighbors try to "punch each other out, " or when a union strikes a company, or when one country invokes sanctions against another. War is a more extreme level of violent fighting in which the parties to the struggle *take up weapons* to extend their power to hurt and destroy. War is destructive of people, resources, facilities, and relationships. Most and Starr (1983) pull together a number of definitions of war as follows:

> A "war" is a particular type of outcome of the interaction of at least dyadic sets of specified varieties of actors in which at least one actor is willing and able to use some specified amount of military force for some specified period of time against some other, resisting actor and in which some specified minimal number of fatalities (greater than zero) occur. Unlike situations involving structural violence, wars involve . . . an influencer, an influencee, and a mode of influencing—in which the mode is military force and at least some fatalities result. To the extent that all involved parties are nation-states, wars are the resultants of attempts by one to use particular means for influencing another, resisting nation. (pp. 140-141)

Thus, a fist fight becomes a "war" when one or both of the parties takes up a gun or another kind of weapon and fires at the other. An economic sanction becomes a warlike act when the military is used to enforce the sanction and shooting occurs. Many times people use the term *war* to apply to struggles that are less than destructive, but still have potential of becoming violent. *This is usually faulty use of the metaphor in which the results of the use can be very misleading and may actually contribute to escalation.*

The frequent use of the term "trade war" to describe the struggle between nations to market their products and to find reasonable compensation for these products can lead to a concept of the competing nation as an "enemy." Gradually the concept of a more violent war emerges in the minds and behaviors of the constituents.

> *Jane and Jack moved into violence and "war" when she struck him. But they de-escalated to litigation and campaign. However, these did not work and finally violence through the use of a weapon emerged when Jane faced Jack behind the barrel of a pistol.*

All the prior stages in the Struggle Spectrum have alternatives that do not involve violence and destruction. The use of violence and destructive behavior is the ultimate stage of unresolved struggle. When parties reach this level of a dispute the only alternative, short of the outcome of the battle, is to de-escalate into other levels of the Struggle Spectrum. When we reach this level we have come to a point from which it is very difficult to retreat. Rational processes no longer function in the relations between the parties except as tools of destruction. Polarization is so great that changes in position are extremely difficult, if at all possible.

Conditions of Stage 6

It is important that we recognize that all fighting and war are not purely physical in nature. Physical violence is the most typical characteristic of the process, but psychological and economic violence can be equally destructive to the human condition. Every tool that can bring enemies to defeat are used, and psychological warfare is very powerful whether between persons or nations. Economic violence is similar. Tariffs, for example, can destroy the economic base of a targeted country and result in actual physical deprivation and death.

Parties to the dispute view each other at this stage as enemies and their goal is to eliminate each other or to so reduce each other's capacities that they cannot respond or in any way prevail in the dispute. The essential goals of fighting war are to defeat the enemy. The goals of the parties are irreconcilable.

> *In the 1990-91 stages of the Middle East crisis between Iraq and the U.S., the U.S. insisted that Iraq leave Kuwait. Iraq persistently refused to do so. It is that irreconcilability that brings on the violent action unless some significant de-escalation takes place. No de-escalation took place and war ensued.*

It is also apparent that when two sides are strongly committed to opposing positions it is even more difficult to find grounds for de-escalation, negotiation, or another form of management because of the very polarization between the parties. Each side faces significant loss of face and stature if it abandons its stated goal. In spite of the often-cited instances in which a single mistake or error triggered a war, the essential context that makes that war possible is the existence of *perceived mutually irreconcilable goals* within structural conditions that make the war inevitable.

There is *communication* in warfare. It is of a closed system, however. The throwing of a punch, the firing of a shell, the dropping of a bomb, all are messages about the intent and desire of the source. When an enraged wife slaps her husband or pulls a gun and shoots him she has sent a clear message. If he is destroyed, her message is total and complete. If he lives, he then must decode that message as to its potential significance. The nature of violence itself may send messages in fights and warfare. There is a difference between dropping an atom bomb on a country and setting up a blockade of its commerce. Both represent levels of violence but one is more conclusive than the other.

Each side in war and fighting seeks control by using physical (including weaponry), economic, political, and psychological force against the other. By threats of destruction or by other means the main direction is to overpower the opposition. The only interventions that are available in fighting or war are those of physical, psychological, or economic force.

> *When neighbors become embroiled in acts of physical destruction of each other or each other's property, the basic intervention is from the police or others who may have to use physical force to subdue the combatants. Sometimes others in the neighborhood will boycott the fighters or use psychological pressures to force them to abandon their destructive behavior. These interventions, however, rarely actually resolve the struggle between the parties and may initiate other struggles. There are many examples of this in Middle East affairs.*

It often occurs that some parties, frustrated at their inability to resolve a dispute, will resort to police action to gain control and thereby trigger responding physical violence.

The *outcomes* of fights and war are destruction of one or both of the disputants, one of the parties prevails and subsequently dominates or destroys the other, or both of the parties are seriously harmed. However, as we noted above, the losing party or nation may reorganize itself and plan to gain its ends by other means or by subsequent violent acts.

SOME GENERAL OBSERVATIONS ABOUT THE SPECTRUM: USING THE STRUGGLE SPECTRUM IN SELECTING STRATEGIES FOR DISPUTE MANAGEMENT

The function of the Struggle Spectrum is to provide a framework in which we can study conflict and struggle and the means of managing the processes involved. It is far from complete, and there are many variations that can be developed with it. There are, however, several basic assumptions that underlie its existence:

1. Violent struggle, as defined here, does not emerge suddenly from a nonstruggle context. It has antecedents in the relationships between the parties to a struggle and the contexts of those relationships.

2. It is important for us to know and understand these antecedents if we are to mount effective systems of managing the process of struggle so that it does not escalate to the destructive stages.

3. Struggle is not a singular phenomenon. It is a multiple condition that effects individuals, partners, groups, states, and nations. The Struggle Spectrum does not separate these in its continuum. The spectrum applies to all of these units. It is just as descriptive of what happens between nations as it is of what happens between husbands and wives.

4. The structure of our present society is such that it encourages and literally forces us to the dispute level of struggle in many contexts. The win-lose orientation is rampant. If we expect to reduce the dangers of escalating to the violent end of the struggle spectrum we must address those personal, social, political, national, and international structures that make disputes a vital part of their existence and that leave no room for the management of mild differences and disagreements.

5. The elimination of fighting and war as a means of resolving struggles can only be achieved by restructuring the societies that allow unresolved disagreements to escalate to violence.

6. The restructuring of those societies and the management of struggle must begin with

individual behaviors and perceptions before it can be expected to occur in groups and nations.

7. The use and development of neutral third parties as agents in the management of struggle is a critical process and needs to be addressed more thoroughly in our present society. It is clear from the nature of the spectrum that there are levels at which the neutral third party can play a vital role in struggle management. There are other stages at which these agents are relatively helpless. It is important for us to know the difference.

8. The relation of internal intentional competition (the desire of a person to be "number 1") and external structural competition (the win-lose condition) needs to be more thoroughly studied. We have evidence that structural competition can induce internal competition. Are we similarly able to predict structural competition from the presence of internal intentional competition (Kohn, 1986)?

9. By looking at the spectrum we can recognize points at which interventions can be most useful and when they are not functional. Thus, although no intervention is needed for mild differences, it may be useful at the level of disagreement.

10. Also, the type of intervention varies with the particular stage of development of the struggle. Whereas arbitration is hardly needed at Level 2 (disagreement), it is highly useful in Stages 3 (dispute), 4 (campaign), or 5 (litigation). Mediation, for example, is most practical at Stages 2 and 3. It has increasingly limited use at Stage 4 and is impossible under the conditions of Stages 5 and 6. When we get to the place where a struggle has escalated to the stages of litigation and/or war, mediation is very difficult to obtain and to accomplish. Parties are not, by that time, willing to seek mutual solutions and are heavily committed and polarized on their position. (For example President Bush and Saddam Hussein became highly polarized in their positions during the latter months of 1990 and actually resisted efforts to be brought together to seek a solution. No mediation was possible at that stage simply because each party was locked into its demands and each side was unwilling to change its position.) In Stages 5 and 6, win-lose has become the essential condition. To get mediation into a setting in which this has taken place would mean that the parties to the dispute would have to either abandon or attenuate their fighting by choice or by an external force that is greater than either of the parties in the dispute.

Thus, when Jane and Jack went to court over their dispute they were already committed to fighting each other until one won or the court made the decision.

When a union strikes an employer it is difficult for mediation to take place until the parties begin to attenuate (or de-escalate from) their positions and indicate a willingness to try to work the solution out together by other means. (It is often the case that during a strike the parties may be meeting in mediation trying to settle the issues over which they are fighting. What this means is that there are really two or more levels of the dispute going on at the same time. The mediation is operating at a level where the parties are at least trying to settle and to stop the violent end of the struggle.)

When two countries are at war mediation is very difficult until the effects of the warfare and the struggle for power change the situation, or until the situation de-escalates and undergoes significant change and the parties are willing to attempt other means of settling the dispute.

11. De-escalation is always an option although it becomes more difficult as we move toward Stage 6 (see Chapter 7, this volume).

CONCLUSION

This spectrum provides us with a tool for determining the kinds of management and/or intervention processes appropriate, and indeed functional, for any given disagreement-dispute as well as a model for understanding the manner in which mild differences may escalate into fights when they are not resolved. It also demonstrates clearly that skill in problem solving, decision making, communication, and negotiation are vital to the process of coping with our constant involvement in struggle.

CHAPTER 2

//

Management of the Struggle Processes

Because struggle is ubiquitous it is important that we use the spectrum of struggle to guide us in managing the process so that it doesn't escalate into violence and destruction. I am not trying to eliminate struggle as a human process of interaction. My concern is to find ways to *manage* it so that we can benefit from the products of struggle while at the same time controlling it so that it doesn't become a dangerous or unnecessarily destructive activity.

A necessary part of understanding the management process is to examine the antecedent and concomitant conditions or factors that lead to and accompany struggle. Historically there have been many attempts to locate the causes of conflict, both those that precede the genesis of the process and those that appear to escalate the process. To list all the accumulated hypotheses about the causes of conflict would be impossible in this document. What we will do is provide a general identification of some of the more consistently identified antecedents and concomitant factors that seem to generate and escalate the struggle process.

ANTECEDENT AND CONCOMITANT FACTORS OF STRUGGLE

We can clearly identify two sets of factors that seem to have some connection with the appearance of struggle in human relationships: They are personal and contextual (or situational) factors.

Personal Factors

Take a look at the following human conditions (all of which can lead to struggle within and between people) and identify any of them that describe your state of being at any time.

Authoritarian	Dogmatic	Defensive	Aggressive
Self-doubting	Fearful	Frustrated	Rejected
Alienated	Hopeless	Apathetic	Rigid attitudes
Despairing	Cynical	Distorted perceptions	Suspicious
Cognitive dissonance	Prejudiced	Conforming	Distrusting

Some others are: inadequate or poor communication, failure to be appreciated, possessiveness, lack of confidence, compulsiveness, carelessness, irresponsibility, irritation at interference, irritation at inappropriate behavior of others, and negative attitudes toward others.

> *Can you think of others? Make a check list for yourself identifying those attitudes, behaviors, and personal conditions affecting your cooperation or struggle with yourself and others. What you will have when you are finished is an introduction, and maybe a key, to your struggle potential.*

Among these lists are some personal factors that appear to have more than passing influence on people in relation to their struggle potential.

Terhune, a researcher at Cornell Aeronautical Laboratory, found that those who mistrust others, have unfavorable views of human nature, and are Machiavellian (manipulative) in their relationship with others will be likely to exploit and retaliate against others. He also found that those who are passive, docile, dependent, and submissive, and who need abasement and deference are likely to avoid struggle or to cooperate in joint efforts. Those who have a high need for achievement, are able to think abstractly, have a tolerance of ambiguity, are open minded, and are able to work alone effectively will follow a policy in which cooperation is the better way to maximize gains. Those who are generally trusting and egalitarian, conciliatory, and have a favorable view of human nature are likely to be cooperative with others when differences arise (Terhune, 1970).

It appears that the potential for violent and destructive behavior increases in direct proportion to the number and intensity of characteristics such as defensiveness, authoritarianism, prejudice, aggressiveness, frustration, stress from overload, high need status, and so on, which appear within the participants to an interaction. If these characteristics are added to interaction patterns of competition, domination, and provocation, the potential for violent struggle is going to increase (Nye, 1973).

Nye points out that once a struggle has started between persons or groups and becomes recognizable, it tends to increase the number and intensity of struggle-promoting characteristics—a "snowball" effect. As the struggle triggers added struggle, producing stronger personal orientations, it also begins to spiral into more competition, more attempts at domination, and more provocation incidents (Nye, 1973). This tendency is clearly represented in the Struggle Spectrum described in this book.

Another personal factor that most writers agree has an influence on the escalation of struggle is aggressive behavior. Aronson, a leading social psychologist, defines aggression as "a behavior aimed at causing harm or pain" (1972, p. 143). Terhune (1970) found that when tendencies of a generally aggressive and rigid nature are present in persons who are interacting, struggle is likely to arise. This aggressive behavior was identified as appearing in the presence of authoritarianism, the need for power or dominance, isolationism, concreteness in thinking, dogmatism, and paranoia.

Terhune also found that when it is impossible for the parties to withdraw from the interaction, when one or more are defensive, fear being rejected, and are unwilling to forgive, struggle is likely to emerge. However, when offered unconditional cooperation by others in the interaction these types are likely to be cooperative because of their affiliative needs, fear of rejection, and mild schizophrenia.

Coser (1956) wrote of cases in which struggle arose "exclusively from aggressive impulses which seek expression no matter what the object, where . . . the choice of object is purely accidental. In such cases no . . . limitations exist, since it is not the attainment of a result, but rather the acting out of aggressive energies which occasions the outbreak" (p. 49).

Persons with an obsession for winning and lack of concern for others are usually highly aggressive (Ruben, 1980). They are the "tough battlers" who are high in internal control, take risks, and are belligerent. According to Filley (1975), "they believe strongly that they are right and will do almost anything to avoid losing . . . and destroying their egos" (p. 54). They are normative, controlling, judgmental, make sharp distinctions between right and wrong, and think in terms of fixed rules and values. We can expect the highly aggressive person to move easily and quickly beyond a mild disagreement to dispute and even more violent levels of the spectrum.

It is common knowledge that each person views the world from a different physical and psychological space. When persons experience wide variations in their perceptions of common situations, the situation may lead to struggle between the parties.

Two roommates in a fraternity were interested in the same sorority sister. Joe saw the woman as a friendly companion, Harry saw her as a "hot date" and sexual partner. If she accepted a date with Joe, Harry would perceive his roommate as trying to cut in on his "territory." If she accepted a date with Harry, Joe would perceive his roommate as attempting to defile a fine young lady. Regardless of who got the date, they would become agitated with each other. A fight eventually ensued.

In another situation Myra admired her roommate's collection of records and said so to Su. Su, however, perceived Myra's statements as being expressions of jealousy and proceeded to accuse Myra of just such a feeling. A minor dispute ensued.

Differences in styles of behavior appear to affect the struggle between people. In the past few years a great deal of attention has been directed toward the work of Katharine Briggs and Isabel Briggs Myers, her daughter, in applying some of the concepts of psychological types developed by C.G. Jung, a Swiss psychiatrist. They have developed a tool for describing the personality preferences of people and fitting them into various types. The instrument is the *Myers-Briggs Type Indicator* (MBTI). They have divided the preferences into four scales with two opposite choices on each scale.

The *Energizing* scale describes how a person is energized and has two extremes: *E*—Extroversion (draws energy from outside, from people, activities, or things) and *I*—Introversion (draws energy from the internal world of ideas, emotions, and impressions).

The *Attending* scale describes what a person prefers to attend to and its alternatives are *S*—Sensing (gathering information through the senses and focusing on what is actual) and *N*—Intuition (gathering information through the "sixth sense" and attending to what "might be").

The *Deciding* scale describes how we make decisions and identifies the alternatives of *T*—Thinking(organizing and structuring information to make decisions in a logical way) and *F*—Feeling (organizing and structuring information to make decisions in a personal value-based way).

The fourth scale, the *Living* scale, identifies the life style a person adopts or prefers and identifies the extremes as *J*—Judging (a planned and organized life) and *P*—Perceiving (living spontaneously and flexibly).

By taking the inventory, people can discover their preferences on each of the scales and learn which combine into a type which represents their particular styles.

> *For example, ISTJ means an introvert (I) who likes to process information with sensing (S), who prefers to use thinking (T) to make decisions, and who mainly takes a judging (J) attitude toward the outer world. A person with opposite preferences on all four scales would be an ENFP. This means an extrovert (E) who prefers intuition (N) for perceiving, feeling (F) for making decisions, and who takes a spontaneous and flexible attitude (P) toward the outer world. (Myers, 1987, p. 7)*

Because of their differences, when the above two types need to work together, we can expect some struggle between them as they attempt to deal with the task and each other. The significance of the MBTI to interpersonal struggle is that it provides us with some cues to the types that are likely to struggle with each other. For example we would expect Extroverts (E) to have more difficulty relating to and working with Introverts (I) than would other Introverts. An area in which struggle could very likely emerge is between those who make decisions through Thinking (T) and those who make decisions by Feeling (F). Even so, each difference has some positive as well as negative aspects, but when there are differences there is a potential for struggle.

Kiersey and Bates (1978) merged the Type theory with what they call "Temperament" theory. They observed styles of managers and their leadership behaviors and worked out the Temperament theory by grouping Types into SJ, SP, NF, and NT.

An SJ manager is one who needs appreciation and is irritated by others who do not use standard procedures, ignore deadlines, and do not play by the rules. This type of manager tends to irritate others by doom and gloom positions, sarcasm, sharp criticism, and failure to see humor. The pitfalls of these types of managers are that they are impatient when projects get delayed, may decide issues too quickly, tend to be overly concerned with dire happenings, and believe hard and long work is the way to success. The SJ manager focuses on the hierarchy of the organization, and his or her abilities lie in establishing policies, rules, schedules, and following through, along with patience, thoroughness, steadiness, and reliability. The SJ manager believes that self and others must earn their keep and that the organization must run on solid facts. The SJ values caution, carefulness, and accuracy of work.

Contrast this SJ manager with the NF manager who appreciates him- or herself as having high energy and an ability to value others and to make unique contributions. The NF managers need approval. Irritations at work are impersonal treatment, criticism, and lack of positive feedback. The NF irritates others by taking emotional stands, moralistic positions, and by getting overextended and creating dependencies. The NF's pitfalls to managing are sweeping problems under the rug, playing favorites, observing priorities other than one's own, and anxiety to please. The NF focuses on the growth needs of the organization and is skilled in communicating organizational norms, making decisions by participation, and is personal, insightful and charismatic. This manager believes that the strength of the people in the organization is the strength of the organization and that the organization must utilize the talents of the workers. The NF values autonomy, cooperation, harmony, and self-determination.

Now, if these two types of managers are operating within the same organization in a fairly close working relationship with each other, we can assume that there is going to be sparks and some struggle between them and their subunits. Each type (and temperament group) has important contributions to make to a group and the group would be weakened without them. But the differences can create tension. Some styles and temperaments need each other in order to maximize a group output and a little struggle between them is positive.

There is a great deal of research being done on the MBTI instrument and it appears to be quite effective in identifying style preferences. It has great promise as an instrument to be used in helping people to understand each other so that accommodations can be developed. It is apparent, also, that the information from the inventory can be helpful in putting people together in teams in order to minimize the potential for unproductive dispute.

Anxiety

Another factor that seems associated with struggle is the presence of anxiety. This is very closely related to the presence of *stress*. High levels of anxiety seem to cause people to be excessively rigid and inflexible (Folger & Poole, 1984). These rigid and inflexible tendencies often cause people to persist in compulsive acts that have destructive results. Many find that the performance of compulsive, repetitive behaviors is somewhat rewarding and removes some of the anxiety because such behaviors provide a certain level of control over a situation even though it may lead to undesirable consequences. The result is a cycle of escalation. Anxiety leads to compulsive behaviors, which give a sense of mastery over a situation, which in turn reduces the anxiety but also increases the struggle. The increase of the struggle then produces more anxiety.

Three partners were engaged as instructors in a high pressure-high stress training program that required intense concentration and delicate interactions with the trainees. The situation was such that the partners, although very effective in their work, ended each work day with much anxiety about the effectiveness of their performance for the day. So, before bedtime, the three would gather in their living quarters, eat lots of junk food, drink beer, engage in high tension-manic type laughter and create absurd scenarios involving themselves. All quite relaxing, they thought, while providing release from the tensions of the day. However, instead of providing relaxation and actual stress reduction, the behaviors seemed to escalate the tension and stress so that they could not sleep and would inevitably start the next day in a state of semi-exhaustion. The combination of being tired and under pressure made the next day stressful; minor struggles with colleagues would escalate into tense exchanges and the whole process escalated again. By the end of the training week, the team was in serious physical-emotional disarray.

Jerry was very anxious about getting his term paper completed on schedule and was working late one night when his roommate came in with a case of beer and a demand that Jerry join him in a little relaxation. Jerry cursed him, threw a book at him, and locked the door, thus feeling that he was getting some control of the situation. His roommate, in turn, became angry and started pounding on the door and yelling. Jerry at that point experienced another anxiety . . . the cost to him if his room door was destroyed by the roommate. Thus the original anxiety had been assuaged for a moment but now another arose and the struggle between the two friends escalated and that brought still another concern to Jerry.

A commercial artist experienced a frustrating day at work where things went wrong and his work was ruined. He came home with high anxiety about his job. When his young son asked him to let him go out and play, the man spanked the son heartily. Afterwards the man felt very guilty about what he had done and at dinner-time got into a heated controversy with his wife over who should wash the dishes.

As Folger and Poole (1984) suggest: "Anxiety results when people disapprove of the very behaviors they are engaging in" (p. 15). But the anxiety does not decrease the tendency to continue in the undesirable behaviors because it clouds clear thinking. Thus, in struggle situations people may act out of anxiety and those acts serve to escalate the struggle.

Internal Struggle

Most of us experience internal struggles. Some psychologists indicate that these internal struggles are part of contradictions or differences in our values, expectations, and personal orientations. An analogy (metaphor) that has considerable acceptance is that there are "many selves" within us. At times these selves come into opposition with each other. The concept of "cognitive dissonance" advanced by Festinger (1957) lays the groundwork for the understanding of these internal struggles. His hypothesis was that dissonance is psychologically uncomfortable, therefore we are motivated to try to reduce it and achieve consonance or consistency. This attempt to bring about consonance often leads us into conflict with other values and concepts.

> *I often find myself experiencing an inner struggle between competing values and/or wants. Recently I had to make a decision as to whether to buy a really fine sweater that I saw in the men's store. One side of me said that I would look good in the sweater, that it was a warm one, and I needed a warm sweater because my old one had elbowed out, and that new one would last a long time. Another side of me seemed to say that the sweater cost too much, was really not as warm as it looked, and that I really didn't need it as much as my ego wanted me to think.*

When one set of personal values clash with a contradictory set of values within ourselves inner struggle results. We see this often in the love-hate relationship that is felt for a partner, in the approval-disapproval of a colleague, in the acceptance-rejection of a friend. That inner struggle can cause stress, tension, anxiety, and other ills unless the differences are resolved. I believe that persons who have many unresolved struggles within themselves are also likely to become involved in struggle with others as ways of avoiding their own inner struggles or as ways of neutralizing the inner dissonance. *This means to me that before we can have peace between us we must have peace within us.*

Contextual or "Situation" Factors

Struggle between persons occurs in context frames in which the behavior is in response to the actions of others or a set of circumstances. The actions that individuals perform are shaped by these contexts as well as by the internal conditions of the person (Folger & Poole, 1984).

The basic contexts of human interaction are intrapersonal (within the self), interpersonal (between persons), intragroup (within a group), and intergroup (between groups). Most of the specific or subcontexts are within these major context frames.

There are many subcontexts within these frames which seem to aggravate or encourage struggle behavior and to trigger escalation to more violent levels of the spectrum. I shall deal here with several of the more obvious ones. These contexts are not mutually exclusive and sometimes merge to create unique combinations.

Win-Lose or Competition

Probably the context that most clearly contributes to the escalation of struggle is that of *competition* or the "win-lose" situation. It seems to be universal. Kohn (1986) draws a distinction between *structural competition* and *intentional competition*. (Structural competition is characterized by mutually exclusive goals—"my success requires your failure," as in the zero-sum game. The goals of the parties to the interaction are simply incompatible. War is a version of structural competition in which one side must make the other fail in order to succeed. Competitive games such as football, basketball, hockey, volleyball, tennis, poker, and bridge are others.

> *I have experienced numerous situations of structural competition in which the struggle between the parties has led to violence by the direct participants and the onlookers. In a school where I once taught, the basketball team was forbidden to compete with the cross-town team because on one game night the two teams became embroiled in fist fights and other mayhem with each other on the court while the spectators threw bottles and other hard objects at each other, injuring fans as well as players.*

Intentional competition is "an individual's competitiveness, his or her proclivity for besting others," the desire to be Number One (Kohn, 1986, p. 5). This can take place outside the structured competition situation as when a person is constantly evaluating him- or herself against others even though there is no prize or accolade offered.

Within the competitive context people seem to focus their efforts on goals and interests that are antagonistic to each other and on efforts to block or constrain each other. In the competitive context, the opposing parties develop hostility toward each other that did not previously exist. Differences are emphasized, opponents are perceived as being dishonest, cheating, and unfair, communication is often misleading, and important information is withheld The result of these conditions is escalation of the struggle. "Competition breeds competition" (Deutsch, 1973, p. 367).

What Is Winning?

Throughout our lives we have been conditioned to perceive winning as the overcoming and defeat of the antagonist who then becomes the "loser."

Ruben (1980) puts it dramatically:

> Competition is an inescapable fact of life. From the nursery to the nursing home, from the bedroom to the boardroom, in politics and business and school and sports and everyday conversation, human beings are in constant competition with each other. We compete for jobs, grades, social position, sex, friendship, money, power, even love. So pervasive is the competitive urge that it frequently governs our behavior even when we are unaware of its influence. From the time we are very small, it is a fundamental aspect of the process by which we develop our self esteem, our social assurance, our very identity. (p. ix)

Winning, by definition, means primarily that one gains victory in a contest by overcoming an opponent (Websters Third New International Dictionary, unabridged, p. 2618). Losing means a failure to win and is thereby a deprivation (NID, p. 1338).

We have also been conditioned from childhood to seek to be "winners" in almost all of our relations with each other, that is, to overcome and supersede our "opponents." According to Ruben (1980), "there are virtually no areas of human interaction which are free from the urge to win" (p. 3). Whenever the perception of "win" appears we expect there to be a loser.

Win-Lose = Zero Sum

In many struggle situations, the escalation leads us to a "zero-sum" or "win-lose" state of affairs. That is, the forces present move us to a situation in which, by attitude of the parties or by actual circumstances of the situation, only one side can prevail and the other *must* lose. In those conditions the critical goals of each side are exclusive and incompatible. There may be other subgoals that are not related to the interaction that are not exclusive. They, however, do not have compelling influence on the interaction. There is only one way to realize the payoff for this kind of struggle condition. There is only one winner and therefore there must be a loser. There cannot be a loser without a winner. The structure is clear and finite.

By definition, the win-lose state of affairs means one side will win and one side will lose. The existence of the win-lose state of being does not allow for both sides to win because it is the very presence of the threat and the reality of losing that makes the struggle significant. If both sides could *win*, there would be no *lose* in the configuration. The win-lose condition presumes the inescapable effect of one side losing—A "winner-take-all" condition. The costs of the struggle are not always constructively resolved or removed.

We have numerous situations in life in which this condition exists. When two persons are seeking the hand of a third in marriage, our Western culture allows for only one of the suitors to win the hand of the third. When we run for a single public (or any politically based) office, only one person can be elected for a specific position. Our U.S. Constitution does not allow for more than one President at a time.

Blake and Mouton (1984), leading social psychologists over the past 40 years, write that

> When groups are vying with one another, a win-lose mentality characteristic of many interface relationships may come to replace necessary cooperation and problem solving. Each group has a vested interest in its own success, even if one group's gain is at the expense of the other. The desire to win becomes an end in itself. This win-lose competitive motivation can be and often is exploited to encourage increased motivation and effort from group members. Then winning becomes the name of the organizational game, and members are pushed to work harder, faster, longer, or better . . . Once established, a competitive mind-set evokes more distrust, which can lead to increased tension, hostility, and conflict. (pp. 9-10)

This win-lose state of being is very compelling and appears to fuel the escalation of struggle by creating forces that aggravate the struggle. It does nothing to de-escalate struggle and actually does little to facilitate the discovery of innovative constructive solutions acceptable to both sides (Likert &

Likert, 1976). In fact, there is considerable evidence to show that groups who continue to lose in win-lose struggles in intergroup situations become debilitated and exhibit destructive behaviors. They divide into warring subgroups, isolates appear in the groups, rumor becomes abundant, the groups lose attractiveness to their members (losing football teams have a hard time recruiting top-level players), the better members leave, insecurity in the group develops, innovations and initiation of ideas diminish, bureaucratization of the group increases, other groups are perceived as competitors against whom this group cannot win, and the groups' capacity to respond deteriorates (Shepard, 1964).

Basketball, baseball, and many competitive games and sports are win-lose struggles. It is not possible for both sides to win. *There can be no such thing as a win-win when a win-lose condition, structure, or intention exists* (see discussion below). The win-lose condition may be the result of a set of predetermined rules, as in competitive sports and other contest activities, or it may be the result of a state of mind or perception of the situation by the parties to the dispute. If one party to a dispute *perceives* that it must supersede the other, the win-lose condition is present regardless of whether or not that is actually the objective state of affairs.

> *What started out as a friendly shooting of baskets by two persons with no competition assumed, turned into a contest when one of them decided that she wanted to make more baskets than the other. It wasn't long until the friendly "shoot" became a hotly contested game.*

The nature of the goals of the parties to the dispute determine whether the condition becomes win-lose. If the goal is a resource that cannot be divided and only one can achieve it, the win-lose structure is inevitable as, for example, when two persons seek a prize that only one can have. As we have noted before, there are some win-lose conditions that are inescapable due to the nature of things (called "zero-sum," condition, or structural). Some are present because the parties *perceive* the situation in that way.

In employment situations, a given job may be available to only one person. Thus, when a dozen or so apply and compete for the job they are involved in a win-lose situation. Similarly, in bidding in commodity or product purchases, only one bidder gets the bid and the others lose. A great deal of our social, economic and political life revolves around the win-lose process. I have more to say about that in the chapter on Negotiation.

The win-lose condition in group relations typically exhibits the following characteristics: in-group cohesion grows rapidly against the "enemy" before and during the contest; leadership and power become more concentrated; within the group there is less opportunity for disagreement and questioning of the alternatives; diversity is eliminated; internal strife (particularly within the losing group) arises after the battle is over; perceptual and judgmental distortions increase significantly on both sides; objectivity decreases as the contest is heightened; attitudes toward the other become increasingly hostile; confidence and trust disappear; and the representatives of each group are put under great pressure to win at any cost (Likert & Likert, 1976).

As I explained in Chapter One, the struggle-conflict phenomenon seems to spread out over a continuum. At one end of the continuum there are opportunities for joint decisions and sharing of rewards or payoffs so long as the parties have not become polarized. But, when the struggle escalates toward the dispute phase and beyond, it becomes more polarized and each party feels that its goals must be met. Not to reach them is to *lose*. To reach them is to *win*. When parties become polarized against each other with their goals mutually exclusive (that is, if one reaches the goal the other cannot), they find it extremely difficult to see or seek a middle ground on which they can agree.

There is no avoidance of the "win-lose" type of interaction when we are in a zero-sum payoff context or structure. They are one and the same. Furthermore, it is extremely difficult to retreat from this structure once we are in it. That is, when I, by choice, get involved in an organized basketball game, there must be a winner, and I must behave in reference to that set of conditions or leave the game. It is not very realistic to hope to change the rules of the game, once started, to make it possible for us to come out with a tie and a claim for both of us to win.

Traditional approaches to negotiation and bargaining are also forms of win-lose interaction. However, there are ways in which these processes can change the game so that more integrative approaches can emerge. I have more to say about this in the chapter on Negotiation and Bargaining.

Cultural Differences

Another contextual factor that seems to aggravate struggle is *cultural differences*. Differences in language, dress, perceptions of the world, rituals, and goals within close proximity to each other seem to trigger disagreements, disputes, and on up the spectrum to violence. These differences occur in interpersonal relations and intergroup relations. The failure to provide for adequate communication between cultures establishes a framework for struggle. Many universities have formed offices of intercultural affairs in order to help de-escalate the struggles that emerge when two cultures clash on the campus.

Mary Jane Collier, an intercultural communication specialist at Oregon State University, in a professional discussion, defined culture as a systematic *process* that is a *conduct* created and changed by people, and that any group of persons creates a culture when their conduct becomes patterned with recurrent symbols, shared interpretations and language codes, and evident norms. She also pointed out that the cultural diversity in our society is increasing.

We are experiencing, in the United States, an increasing amount of overt confrontation and struggle between cultures. The confrontation of different cultures in the ghettos of New York, Chicago, Los Angeles, New Orleans and elsewhere is spawning many instances of violence. On one college campus I know, there is a growing number of people enrolling from the Pacific Rim countries. The impact of these different cultures on a rather conservative Western-U.S.-university culture has created some tense situations. Recently, for example, a fraternity whose members were mostly black withdrew from the Interfraternity Council of the campus due to alleged mistreatment of its members at the hands of the fraternities populated by mostly white members.

Different religious practices seem to generate distrust between the cultures and struggle emerges as the immigrant culture tries to find ways to practice in a climate that is resistant to these practices.

> *The crises in the Middle East and the Balkans have persistent and violent religious struggles in their contexts. On many campuses in recent years we are uncovering strong anti-semitic groups who are attempting to destroy and reject the semitic peoples. Similarly, Neo nazi and White Supremacy groups appear determined to destroy the rights of the black, brown, and otherwise different cultures in our midst. Recent trials of the leaders of one of these groups in the Northwest revealed very violent tendencies that led to the brutal death of several blacks in the area.*

Not the least of the problems in a multicultural society is the difficulty in coping with the varying interpretations assigned to nonverbal symbols. The effect of distance between people as they interact, the variations in the significance of certain hand movements, and so on, are all cultural elements that create a context in which struggle takes place that can easily escalate when the issues are not resolved. (The U.S. Peace Corps was an effort to circumvent the potential struggles that arise between cultures by providing opportunities for U.S. citizens to live and work with different cultures and thereby learn how to relate to them.)

Interference

Another contextual factor that has some effect on struggle is the *interference* with the goal-efforts of people. As a campus parking hearings officer, I was introduced to the almost violent struggles that occur between those who park illegally as they attempt to get to a class, meet a friend, move their belongings into a dormitory, or take care of an emergency, and the Parking Officers who are perceived as interfering with the goal efforts of the violators of the parking code.

I remember quite vividly when I was preparing to take off on a long-anticipated holiday and a colleague intervened with an urgent call for help regarding his car. I did not respond too pleasantly to his request, and a potential struggle between us arose.

> *A committee chair who was trying to keep the meeting going smoothly was constantly harassed by a member of the committee who would break in with ideas and subjects that were out of order and that served to interfere with the business of the group. The chair finally responded with an angry attack on the troublemaker, inviting him out of the meeting. When the meeting was over, the chair was met at the door with threats and harsh words by the rejected member and his compatriots.*

As an arbitrator I encounter frequent objections from one side to the presentations of the other side. These interferences are usually attempts to restrict the information coming from the opposing side, to confuse the other side, to make the constituency feel that it is being represented well, or to influence the arbitrator. What I have noticed is that as the objections increase, the tensions between the parties increase (see Chapter 6, this volume).

Institutional and Organizational Factors

Institutional or organizational contexts are a persistent source of struggle, as are differences in needs and goals. Some of the more significant areas relate to the difference in the goals and purposes of those at the top of the organizational structure and those at the bottom. Thus, the president and management team of the Gizmo Company seeks to realize a profit from the manufacture and distribution of gizmos. To do this requires that a large number of gizmos be produced with the least amount of cost, time, and effort. The management group sees this as its goal. The workers on the assembly line and at the distribution centers seek to make a living wage or better with the least amount of effort required per unit. The difference in the basic goals of the workers and management sets the stage for struggle throughout almost all business phases.

In bureaucratic service structures in government, the struggles between those who deliver the services and those who design the services and engage in the politics of maintaining their agency are common. Often the director or executive officer of an agency is more concerned with maintaining the role and status of the job than in actually providing the service that is the reason for the existence of the agency. Quite often, also, the workers in the agency seek ways to advance their position in the agency hierarchy, to gather icons of authority, and/or to access resources rather than attend to the services for which the agency exists. These differences in goals are often seen as exclusive and struggle results.

Struggles between lateral units in an organization often emerge in efforts to gain more attention, a greater part of the financial resources, better working conditions, and so on. One of the most recognized factors in these struggles between lateral units is the lack of useful and pertinent communication between them—one hand does not know what the other hand is doing. A similar problem arises in the vertical relationships between units in an organization.

Realistic and Nonrealistic Factors

Coser (1956) describes another set of contexts, the *realistic* and the *nonrealistic* forms of struggle. Those struggles are *realistic* which rise from "frustration of specific demands within a relationship and from estimates of gains of the participants, and which are directed at the presumed frustrating object . . . insofar as they are means toward a specific result." Those struggles involving interaction between persons are *nonrealistic* that:

> are not occasioned by the rival ends of the antagonists, but by the need for tension release of at least one of them . . . the choice of antagonists depends on determinants not directly related to a contentious issue and is not oriented toward the attainment of specific results. (p. 49)

Thus, realistic factors include such things as opposing claims to scarce resources, power, values, position, mutually incompatible goals, and when the struggle is perceived by the parties as a means toward some specific goals and desires. Nonrealistic factors involve those conditions in which frustrations and deprivations are occurring, in which realistic factors were never allowed expression, and in which there is a release of tension in aggressive action that provide sufficient satisfaction (Coser, 1956, p. 54).

Nonrealistic struggle was demonstrated when a young preschooler became frustrated because he wasn't getting the attention he felt he deserved in the family and would verbally and physically attack almost anyone who appeared.

However, when two roommates get into a scuffle over the use of a jointly held vehicle the struggle is realistic because it concerns a means of obtaining specific results. Most labor-management struggles are within the realistic context.

Interdependence

Struggle arises in a context in which the parties to the matter are *interdependent*. That is, the actions of one party has consequences for the other party and visa versa. If there was no dependence on each other for anything, two people would not engage in struggle behavior. If Jane and Jack had no dependence on each other, they would not have had trouble. Further, we can probably also suggest that the more interdependent people are with each other, the greater the chances for disagreements to arise. The more that the actions of my partner affect my life, the more likely we are to encounter some disagreements about what she does or does not do, and visa versa. Some of this is the result of the potential that each of us had to aid or to interfere with the other (see Folger & Poole, 1984, p. 5).

Deutsch (1977) identified two levels of interdependence: "promotive interdependence" and "contrient" interdependence. In the "promotive interdependent" situation the relation between the parties is essentially cooperative in that the parties share goals and what one attains satisfies the other also (a positive correlation between the the sets of goals). The "contriently interdependent" situation exists when one party reaches the goal and the other fails. It is quite possible for two persons to have high promotive interdependence on one set of goals and contrient interdependence on another set of goals. Deutsch also relates the two interdependencies to the nature of the struggle interaction. The promotively interdependent relationship in relation to a goal leads to cooperative interaction. The contriently interdependent relationship leads to competitive interaction. Thus, in the Struggle Spectrum, a promotively interdependent relationship between the parties may lead to resolution of differences at Stage 1 or 2. As we move into Stages 3, 4, 5, and 6 the contriently interdependent relationships appear to dominate.

Scarce and Undistributable Resources

One of the most common contexts of struggle is when people with similar needs, values, and conditions encounter *scarce and undistributable resources* or goods that are required to satisfy their needs, values, and conditions. For example, two fraternity brothers want the same single room in the fraternity house. They have similar needs for a quiet study space. They both value privacy. The particular room is the only single room in the house and is located away from the major traffic flow of the facility. Clearly, if the men had different needs in terms of rooms there would be no struggle.

Different Needs and Values.

The opposite context also creates a potential for struggle. When *needs and values are different* within an organized system or group the participants will encounter struggle when those needs and values push the participants in different directions or to the use of different methods. Thus, in a situation in which a family of four is traveling on a vacation in the family station wagon, Mom and Dad want to stop at campsites and pitch the tent. Their teenaged children hate camping out and are unalterably opposed to tenting in any form. The struggle within the family can become serious.

All of these contexts are capable of spawning struggle. There are others, and your own experience can uncover them. They do not usually exist in isolation from each other, but can be part of a more complex scheme that combines several contexts. For example, when different needs and values within a group merge into a win-lose context, disputes are usually intense and escalate rapidly.

PREVENTION AND INTERVENTION IN THE MANAGEMENT OF STRUGGLE

The management of struggle can be approached from two directions: preventive and interventive. The *preventive* occurs when we discover, train, educate, and install processes that facilitate the control, avoidance, or deterrence of the contexts and other divisive conditions that lead to undesirable levels of struggle. The *interventive* occurs when we bring third parties into struggles that have escalated to disputes and more intense levels and charge them with the responsibility of facilitating the parties in resolving the disputes.

Preventive actions are those that anticipate difficulties in managing the struggle process and seek to change or manage the conditions that cause it to escalate. The interventive process occurs when the parties to the struggle themselves are willing to get the help of uninvolved third parties to reach settlement or resolution of the dispute. It also occurs when, because of the effect of the struggle on the parties and others closely related to them, third parties are imposed on the disputants by force or mandate, as when the police intervene in a fight between two warring gangs on a street or when the court mandates that a divorcing couple must go to mediation (see the discussion of this in Chapter 5).

Preventive Processes

By looking at the struggle spectrum you can see that we can often prevent one phase from developing by resolving the preceding one. Thus, one way of preventing the escalation of struggle is to train people to recognize the conditions and contexts that lead to escalation and the methods whereby those conditions can be controlled or managed.

Training in related skills and understandings also has preventive value. Preventive systems include programs aimed specifically at developing skills and understanding in interpersonal communication, the struggle spectrum and the nature of conflict, problem solving and decision making, negotiation, self-awareness, small group behavior, leadership, and other areas.

It is also valuable in helping parties with potential disputes to understand each other better and to develop effective communication systems. In a sense, teachers, therapists, lawyers, administrators, and other community and professional leaders can be deeply involved in the prevention and/or management of struggle escalation. I have discovered that skilled mediators, when not mediating, can provide excellent preventive guidance as a result of their direct experience with how struggle escalates. In order to facilitate the development of conditions that prevent the escalation of differences to destructive disputes, the Federal Mediation and Conciliation Service has for many years provided special assistance to labor and management outside of dispute settings.

It is also possible, in some situations, to *de-escalate* a dispute to a level at which preventive processes may be introduced. A dispute between a divorcing man and wife may have gone to the litigation stage. At this point the two have rejected the alternative of taking any further responsibility for reaching a solution to their problems. The actions of a counselor or judge may cause them to de-escalate from this stage to a stage at which they are willing to attempt to discuss their problems and reach a solution. Labor-management mediators often do not get drawn into disputes until the parties are highly polarized and in strong contention. One of the early tasks of the mediator is to create ways in which the parties can de-escalate without losing face (see Chapter 5).

There are any number of processes that can be used to prevent and/or manage struggle emergence and escalation. Again I deal only with some of the more outstanding ones.

Self-Awareness

In trying to prevent the effects of antagonistic intrapersonal characteristics on ourselves and our relationships with each other it is important that we develop considerable *self-awareness, self-esteem and trust in ourselves.*

Robert (1982) identifies self-awareness as a key to the management of struggle.

No one knows exactly how he or she will behave when faced with difficult interpersonal or intergroup confrontations, because rational responses are usually short-circuited by the stress . . . But the more a person learns about how he or she might react, the greater the chances for selecting the appropriate course of action. Unfortunately, this self-knowledge is extremely difficult to obtain. A self-help formula that promises to make people more assertive, lovable and effective as they deal with conflict [or struggle] in their lives will not work if it does not fit the style of the person using it. To accept suggestions for handling conflict [struggle] without spending some time on personal awareness and self-understanding is like buying mail order clothes—they will fit only if you are lucky. One must always ask, "Will this work for me?" Without understanding your potential as a conflict [struggle] manager and examining your strengths, weaknesses, natural inclinations, and preferences, you will find limited value in "canned" suggestions, and they may even be detrimental. (p. 14)

Robert developed a "Conflict-Management Style Survey" that is very useful in helping persons identify their styles of responding to struggle situations (1982, p. 24 ff). Taken along with the MBTI, a helpful set of information can be generated about our selves in relation to struggle. There are numerous other avenues for reaching this condition. Studies in personal psychology are valuable.

Having looked at some of the characteristics that make our relating to each other in struggle situations more likely to become destructive, what can we do to overcome or control these characteristics?

Remember that such characteristics as authoritarianism, defensiveness, dogmatism, alienation, despair, and prejudice may come from a long way back in our lives. Certainly a great deal of the treatment we receive as children affects the way we behave now (for example, children who have been abused tend to become abusers as adults more frequently than those who were not abused). The kinds of behaviors we were rewarded for are the kinds of behaviors we are probably following now. If we were rewarded for winning a fight and punished when we lost, our present orientation is likely to push toward a win-lose condition pretty fast. The first step, of course, is to find out what our behavior tendencies may actually be. If they are not what we would want them to be, then our problem is to find ways of changing them.

It may be that we can do this alone or with the help of close friends. But failing that, there can be other ways of getting help. When the problems seem to be affecting us more than we can control, a common suggestion at this stage is to go in search of a psychotherapist. The image of the therapist is such that we think we should be able to get help immediately. It is possible that a therapist can be of help depending on the background and the basic orientation to practice that represents his or her work. However, we should be aware of the significant difference between therapists and counselors and/or educators. The therapist usually works from a model resembling the medical profession, that is, on the basis that the person coming for treatment is sick, disabled, or otherwise debilitated. Therefore, in order to put things right, a treatment or healing process must take place.

In contrast is the counselor and/or educator who works from a model of normalcy or relative health. The educator views the student and the counselor views the client as a healthy person who is having some difficulties in normal growth and adjustment or just wants to become more effective in coping with the world. There is no call for healing or therapy in the counselor's or educator's model. The thrust of the work of the counselor and the educator is to *facilitate* the growth of the client-student. In this respect, the counselor-educator and the therapist are vastly different.

There are other areas in which they overlap. Both may use similar means to help the patient-client. Therapists are discovering that many of the methods useful in learning and growth are also effective in treatment and therapy. Educator-counselors are discovering that many of the techniques used in therapy and treatment are quite useful in growth, development, and learning when used carefully and discriminately. In a sense both are dealing with the person, but at different phases or conditions in the existence of the patient-client.

Therefore, rather than go to a therapist when you feel you have difficulty in recognizing and coping with struggle, try the education-counseling route. There are numerous types of programs in higher education, in extension courses, and on the open market dealing with personal growth and development. Self-awareness and interpersonal communication seminars and workshops aimed at coping with just such matters as we are discussing here have been held in Oregon for over two decades (see Keltner, 1990). There are many types of personal-growth programs around the country. They have a variety of names and styles of presentation. Most of them, however, aim at facilitating change and growth in personal behaviors and orientations. The T groups, as initiated by the National Training Laboratories, are probably the most well known and, in the hands of well-trained personnel, are educationally solid and reliable. Encounter groups were developed 30 or more years ago and swept across the country at a great rate. They still exist in modified form and name. Unfortunately, the basic concept of encounter was contaminated by some less substantial offshoots.

One of the fundamental concepts of encounter came from the work of Carl Rogers, Will Shutz, and others. It is fundamentally a process of facilitating each person to confront intra- and inter-personal relationships in the group setting. Inevitably the issues and coping problems of inter- and intrapersonal conflicts come in for attention. A principle concept of coping is based on a loving and supporting atmosphere so that each member can feel secure in dealing with problems. Certainly, if the approach is well designed and the group is led by a qualified person who has demonstrated effectiveness there is much to be gained from participating in groups such as growth groups, awareness groups, T groups, or some form of encounter group.

Use caution, however, in selecting the group and the leader-trainer. There are very many unqualified and inept persons attempting to perform as trainers of T groups, encounter groups, and so-called growth groups. Their ineptness and lack of preparation often allows for behaviors in the experience that cannot be handled or coped with in that context in a constructive manner.

One of the important contributions of effective-self awareness training is that it will help us become conscious of our physical and emotional states in various situations. Sometimes this can be startling.

> *One time a friend of mine, named Steve, was participating in the POWERPLAY game invented by George Peabody and Paul Dietterich (Peabody & Dietterich, 1973). During one of the balloting periods, someone from another group grabbed his ballot and ran off with it. Steve took out after him and caught the "thief" just outside the door and tackled him on the grass. Suddenly Steve froze in his position . . . then got up and shook his head and came back in to where I was standing.*
>
> *He burst out angrily, "Sam, what the hell did you do to me?"*
>
> *I replied that I hadn't done anything.*
>
> *"But you made me do it!" he shouted.*
>
> *"Do what?" I asked.*
>
> *"You set up the conditions where someone would steal my ballot and I would go after them, didn't you?" he accused.*
>
> *"No, I did not set up conditions for that to happen." I replied. " This is simply a game. Lots of things can happen. But what are you talking about?"*
>
> *"I'll tell you what I'm talking about . . ." he shouted, waving his arms. "When I tackled Joe out there, and he's a close friend of mine, I had a pencil in my hand and for a second or two, My God, I could have shoved it into his belly and thought nothing of it. Look, I'm a peaceful guy. I don't hurt people. What in the hell was going on that I suddenly felt I could hurt one of my best friends?"*
>
> *I asked Steve to stop a moment and get in touch with his inner feelings. He reported, after a while, that he felt all the turmoil inside but there was also a good feeling that he got his ballot back. But the violence really upset him. I tried to help Steve get in touch with the conditions he faced when he took off after his friend, of the feelings he had, of the pressures he felt, etc.*

Hopefully, Steve will be a bit more wary when he finds himself in pressure conditions and emotional states in which he can suddenly turn destructive and enact a punitive destructive process. This is a form of self-awareness. Through the simulation Steve and others were able to get in touch with many of the factors within themselves that lead to destructive conflict. There are too many people unable to get in touch with these inner elements. Good negotiators, mediators, facilitators, and arbitrators must be in touch with themselves.

One of the functions of self-awareness training is that when we find ourselves slipping into struggle conditions or states in which our feelings and behaviors are out of control we can seek qualified help. Most of us who have been involved in this kind of work realize that everyone needs help at one time or another. An important achievement is to be able to ask for help when we need it.

There are several benefits that emerge from self-awareness and the training that facilitates it. It will:

- help us be more perceptive about other people's thoughts and feelings and to be empathetic with their state of being;
- allow us, in turn, to determine our strategy for dealing with others as they move through various states of being. In other words, if I can sense what you are feeling I can estimate the reactions you will have to what I am doing and prepare to cope with your reactions in a nondestructive way;
- also help me be more tolerant of the emotional extremes that others reach and the competitive alternatives that they might use;
- give us greater control over our own responses. By being in touch with our inner selves we can be aware of more alternatives we may have so that we can select responses in conflict situations that will not cause escalation toward violence; and
- also help us to be more centered or balanced and to be able to maintain a centered state of being in the midst of heavy struggles when losing our balance would lead to violent conflict and probable destruction and/or defeat. For over a thousand years martial artists have studied the art of being centered, not just to be able to use the tools of war, but to enable them to meet the struggles around them alert and relaxed. The art of balance and centering is still taught today by masters of Aikido, Karate, and others who teach the merging of body-mind in social interaction (for an interesting discussion of these processes see Dobson & Miller, 1978).

Cooperative Contexts: Changing the Game

How do we prevent the development of win-lose contexts in our relations with others? This is one of the most significant areas in which work is needed. As I have indicated, there are some win-lose conditions that are productive and useful. It is when the win-lose situation leads to undesirable consequences, to violence, decay, and destruction that we need to find ways to avoid or "detoxify" the condition.

One of the most highly touted but little understood processes in preventing the dangerous effects of win-lose contexts is the development and use of a *cooperative* context. This means that we must *change the character of the win-lose game. That is, those interactions that are structured for competition must be restructured so that they are cooperative.* We need to restructure or, to use a currently popular word, "reframe" our relationships so that there are not winners or losers. The way to do this is to develop more cooperative interaction. Deutsch (1985) explains:

> A cooperative process leads to the defining of conflicting interests as a mutual problem to be solved by collaborative effort. It facilitates the recognition of the legitimacy of each other's interest and of the necessity of searching for a solution that is responsive to the needs of all. It tends to limit rather than expand the scope of conflicting interests. (p. 255)

Kohn (1986) points out that "competition interferes with communication. The difference between cooperation and competition is the difference between listening to each other's points of view and twisting each other's arm" (p. 157). He points out that "we try to beat others in order to prove our own worth," and that the way to find better (than competitive) ways of gaining self-esteem is to build trust in ourselves so that we do not have to keep proving our superiority. "The better I feel about myself, the less I will need to make you lose" (p. 183).

What we need to do in order to prevent escalation of struggle is to design contexts that are cooperative rather than win-lose or to minimize winning by not keeping score or directing our attention to the results of the activity, but enjoying the activity for its own sake. Thus we can shoot baskets together and even play "horse" without being too concerned as to who wins or loses and primarily enjoy the action.

This means that the concept and practice of "winning "must be changed to another model.

We're All Winners? The Fallacy of the "Win-Win" Strategy

During the past few years we have heard a lot about the way to solve our conflicts, to resolve our struggles with each other, and so on by using a dubious concept, strategy, and attitude called "Win-Win." The essence of this theme is that each party to a struggle "wins" instead of one winning and the other losing. On the surface it sounds like a brilliant idea. A way for EVERYBODY to "win" in the SAME GAME! WOW! Heaven at last! We've WON the Revolution . . . ALL of us! Advocates of this "win-win" solution are widely represented in many fields.

There is much amiss about this concept, strategy, and attitude. (It appears in all three forms.) Let's examine the matter more closely.

If the concept and its application were thoroughly understood I would not be concerned. But the evidence is clear that many people are misunderstanding and misusing the idea. I have even heard well meaning people ask why we cannot use the "win-win" approach in a basketball game when two evenly matched teams are sweating it out. One of the strangest situations was when two men were vying for a single available job. An observer suggested that they should approach the whole struggle with a "win-win" attitude and that the one who did not get the job could feel that he had done a good job of competing and that this was a "win" too. Only one man won the job. The other did not get the job. Did they both win?

It is very important that we recognize that it is extremely difficult for a "win-lose" game or situation to be transformed into another kind of game or situation once it has become active. Thus when we are in a "win-lose" context or structure there cannot be a "win-win" result. (See the win-win chart on the next page.)

Society is not structured at present to eliminate the win-lose context. All of our lives we have been conditioned to glorify the winners and castigate the losers. Winning has been "good," and losing has been "bad."

THE WIN-LOSE CONDITION AND
THE IMPOSSIBILITY OF WIN-WIN

The win-lose condition is a binary state of affairs that is characterized by *mutually exclusive goals,*
polarized positions and *"winner-take-all"* perspectives. **Whenever that condition exists it can be resolved
only by one person winning and the other losing.**

IN THE BINARY STATE OF AFFAIRS
IT IS NOT POSSIBLE TO MERGE
THE TWO POSSIBILITIES OR
TO ELIMINATE ONE OF THEM.

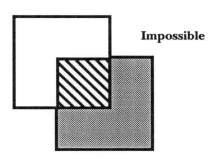

Impossible

To eliminate losing and provide for integration,
a new and/or different **context, condition, or situation**
must be created that is not a binary or bimodal condition.

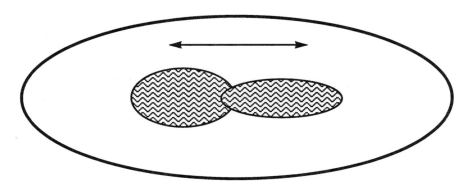

This is a different kind of game

Kohn (1986) points out that:

. . . our schooling, from the earliest grades, trains us not only to triumph over others but to regard them as obstacles to our own success. Our leisure time is filled with highly structured games in which one individual or team must defeat another. Even within the family there is rivalry . . . that turns love into a kind of trophy.

Our collective creativity seems to be tied up in devising new ways to produce winners and losers. It is not enough that we struggle against our colleagues at work to be more productive; we must compete for the title of "Friendliest Employee." . . . No corner of our lives is too trivial—or too important to be exempted from the compulsion to rank ourselves against one another.

Our lives are not merely affected by, but structured upon, the need to be "better than." We seem to have reached a point where doing our jobs, educating our children, and even relaxing on the weekends have to take place in the context of a struggle where some must lose.

Bookstores have been deluged with guides to winning in the marketplace. (pp. 2-3)

What if we had learned just the opposite—that losing was "good" and winning was "bad?" Would we not struggle to lose just as hard as we now struggle to win? Because we have been given rewards for winning, we tend to expect rewards or payoffs whenever we win. Thus, any rhetoric that attaches the concept "win" to any expected outcome of a dispute is bound to be attractive.

It seems that many times we get involved in rather destructive conflicts and struggles so that when we have won, we have actually lost more than if we had been defeated. Hemingway (1933) wrote:

Unlike all other forms of battle or combat, the conditions (of gaming) are such that the winner shall take nothing; neither his ease, nor his pleasure, nor any notions of glory, nor if he win far enough, shall there be any reward within himself. (title page)

> *I am reminded of a football game where my team won by a field goal but only after it had lost its quarterback, fullback, tailback, and center to injuries which put them out for the rest of the year. We won alright but was it worth it? We didn't win another game the entire season.*

It has been suggested that there is more than one goal in every dispute and that although in the instance in which two persons were seeking the same job one person did not get the job, he or she did gain some experience and learned some additional skills that would allow him or her to survive in another situation. We must remember that we operate with primary and secondary goals. Thus, the loser in the job situation may have gone into the situation with not only the goal of getting the job (his primary goal) but of learning something about the situation and practicing his or her skills. The significant thing here is that there are at least two kinds of goals. One—the getting of the job—is an exclusive goal and only one person can reach it. The other is an inclusive goal that can be achieved by each person involved. These multiple goals can exist in any struggle situation but *when at least one exclusive goal is present the win-lose context is controlling.* It is rare that the inclusive goals overcome the exclusive goals when the exclusive goals are primary in nature. To say that the acquisition of skills and understanding gained from experiencing the loss of the job is a "win-win" is simply an oxymoron.

Winning and losing are based on what we *value.* Thus, to get a clearer understanding of winning and losing we need to understand the process of valuing, the kinds of things people value, and the sources of these values.

Can We Win Without A Loser?

The concept of both parties to a dispute winning and no party losing is indeed a tantalizing theme and when the perceived situation of "win-lose" is *not* really an actual win-lose or zero sum game, it may be possible to convince people that they both can "win" if they follow some given procedure or accede to a predetermined decision. But it is functionally and realistically impossible to reach a win-win solution *when the context provides that only one of the parties can win.*

If by accepting a certain predetermined decision or by following a process not desired by the parties they can be led to feel that they have "won," they will likely accept those conditions simply because they have been conditioned to consider winning as a major value and one for which considerable sacrifice must be made. Winning becomes the carrot to lead them to accept what otherwise might be viewed as less than the goal they actually wanted. The fatal fallacy is inescapable.

Fallacies of Win-Win

This condition makes us easy prey for those who would promise us great rewards by providing a "win-win." If we can feel we have won we will likely accept a decision. But there is a fatal fallacy here. Actually "win-win" may be only a manipulative ploy to bring people to accept a condition that *they might not otherwise accept if it were not identified as "winning."*

Greenhalgh (1987) argues that "the notion of winning is a metaphor that has the power and potential to create tunnel vision, and lead people to visualize conflicts in counterproductive ways" (p. 167). He sees the metaphor of winning as both inappropriate and dangerous in situations in which it is used to characterize negotiations. Thus, according to Greenhalgh, the win-win notion is not only illogical but conjures up the wrong images. He asserts that "when writers describe a positive-sum outcome as 'win-win' it suggests to me that they not only are using sports or military metaphors inappropriately, but are also inducing their audience to adopt the same potentially misleading interpretation" (p. 170). Greenhalgh talks of using the win-win metaphor in positive-sum outcomes as inappropriate. Note here that the positive sum game is one that is non-zero sum and in which the parties can positively share in the outcomes.

Currently in the mediation process (see Chapter 5, this volume) a number of the advocates of mediation are attempting to identify the process as a "win-win" process. This is an error. What mediation demands is a change in the character of the interaction. This means a change in the game.

> *One mediator, working with a divorcing couple mandated to mediation by the court, attempted to convince his clients of the value of mediation. In the intake or orientation session with the parties he frequently referred to the "win-win" characteristics of the process. The couple agreed to go forward to the mediation. The outcome of the mediation was a compromise agreement in which neither party got all that they originally sought. Each had to give way on some of their goals. After the mediation was over both parties were very angry, each complaining that instead of winning what they sought they really lost. The use of the "win-win" phraseology in describing the process was a rhetorical tool to bring the parties to accept mediation. What it actually did was to alienate the parties to the mediation process.*

It appears to me that we may be victims of another oxymoron or "semantic antic." Words do make a difference because they have referents in our experience and expectations. So, when we use the word "win" we expect because of our deep conditioning that there is a loser. Actually, what frequently happens is that when the "win-win" words are used in the "win-lose" context and structure, we can expect some manipulative ploy to bring about conditions that might not otherwise be accepted if they were not identified as a "win." "Win-win" is unfortunately a metaphoric set of words that reflects a concept, strategy, or condition that is at best confusing and at its worst a very subtle manipulative tool. Additionally, bookstores are also carrying a number of books hawking a "win-win" theme which turns out to be another way to manipulate others to do as one wishes. It has become, too often, a rhetorical device aimed at convincing people to accept a process that they would not otherwise accept because it promises them a "win." I recently saw an automobile ad touting the purchase of the advertised machine as a "win-win."

What many people mean when they use the term "win-win" in a win-lose context is that they want to avoid the presence or experience of a loser or of losing and the unhappiness that accompanies this. What many seem to hope is that by using the term "win-win" they can spirit away the win-lose context in which the situation exists. Such contexts or structures are simply not changed by such behavior. The basic win-lose structure of the game itself must be voided, changed, or abandoned before the mutual sharing of the rewards can take place. *If the concern of those who herald the "win-win" philosophy is to increase cooperation, collaboration, and joint problem solving then something more substantial than playing with the words and oxymoronic language will have to take place.*

Changing The Game

The key to all of this is that *if what we want to bring into focus is a condition in which both parties can distribute or share the payoff, we do not want the concept of "winning" in the structure at all.* In the win-lose context the emphasis is on winning. We need to change the context to one in which the emphasis is on the relationship between the parties and the mutuality of their goals.

In other words, instead of talking about achieving a "win-win" in a "win-lose" game we should be *changing the game or altering the basic structure of the process.* What this means is that we should carefully monitor our relationships with others so that joint deliberation and decision making can maximize the distribution of the rewards. That is, we need to seek and create more situations in which the rewards can be distributed between all who are involved and are not mutually exclusive for just one person or side. This would mean that both or all parties to the struggle would not be losers in the sense we have used the term in the win-lose context.

Instead of a "win-win" terminology for such joint processes I would suggest such terms as "shared," "sharing" or "joint resolution." Greenhalgh (1987) suggests "synergy" or "symbiosis" as better terms than competition for identifying interdependent relationships (p. 173). Again, the problem we face is that once a situation has escalated into a win-lose situation there is no way it can become a "win-win." The impossible nature of the situation can be demonstrated by the absurd equation: Win-Lose = Win-Win.

There are many kinds of situations in which the payoffs can be *shared* and in which the relationship is primary. In these conditions both the contestants may share in the available resources. In other words, the parties to the struggle may distribute the reward between them based on their agreement. Thus, the total results of the payoff will not equal zero. Hence, this is called, in game theory, a Non-Zero sum game. The process of working out the division of the rewards is either determined by the rules of the contest or is worked out through the deliberation and cooperation of the parties to the struggle. This cooperation can only be achieved by a different relationship brought about by a joint deliberation of the parties through some form of communication.

An example of this form are the golf tourneys around the country at which the top two or three players divide the winning money. Even so, the top winner gets the most money according to the rules set out before the game began. However, this is not called a "win-win" game. Many collective bargaining situations between management and employees are of such a nature that the outcomes can be *distributed*. That is, the resources can be split up evenly between the participants if they agree. However, at points in the bargaining over certain issues such as wages, the struggle becomes clearly win or lose. What the employees get comes out of the profits of the employer. That is a clear case of win-lose.

Because so much of our life is based on win-lose conditions, they simply cannot be avoided by the rhetoric of giving them another name or by trying to assume that they do not exist. Thus, to talk of "win-win" as a way of resolving a win-lose conflict is logically and practically absurd. To accomplish what well-meaning advocates of "win-win" seem to desire, we must *eliminate the concept and condition of "winning"* as a desirable dispute resolution and put in its place more mutually inclusive conditions and structures that will allow the parties to a struggle to find common ground and to *share in the rewards* emerging from the resolution of their dispute. This means a deeper understanding of the spectrum of struggle and of the ways in which it can be managed to avoid the extreme violence that emerges from unresolved disputes.

Certainly, winning has been identified as a pleasant process so long as the loser has also enjoyed the game or has gained something of value not otherwise available. But when we move to the extremes of disputes—fighting and war—there can be no enjoyment of the game by the participants. There may be enjoyment by those who sit on the sidelines and provide the warriors with the tools of war and thereby profit. But the participants themselves do not enjoy either winning or losing such conflicts for the most part except when they emerge unscathed or unharmed. There are a few, of course, who delight in the struggle, the danger, and the risk of being destroyed, and in the sadistic mutilation of the enemy. But they are not the core of our society. In our society's future the level of struggle called war will leave neither side untouched with death, destruction, sorrow, and pain. We must find ways to resolve disputes short of violence. That is the preventive way.

Setting Mutually Inclusive and Superordinate Goals

Part of the preventive way toward dealing with win-lose contexts is the establishment of goals that are mutually inclusive. When two persons can be brought to seek goals that are not exclusive the possibilities of future struggle between them is reduced.

A couple were seeking divorce and custody of their children. Each was demanding all of the children's time and their exclusive protection and parenting. After several sessions with a mediator they agreed to seek a division of the custody that would meet their children's needs, give each parent some important time with them, and guarantee that the children would suffer as little as possible as a result of the parents' separation. What really happened here was that the separate and private goals of the couple were replaced by goals that were more inclusive and included the interests of the children. The new goals were what is called "superordinate."

In an experiment some years ago two boys' teams who were competing and hostile with each other were deprived of their water supply whereupon they abandoned their struggle with each other and joined forces to find the cause of the loss of water, a more superordinate objective (Sherif, 1966).

> *The union and management of a textile company were locked in a struggle over wages and working conditions. The union was demanding a wage figure that, in effect, would threaten the ability of the company to continue in operation. The company was demanding an extension of hours of work in order to increase its production and remain in a market that was very competitive. Their goals were perceived as exclusive and the polarization created additional separation between the parties. Hostilities were emerging between the managers and the union personnel. By mutual consent they brought in a mediator. The mediator encouraged them to explore their mutual needs in the situation. The workers, facing inflation, wanted higher wages in order to protect and increase their purchasing power. The company, facing the destructive effect of its competitors and the downward trend of the selling price of its product wanted to reduce its total costs of production. By looking at the situation together they developed a set of goals that would meet the cost of living needs of the workers, increase the production in the plant to overcome the price reduction of the product and the pressure of the competition, and set up cooperative committees to deal with future issues that would arise between them.*

Setting New Rules for Interaction

Struggle between two parties implies the existence of rules that reflect and support the structure in which the contest occurs. Shimanoff (1980) defines a rule as "a followable prescription that indicates what behavior is obligated, preferred, or prohibited in certain contexts" (p. 57). Rules in a relationship occur in both explicit and implicit forms. Explicit rules are stated, and implicit rules are those that control behavior but are unspoken and unwritten.

When two parties discover their disagreement escalating toward the dispute level, further escalation can be managed, in part, by working out new rules of procedure for dealing with their differences. That is one of the reasons for the development of parliamentary procedures. It was an attempt, I suspect, to allow disputes to be aired and discussed without the mayhem that took place during early attempts at group decision making. The rules of procedure arose in order to contain differences and to encourage open discussion.

In families there are often implicit (unspoken) rules about how people relate or deal with each other. In new families the parents need to develop some rules for handling disputes that are bound to arise.

> *One couple I know have a firm understanding that they will never go to sleep as long as there is an unresolved difference between them. They seem to live by the rule. The wife told me once that sometimes they didn't get much sleep but that things seemed to get worked out. In another family it was understood that no decision involving the family as a whole was made without all members having an opportunity to provide their input. Another couple, anticipating marriage, worked out a contract between them which provided for ways in which they would deal with dis-agreements that might arise in the future. Two partners in a commercial enterprise wrote into their partnership agreement a set of rules whereby they would resolve any differences that might arise between them concerning the operation of the enterprise and the distribution of the profits.*

When it appears that a struggle may escalate partly because of the nature of the rule structure, some new rules or changes in rules may be useful. Hocker and Wilmot (1985) suggest some steps for discovering the rules that are present in a struggle situation and for generating new ones:

Parties independently list explicit and implicit rules that are operating in the situation.

Identify how and when the rules have been broken and how the violations have been communicated.

Generate rules for behaviors that should and should not be performed.

Review the list and make each rule clear and prescriptive.

Code each rule as to whose it is, what keeps it going, who enforces it, who breaks it, and what function it serves.

Discuss how the rules aid or inhibit the management of the struggle and make changes as they are perceived as useful. (pp. 141-142)

There are conditions, however, in which the emphasis on rules may become counterproductive. They must be approached carefully. Greenhalgh (1987) points out that rules coming from the sports metaphor have a negative effect on the reduction of struggle by increasing the tendency to litigate rather than to mediate and by "inducing the disputants to focus on the immediate . . . episode rather than take a longer-term perspective" (p. 171). Thus the union that went to arbitration over the matter of the management's violation of a nondiscrimination rule in the case of a woman worker who claimed she was being paid less than the standard rate for a job may have been ignoring the larger issue of discrimination that existed throughout the company.

Joint Problem Solving

A very useful preventive system is to develop skills in problem solving. These skills are not as common as they should be and as a result many mutual problems lead to struggle between the prime participants. The whole process of joint problem solving is a subject of special study. It includes the working out of mutual goals, exploring obstacles together, establishing criteria that will meet the needs of both parties, exploring alternative solutions to the problem, evaluating those solutions in terms of the criteria, and selecting the solution that meets the criteria.

Too often two parties will encounter a problem and without any careful study both will introduce solutions that are incompatible with each other. The argument over the solutions quickly escalates into dispute as each party takes a position that is contrary to the other. What is needed is a more careful examination of the goals of the parties that gave rise to the problem and of the conditions under which those goals can be met.

The joint problem-solving process can be introduced into many situations. The process of working together as a team on mutual problems requires considerable understanding of the dynamics of working together as well as skills in group communication.

The departments in a liberal arts university found themselves unable to work out a curriculum for the undergraduate program. Each department wanted its subject matter to have the most available hours for the students. The matter was not resolved until a new dean arrived and brought all the departments together in a joint effort to design a curriculum that would fit the school, not just the departments. At first the departments did not seem to respond to the change. But after the dean financed a retreat at which all the faculty were exposed to special training in joint problem solving, the group began to develop a significant curriculum.

Joint Decision Making

When we make a decision we are involved in making a choice among the alternatives available to us. When two people are involved in making a decision they both have to agree before the decision is made. When more than two people are involved in making a decision, the situation changes. The individual choice of each group member must be considered as part of the group decision. Sometimes one person will make the decision for the group (a "onefer"). At other times two people will join forces and bring the group to the decision on which they agree (a "twofer"). Another way group decisions are made is by majority vote (51% or better). Still another way is by consensus (100%).

Decision making by consensus is highly desirable so long as everyone has an opportunity to express judgments, points of view, and so on. It is dangerous, however, if in order to get consensus the group forces members to agree or members agree because they do not want to go contrary to the majority. In group decision making minority opinions must be heard to test the quality of decisions. Ideally, if we can develop real consensus in a group (that is, everyone reaches the same choice after all differences are aired and resolved) we will go a long way toward preventing differences from escalating to more combative levels of the spectrum. For example, the Quakers are skilled at the process of finding the "sense of the meeting" and will often spend a great deal of time allowing all to be heard.

Communication Processes

One of the most important of the preventive processes is the development and maintenance of open communication between the participants. The presence of barriers and interferences to communication between people clearly encourages escalation of differences. When people are unable to communicate effectively with their counterparts over differences there is greater chance for hostility to emerge. As the hostility emerges the differences become viewed as more and more significant, and this leads to additional communication difficulty.

Within organizational structures the failure to provide open communication up and down the ladder of the hierarchy tends to breed dissension between hierarchical levels. On a lateral level, when two departments who must share resources do not have open communication between them, there is an increasing tendency for them to become highly competitive and to escalate their differences.

Among the elements of communication one of the most important is skill in *listening*. If we are unable to listen to the other and get some idea of how the other perceives the world and the situation, we cannot expect to find joint resolution of our differences. Actually, we may not even be aware of the existence of differences until they suddenly emerge in violent form. Listening is a complex skill and one not easily learned. It is more than just hearing. Of all the communication processes (reading, writing, speaking, and listening) it is the most used and the one for which we have been least trained. Even though the normal person has hearing capabilities, these do not guarantee listening skill. It is estimated that the average person's efficiency in listening is between 25% and 30%. If we had to depend on that level of efficiency to maintain a business it would probably fail. With this low level of skill in listening to each other is it any wonder that we have so many unresolved disputes in our society and that even nations are unable to resolve their differences short of war.

Relationships vs Content

In many struggles there is great confusion over what is at issue—the content, the subject under scrutiny, or the relationship between the parties. Is it the people or the problem? Many times they are so intertwined that it is impossible to separate them. In many situations antagonism between two parties may spill over to any matter discussed. It takes people to make problems between people. Thus, if we wish to prevent future violence over issues that can be resolved jointly, it becomes necessary to work on repairing or creating relationships that allow for nonviolent interaction. The same is true when the task is to reduce violence and to de-escalate the struggle to levels at which it can be dealt with by other means.

> *The gang on 12th street (mostly African Americans) and the gang on 33rd (mostly Italian-Americans) both perceived the other as alien and primarily concerned with destroying them. Their relationship was such that any content issue that arose immediately became a cause for fighting. Social workers in the area tried to get both sides to join together in friendly games, or in joint service projects, but were quite unsuccessful. Each game would result in a fight. Each service project would result in a violent competition that would negate the value of the service (as when they got into a fight over who collected the most canned goods for a Thanksgiving food drive and destroyed the canned goods that each had collected). In one fight a member of one of the gangs was killed. It wasn't long before his death was followed by another in the opposing gang.*
>
> *Finally, in desperation, the community leaders brought the groups together to talk about their relationship. The confrontation was a difficult one, and took some careful strategy and delicate negotiations. But under the skilled leadership of a highly trained facilitator the gangs began to see the effect of their relationship on their behavior and slowly began to seek friendlier relations with each other. It took many months of careful work to bring this about.*

Interest vs Positions

A similar concept is the matter of *interests vs. positions*. A *position* can be one side's perception of a desirable solution to a problem, a perception of a situation, or a proposition that one side will advance and defend. *Interests* represent the underlying goals that are being expressed through the positions. They are difficult to find when covered up by positions, but they are the controlling factors over many positions.Hence, in the preventive processes of struggle management it is important to *facilitate the exploration of interests of the parties to the dispute* (see Fisher & Ury, 1981, for an extended discussion of this concept).

Trust

When struggle escalates to competition and dispute it breeds and is accompanied by distrust. One tool to help prevent the escalation to undesirable levels is to develop trusting relations between those involved in the interaction. The development of our own trusting behavior hinges very closely on our self-concept and self-awareness. Our interaction with others gives us opportunities to affirm our view of ourselves. Thus, my trust of another is a function of my own self-concept and my own self-trust, as well as my acceptance of the other.

When we feel that we can anticipate another person's actions with considerable accuracy and have confidence that he or she will respond as we anticipate there is a kind of trust present. In this sense, it is possible to trust a rival, opponent, antagonist, or enemy by anticipating accurately how that person will behave under certain conditions. However, most of the time that we refer to trust we are referring to an expectation that the behavior of another will be positively responsive to us and our goals and will be to our benefit. I can trust my partner to perform in such a way as to enhance my perception of myself and to aid in the realization of my goals. When my trust is not fulfilled I suffer unpleasant consequences that are worse than what I would have experienced if my trust had been fulfilled (Giffin & Patton, 1971).

When we trust each other we have confidence that we will not act in ways that will hurt us or someone we care about. The presence of distrust or the lack of confidence that another will act in our interest or welfare also has a generating effect on struggle escalation. One of the most significant preventive measures that people can create is the development of trust between them. When I perceive that you accept me and I value your acceptance, I am more likely to trust you than if I did not perceive you in that light. This again brings the matter of trust back to the matter of self-awareness as a preventive process.

Negotiation and Bargaining

In a later chapter the processes of negotiation and bargaining are explored. Negotiation can be an effective preventive process as well as a method of managing the whole struggle context. In the early stages of the spectrum it can prevent escalation. In the later stages bargaining can be used to start de-escalation so that better problem solving and negotiation can take place.

In short, many of the preventive processes relate to the personal behaviors, styles, attitudes, and skills that the participants in an interaction possess. Modifying and developing these elements can be very useful in preventing the escalation of struggle. In a later chapter we talk about negotiation.

Interventive Processes

Another process that has demonstrated considerable usefulness in managing struggle is third party intervention. Intervention can occur in several forms and with varying results. You will notice on the Struggle Spectrum that there are several stages when intervention can be used.

Intervention is basically an infusion of a person or persons, other than the disputants, into the interpersonal situation. Or, as in the case of international relations, the infusion of a third nation into an international dispute.

The dynamics of the struggle situation are changed immediately with the introduction of an intervenor. The first change is that the number of parties involved in the total interaction is increased. This brings about a change in the nature of the communication in the interaction. A third party changes the total direction, flow, and nature of the communication between the disputants. Intervention can have a significant effect on the outcomes of a dispute.

Intervention can range from a facilitative process to a controlling process. Intervention can be punitive, as in the case of a police action, aggravating, as in the case of meddling, facilitative, as in the case of mediation, and judicial, as in the case of arbitration and the courts.

Controlling

A *controlling* intervention is when the intervention takes the form of enforcement of rules, police action, punishment of the disputants, or manipulation of the disputants. When a parent intervenes in a dispute between children and sends them off to their respective rooms there is a controlling intervention. Other examples are when police are called in by disturbed neighbors to stop a violent fight between a husband and wife, or when referees intervene in a ballgame (or other game-type situation) to enforce the rules. Controlling interventions take place in organizations where managers may intervene in worker disputes and order the participants to stop by invoking sanctions or punishment. Too often these interventions are couched in terms that tend to shield the manager from the implications of the practice.

For example, a number of programs have developed recently under the title "Mediation for Managers." No one will dispute the fact that managers could use many of the basic skills of good mediation such as listening, problem solving, reasoned decision making, and so forth, that are not exclusive to mediators. But to suggest that a manager can intervene as a neutral mediator in a dispute among subordinates that effects the welfare of the enterprise and therefore the welfare of the manager is pure sophistry. The manager cannot, by the nature of the position, function in a *neutral* mediatory facilitative way in matters in which he or she has a direct or even secondary stake in the outcome. This is not to say that a good manager should not be able to assist the disputants in resolving their difficulties along lines that benefit both the manager and the enterprise (and even the disputants). Such intervention, however, is simply not mediation as it has been conceived and practiced by trained specialists. It is fundamentally a controlling type of intervention.

Facilitative

A *facilitative* intervention is when the intervention takes the form of a neutral third party who aids the parties in working out a resolution to their struggle. Mediation is the most common form of this process. The mediator, as you will discover later, has no stake in the outcome of the dispute and serves as a process facilitator to enable the parties to solve their own problems. I devote a whole chapter to the process of mediation.

Judicial

A *judicial* intervention is when the elements of the dispute are resolved by the decision of a third party such as the courts or in arbitration. There is a difference, however, between the judicial intervention of the courts and the intervention of an arbitrator. Usually, in the courts, the parties do not have a full choice as to in whose court a matter will be heard or who those making the decision will be. In arbitration the choice of the arbitrator is in the hands of the parties to the dispute or by prior agreement of the parties or their agents. I devote a whole chapter to arbitration.

Meddling

A *meddling* intervention is when a third party, interested or disinterested, intervenes in a dispute in order to become a party to the dispute, to enhance their self-image, to aggravate the dispute, or for other reasons not necessarily useful in the settlement of a dispute. Many well-meaning but unskilled people try to intervene in disputes, and the result is acceleration of the dispute or damage to the parties and themselves.

As the mediation process has become more prominent in the managing of disputes more and more people have decided that being a mediator is just what they want to do. So, many people will read a manual on mediation, take a weekend workshop on mediation, and hang out their shingle. They are hardly qualified to mediate on the basis of such preparation. But some unsuspecting clients are eventually seduced into using their services. The outcome is usually not what it could be with an experienced and highly trained mediator. I have more to say about this in the chapter on mediation.

> *I remember a playground incident where another fellow and I were throwing fists at each other for some reason long forgotten. Aiding and abetting us was a fellow who kept placing sticks on our shoulders and demanding that our opponent knock them off. I remember he kept shouting at us both to fight, not just wave our arms, to hit harder, and to "clobber the clown." In the melee that followed, the meddler got his nose broken because he didn't duck one of the swinging haymakers I aimed at my opponent. It took the forceful intervention of the principal to stop the dispute. The meddler was treated to the same punishment as the two of us.*

Neutrality and Intervention

Another aspect of intervention is the neutrality of the intervenor. A neutral third party is a person who is not an advocate for either side to a dispute and has nothing to gain personally, professionally, or ideologically from an advantage of one party over the other. The neutral's basic concern is the agreement or settlement of the dispute, regardless of the direction it may take. The settlement agreement must have the approval of both parties, but not that of the neutral. Neutral intervenors are agreement-settlement centered rather than client centered.

Some professional roles that appear to be interventive cannot be neutral ones. The attorney-as-advocate functions to champion the cause of a client against the cause of another party. The attorney-as-advocate cannot be a neutral advocate or intervenor in a dispute involving clients for whom he or she has served as an advocate. Similarly, the counselor-therapist who seeks to aid a client in coping with personal problems resulting from a dispute cannot be a neutral intervenor between the client and the person with whom the client is in dispute. Most lawyers and counselors are client centered in their professional assumptions and perspectives and as long as these assumptions prevail in their practice they cannot function as useful neutrals.

This difference is not clearly perceived by many people who seek to get on the bandwagon of dispute resolution. This is not to say that lawyers and counselors are inadequate neutrals. However, most lawyers are still taught to be adversaries, and counselors to be therapists. These functions do not fit well in a neutral process. Seasoned attorneys who are able to see the many dimensions and sides to a dispute may, with some retraining, become effective judges and/or arbitrators. They may, if carefully retrained become effective mediators. The same is true for counselors. But without special training and/or retraining they usually are unable to function effectively in neutral roles.

SUMMARY

The Struggle Spectrum guides us in the management of struggle so that it does not escalate into violence. In order to understand the management process we have examined some of the antecedent and concomitant factors of struggle. These factors fall into two general categories: personal factors and contextual factors.

Personal factors were identified as aggressive and rigid behavior tendencies, mistrust of others, aggressive impulses, variations in perception of common struggle situations, differences in styles of behavior, anxiety, stress, and internal struggle. Contextual factors explored were win-lose competition, cultural differences, interference with goal efforts, institutional and organizational contexts, realistic vs. nonrealistic forms of struggle, interdependence of the parties, scarce and undistributable resources, and differences in needs and values.

The management of struggle was discussed in relation to preventive and interventive processes.

Preventive processes include training, education, facilitation, avoidance, and other processes of deterrence. They anticipate difficulties and seek to change or manage the conditions that cause escalation. Preventive processes involve increasing self-awareness, self-esteem, and trust in ourselves through special training and development. Another important preventive process is moving the win-lose context to a cooperative context.

We discussed the confusion and the fallacy of the overly popular "win-win" type of solution to win-lose contexts. Changing the game from win-lose to cooperation is a particularly important preventive process. Also important to the process is the alteration of the basic structure of the struggle. Setting mutually inclusive and superordinate goals is a powerful way of changing the game by shifting the direction of the energy of the participants to the struggle. Setting rules for interaction is another preventive process in which the obligated behavior is altered to provide less violent and divisive interaction between people. We warned about overemphasis on rules as being counter-productive, particularly when they are drawn from the sports metaphor.

Joint problem solving is identified as one of the more useful preventive processes. Decision making by consensus was recognized as being a highly desirable method of prevention under the conditions in which everyone has opportunity to express judgments. We pointed out the danger of forcing consensus when there are those who do not agree with the group. Improving the communication between parties was also identified as an important preventive process (a key communication process is listening). When relationships and content are involved in situations that have escalated, in most instances the matter of the relationships needs to be addressed if the content issues are to be resolved. Similarly, interest vs. position was discussed and the importance of understanding interests as a preventive action was emphasized. Trust, too, came in for some attention as a preventive process. Distrust plays an important role in the escalation of struggle. The nature and development of trust and distrust, their relation to our self-concept, and the role of expectations in trusting behavior were discussed. Another preventive process is negotiation. This process will be discussed in more detail.

Interventive processes are the infusion of a person or persons other than the disputants into the struggle situation. The intervention of third parties changes the dynamics of the interaction. The types of intervention include controlling, facilitative, judicial, and meddling. Controlling interventions are those used by police and others who are enforcing laws or imposing controls over disputants. Facilitative intervention is the predominant function of the mediation process. Judicial interventions involve the courts via judge and jury and arbitration via the arbitrator. Meddling occurs when third parties intervene in order to become a party to the dispute, to enhance self-image, or to aggravate the dispute for personal reasons not necessarily useful in the settlement of the dispute. Reference was made to "meddling mediators" or those who want to mediate but are neither qualified nor neutral.

The neutrality of the intervenor was identified as an important condition of the use of intervention in the management of struggle. We discussed some of the professional groups that have a great problem with neutrality when their basic purpose has been to advocate their client's interest or welfare.

Mary Tjosvold, an administrator in a children's home, identifies some of her rules for the management of conflict. They are:

> Develop a cooperative approach in which all persons recognize they have contributed to the (struggle) . . . and need to help solve it. Avoid trying to win and to show that you are right and the other is wrong. Attempt to identify and solve the underlying problem . . . Develop open communication with and trust for each other. Describe the other's behavior rather than label or accuse. Focus on the changes that can be made. Identify resources that each person can employ to solve the problem. Select a solution that helps all concerned. Identify what each person has learned. (Tjosvold & Johnson, 1983, p. 229)

CHAPTER 3

///

Power and Struggle
Some Concepts of Power and Empowerment in Dealing with Disputes

> The cooperative, loving side of existence goes hand in hand with coping and power, but neither the one nor the other can be neglected if life is to be gratifying. Our appreciation of the earth and the support of our fellows are not gained by abdication of our powers, but by cooperative use of them. (Rollo May, 1972, p. 30)

Everyone has it. Many deplore it. Many fear it. Many revel in it. Multitudes fight for it. Other masses fight against it. Person-to-person struggle is involved with it. Many try to hide it. Group-to-group is engulfed with it. Nations struggle with it. It is used on the job, at home, in the marketplace, on the street, in the church, in the school, in every place where people and groups interact with each other. This ubiquitous thing is *power*.

Power exists universally among humankind. It is neither negative nor positive. It is neither good nor bad. It can be used to enhance or destroy, to protect or abuse, to glorify or condemn, to achieve or fail, to depress or exhilarate. It is probably the single most important element in the struggle spectrum. Siu (1979) perceives power as a "universal solvent of human relations" (p. 40).

In any dispute each party to the dispute has power. Many differences and disputes arise because of the efforts to exert power over another who resists. The resolution of some disputes depends on who has the greater power. Sometimes a power balance appears vital to the resolution of a dispute. Negotiation and bargaining processes are systems of applying power to the settlement of differences. The mediation process is a system whereby power can be adjusted to lead to a resolution. The arbitration process is a testing ground where certain powers of the parties are applied to get a decision that will lead to the resolution of a problem.

Let's examine this universality more closely by putting together a concept or definition of power with which we can explore its nature and application.

THE NATURE OF POWER

Power is an intentional communicative influence process.

Certain basics appear in most attempts to define power:

- Power is a potential and actual process
- of intentionally influencing events, beliefs, emotions, values, and behavior of others
- in order to satisfy self and/or others' needs and desires
- by performing some actions
- which are basically communicative in nature.

Let's look more closely at some of the factors emerging from this definition.

Potential and Actual

Potential power is the nonexercised ability to influence the conduct of others. It is not the act or event of power itself, but the existence of conditions that make possible the exercise or act of power. For example, status in an organization carries with it certain levels of potential power, both implied and explicit. The president of a company has potentially more power than does the secretary. Thus, when the company president issues an order it will usually carry more weight than if the secretary issues it. In a paternalistic society the father has more potential power than does the mother (the opposite is true in a matriarchal society).

Actual power is the intentional influence exerted by persons or groups over the conduct of others. A traffic officer by the nature of his position, his uniform, and his behavior may have the potential power to direct the flow of traffic through an intersection. When he acts through arm signals, by blowing a whistle, and so on, and the drivers respond appropriately, the power becomes actual.

However, because of the many other factors affecting the exercise of power, often people with lower status within an organization may exercise more actual power than those with higher status. A new director of a service organization has, by the nature of the position, potential power over the affairs of the group. However, a secretary who has been with the group for over 15 years and has outlasted two other directors will likely have more actual power over the processes and decisions of the group.

Simply because you can or could influence the conduct of your neighbor means you have potential power. Potential power does not become actual power until you influence your neighbor (see Gould & Kolb, 1964).

Influence

Influence is the ability to induce change in human behavior, attitudes, and values. Power is a kind of influence that emerges within relationships. One way of saying this is that "A has power over B to the extent he or she can get B to do something that B would not otherwise do"(Jacobson, 1972, p. 9). ("A" is usually referred to as the "agent" and "B" the "recipient".) The power relationship is not a one-sided affair. B may also have power over A in that B makes choices that effect A's intents and goals. The power balance may shift from time to time between A and B.

Power may also be viewed as the "ability to cause an event to happen or not to happen . . . the ability to influence or control events and people . . . and to influence how events are interpreted." This concept of power implies control over the total personal, social, and physical environment (Kennedy, 1984, p. 4). Most parents, during the early months and years of their children's lives, control the environment in which their children live.

Robbins (1986) says power

is the ability to change your life, to shape your perceptions, to make things work for you and not against you. Real power is shared, not imposed. It's the ability to define human needs and to fulfill them . . . It's the ability to direct your own personal kingdom—your own thought processes, your own behavior—so you produce the precise results you desire. It is the "ability to act." (pp. 21-22)

Ability to Reach Goals and Satisfaction

Another way to look at power is that it is the ability to get what one wants. It is "the process by which people do things and get other people to do things" (Funkhouser, 1986, p. 5). The goals that a person has are achieved through power, by getting others to do things consistent with the achievement of those goals. Power is "the ability to act effectively and to accomplish objectives" (p. 10).

Hobbes (1588-1667) in his *Leviathan* claimed that "humans have a restless and perpetual desire for power and that the power of an individual is . . . to obtain some apparent future good" (cited in King, 1987, p. 104).

Some scholars assert that power is simply the capacity of a person (an initiator) to increase his or her satisfactions by intentionally affecting the behavior of others (one or more responders) (Craig & Craig, 1974). They point out that any attempt to affect the behavior of others, whether subtle or direct, effective or ineffective, is an attempt to exercise power.

Involves Several Relationships and Acts

Many students of the nature of power identify several components that have commonly been ascribed to the power act. Among the most consistently identified are (a) the *agent*—the initiator, the influencer; (b) the *recipient* of the power act—the target, the object, the responder; (c) *pressure* or *incentive* in the form of punishment or reward; (d) the *goal* or outcome of the changed behavior, belief, attitude, and/or value; and (e) the *relationship* between the agent and the recipient that allows for a sharing of the process. Surrounding these components is the environment in which the acts take place and which enhances or obstructs the efforts of the participants. Communication, as has been mentioned before, is the essential process through which these acts and relationships emerge (see Craig & Craig, 1974, p. 46, for a similar set of constructs).

All forms of power in human interaction are founded on the ability to communicate. People seek order, meaning, and significance in their life. To bring this into being we must have power to act, and power is "a deliberate act of human organization . . . a relationship that is both activated and sustained by human communication. Power is a communication act" (King, 1987, pp. 3-4). Language itself is a powerful tool of influence.

Gaining Compliance

A function of power may be to bring others to acquiesce or to accept without protest or resistance. The teenage daughter who rejects a date because her mother does not like the boy is being compliant. Siu (1979) talks of this aspect as: "One person exerts power over another to the degree that he is able to exact compliance as desired" (p. 31).

"Power is the ability to get what one wants" (Boulding, 1989, p. 15). Another way of saying this is,

> the probability that one actor within a social relationship will be in a position to carry out his own will despite resistance, regardless of the basis on which this probability rests . . . All conceivable qualities of a person and all conceivable combinations of circumstances may put him in a position to impose his will in a given situation. (Weber, cited in Duke, 1976, p. 40)

This concept is certainly all inclusive. It includes legitimate and illegitimate ways of gaining power through economic, political, sexual, religious, educational, or any other means of action or no action at all.

A Process that Can Be Used for Good and Bad

Although I believe that power is neither good nor bad in and of itself, it is clear that it is viewed as being both good and bad; benevolent and malevolent.

The *malevolent* face is that which is based on a perception of life in which people function from fear, positions of dominance, and control of submissive others for their own welfare and satisfactions. The malevolent world is perceived as a primitive jungle in which only the strongest survive. People who view power from this perception usually feel threatened and feel they must destroy others before they themselves are destroyed, and they treat others as pawns with no power or ability to create and make their own decisions. Persons viewing the world from this perspective are apparently more aggressive and collect items and resources that enhance their prestige (cars, property, huge houses, awards, membership in exclusive clubs, control over others, etc.). They also appear to take more chances (as in gambling), engage in more physical fighting behavior, and encounter violent accidents (see McClelland, 1980). The recipients to this kind of mode tend to be passive like slaves and when the leader or power is removed they become violent (see Boulding, 1989).

The *benevolent* face is that which is based on exercising power for the benefit of others. It is more socialized, exhibiting a concern for the goals of the group, for helping groups find goals, and for facilitating members of the group in reaching their goals. Along with this concept is an ambivalent feeling about holding power, a realization that for every "win-lose" victory someone loses and that victories must be planned carefully. Members of groups led by persons viewing power in this mode are likely to feel that they are capable of originating ideas and actions on their own. People living with this more socialized face of power tend to become involved in politics, to join more service organizations and become officers in them, and tend to join in organized informal sports.

At one extreme is the power to destroy. At the other is the power to integrate. In between is the power to exchange (negotiate). Boulding (1989) calls these "the stick, the carrot, and the hug" (p. 10).

Unstable and Unequally Distributed

In almost all of the arenas of human behavior power is hardly ever equal. As human beings become involved in organizations, hierarchies arise with greater power massed at the top of the system. Democratic societies tend to control and limit this power, but autocratic societies allow a wide variance between the power at the top and that at the bottom of the system.

This instability and inequality leads to human struggle from the one-to-one relationship to the one-to-many to struggles between large groups such as nations or coalitions of nations. Many fights and disputes arise over efforts to gain more power over people and to reduce the power of others over us. The gangs in large cities are constantly involved in struggles to gain or sustain power over social and economic groups of people.

King (1987) points out that history reveals all power as unstable. That is, it is not held constantly by one unit. "Great leaders are constantly overthrown, and the most secure dynasties lose coherence and crumble away. The children of heroes are degenerates. Dominant classes are replaced or subordinated by new conquerors" (p. 85). King (1987) also claims that power is produced by human transactions. It is not a finite quality. If one person gains power others do not necessarily lose it.

SOME MYTHS ABOUT POWER

There are a number of myths, concepts and beliefs about power that are false and not supported by evidence. Funkhauser (1986) organized these into the following and debunked them in the process:

1. Power is bad.

All power is not bad. Without it life could not exist. There is both good and bad use of power, benevolent and malevolent (as we described above). The abuse of power by persons, systems, and governments has caused us to dislike the idea of power. When we see a nation and its people suppressed by dictatorial methods we often reject the use of power instead of the persons using that power. Often persons who complain about power are the ones who have little or did not prevail in some power struggle.

2. Our concern with power is an outcome of the stresses of the modern world.

Power struggles and the exploration of power have existed throughout all recorded history. The Old Testament is filled with stories of power. We have always been interested in power. Writers, philosophers, teachers, and politicians throughout recorded history have addressed the matter. Greek dramatists, Latin philosophers, Plutarch, Machiavelli, Chaucer, Shakespeare, Tolstoy, and many others have written about the subject. The history of the Asiatic world is similarly filled with stories and traditions of an ancient source that indicate power has been a central concern for as long as records exist.

3. We have no business influencing what other people do.

As long as we are interacting with each other *we cannot avoid influencing each other*. Even so, there are special influential individuals who play significant roles in our society: doctors, teachers, pastors, friends, parents, bosses, and many others. Harm may arise when someone controls another for his or her own benefit and at the other's expense. This condition represents what I call *manipulation*. Manipulation, by definition, is control of others through fraud and deceit. It is a form of power that is harmful.

4. Powerful people are outgoing, self-confident, and aggressive.

The overt, aggressive, self-confident "super salesperson" is not necessarily the only powerful type. Sometimes such people create rejection through their assertiveness and aggressiveness. There are many people who are powerful and are soft-spoken, shy, and even appear helpless.

5. With "sales resistance" we can keep from being influenced by others.

Some agents are so skilled that they can persuade you to act or believe without your being aware of the influence. This happens all the time. The more you understand the power processes the more likely you will be able to recognize them when they are being used on you. Knowing and recognizing the techniques being used, you are then in a position to decide whether to accept the influence or reject it on the basis of its ultimate value to you. Although I do not claim to know all there is to know about power I do actually enjoy watching a good salesperson work on me. In one case, I became so engrossed and intrigued with the techniques that were being used that I bought the product, to my later disgust.

6. It is easier to influence weak than strong persons.

Weakness and strength are relative. If we define weakness as being easily influenced and strength as the opposite, then, of course, the weak will be more easily influenced. But that is circuitous reasoning. Actually weakness or strength do not seem to have much to do with influencibility. History is filled with "strong" persons who were influenced significantly by "weak" persons. Tiny babies, for example, weak in their physical being and in their mental-social development, exert a powerful influence on the adults around them.

7. The key to power is a powerful position.

Although position or status contributes to the power of a person other factors must be present. Many persons in significantly "powerful" positions are themselves inept and weak persuaders. Also, many people who do not function in positions of status have great influence over the group in which they operate. Although status or position has relevance to power potential it is not sufficient alone to be the key to power. The President of the United States, one of the most potentially powerful positions in the world, can be made powerless by a recalcitrant congress that blocks his efforts at every turn.

8. Power is mysterious. Some have it and others do not.

Everyone is capable of influencing the acts of others. The power we have is a matter of degree. Also, sometimes we have more power than at other times. There is no mysticism about power. The factors of power are known and identifiable.

9. The more we openly discuss and study power the easier it will be for people to control and take advantage of each other.

Power can be used in a positive way. Knowing about it does not increase the negative use of power. A great many of our institutions are directly concerned with increasing the power of people: Education and religion are two such institutions. It is essentially the motives of the person using the power that determines the goodness or badness of the results. Power in and of itself is neither good nor bad (Funkhauser, 1986).

THE BASES OF POWER

The source of power is within a person and within the contexts in which we operate. Human power does not exist except as people generate it and use it. There may be a great deal of potential power in a position but unless a person acts on that potential there is no power actually exerted. People acquire power by using it. Thus, even though the traffic police are perceived as powerful because of their uniform, the power act is the point at which the power emerges.

When we experience change in our behavior, habits, beliefs, and so on, it originates in our own internal responses to another person or group. The power of a person is usually identified as the observed ability to shape another's behavior, but it depends on the response of the other.

Your ability to influence my behavior has several bases: information, reward, coercion, expertise, reference, identification, and legitimacy (see Raven & Rubin, 1976). Let's look at each of these briefly.

Information provides us with a power resource by the manner in which it can change others' perceptions and behavior.

> *If I am driving around town seeking a certain residence at a given address and do not know where the street is or the number arrangements of the residences I am pretty helpless. A person or source of information that gives me the name and placement of the streets and the numbering arrangements will provide a basis for considerable change in my behavior. Once I have the information I need it becomes independent of the one who gave it to me. It is the information and not the person who gave it to me that is significant in the changes I make.*

However, the source of the information may still have some affect on my use of it. That is, the information may be used differently were it to come from a friend in whom I had great confidence in contrast to a stranger who appeared unshaven, decrepit, and not too coherent.

Those persons who have information of relevance or importance to others have a significant basis on which to build their power over those others. By sharing that information they are able to influence the behavior of those to whom the information is given. Unshared information can also control behavior.

> *I may know that an automobile I am trying to sell you has a defective fuel injection system. By not sharing that information with you I can influence you to buy the car at a higher price than you would offer if I shared all I knew about the car.*

In organizations, the kinds of information that seem to provide power resources are about what people think, what they say, and what they do. Technical information as a special power resource is useful only to the extent that it can be coordinated and woven into the information about the behaviors of people.

> *The displacement capacity of an automobile's cylinders is of no persuasive value unless the prospective owner understands its significance to the performance of the vehicle.*
>
> *If my boss can't hear or read lips then no amount of information about a prospect or program can be delivered by talking with him.*
>
> *If one of my staff members is a strong conservative Catholic and a devout follower of the Pope, all the information about the efficacy of birth control will likely be of little use.*

The "gatekeeping" role of persons who have critical information is powerful. By releasing information carefully on a selected basis they demonstrate a great deal of power.

> *The eyewitness in a murder trial can affect the outcome of the trial by controlling the information released.*
>
> *Many secretaries are in control of a great deal of information about their boss and the operation. By controlling the release of that information (who it goes to, when it is shared, and how much is shared) they can affect the function of the entire organization.*

Reward and coercion are not as potentially independent of the influencing agent as information. However, the promise of reward and the threat of punishment by the agent provide a significant base for influencing others.

> *The section supervisor of a work crew has a strong base for influencing the workers on the crew because of the inherent power of providing pay increases, decreases, promotion, and termination.*

Reward and coercion depend a great deal on the ability of the influencing agent to observe whether the recipient of the action complies with the influence effort and to make the decision to put these factors into effect.

Reward and punitive behavior also depend on the recipient. *The effect of coercion on the attitudes and behaviors of recipients determines the power of the agent.* If the recipients respond so that agent's goals are reached, the method is more effective than if the recipients reject or resist the coercion. Receivers of coercive or punitive actions often tend to reject or dislike the agent using the coercion and will seek ways of retaliation through displacing the coercer or negating the power used.

> *The worker who loses a day's pay because he didn't follow the directions of the supervisor will probably not like the supervisor who initiated the rule and administered the punishment and may seek to retaliate through the union or other means.*

The receiver of reward actions will tend to like and accept the agent. Parents who legitimately reward their children for good deeds are more likely to be respected and loved than those who punish for bad deeds alone.

Similarly, the surveillance necessary for the use of reward and coercion may bring doubts and other influences to bear on both agent and recipient.

> *The more police perform surveillance actions in a community in order to maintain control over possible unlawful activity the more stress and tension will develop between townspeople and officers. The more the teacher keeps a punitive eye on the behavior of the students the more likely the students will dislike, distrust, and find reason to disobey. The "carrot, stick, and hug" system is a significant element in the power of people over people.*

Expertise is clearly a significant basis of power. Look at the degree to which we allow doctors, teachers, engineers, science specialists, and so on to influence our behavior. There is a reverse of the expert influence, however, called "negative expertise," when the agent (influencer) is perceived by the recipient (influencee) as using his or her expertise for personal gain and not for the recipient. In these cases the recipient is likely to do just the opposite of what the agent suggests. Expertise is different, also, from information. Although in many instances the "expert" is one who has a lot of special information, it is the manner in which that information is used that is the difference.

> *The teacher who has accumulated a great deal of information about a subject but does not have the skills or "expertise" to make it available to students is less powerful than one who can provide an instructional context in which students can learn. Expertise is the special ability to perform.*

Referent relationships are also significant bases of power. Our memberships (formal and informal) in groups of acclaim or popularity provide us with an acceptance that might not otherwise exist. The degree to which the influencing agent can be perceived as having common experiences and memberships with the recipient will provide a basis for the influence the agent exerts on the recipient.

> *In a town where golf is a prime recreational interest, membership in the town's only golf club is necessary for the acceptance of a person into many aspects of the community. The so-called elite clubs and organizations provide their members with a kind of referent power over the nonmembers.*

Legitimacy is a strong power base in our society. It is essentially related to the factor of status. Those persons in formal social organizations who hold positions of responsibility over others in the organization have a legitimate power base. Business organizations, the military, government agencies, and the church are prime examples of where this base can be found. But legitimacy is also found in informal social organizations such as the family, the neighborhood, and so forth, in which certain members, by common practice, hold some status within the group. Parents are persons with a legitimate power base. A vital aspect of the legitimacy base is the fact that those in legitimate power situations also have high potential reward and punishment power. (Note the subsequent discussion of the "structural" type of power. I make a distinction between the bases or sources of power and the kinds of power that emanate from the sources.)

A paradoxical situation arises, however, in relation to the weak, the helpless, and those without a legitimate power base. We are regularly influenced by the pleas of the helpless child, the weak and helpless patient, the apparently innocent person, and so on.

Skill in *communication* provides for potential power. Efforts to exercise power are enhanced by skilled communication, and communication assists in making the efforts to exercise power successful. Efforts of the agent to influence the recipient are carried through communication processes. Robbins (1986) claims that "all behavior and feelings find their original roots in some form of communication" (p. 23). Those persons who are able to manage the communication elements are going to be more powerful than those who do not have this ability.

The core of the communication process is *the self.* Awareness of the self is therefore a vital process in communication and the use of power (Keltner, 1973). The reasons for this are not often perceived.

All the things that happen to us, the messages we receive, the experiences we have, and the contacts we make, are not the things that effect our behavior directly. How I feel and behave is the result of my *perception* of what I experience and the significance I put to the things *as I perceive them.* Each person sees the world from a different locus of perception. Therefore, my image of what is happening is going to be different from yours. I respond to my image and perception and communicate with you on the basis of my own perceptions of you. The degree to which I can separate out my own images of the world and discover your images will allow me to construct messages that can be communicated so that you will be able to comprehend what I am experiencing, seeking, perceiving, and feeling. This, in turn, is then interpreted by you and provides some influence on what you do. I comment further on communication and power later in this chapter.

Practitioners in the field of Neuro-linguistic Programming (NLP) contend that the "states" we are in determine our success or failure in given situations. A "state" is defined as "the sum total of our experience at any moment in time" (Robbins, 1986, p. 47). It is a neurophysiological condition that can be enabling or paralyzing. Conditions such as confidence, joy, ecstasy, and the feeling of strength are enabling because when we are in these states we are able to accomplish things we cannot accomplish without them. In contrast, when we are confused, depressed, fearful, anxious, sad, and frustrated, our power to be effective is reduced. Robbins (1986) claims that the ability to put ourselves into enabling states is the difference between those who succeed and those who fail to achieve their goals in life.

Thus, *self empowerment* is the process of learning how to select those states that are most enabling for us and to bring them into being within our inner self-structure. Robbins (1986) claims that "your behavior is the result of your state, and your state is the result of your internal representations [of the world around you] and your physiology, both of which you can change in a matter of moments" (p. 55).

In addition to this there is a factor called *will to power* that represents the struggle to achieve, to overcome, to win victory, and to ascend social, political, and professional hierarchies (Korda, 1975).

Another way of looking at "bases" of power is in terms of *control over resources.* This includes material resources, psychosocial resources, information, and organizational resources. Property ownership, for example, has since the origins of the industrial revolution been a significant base of influence. Although it may not be as significant today as it was at the time of the industrial revolution, it still retains some weight in providing a power base among certain classes and groups of people. Psychosocial resources are found in our sense of identity, our values, habits, interests, aspirations, the way we view the past, our ability in decision making, and our membership and acceptance in groups. Organizational resources are our access to media, our control of systems of distributing information, kinship or family ties, religious affiliation, and other factors found in the structure of an organization that provide influence for its members (King, 1987). Informational resources are the availability of critical data and our control over the collection and dissemination of that data.

Most of the bases of power reside in ourselves. Our understanding of ourselves, our ability to determine and control the "states" in which we exist, the use of communication, resources, our ability to provide rewards and punishment, our referent relationships, and our "will to power" all provide the foundation on which we build our influence on other people.

KINDS AND TYPES OF POWER

Several types or kinds of power exist in the spectrum of power system. Early research by French and Raven distinguished five types of power: referent, expert, reward, coercive, and legitimate (French & Raven, 1959). Since that time the research has elaborated on these types. They seem closely related to the bases on which power develops. The kinds and types of power emanate as constructs from the bases that we have just discussed. In some instances the kinds and bases seem similar. This occurs because of the common source and character of the power act.

In the following section we look at how several writers describe of the kinds and types of power. Note how they all have basic similarity to the French and Raven categories but note, also, how they differ.

Rollo May

May (1972) contended that all of us have five different kinds of power and use them at different times.

Exploitive power is used to dominate and control others. It is the simplest and most destructive. Cult leaders, dictators, and those who know of no other way to relate to others use this kind of power. It is closely connected to the use of force of all kinds, and the victims have no choice or alternative but to submit or die. Violence and the threat of violence are assumed.

Manipulative power is less overtly violent and destructive than exploitive. May describes it as a "con" man process in contrast to the "gunman" process of exploitive power. A great deal of it depends on pretense. It is a way of changing behavior by artful and unfair means in order to control. May argues that operant conditioning is a manipulative form of power. This is the conditioned response described in the basic work of Pavlov and B.F. Skinner. It is a very common form of power in our society.

People who are depressed, anxious, frightened, and in states of confusion are easily controlled by manipulative power because the agent promises them a way of overcoming their deficits. Hitler used this kind of power when the Germans, after the United States's Smoot Hawley Tariff and similar actions by other states, were in such dire economic straits that they were easily manipulated by someone who would promise them freedom and release from their troubles. James Jones used manipulative power when he took members of his flock to Guyana and destroyed them.

Competitive power is the essential element of the "win-lose" context. When one person wins the other loses. It is present throughout most of our social, political, economic, and athletic worlds. The desire to be the winner drives most of us in much of our life relationships (see Chapter 2). At the same time, it has some constructive aspects as when businesses improve their product and efficiency in order to win the market, or when students compete for scholarship prizes. Many great advances in human society have taken place in a competitive situation. It has its positive forms as well as negative and destructive forms.

Nutrient power is exhibited in caring for others. Parents caring for their children, teachers providing students with skills and information that benefits them, and leaders providing direction and resources for the benefit of others are typical uses of nutrient power.

Integrative power is that which provides cooperation with others in order to accomplish mutual needs and desires. Two leaders challenging each other but reaching for joint efforts are using integrative power. It is, in May's thinking, playing the "devil's advocate" with ideas and themes in order to improve them. It is a way of providing for growth and advancement. It is an important power function in the management of struggle.

Funkhauser's Spectrum

Another way of looking at the kinds of power is described by Funkhauser (1986) who divides power into a spectrum comprising four types; structural, agreement, persuasive, and performance.

Structural power emerges from the nature of the organization and the social roles that are associated with the structure. It is similar to what we have previously described as "legitimate" power. Thus, the president of an organization inherently has certain power simply by being president. The organization need not be a formal one to convey structural power. Informal groups such as the family have roles that are a part of the structure and society defines, to a variable extent, the nature of these roles. Thus, the role of the father in a patriarchal society carries with it certain potential power that the person in that role translates into action.

Agreement power is achieved through mutual decision by two parties. It is arrived at through the process of negotiating an understanding (either unwritten or actually contractual) of what each of the parties to the agreement "can and cannot do." This kind of power is very important in the management of struggle.

Persuasive power is "engineering other people's action decisions so that they do what we want them to do" (p. 32). Persuasive power comes into play as structural and agreement power declines or is unavailable (notice how this develops in the Struggle Spectrum). Thus, the salesperson, the advertising industry, and all of us at one time or another use this power in our daily lives.

Performance power comes from our ability to make decisions to take action. A person who has high performance power is a person who does the right thing at the right time in order to accomplish his or her goals. High performance power people make maximum use of their abilities.

Craig and Craig's Destructive and Synergic Power

Craig and Craig (1974) divide types of power into directive and synergic. *Directive* power is when the agent intentionally advances his or her own interests and satisfactions by using the behavior of others to advance those interests. It is that type of power in which "the initiator intentionally makes people act against their will, their judgment, their interests, or leads them to act blindly without considering their interests and those of others, or without considering their personal responsibility for outcomes" (pp. 60-61). This is similar to what May calls manipulative power. Craig and Craig view this power as dehumanizing and destructive of human capacities and morale. Typical of the use of this type of power are the Nazi prison camp administrators, dictators, authoritarian leaders, and so forth.

In contrast to directive power, Craig and Craig identify synergic power. *Synergic* power is "the capacity of an individual or group to increase the satisfactions of all participants by intentionally generating increased energy and creativity, all of which is used to co-create a more rewarding present and future" (p. 62). This, again, is similar to what May calls nutritive and integrative power.

The differences between directive and synergic power are obvious. Directive imposes and synergic composes. Synergic power takes into consideration the needs and desires of the recipients. Education is synergic at its base (although there are some directive teachers). Therapy is synergic. Neither directive nor synergic represent any forms of power absence. Both involve the use of influence in effecting behavior. Craig and Craig take the position that the extremes of these two types are rarely present and that we usually fall somewhere in between. We can see clearly that the effective management of struggle will depend on the use of synergic power.

Kennedy's Ways of Performing

Kennedy (1984) writes of power styles as *ways of performing the act of power*. Her interesting system defines the styles in terms of various behaviors. According to her, persons use *consensus* style when they blend many ideas into a concept or action that everyone will support. The *manipulative-consensus* style is when the person appears to use consensus but eventually makes the decision to suit his or her own wishes and goals. The *sales* style involves persuading superiors, co-workers, or subordinates to do what the agent wants done. The *decisive* style is when the agent is more interested in making immediate decisions than looking at alternatives. The person who examines all actions in terms of the effects on career or superiors is using the *political* style. The *manipulative* style uses insinuation, guilt, emotional approaches, and fraudulent means to get what the agent wants. The *social worker* style focuses on keeping people happy and content as much as completing tasks. The *command* style is a "quasi-military" style of influence and is probably one of the more universal styles used. The *fire fighter* style is characterized by putting off decisions until a crisis occurs. The *legal* style follows procedures, rules, policies, and laws precisely and attracts people who feel they need safety. Persons who want to keep information, resources, and decisions under control are using a *tight* style. The person who lets people do what they want to do as long as they get results is using an *abdication* style. The *secretive* style uses the closed door, secret meetings, and other means of hiding the decision making and actions that affect the larger group. The agent who balances alternatives and makes a decision when absolutely necessary is using a *conditional* style. Comparing these styles to the behaviors in the Struggle Spectrum shows a high level of correspondence with the spectrum and the Kennedy descriptions.

By comparing these various descriptions of the kinds of power we can see that they are many and varied. I have pointed to some of the common threads or themes. Each of us apparently develops our own particular combination of styles of exhibiting or using power and adapts them to the level of struggle in which we find ourselves. The significant matter, however, is that in the whole process of struggle and struggle management we are dealing with power in its many forms. Each person involved in struggle is also involved in power acts as both agent and recipient. The management and control of struggle is therefore the management and control of the power systems being used.

WHO ARE THE POWERFUL?

Leaders

Probably the most constant answer to the question who is powerful is *leaders*. Leaders, by the nature of their situation, are persons who exert considerable influence over those whom they lead. At the same time, once they are in power, leaders tend to shift their psychological orientation to one in which maintenance of their position may become more important than serving their constituents. (Duke, 1976). Leaders, from the outset, are those persons who have come to that position by virtue of their being able to influence others to place them in the leadership role. Even those leaders who seem to inherit structural leadership positions must have some influence over their constituency in order to gain and hold the actual leadership role. Much has been written about the role of the leader as a servant. Indeed, some of us believe that the effective leader exists to the degree that the constituents' needs and desires are served by the actions of the leader.

> *There is an ancient story about a village whose leader had died. A carefully selected team was then sent out on a journey to find someone who would lead the village. Along with them went a valued and respected servant who, among other things, helped them take care of the daily duties of food preparation, organizing the pack animals, charting the routes to follow, arranging for interviews with the village leaders they encountered, providing medical assistance when needed, and serving as a listener to their stories of glory and pain. The journey took the group far and wide. Each person they interviewed seemed inadequate. Some were good in one thing but not another. None fulfilled their expectations. Eventually the team returned to its village to report failure in their search. As they were disbanding, the servant continued to direct and provide the duties that he had provided all during the trip as well as helping each member of the search group return back home. Some of the villagers seeing this realized that the servant was performing the very duties that they were seeking in a leader. The leader was among them. The true leader was the servant.*

All of Us

Most writers on power agree that anyone with energy, concern for others, and a drive to accomplish anything exercises power (Siu, 1979). Parents, teachers, ministers, police, athletes, managers, club and society officers, committee chairpersons, department heads, executive officers, and elected government personnel all exercise power to one degree or another. This does not eliminate anyone who has the desire for power and the basis of power.

There is, as I have mentioned before, a hierarchy of power in our societies. Those persons with the greater energy and drive for ascendancy are usually at the upper level of the power hierarchies. Notice the difference in power level of the business manager who is satisfied with maintaining a reasonable return on investment and a steady growth rate with the executive who wants very much to be at the top, to increase the size of the business and the amount of return, and to increase the scope and influence of the executive role. The manager may surely have power and may exercise it well, but the executive has more power and runs greater risks of being challenged and of losing power.

Robbins (1986), in his discussion of the "power of state" (meaning the power of the internal state of being) notes that our behavior is the result of our state of being. He points to the story of Karl Wallenda of the Flying Wallendas who after years of successfully negotiating the high aerial routine in circuses fell to his death after he had begun to "see himself as falling" (p. 55). Our state of being, according to Robbins, sets in motion the energy that directs our behavior.

Even the Weak and Defeated are Powerful

What seems like a paradox is that those believed to be powerless may often assert power by using their so-called helplessness. Powerful people might include babies, aged people, and others who are able to gain their own ends (Duke, 1976). Children consistently gain the assistance of adults by requesting help to perform acts they cannot themselves perform. Some handicapped people consistently influence others to help them by calling attention to their handicap either overtly or covertly, or both. "The powerless often assert their power by emphasizing their helplessness" (Raven & Rubin, 1976, p. 217).

Haley (1969) points out that Jesus built a great power base by organizing the poor and the powerless. He points out that one of the most powerful tactics that Jesus used was the "surrender" tactic also used by wolves and other wild animals.

> When two wolves are in a fight and one is about to be killed, the defeated wolf will suddenly lift his head and bare his throat to his opponent. The opponent becomes incapacitated and he cannot kill him as long as he is faced with this tactic. Although he is the victor, the vanquished is controlling his behavior merely by standing still and offering his vulnerable jugular vein. (p. 51)

One of the many concepts developed in the ancient art of Aikido is that of the weaker opponent overcoming the stronger by going with the flow of energy of the opponent and turning it to the advantage of the weaker.

COMMUNICATION AND POWER

As I have indicated earlier, communication is at the heart of the power process. Each of us uses communication to bring our power acts into being. All forms of communication are at play in the power processes. Speaking and listening are the most used forms of communication in which power is exerted. Reading and writing account for about a third of our communication and, thus, for about a third of the power processes. The many forms of nonverbal communication, including smell and particularly touch, play highly significant roles in power processes. It is through communication that the bridge between agent and recipient is established that allows the beliefs and behaviors of the recipient to be effected.

We know that power holders in a social situation communicate more frequently than other members and occupy a central position in communication networks (Jacobson, 1972). High power persons initiate messages more frequently than do low power persons. Low power persons initiate fewer messages and direct most of them toward high power persons (Jacobson, 1972).

It is a commonplace that whomever controls the flow of information controls the distribution of power. We have all experienced the manner in which an office secretary or receptionist can control the flow of information and, thus, the power of those in an office. In many offices the most powerful person is the one who operates the communication system. Notice the influence that the character "Radar," the communications officer in the television series *Mash*, had over what went on in the personal and professional affairs of the medical unit.

We talk to each other in several contexts. The personal, private, and informal level is the most frequent form of speaking and listening. Here we talk with our family, our friends, our neighbors, with casual acquaintances, and so forth. Of all our communication time, written and spoken, we spend most in this context. The next most frequent context of our talk is the professional and semi-private. Here we engage in conversation and discussion with our colleagues, our bosses, our subordinates, with clerks, salespersons, and others in the pursuit of our professional interests. The least frequent of our talk contexts (for most of us) is the public performance. In this context we appear before a group of people and give a speech. Thus, the range of talk runs from the personal and private with one or two others to the public and relatively impersonal when we talk with groups in a speaker-to-audience situation. In all of these there are communication factors that affect the power of the communicator.

The Power of the Speaker

One of the most significant power elements in all of the contexts is the perceived credibility of the talker (usually the talker-initiator is the agent in the power transaction). Credibility comes from two directions. The first is the premessage-event status, experience, and general recognition of the speaker. Affiliations, accomplishments, position of authority, and so on play a part in affecting speaker power. The second direction is from the event itself. The manner in which the speaker behaves, the skill with which the message is delivered, the perceived sincerity and credibility of the message, and the rhetorical quality will affect the power of the speaker. All the factors in the elements of persuasion are power-building factors.

Factors that reduce power in speakers have come under scrutiny. Johnson (1987) reported the following forms of communication as *powerless*: hedges and qualifiers; hesitation forms: "uh," "um," "and uh," "you know," (I call the use of these and other forms "medial grunt disease"); Y tag questions: adding "isn't it?" at the end of a statement; diectic phrases: "That man *over there* looks like the one;" and disclaimers or introductory expressions that excuse, explain or request forbearance.

We have already noted that persons who talk more than others, who take more turns, and produce a greater volume of talk and messages in a group are usually more powerful than those who perform fewer of these functions.

Nonverbal Factors

Nonverbal factors effect the power of the speaker in any situation. These include the use of eye contact, gestures, body positions, voice variation, and tone that work on the margins of attention to influence the listener. King (1987) notes several other nonverbal characteristics of powerful people:

> Powerful people are more relaxed than their subordinates, less attentive to the communication of others, less vulnerable to spatial invasion, more in control of floor space . . . less frequently interrupted, take more turns in conversation, talk more of the time, and are touched less often. (p. 17)

There is a belief that relative height also effects the power of the speaker. The person perceived as taller is usually considered to be more powerful (King, 1987).

A lot of nonverbal factors are considered symbols of power status and, in turn, provide some power granting conditions in the communication context.

Korda (1975) identified several power symbols in the modern business society:

Foot power comes from wearing the accepted type of shoes in the condition that is most acceptable to the recipient, and in the placement of the feet. High power executives wear relatively simple shoes that are polished and that are purchased in socially elite establishments. They work seriously with both feet on the floor. They do not reveal the soles of their shoes.

> *I used to be a shoe-shine boy in a barber shop when I was in junior high and high school. I became quite aware of the influence of nicely polished shoes on the appearance, and thus the power, of the wearer.*

Telephone power comes from having several telephones, or having a car phone or a pocket phone. Nowadays we are also becoming aware of *fax power* with the increasing use of fax machines to transmit documents and messages.

Office supplies and their arrangement such as small calculators hidden in the pocket, yellow legal pads, computer terminals, thermos bottles and cups, and so on. The items placed on desks also play a role in representing the power of the owner.

Furniture power comes from hidden file cabinets with locks, low soft sofas, and other functional furniture placed in various arrangements to provide a power position for the owner of the office. The most powerful arrangement, according to Korda, appears to be one with the window behind the owner so that the visitor must view the owner across the desk and against the light of the window, and thus in some shadow. This arrangement also allows the owner to watch the visitor with the light full on the person. Further, the placement should be such that there is more room for the owner behind the desk than for the visitor in front of the desk.

Time power is, according to Korda, one of the ultimate power symbols. Examples include clocks in the office, using wrist watches face up and face down on the desk, rushing at the last minute before appointments and departures, and a full schedule of appointments. Have you ever noticed how much more important a person seems with whom it is difficult to schedule an appointment?

Waiting and Stand By tactics are also included by Korda in his list of symbols. Examples include allowing a half hour for meetings that will run an hour or more so that the next appointment will have to wait and having aides and assistants standing by to provide services on instant notice.

Insulation from small tasks seems to be a symbol that many high power people use. Serving coffee, cleaning desks, fetching mail, opening mail, dialing telephone numbers, arranging facilities for meetings and travel, and so on all are tasks that the high power executives appear to avoid, even when they have the time to perform them.

Cleanliness seems to be a symbol of power to the executive officers. Desks are clean and there is little on the top of the desk to show that any work is being performed. Dress is always clean, fresh, and ironed.

> *I remember walking into the office of a very busy senior executive and being astonished at the desk being absolutely clear except for a desk pad and pen-pencil set. I recall that I was very impressed.*

Other Symbols

There are many other symbols that communicate power. Membership buttons and pins often suggest affiliation with highly respected societies: honor keys, woven emblems, labels, and so on are common. Degree certificates hung on the office wall, the location of the office in a building or on a level of an office building, the kind of automobile one drives (from a second-hand rusty Volkswagen "Beetle" to a stretch limousine), the kind of clothing one wears, the value of the artwork in an office or home, and places where one eats are all good examples. All of these symbols, however, are related to the social standards of the immediate society in which a person lives and works. A stretch limousine would be simply out of place and viewed as ostentatious for an elementary school teacher. On the other hand, Ross Perot, a Texas billionaire, drives himself around in a sedan that is several years old and inconspicuous to those around him. The contrast of his riches and his conveyance suggests power.

The Power of the Listener-Audience

Because the listener is usually the target of the power act he or she commands a great deal of influence over the outcome of the interaction. In the private person-to-person context this power is singular and yet potent. In the public speaking situation the number and attitude of the listeners presents a formidable power source to deny and block the efforts of the agent and/or to provide a reciprocal influence effort that will cause the speaker to change course, approach, and other intents. There is massive evidence over the centuries to show that an audience will give power to a speaker when the conditions are right.

The first act of power granting is when the listener decides to hear what the speaker has to say. The decision to listen is almost totally within the ability of the listener. In public and private contexts alike the audience can change a speaker from a passive, taciturn, anxious state to an impassioned, excited and confident person by showing support, affection, veneration, and confidence in him or her.

POWER IN GROUPS AND ORGANIZATIONS

All groups have a continuing flow and exchange of influence among their members. In the more formal organizations, such as industry or government, the influence levels become levels of authority or managerial subsystems of the organization. During the entire life of a group there is a continual "jockeying for position" by the members. These "positions" represent roles that are devised to perform those activities necessary for the survival of the organization (Katz & Kahn, 1966). Out of this process comes a structure commonly called a "hierarchy." This has often been called the "pecking order"—first observed among chickens where the dominant one is able to peck each of the others and the others are not able to peck the dominant one in return. This structure is composed of a set of role relationships between persons within the organization wherein the roles are developed as parts of an influence structure which provides for who must transact with whom and the influence aspects of those transactions. This has been identified as the supervisor-subordinate relationship. Each supervisor, therefore, has a specified span of control over which he or she has influence and power. This power is what some call "legitimate" power.

A significant condition of this hierarchical power arrangement is that those lower in the hierarchy tend to direct communication upward to those at the higher levels of power. Those at the top seem to spend most of their communication time in communicating with others at their level (Raven & Ruben, 1976). There is some evidence that downward communication through the system is not very efficient nor effective and that the different levels of control in a complex hierarchy act as barriers or obstacles to the downward flow of information (Budd & Ruben, 1972).

Downward Communication

Most important messages going downward from upper power levels in a large organization are communicated orally with some combination of written communication. This seems to be the most effective procedure used (Budd & Ruben, 1972).

The communication flow data shows that those with the most influence power are usually at the upper levels of the organization. Along with this, their power position is bolstered by the presence of available rewards and punishments built into the system (such things as promotions, pay raises, suspensions, discharges, etc.).

The types of communication that flow downward are usually instructions about the nature and performance required in a job, rationale and relation of the job to other organizational tasks, procedures and practices followed by the organization, reports back to the subordinate about the quality of performance, and indoctrination as to the goals and purposes of the organization. Of these the instructions about the job are usually first priority and receive the greatest amount of attention. The least used type is the report back and appraisal system of the worker. Functionally, all types should be fully used in an effective system. When the system is not working, struggles over power arise and when they are not resolved they escalate into the more violent levels of the struggle spectrum.

Horizontal Communication

An effective system needs to have good lateral communication. Here is where teamwork develops around similar jobs. In addition, there is evidence to show that horizontal communication among peers provides emotional and social support for the individual (Katz & Kahn, 1966). These supports and teamwork serve to increase the power of the group at that given level of the organization. Peer groups without the stimulation of coordinating their work tasks and relationships will tend to become bored and direct the content and direction of their communication toward destruction of the organization (Katz & Kahn, 1966).

It would appear, also, that the more effective the horizontal communication is among peers the more difficulty the higher levels have in performing in the power sector as defined by their position. In a highly pyramidal and authoritarian structure in which the key information is received and retained by the top levels there is a tendency for the top levels to use this information for control and punishment of the lower levels. One of the results is that the amount of horizontal communication related to the functions of the organization becomes reduced, and the horizontal communication directed against the organization tends to increase. The struggle quickly escalates if it is not controlled or eliminated.

Upward Communication

The content of upward communication usually involves such things as personal problems, performance, and perceptions; problems and information about peers and others; matters about the organization and its practices and policies; and perceptions of what is needed and how it should be done (Katz & Kahn, 1966). The nature of the hierarchical structure usually allows for those at each level of the structure to listen to those in the next higher level and not to listen to those below.

Sometimes information passed up the line is used to control and punish the persons about whom the information is passed. For this reason there is a hesitancy to pass information upward. Many struggles in management arise from the nature of the information that is passed upward. This struggle for power seems ubiquitous.

The Group as An Agent of Power

For a long time we have been concerned with the effect that group membership has on the behavior of the members. Great concern has been expressed over people who become involved with groups called "cults" (in the lay language). The effect that membership in such groups has on those who become involved has been touted as a reason for elimination and/or destruction of the "offending" groups.

But the reality is that any group is bound to have an influence on the actions of its members. Again, the members become the recipients of the group's agency. In that sense, the members have power as recipients to select or reject the power moves of the agent. The original choice to join a group can be modified or abandoned although as time goes on there are increasingly powerful bonds of friendship, affiliation, loyalty, and sometimes fear that may pull toward the group. It has been found that group influences continue for a long time after the actual power act (Jacobson, 1972).

Jacobson (1972) reports that there is evidence that membership in a group tends to bring members to conform to the standards and ethics of that group. It appears that even when the group opinion is incorrect or distorted the members will tend to shift toward that opinion. The reasons for this seeming "conformity" may be found in the basis on which people join groups. Usually there is some attraction toward a group for the person before joining. That attraction may be personal, social, psychological, religious, emotional, economic, educational, or physical. Thus, the perceived expectancy that the group will provide the things the potential member wants and/or needs will add pressure to join. Once in the group, the affiliations with other members, the sense of common cause, and other bonding conditions may be stronger than the negative effects of behaviors that do not meet the standards of the member, of excesses that are not acceptable to the member, and of philosophies that turn out to be less than expected. Thus, the member will weigh the factors but will tend to stay with the group unless the negative aspects become so overwhelming that they overcome the positive aspects.

It is an error to assume that only cult and "undesirable" groups "brainwash" their members and overpower them. Almost every organized group we know surrounds its members with rules, norms, behavior expectancies, and rationales to which the member must conform or leave. Churches, social clubs, fraternities, professional organizations, and educational institutions all have their rules and standards of membership. Further, a group that is rejected by the larger society today may in the future become a highly accepted group and visa versa. The KKK, for example, has lost a lot of its acceptance over the past three decades. Anti-smoking groups have grown from barely tolerated radicals to highly accepted organizations today. The flow of society results in the rise and fall of various groups over time.

Some groups, more than others, make special efforts to solicit membership and then to retain their members. *Again, the power of the group over a person (recipient) is very much a matter of the degree to which the recipient (the member) gives power to the group.* But let us not ignore the special power that comes to a group from the collected grants of power from a number of recipients who are similar to and peers of the particular member.

It may be that we will need to redefine what we have popularly called "brainwashing" so that it refers specifically to those situations in which the tactics used by the group are manipulative (fraudulent and deceitful), contrary to the wishes and purposes of the individual, and depend on various forms of violence and deprivation as a means of control. Most groups in our society do not fit those criteria. Although, when we discover groups that do fit those definitions we encounter a particularly difficult task in providing members with alternatives that can break them out of the choice they have made (see the articles on brainwashing in *Society*, 1980, *17*(3), 19-51).

Groups provide many opportunities for struggle and conflict. Internally, the struggle for power and control over the group is found in every group. Externally, the struggles between groups for territory, ascendancy, recognition, and resources is a constant in our total society. To understand these struggles for power within and between groups we must be more aware of the nature of groups and their processes.

CONCEPTS AND THEORIES OF WAYS TO BE POWERFUL

The understanding of power is an important prerequisite to developing understanding and skills in the management of struggle. The very nature of many aspects of power relate directly to the processes involved in struggle. We deal with many of these power factors as we address the specific methods of negotiation, mediation, and arbitration. It is not my intention to provide a complete manual of rules and techniques by which you may become more powerful than you are. My concern is to look at power as an important factor in the management of struggle. I have tried to summarize some of the concepts, advice, and suggestions offered by various writers dealing with power. In doing so I have tried to avoid judging these propositions as good or bad and have attempted to present them in an objective manner so that you may view them and select from them the kinds of actions that will facilitate you in your endeavors.

Jacobsen (1972) provides us with an excellent general summary of research on power. All power involves an agent, as we have indicated, a method, and a recipient. Research has helped us to define and identify elements of each of these factors. The *power holder (agent)* may be either an individual or a group but power itself is a social relationship rather than a personal attribute. The agent exerts power over the recipient if (a) the agent controls the resources that the recipient wants or values; (b) the agent is in a higher position than the recipient in a hierarchy or social structure; (c) the agent can reward or punish the recipient; and (d) the agent can influence the recipient no matter what the recipient does (called "fate" power), by talking more often, and when there is a past record of successes.

Usually the successful power agent makes more successful power attempts than does the recipient, enjoys using power, and is less susceptible to other power attempts than is the recipient. Even so, the power holder incurs costs as a result of the exertion of power. When the agent is a group, the power over the members is greater when they expect common outcomes for all in the group, when the group has a record of past success as a group, and when it is apparent that the group product is superior to individual efforts. The *recipient* is vital to the power act. Power actually depends on the recipient, and the recipient depends on the act of power. The recipient's dependency on the agent is in proportion to the investment the recipient has in the goals that the agent provides. The recipient's dependence on the agent increases as the availability of the recipient's goals outside the relationship with the agent decreases.

The recipient conforms to the power attempts of the agent when they are consistent with the recipient's own values and beliefs and if it helps the recipient to attain his or her own goals. The recipient will also conform to the agent's power attempts when he or she perceives that the agent can observe his or her behavior and reward and punish for it. Similarly, the recipient will conform if the agent gives the recipient positive responses, if he or she admires the agent, if the agent is perceived as having a legitimate right to influence the recipient, and if the recipient admires the agent and wishes to emulate him or her. If the recipient believes that the agent is an expert he or she will conform to the agent's power attempt. However, if the agent attempts to use his or her power outside his or her own area of expertise the recipient will resist the "expert" power.

When a recipient deviates from the group he or she will receive a number of power attempts until it is apparent that he or she will not conform. At that point the communication toward the recipient will drop. The recipients in a group attempt to reduce their dependency on the agents by such means as cost reduction, withdrawal, giving status, extension of the power network, and by forming coalitions. The communication of low power members of a group is less frequent than that of high power members but what communications they have are mostly directed to high power members.

The *methods* of exerting power are activities that put the agent in a position of trying to force compliance by the recipient when the recipient has some alternatives from which to choose in responding. There is a time lag between the power attempt of the agent and the response of the recipient. *Power attempts are successful if they result in behavior that the recipient would not otherwise perform.* The exertion of physical force will give the agent power over the recipient. The agent can also exert power over the recipient by offering rewards or punishments or by increasing or decreasing the alternative choices that the recipient has. Perception plays an important role in power methods. The agent can exert power over the recipient by changing the recipient's *perception* of reality rather than changing the reality. Persuasive communication is a significant method of exerting power.

Legitimate authority, reducing the power distance between agent and recipient, displaying cooperative behavior, and participating actively in discussion are methods whereby the agent can exert power.

Whatever method the agent uses there is some cost to him or her for exerting power. These costs involve the risk of rejection, the failure to gain objectives, and, even in the case of success, there is some danger of future rejection by the recipient.

Cannetti, in his book *Crowds and Power* (1963), identifies what he calls the "elements of power."

Speed of performance is an important element.

Questioning is a power tool whereby the questioner gains control of the respondent by getting attention and directing the nature of the answer.

Secrecy, according to Cannetti, is at the core of power. The powerful person reveals only some of his secrets to any one person and never reveals all. "Power is impenetrable. The man who has it sees through other men, but does not allow them to see through him. He must be more reticent than anyone; no-one must know his opinions or intentions" (p. 292). Secrecy is dangerous. For example, modern technical secrets are more concentrated and dangerous than any that have ever been created. They concern everyone but only a few have real knowledge of them.

Condemnation. We exalt ourselves by abasing others.

Pardon and Mercy. "The supreme manifestation of power is the granting of a pardon at the last moment" (p. 299).

In discussing the strategies and tactics of power, Siu (1979) lists eight axioms as the basis for developing agent strength in power acts. They represent advice to an advocate or warrior as to how to deal with their adversary in a struggle. The list is quite similar to many Machiavellian concepts for control.

1. Adjust the objective to the resources, expending neither more for an intermediary target than it is worth in its contribution to the ultimate objective nor less than is needed to gain it.
2. Keep the objective always in sight, ensuring a clear line of attack without ending in a cul de sac.
3. Shape the operations so as to allow alternative tactical targets, thereby placing the opposition in the horns of a dilemma.
4. Exploit the line of least resistance, always pointing in the direction of final objectives.
5. Pursue the course of least expectation on the part of the opposition, deceiving and beguiling to widen his miscalculations.
6. Maintain a flexible posture, responding to exigencies of the unexpected.
7. Refrain from repeating a line of attack that has just failed, recognizing that the opposition have in all probability reinforced themselves in the interim.
8. Dislocate the opposition—upsetting their strategic balance and disjointing their psychological reserve with goading lures and traps—before striking the decisive blow. (pp. 87-88)

Siu's axioms are clearly designed to provide antagonists with tools for fighting. We must not make the mistake of assuming that all power methods and strategies are related to the more violent struggle situations. We use our power in many situations in which the recipient is neither competitor nor enemy but a friend and colleague whom we want to believe something and/or behave differently.

Power on the job has attracted a great deal of attention. Typical of many suggestions are those by Kennedy (1984) who tells how we should "influence the boss."

Influencing the Boss

1. Have your boss become dependent on you for special service.
2. Find where the boss's style or procedure is lacking and fill the gap by motivating others to deal with you.
3. Gain control over sources of information and become the primary conduit for information going outside your department.
4. Subtly "train" the boss in procedures and methods useful to your own career.
5. Anticipate the boss's wants so you can provide these things for him and thus gain his confidence and support.
6. Make the boss dependent on you for information about what is happening inside and outside the department. (pp. 95-104)

Korda (1975), writing in the same manner, lists several rules that he feels apply in any situation involving power.

1. Act impeccably! Perform every act as if it were the only thing in the world that mattered.
2. Never reveal all of yourself to other people. Hold something back in reserve so that people are never quite sure if they really know you.
3. Learn to use time, think if it as a friend, not an enemy. Don't waste it in going after things you don't want.
4. Learn to accept your mistakes. Don't be a perfectionist about everything.
5. Don't make waves, move smoothly without disturbing things. (pp. 259-261)

Whatever rules you follow there is general agreement that "effective power involves restraint in its use in order that it can be retained, while persons with this power who use it for their own gain ultimately have to face organized resistance to their power"(Duke, 1976, p. 263).

There are several other concepts in the process of powermaking that have been found useful. Try these:

- *Find as many sources of power as you can. The more power resources you have the more effective will be your use of the process.*
- *Do what you can to facilitate the development of your own prestige without making a fool of yourself.*
- *In your organization, try to make the power structure as flexible and adaptable as possible.*
- *In your organization, seek to develop and maintain order, conformity, consensus, and integration of the people and the processes.*
- *Seek new members for your group who are willing to conform to its norms and standards.*
- *Seek to emphasize cooperation, love, and friendship as themes for the existence of your group.*
- *Bridle and limit the uncontrolled, exploitive use of power for simple personal gain.*
- *Study the ones in power. Take note of their style. Watch for the strengths and the weaknesses in their power moves.*

THE USE OF POWER IN STRUGGLE MANAGEMENT: BALANCE AND UNBALANCE

In every struggle, from mild disagreement to war, reaching agreement depends to a high degree on the distribution of power among or between the participants in the relationship. In situations in which one party has more power than the other, the more powerful side is more likely to impose an agreement on the weaker. Thus, in a divorce dispute involving custody of the children, the person in the partnership who has the greater power will be able to control the custody allocations. Unless the weaker party in the relationship finds some way to gain a closer balance of power, the inevitable control of the stronger must be expected.

When the power between the participants is relatively equal or balanced the struggles may be resolved through skilled negotiation. However, when that fails the struggle is likely to escalate to more violent levels very quickly. The holding of power thus becomes an issue in the relationship. Sometimes when the power relationship has not been resolved a fight for power ensues. It can become very violent. (This may have been one of the critical situations in the American Civil War.) It is quite frequently the source of violence between siblings, as well as parents, in a family. Good negotiations usually require a level of some balance between the parties so that effective joint decision making can take place. When there is high unbalance in the situation there is simply not much negotiation because the more powerful control the action and the decision making. Only when the low power side develops methods and strategies to equalize the difference can effective negotiations begin to take place.

When the power unbalance is present in a struggle situation there are several ways in which it can be altered. One is for the low power side to withdraw from the situation. This has many dimensions to it. The withdrawal itself may shift the balance dramatically.

A couple who had been together for some time encountered considerable struggle over how much time they would spend with each other. One demanded more time of the other than was presently being given. The other, who apparently had more power in their relationship, was pressed with work and other responsibilities and was unable to spend the amount of time wanted by the partner and simply refused to make the changes requested. Intense and heated discussions went on for about a year. At the same time the relationship continued and both seemed, in spite of the power differential, to want to be together and to enjoy the relationship, even though one appeared to have the greater control. Finally, when they failed to resolve the time issue, the weaker partner broke off the relationship and began seeing another person. The person left behind made many futile attempts to bring the other back into the relationship. All the agent power tools available were tried and to no effect. The person who had exited from the relationship had the ultimate power to destroy the relationship and did. The power unbalance was actually reversed with the demise of the relationship.

Another method of dealing with unbalanced power is for the low power person to gather together a group of friends or others who will provide the gratifications that are desired but unavailable from the person with the greater power. (Jane attempted this in the story in Chapter 1.) The establishment of such a network becomes a substitute for the gratifications wanted but not received in the relationship. This happens often in group situations in which the dissatisfaction with the power in the group will lead persons to seek relationships outside the group to satisfy their needs and wants.

> *A team of trainers had developed a highly effective training system. The team was led by an older person who had initiated the project and who, for many reasons, was the dominant power in the group. Other members of the team received a great deal of satisfaction from being on the team, and the dominant person used power benevolently with care and concern for the welfare of the others. So long as the lower power persons were satisfied with their dependency on the dominant person there were no problems. Some in the group, however, became more independent and resented the power exerted by the dominant one and repeatedly tried to challenge and reduce the influence of the leader on the group. Finally, the persons who had challenged the leader brought in others and extended the in-group networks so that the new members could provide satisfactions that the old leader could not. When that did not work the dissenters abandoned the team and went to other groups doing similar work. They became competitive with the group they had left and tried to destroy it.*

A third way of dealing with a power unbalance is for the low power elements to create coalitions that will challenge the high power elements and provide more satisfactions than the high power elements can. It is often the case that within groups the weaker persons will join together in coalitions to control the strong. Thus, in the above situation, two or three of the group formed a small "clique" that began to control the areas of decision making that the leader had benevolently left to the members. Soon this strategy placed the originally powerful person into a weaker position, and the coalition took over.

A fourth way of dealing with power unbalance is to give added status to another in the group or in the relationship. Thus, several members of the group who had been with the group for some time presented themselves as having more status and greater influence than the leader, and one of them eventually challenged the leader on a more equal footing. In all of these situations it is clear that as long as members in a relationship are dependent on one another for benefits, the power in relation to those benefits will be out of balance. To the degree that the lower powered persons (recipients) can become independent of the benefits provided by the power agent, the balance of the power may increase.

Another power balancing process is when B (the recipient) develops skills or services that A (agent) wants and cannot get elsewhere thereby shifting the relationship—B becomes the agent and A becomes the recipient. This shifting of roles is often subtle but it can be very effective in balancing a relationship. What is happening is that those who were dependent now become more independent. Those with the least dependence on the leader or the group are the most likely to exit.

Deutsch (1977) summarized his discussion of how low power persons could deal with the high powered who controlled them by saying,

> apathetic resignation or destructiveness are not the only responses available in the face of contrary authority. It is possible to increase the power of the have-nots by developing their personal resources, social cohesion, and social organization so that they have more influence. And in jujitsu fashion, it is possible for the have-nots to employ some of the characteristics of the haves to throw the haves off balance and reduce their effective opposition. (pp. 399-400)

At those levels in the Struggle Spectrum where intervention becomes usable the effects of that intervention are usually to alter the power structure in the situation. Thus, when a mediator intervenes into a situation the power balance is changed. When the arbitrator is called in, the power situation may be less dramatically changed, except that there may be a greater balance already present which led to the stalemate in the dispute. I have more to say about these situations in Chapters 5 and 6 on Mediation and Arbitration.

PROBLEMS AND DANGERS OF POWER

Intoxication of Omnipotence

Power over others is an intoxicant. It is headier than drugs and alcohol. The higher up you go in an organization the more you begin to feel that you know all that is needed and what is best for people better than they themselves know. This is a dangerous state of being for it makes you immediately vulnerable to attack and destruction.

> *The wise man soon learns that omnipotence is servitude. Too much power over other people can be almost as bad as falling into the clutches of people who think they have the right to run your life. (Korda, 1975, p. 47)*

Compensation and Illness: Stress

When power is used to compensate for physical defects, real or imagined, the result is frequently bitterness and anger. As a person's power increases it is known that a number of illnesses seem to arise. The drive for achievement and power correlates highly with the presence of an acid in the blood that makes us more vulnerable to gout, to coronary heart disease, and to various disorders of the gastrointestinal system. The more we strive for power in our jobs the more stress we seem to encounter. Many powerful people are paranoiac and live in constant fear of attack and destruction. Others are schizophrenic: They want to control, to give orders, and to punish, and at the same time they want comfort, appreciation, and love. The result of these conflicting demands is exhibited in stress-allergic reactions of all kinds.

The Guilt of Power

For some the acquisition of power is accompanied by guilt feelings brought on by the myth that power is bad ("power tends to corrupt and absolute power corrupts absolutely") and the use of it is unethical. These guilt feelings lead to increased defensive behavior and alienation from society and may eventually lead to mental breakdown.

Power, Struggle, and Violence

In spite of our modernization and sophistication in today's world we are certainly no more safe or protected from sudden violence than primitive people. In fact, we may be more unsafe than ever before in the history of human society. Part of that danger comes from the developing use of destructive forms of power and the escalation of struggle in ways that deplete rather than enhance human life and that escalate rather than diminish or de-escalate violence as a way of managing struggle.

Although power is ubiquitous, as I stated at the beginning of this chapter, it is also subject to misuse and inhuman application (the "bad" image of power). This is one of the prime dangers that besets us. The tools of power are available to anyone. As tools they can be used for good or evil. Power is just like a scalpel that can be used to save a person's life or destroy it, to resolve a struggle or escalate it. The ethical and productive use of power becomes a *personal* responsibility that needs more and more attention. The effective, positive use of power leads to survival and helps to overcome the desolation and destruction of a brutish world. With it comes a feeling of health and goodness that uplifts the human spirit. The ineffective use and/or use of power in the "bad" image makes the world more brutish, escalates peaceful differences into violent conflicts, brings on our own destruction more rapidly than otherwise, and creates social, psychological, and physical invalids.

The use of any kind of power, however, has its costs.

AND SO..................

If we seek power with greed, self-interest, and fear of the more powerful we will surely put ourselves, our fellows, and our freedom at risk.

If we seek to enhance the lives of others through the management of struggle, to discover a sense of significance, to realize that we count for something, then we will use power in a joyous endeavor that will enrich our life and the lives of others.

We cannot avoid the "power play." It is all around us. Every interaction with another leads to a power transaction. There is no way to escape this game. It is possible, however, to make that game a joyous one which enhances the human condition.

//

CHAPTER 4

Managing Struggle Through Negotiation and Bargaining
A Look at Struggle Management Through Problem Solving, Negotiation and Bargaining

INTRODUCTION

> *Dean, age 7, his sister, age 5, and his parents had just assembled at the dinner table for their evening meal. His father, Jim, looked over at Dean, who was busy with a crayon and a coloring book and said,*
>> *"Let's put the crayons and the book over on the toy table for now, Dean, it's time for supper."*
>> *Dean replied, "Okay, in a minute, I want to finish this drawing."*
>
> *Jim was quiet for a several minutes, and Dean did not cease his activity. Jim quietly reached over and quickly took the coloring book and crayon and placed them on the toy table. Dean started to object but for some reason stopped and reached for a plate of crackers. As he was crunching away, Jim asked, "Well, what happened at school today, Dean?"*
>
> *Dean did not answer but kept munching on the cracker and started teasing his sister by poking a cracker at her. Jim intervened again, "Dean, leave your sister alone. I'd like to know what you learned at school today. Please tell me. It's important."*
>
> *Dean was silent a moment then looked up at his father and said, "Why do you want to know?"*
>
> *"We like to know what's happening at school so that we can help you here at home if we need to," his father answered.*
>
> *"Well," Dean answered with a solemn look, "That'll cost you fifty cents."*
>
> *Jim shook his head a bit, grinned, and replied, "That's too high. I'll give you five cents."*
>
> *"No way!" Dean answered with a shake of his head as he pushed another cracker at his sister. "That's not enough."*
>
> *"Seven cents, then. A nickel and two pennies and not a bit more," replied Jim.*
>
> *Dean was quiet a while and then, putting his elbows on the table and looking straight at his father, said, "Well, then, I guess I won't tell ya."*
>
> *Jim smothered a laugh and tried to look serious. Then, appearing to think it over he said, "Well, I guess I can go to ten cents, a dime, but that's it. Don't forget what a dime will get you."*
>
> *"What will it get me?" Dean shot back.*
>
> *"Well, ..." Jim hesitated.*
>
> *"Nothing, Dad! You know you can't buy anything for a dime that's any good." Dean grinned at his Dad. "But for 25 cents I'll tell you what happened in just the art class. Is it a deal?"*

(continued)

> "Quit trying to play games with me, Dean. I really want to know," Jim grunted.
>
> "I'm not playing games, Dad, you are. If you want to know what I did, pay me for it," Dean said earnestly.
>
> Jim thought a moment then proposed, "Okay, here's my final offer: I'll give you 25 cents if you tell me the whole story, including what happened on the playground. And, here's the quarter." He pulled a shiny new quarter from his pocket.
>
> Dean looked at the quarter, giggled, and reached over to take it. His dad jerked the quarter back saying, "Wait a minute, young man, you haven't agreed to my offer. I'm not giving you the quarter until you agree. And I won't give you the quarter, then, until you've told me what I want to know."
>
> Dean shouted, "That's not fair. Don't you trust me?"
>
> "Of course I do, Dean, it's just that it is not good practice to pay for something before you have an agreement on its price and until you get what you want. When you go to the store you don't pay for anything until you get it, do you?"
>
> "Yes, but . . ." Dean started, but his father interrupted,
>
> "Just agree to the deal and I'll trust you to live up to your word. Okay?"
>
> Dean's black eyes twinkled and with a grin he said, "Okay," as he reached for the quarter now held in his dad's tightly held fist.

Not many 7-year-olds are this sophisticated in the negotiation process or in their relationships with their parents. But this is a true story of a young fellow and his father. The father, an MD and PhD, is an international development broker of scientific and medical systems, instruments, and techniques. His skill in negotiation is the essence of his work. Early on, he and his wife, a pediatrician, quietly, lovingly, and joyfully led their son into the intricacies of negotiation. It will be interesting to see how they deal with more difficult problems.

But certainly, young Dean has grasped some of the key techniques of the negotiation process. But from the day he was born, and probably before, Dean and his parents and the people surrounding him have been negotiating. We all negotiate with each other about many things.

THE NEGOTIATION PROCESS

What Is Negotiation?

Negotiation has been defined in numerous ways ranging from a highly inclusive definition that encompasses almost any type of human interaction, such as "whenever we talk with another we are negotiating," to very specific situations involving specific interactions for specific purposes. For example, when we seek to buy a car and do not want to pay the sticker price we negotiate. My definition is somewhere in-between:

Negotiation is an endeavor aimed at fulfilling needs and interests when they are in some opposition to others. It involves affecting behavior through an exchange between people. It is a peaceful procedure which reconciles and/or compromises differences and which depends on good faith and flexibility. The intention is to change relationships to get what you want from others and to persuade through mutual communication, joint decision making, coordinating interests, and by influencing the decisions of others.

This definition has emerged from my experiences and from my study of others who have written about negotiation. You will find sources of some parts of my definition in:

"a field of knowledge and endeavor that focuses on gaining the favor of people from whom we want things . . . It is the use of information and power to affect behavior" (Cohen, 1980, p. 15).

"a peaceable procedure for reconciling, and/or compromising known differences. It is the antithesis of force and violence. It depends on the two elements of good faith and flexibility" (Rule, 1962, pp. 5-6).

"an exchange between people for the purpose of fulfilling their needs" (Schatzki, 1981, p. 9).

"Whenever people exchange ideas with the intention of changing relationships, whenever they confer for agreement, they are negotiating. Negotiation depends on communication. It occurs between individuals acting either for themselves or as representatives of organized groups" (Nierenberg, 1968, p. 2).

"a process by which a joint decision is made by two or more parties. The parties first verbalize contradictory demands and then move toward agreement by a process of concession making or search for new alternatives" (Pruitt, 1981, p. 1).

"a mutual act of coordinating areas of interest. As these are rarely identical for both parties, this is customarily accomplished through developing compromises that ensure benefit to both. One party dictating to the other is not negotiation. One party manipulating the other with no concern for the other's needs is a cynical travesty of negotiation" (Calero & Oskam, 1983, p. 78).

"all cases in which two or more parties are communicating, each for the purpose of influencing the other's decision" (Fisher, 1983, p. 150).

"a process of potentially opportunistic interaction by which two or more parties, with some apparent conflict, seek to do better through jointly decided action than they could otherwise" (Lax & Sebenius, 1986, p. 11).

"a basic means of getting what you want from others. It is back-and-forth communication designed to reach an agreement when you and the other side have some interests that are shared and others that are opposed" (Fisher & Ury, 1981, p. i).

"The mental ability to observe and put into practice the best means of persuasion in any given situation" (Ilich, 1973, p. 18).

Based on these definitions and my experience, several things emerge as fundamental characteristics of the negotiation process:

- Each party to the matter has different and sometimes conflicting interests, basic needs, goals, perceptions, and concerns.
- The goals of the parties are partially inclusive and partially exclusive. That is, some are sharable and some are not sharable.
- The demands, therefore, are often contradictory; that is, what one wants the other cannot have.
- Joint decision making and agreement are essential for effective negotiation.
- Concession and attenuation of demands are necessary for joint decisions.
- The process is a nonviolent one.
- Communication between all parties is fundamental to the process.
- The larger issues may be a matter of mutual concern to all parties involved when the underlying goals are inclusive (such as the elimination of nuclear war).
- There are usually some time constraints on the parties.
- At least four areas are subject to the negotiation: the *process* by which the parties seek to resolve their differences, the *substance* or content, the *positions* the parties take, and the underlying *interests* or needs involved.
- Persuasion is an important element in the process.

All of these are included in my definition of negotiation.

Negotiation cannot be used at all stages of struggle. It is NOT a process that can be used effectively in judicial decision making, in arbitration, or in unilateral decision making. Furthermore, negotiations are impossible unless both parties are willing to avoid or abandon unilateral decision making by either of the parties or by a third party. Because negotiation is one of the *voluntary* processes for managing struggle it is difficult, if not impossible, to impose it on people who do not want to use it.

Negotiation is a form of struggle management. In the process of such management we seek to:

1. Anticipate and control struggle so that the valuable aspects of the process are preserved, and the destructive aspects are avoided or eliminated.

2. Find that point in all struggle when it ceases to be productive and becomes destructive.

3. Develop personal awareness of intrapersonal struggles that can become destructive and debilitating.

4. Develop awareness of interpersonal struggles and those conditions and points at which struggle becomes destructive to the participants and the surrounding society.

5. Develop an awareness of intra- and intergroup strife and of the factors and dimensions involved so that we can begin to operate on those points and conditions when the struggle begins to become destructive.

6. Develop an understanding of the processes, systems, and so forth that are now available for containing struggle within useful bounds.

7. Encourage the exploration and search for new means of developing struggle control and management.

8. Become aware of the problems in terminating already existing struggles (see Chapter 3).

Within the management of struggle negotiation is primarily a joint decision-making process. That is, both parties to the action are involved in the making of the decisions.

> *Many teacher-school board dealings, in the early years of their bargaining development, were referred to as negotiations. Yet in many states the school board retained the right to make the final and binding decisions. Thus, discussions between the board and the teachers may have had the facade of negotiation, but were actually nothing more than information sharing sessions, unless the board was willing to bind itself to a joint agreement. Newer collective bargaining laws have changed that situation.*

Stages of Negotiation

Most negotiation moves through several stages.

1. Contact. The first stage involves the introduction or contact between the parties in relation to the problem, the disagreement, or dispute.

> *When my neighbor saw me, armed with power saw and ladder, approaching a tree on the boundary line between us she became concerned and came into the yard to ask me what I was about to do. She told me that she did not want any part of the tree touched. At this stage we discovered differences in our needs and interests.*

2. Goals and Positions. The second stage involves the setting of objectives for the negotiations, identifying the areas in which settlement is being sought, and an overview of the goals, positions, and feelings of each party along with a review of background significant to the issues. During this stage, along with Stage 1, an agenda emerges that keeps expanding throughout the subsequent stages. The importance of the agenda is discussed by Pendergast (1990):

The importance of agendas extends to numerous dimensions of the negotiation process: the pacing and flow of the negotiation; the dominance and control of the parties; the preparation and coordination of negotiation team members; the intricate linkages among negotiation issues; the ability to construct "efficient" agreements; and success in achieving acceptance for preferred outcomes. (p. 135)

> *We agreed to talk it over on the spot. I claimed that the tree was obstructing the growth of my garden and I wanted it out while she insisted that the tree provided shade for her lawn and wanted it left alone.*

3. Rule Setting. The third stage leads to an agreement on rules of conduct for the negotiations and sometimes general criteria for a settlement (including both parties agreeing not to coerce the other, a settlement which would consider the needs of both parties).

> *My neighbor insisted that if we were going to argue about the matter we should agree on some rules for our argument. We then agreed to discuss the matter over a lemonade and to explore all the possible aspects of the problem.*

4. **Exploration**. The fourth stage involves a more specific exploration of the issues and establishment of an agenda for dealing with the matter. It is at this stage that the needs and interests of each side are more explicitly discussed.

> *As we sipped her lemonade and walked around the tree, we both acknowledged that the tree pre-existed our ownership of the properties. She showed me how the tree provided shade for her dog's kennel, his run, and for a picnic table where she often entertained her guests. I pointed her to my garden where the shade of the tree had resulted in a stunted growth of some vegetables I had planted. I explained to her that I depended greatly on vegetables in my diet. It was apparent, immediately, that we both had legitimate agendas for action and that each of us had some substantive interest in the tree.*

5. **Focusing**. The fifth stage brings differing perspectives, demands, and positions into focus with each party questioning the other and presenting its own case. Out of this stage may come a recognition of areas in which agreement can be reached and other areas in which further exploration must take place.

> *My neighbor asked me what I intend to do to the tree. I explained that it was my basic intention to cut it down and argued that it was a trash maker because it dropped its many leaves each fall. She then demanded that I leave that tree alone and that from all she could tell it was really on her property. I questioned that but suggested that we go to the court house and get a plot of the lots to see on whose property the tree was growing because that might affect any decision we made. She agreed to check the plot but insisted that she did not want to lose the shade.*

6. **Re-exploration and Agreement.** The sixth stage brings a fallback or a re-exploration of the issues over which no agreement has been reached. It is at this stage that some positions may be adjusted in order to facilitate accomplishment of other demands. Out of this stage comes an agreement on principle and the formula for a settlement.

> *After checking the plot we discovered that the tree, indeed, was growing right on the line between the properties and that its roots, as well as its limbs, extended into both our yards. We recognized that any decision would have to have our mutual agreement. I then proposed checking with a tree service company to see what limbs could be cut without harming the tree and the shade it gave to her lawn. She agreed with that and acknowledged that I did have a problem with the garden.*

7. **Implementation**. The seventh stage results in the parties working out the details of the formula and its implementation.

> *We checked with the tree service and found we could cut the one side to a height where it would not shade the garden while the shade on the other side would not be disturbed. We then agreed on what limbs would come off and all was well.*

All of these stages occur in any negotiation, but not with the same proportion of time or emphasis. Many of the shifts from stage to stage are through implicit communication or nonverbal signals and behaviors. Notice the situation between Dean and his father. Stage 1 was taking place as Jim and Dean interacted at the dinner table and when a difference (or tension) appeared between Dean and Jim as to the revealing of information about Dean's school day. The second stage moved quickly as Jim asked what happened at school. Dean replied "Why do you want to know?" and Jim suggested that it was important to him. The third stage took place as Dean set the price of the information. This overt statement also sent a message that the process by which the information was to be gathered would be through some payment of funds. This became a ground rule for the subsequent events. It apparently existed before in other situations in the relationship and thus was easily and quickly introduced into that situation. The fourth stage appeared when Dean began to divide up the amount of information for the money offered and Jim began to make specific offers. When Jim made a new offer for more information they moved to the sixth stage. When they both agreed and the quarter was on the table they arrived at Stage 7.

Although the time, nature, and complexity of the process at each stage may differ, it appears that such stages are necessary in any negotiation situation. Calero and Oskam contend that the stages represent a kind of ritual and that following the ritual stages is necessary for a successful completion of the process (Calero & Oskam, 1983).

Bargaining and Negotiation

Negotiation and bargaining have often been considered as synonymous terms referring to the same behavior. As I discussed in Chapter 1, they are parts of the larger process of joint decision making within the struggle spectrum and represent different ways of reaching decisions when more cooperative means have failed.

In order to keep the processes and their consequences clear we need to identify negotiation and bargaining as *different* but related processes. They employ many of the same techniques, but they appear to be functional at a different level of the relationship between parties. I see bargaining as including a focus on positions, strong argument, persuasion, threats, deception, and an intense win-lose context between two parties as they seek to win concessions from each other in return for favors granted. The outcomes of bargaining are usually reached through compromise. The bargaining situation brings into play a much higher incidence of argument, persuasion, threat, and exclusiveness of needs-goals than does the negotiation atmosphere. Negotiation, on the other hand occurs in conditions with less polarization, more mutual problem solving, less use of compromise, and greater focus on interests. Key differences between negotiation and bargaining are also established by the degree of mutual exclusiveness of the goals and the elements of argument, persuasion, and concession seeking or trade-offs. Negotiation involves much more joint interest and mutual goal sharing than does bargaining.

The incident with my neighbor over the tree was essentially negotiation. Had it become bargaining, we would have engaged in a much more intense and argumentative affair. We would probably have each hired a lawyer or at least conferred with one. We would have put much more pressure on each other to give in or accept our position. There would have been some heated arguments over the property line. Trade-offs would have been difficult to achieve. Each of us would have tried to persuade the other to accept our proposal. There would have been a longer time of struggle between us before a resolution could have been reached, and either or both of us would have threatened the other with court and police action.

Remember that the negotiation and bargaining processes are part of the larger continuum system of decision making in the struggle spectrum. At one end of the continuum is the full joint deliberation, involving a discussion of *mutual* problems and common goals. As the solutions to the problems become more individualistic, different needs begin to arise, and the joint deliberation moves toward negotiation procedures. As the parties become more polarized in their ideas of desirable solutions and their goals become more mutually exclusive, they move into a bargaining structure. (Note Chapter 1 on the Struggle Spectrum.)

Another way to look at the difference between negotiation and bargaining is in terms of what Fisher and Ury (1981) called "hard" and "soft" behavior. Negotiation is at the soft end of a continuum where we consider the parties as friendly rivals, their goal is agreement, they are willing to make concessions to cultivate the relationship, the parties are soft on people and the problem, they trust the others, change their position without great resistance, make offers, disclose their bottom line, accept one-sided losses in order to reach agreement, search for an answer the other side will accept, insist on agreement, try to avoid contests of will, and yield to pressure.

At the bargaining or hard end of the continuum the parties are clearly adversaries, victory is the goal, the parties demand concessions of each other as a condition of the relationship, they are hard on people, distrust others, dig into their position, make threats, hide or mislead about the bottom line, demand one-sided gains as the price of agreement, search for an answer acceptable to themselves, insist on their position, try to win a contest of will, and apply pressure (Fisher & Ury, 1981).

Fisher and Ury point out that when negotiators bargain over positions alone rather than over interests or needs they become more easily polarized or locked into those positions as they defend them and become more committed to them. Attending to positions and not the underlying problems, concerns, interests, or needs of the parties leads to mechanical splits of demands—not to the resolution of the needs and interests of the parties—and agreements are less likely (Fisher & Ury, 1981).

If, for example, my neighbor insisted that nothing was to be done to the tree with limbs hanging over my garden, and we spent our time arguing whether her or my position was the proper position, we would have never reached a resolution together and the dispute would have escalated to litigation or campaign. It was when we began to explore our separate needs and situations that resolution of the matter became viable.

The desired outcome in all types of negotiation-bargaining processes is change. The negotiation-bargaining continuum is created by the nature of the needs, goals, and methods of interaction used to arrive at the change to be instituted.

Stagner and Rosen (1986) described the bargaining process in labor-management relations as beginning when one side tries to communicate to the other what it sees in the work situation and the changes desired. If both labor and management saw the situation and the changes in the same way, there would be no bargaining. The discussions would be pleasant and would respond to the various interests of the two parties. The joint decision making would be almost automatic.

Although the labor-management context is common and most generally associated with the bargaining process, bargaining also occurs in many other situations. The fruit growers bargain with the food processors over the price to be paid for the crop, the fishermen bargain with the fish-processing companies over the price to be paid for the catch, nations bargain with each other over many issues of international relations, business people bargain with each other over products and prices, and customers bargain with retailers over prices and products. It is said that students often bargain with professors over grades. Husband and wife may bargain over many issues in their relationship. Children bargain with parents. Many of these bargaining situations are preceded by negotiations that have failed to bring agreement, and the relationships between the parties have become more polarized and their attitudes toward each other less cooperative.

The following chart clarifies the differences and relationships between negotiation and bargaining.

NEGOTIATION AND BARGAINING CONTRASTED ON VARIOUS FACTORS		
Negotiation	*Factor*	*Bargaining*
Low polarization	*Situation*	*High polarization*
High inclusive	*Goals*	*Low inclusive*
Interest centered	*Goals*	*Position centered*
Problem solving	*Processes*	*Compromise*
Discussion	*Processes*	*Argument and debate*
Easy "trade-offs"	*Processes*	*Hard "trade-offs"*
Logical, fact seeking	*Processes*	*Emotional, threats, etc.*
Collaborative	*Processes*	*Competitive*
Friendly rivals	*Relationships*	*Adversaries*
Trusting	*Relationships*	*Distrusting*
Soft	*Processes*	*Hard*
Open	*Communication*	*Semi-closed*

Throughout the rest of this chapter I assume distinctions between negotiation and bargaining and call attention to the differences when they are appropriate. Keep in mind that they are part of a continuum and that the chart above identifies the *extremes* of each end of the continuum. Many of the techniques used in negotiation are similarly useful in the bargaining process. At the same time bargaining may require variations that could hardly be called negotiation.

Types of Negotiation and Bargaining

Walton and McKersie refer to four types of negotiation and bargaining: distributive, integrative, attitudinal, and intraorganizational (Walton & McKersie, 1965).

Distributive involves the process of resolving an issue that is bound up in a mutually exclusive goal; that is, what one person or group loses the other gains. *The goal cannot be shared, and thus if one wins the other loses.* The game of poker, international struggles over territory, and most labor-management bargaining are of this type.

Integrative takes place when the goals of the parties are not in direct conflict with each other, thus they can be *shared or integrated with each other*. Integrative efforts may lead to a problem solution that benefits both parties, as, for example, when a class and a teacher work out an agreement to set a deadline for term papers at time most convenient for both under the circumstances. Or, when two neighbors agree to remove a fence that separates their property.

Attitudinal is a process of influencing and *changing the attitudes and relationships of the parties toward and with each other*. It is based on interpersonal processes. It is what occurs when I try to convince my neighbor that I am an okay person and that I will not take more than my share of the apples.

Intraorganizational is the process whereby the representatives of a constituency *bring their principals' expectations into line with those of the negotiators-bargainers and the situation*. It is not infrequent that union and management negotiators return to their constituencies with settlements that they urge be accepted; but their intraorganizational bargaining efforts fail when the constituents vote to reject these settlements.

> *Intraorganizational negotiation and bargaining usually involve another negotiation as when my wife and I must decide on how I am to approach the neighbor about our problem of distributing the apples from a tree growing on our property line. I say the way to negotiate with the neighbor is simply tell her that we're going to take all the apples that grow and fall on our side of the line, take it or leave it. My wife objects strenuously and wants to invite the neighbor over for tea to talk the matter over. The fact is we have to get our own side in order as we try to deal with the other side.*

You will note that each of the types of bargaining brings into play different problems and strategies. But they do not necessarily exist separately from each other. For example, in labor-management bargaining the major style usually involves distributive bargaining, as when the parties are working on a contract. However, outside of contract negotiations they may be involved in a number of negotiations over problems in the workplace that they both recognize and share. Many problems of safety in the workplace involve integrated negotiation within joint committees assigned by the principals to address the issue and to come up with solutions. The representatives at the bargaining table frequently have to negotiate intraorganizationally with their own constituency over what positions are to be taken to the table.

Cooperation and Communication

Both communication and cooperation are required in the problem-solving processes of negotiation and bargaining, and there are some important relationships between communication and cooperative behavior. Communicative behavior is likely to be more effective in bringing about cooperative problem-solving behavior when it contains all of the following kinds of messages:

1. Behavior expected from the other(s).
2. The participants' intended behavior toward the other participants.
3. The sanctions and/or punishments that will be used if the cooperative expectations are violated.
4. The terms and conditions under which the others can return to "grace" if they violate the cooperative expectations (Loomis, 1959).

These particular types of messages represent a kinds of openness and forthrightness between the participants that leads to a clearer understanding of the nature of the problem(s) and the conditions necessary for its removal. As each shares these messages, the grounds on which the problem solving can take place become more explicit and subject to joint accommodation. Bringing about cooperative behavior in a noncooperative contest is a tough task. Deutsch once raised the question, "what do you do if you want to induce a competitor or even an enemy to co-operate?" The strategy he suggested is "firmness and friendliness; a firm resistance to efforts by the other to exploit and to gain an unwarranted competitive victory combined with a continuing, friendly, and generous willingness to cooperate to obtain mutual gain" (Deutsch, 1971, p. 54). Such a strategy may be best accomplished through open communication and clear messages.

The very act of communication in negotiating involves some cooperation between the negotiators. The more cooperative they are the greater the possibility of reaching agreement. The parties in negotiation are characteristically more cooperative and open than in bargaining, but both levels involve cooperation.

Deutsch also suggests that "a conflict is more likely to be resolved cooperatively if powerful, prestigious third parties encourage such a resolution and help to provide resources . . . to expedite discovery of a mutually satisfactory solution" (Smith, 1971, p. 55). The communication of a third party in negotiation changes the structure of the situation. I have more to say about third party intervention in other chapters.

Negotiation-Bargaining is Part of a System of Joint Problem Solving and Cooperative Decision Making

The basic processes with which we can cope with the destructive aspects of struggle are that of joint problem solving and decision making. In one of the classical experiments in the nature of social conflict, Sherif (1984) used problem solving with superordinate goals to bring boys in a violent conflict situation back together. The boys' groups were stimulated to battle with each other through highly competitive win/lose games with rewards to the winner. When the boys actually resorted to violence, the experiment introduced a number of situations that could not be solved by the exclusive action of one group, but demanded joint efforts by all. One such problem was a "break" in the water supply that deprived the camp of water on hot Oklahoma days. The insertion of these superordinate goals led to joint problem solving between the previously "warring" groups.

Problem solving is the attempt to find solutions to problems that confront people. The problem-solving process is an extensive organization of information and attitudes surrounding a situation identified as a problem, and it includes numerous decisions preceding and including the alternative that solves the problem. Effectively used it involves understanding the goals, the obstacles to achieving these goals, and the conditions surrounding the problem situation as prerequisites to setting criteria for evaluating possible solutions. Then the process involves an exploration of alternative solutions, selection of the solution that best fits the criteria, and putting the solution to a test (Keltner, 1957). Effective joint problem solving involves mutual deliberation and cooperation.

In problem solving the focus is on

- solving the problem rather than forcing people;
- dealing with relationships as elements of the problem;
- avoiding votes, trades, chance, or "averaging" as a basis for the decisions;
- seeking facts to cope with dilemmas;
- accepting struggle and some forms of conflict as helpful as long as they do not bring out threats, destructive aggression, and defensiveness; and
- avoiding self-oriented behavior when it tends to exclude others' needs and functions.

You can quickly see that this involves the negotiation side of the negotiation-bargaining continuum.

During the process of joint cooperative problem solving the parties to a struggle develop alternative possible solutions to the problem. These solutions hold varying degrees of attraction for the members of a joint group. At this point some members of each group may attempt to bring the solution they favor to acceptance, and a struggle may occur, splitting the group. In the joint cooperation atmosphere the split may not be rigid or violent, and the possibilities of compromise and accommodation are still very much present. Under those conditions the parties still have considerable flexibility, and commitment to any given solution is still only tentative. If the interaction shifts more to the bargaining mode, the differences become more apparent, positions are more strongly taken and adhered to, and compromises become necessary in order to emerge with solutions that have the support of both or all sides.

Filley (1975) says,

A person using problem-solving methods is saying three things to the other parties involved:

1. I want a solution which achieves your goals and my goals and is acceptable to both of us.
2. It is our collective responsibility to be open and honest about facts, opinions, and feelings.
3. I will control the process by which we arrive at agreement but will not dictate content.
    (pp. 27-30)

This clearly represents the negotiation side of the process.

The problem-solving method is not just a happy dream. Considerable research has been done on the group problem-solving and decision-making process as compared with competitive and individualistic processes. We strongly suspect that joint efforts can create a synergy which can transcend the highest individual effort of anyone in a group.

Deutsch's research suggests that when participants in a competitive game know they will benefit if the other person profits and suffer if the other has losses they are more likely to work cooperatively than if they benefit from the others' losses and suffer if the other gains. Further, he found that a reward structure that is cooperatively developed, as compared with a competitive one, will produce less threat and less aggressive behavior as well as more friendly attitudes among participants and more mutual gains (Deutsch, 1971).

Deutsch (1971) and his colleagues reviewed most of the studies on conflict and carried out a large number of their own. In relation to cooperative behavior they found:

> The availability of a means of cooperating not only permits cooperation but also reduces the likelihood of competition . . . the availability of a means of cooperation reduces competitive behavior disproportionately more than individualistic behavior . . . when a relatively low pay-off is associated with competitive behavior, it is less likely to be selected . . . Relatively high pay-offs for cooperative behavior stimulate both cooperative behavior and the use of inspection procedures that verifies and supports further cooperative behavior; Relatively high pay-offs for competitive behavior stimulate competitive behavior and attack which verifies and supports further competitive behavior. (p. 50)

Throughout the whole problem-solving and joint decision-making process negotiation plays a significant part. It appears almost impossible for negotiation not to occur during the process of problem solving. Parties may negotiate over goals, obstacles, criteria for solutions, alternatives, and applications. When the problem-solving process and negotiation are not handicapped by win-lose contexts but are marked with cooperative efforts to solve joint problems, the resolutions can be more effective and lasting.

POWER AND NEGOTIATION-BARGAINING

The power of the negotiators plays a vital role in any negotiation or bargaining. Indeed, the power of the negotiators may be the most crucial factor in determining the outcome of any negotiation-bargaining context. In Chapter 3 I discussed a number of factors that affects that power relationship between people. I do not intend to repeat that information here, but I do identify some of the power factors that have been identified as having a particular bearing on the negotiation-bargaining process.

Stake in the Bargaining Process

Backarach and Lawler (1981) argue that "bargaining is a dynamic interplay between power and tactics" (p. 40). They submit that the degree to which the parties have a stake in the bargaining relationship provides a basic source of power. "Bargainers negotiate on not only the specific issues at hand but also the nature of their dependence on each other" (p. 59).

Dependence On Each Other

There is, according to Backarach and Lawler's (1981) analysis, a conflict of interest over goals that cannot be achieved without taking the other negotiator-bargainer into account (p. 79). Moving from those assumptions they submit several significant propositions relating to power in the process:

Proposition 1. An increase in the dependence of bargainer A on opponent B increases opponent B's bargaining power. (p. 60 ff)

Proposition 2a. In increase in bargainer A's dependence on opponent B decreases the bargaining power attributed to A and increases the power attributed to B. (p. 69)

Proposition 2b. An increase in bargainer A's dependence on opponent B increases the perception of B's bargaining power, but does not affect the perception of A's power. (p. 70)

Types of Power Most Applicable to Negotiation

Lewicki and Litterer (1985) selected several types of power particularly applicable in the negotiation situation: informational, reward, coercive, legitimate, expert, and referent. They considered informational power (which consists of amount, sources, and persuasiveness) to be the heart of the process. They suggested that persons using reward power are more likely to engender good feelings toward the negotiators using it and that "reward power is far more likely to produce desired consequences" (p. 247). Coercive power moves the situation away from the desired consequences. They proposed that "the use of coercive power is, therefore, likely to be disruptive to negotiation" (p. 246).

Pruitt (1981) considered negotiation power as the ability to get concessions from the other party (p. 87). Perception of one's own power (self-awareness) plays an important function in negotiation. Pruitt posits that:

Bargainers will delay concessions if they label themselves as *more powerful* than the adversary.
If the self label is *less powerful,* there are two possible effects on behavior.
1. It may encourage an effort to build power, however the bargainer defines this term.
2. It may encourage unilateral concession making. (p. 88)

Pruitt pointed out that power in negotiation is expandable and interactive whereby if one party is able to influence the other, the other is likely to be able to influence the first, and so on. He did not, however, indicate that they are fully reciprocal.

BATNA and Negotiation Power

Fisher and Ury (1981) suggested that the better your BATNA, the greater your power (see discussion of BATNA in this chapter). They pointed out that when the negotiator fails to identify the BATNA or any alternatives, his or her power is diminished.

Balance of Power in Negotiations

In Chapter 3 on power I noted that when the power between participants is relatively equal or balanced, negotiation may be useful (p. 63). There is considerable evidence to show that when the parties in a dyadic negotiation have equal power they produce agreements that have higher gain than when the parties have unequal power (Mannix & Neale, 1993). However, the aspiration or goal level of the parties *may also* affect the outcome of negotiations. That is, if a low-power negotiator had higher aspirations than the high-power side, the low-power negotiation might prevail.

Power and the Ability of the Negotiators

A lot of the power differential in negotiation and bargaining is the result of the abilities of the negotiators as well as the resources they have in the situation. Cohen (1980) said that power in negotiating comes from having several options available: having courage and common sense in working the strategy ("Before you can hit the jackpot, you have to put a coin into the machine.'); calculating the odds versus the benefits and failure; avoiding risk for the sake of pride, impatience, or desire to be finished with the process; having the involvement of others on your behalf; being thoroughly prepared; being aware of the needs of the opposite side and speaking to them; having tools and resources to reward and punish; understanding precedent in relation to the situation; and being persistent.

Throughout the discussion of negotiation and bargaining keep in mind that I am dealing with the ability to move the other side closer to your own goals. We are looking at the factors that facilitate and deter this process. Subsequent discussion emphasizes these factors.

NEGOTIATORS AND BARGAINERS

All of us as negotiators have varying values, different backgrounds, emotions, and unpredictability, and because of this humanity bring to the process a variety of conditions that can help or hinder negotiations.

Considerable research has been done on trying to identify and describe the personality of a successful negotiator. It has not been productive. No single set of personality types appears to have the edge on negotiation. Lewicki and Litterer (1985) conclude that:

> most of the factors which affect outcomes are behaviors which are under the negotiator's control. Negotiation may well be more of a 'learned' set of skills and behavior than attributes of qualities individuals are 'born with'; hence, individuals can practice and develop these skills and behaviors to improve their effectiveness. (p. 277)

The professional qualifications of negotiators are primarily human behaviors rather than academic or specialized "on-the-job" experience. What a person can do is more important than what his or her resume may suggest. What a person can do is usually a *combination* of training and experience.

Skilled negotiators and bargainers in every form of social struggle are communication specialists of considerable ability. Not everyone can perform the function of negotiation and bargaining effectively on a high professional level. However, because all of us find it necessary to negotiate, we should know some of the requisite characteristics and skills of good negotiators and bargainers. We make special note of those elements that appear more prevalent in the bargaining mode. Included are skills in listening, message feedback, open responding, self-disclosure, perceiving others, empathy, group participation, and speech.

The Effective Negotiator-Bargainer

Uses interpersonal communication skills

Part of the underlying purpose of our work in struggle management is to facilitate the process of dealing with each other in a constructive and stimulating way and to facilitate cooperative behavior. Our ability to handle disputes and conflict are dependent on some important skill factors. The good negotiator and/or bargainer is an effective negotiator skilled in listening, questioning, and stating positions; uses message feedback frequently ("What I heard you say . . ."); knows how to gain attention and hold it; is able to make a presentation clearly and in an organized fashion; uses nonverbal avenues of expression effectively; does not overly depend on pre-arranged statements or notes but can speak extemporaneously on any area of concern in the negotiations; does not "lecture" but discusses and uses an informal conversational style; uses language that is understandable and when necessary within the idiom of the others; and does not try to "show off" language, voice, or other presentational virtuosity.

Is Self-Aware

The negotiator who has no self-understanding or self-awareness is a dangerous person to be involved in the process. One of the most important ways of managing conflict by negotiation or bargaining is through being in touch with ourselves. This is not something that can be done in the abstract or by just reading about it. Self-awareness needs to be practiced and experienced. Ideally, the first step is to experience your self in a protected setting such as a classroom, training laboratory, or workshop where others are seeking the same understanding. Then, when this has opened up some doors for you, the next step is to begin to use that awareness in your dealings with people from day to day (see Chapter 2 for a more thorough discussion of self-awareness training and problems).

Listens

So much of the negotiator's and bargainer's time is spent in listening to what others are saying that the skill of listening is a primary skill. He or she must be able to listen well at different levels of communication; to listen to the nonverbal as well as the verbal cues; to control the imposition of his or her own thoughts onto what he or she hears others saying; and to avoid hearing what he or she wants to hear. The ability to separate out issues, attitudes, and opinions is vital. Listening for the subtle nuances of feeling and meaning that indicate significant changes in the position or interest of the other is important. Getting the full significance and scope of the interest and position of the other side demands good listening.

Provides message feedback

The ability to reflect back to a speaker the essence of the message spoken through paraphrase or other means is also a vital communication skill. Many situations escalate into heavier struggle because what people thought they heard is not what the speaker said.

> *When the union representative told the company personnel director that delaying a bonus had led to a strike some years back, the personnel director accused him of threatening a strike. Had the personnel director provided some message feedback he would have gotten the message more accurately. He could have said "You are saying that you are going to strike?" Such feedback would have brought clarification. The union representative could have then replied, "I'm not saying that because no such decision has been made."*

Message feedback works for both sides. The sender has a chance to modify the statement so that it more nearly fits the intended information, and the receiver can check to determine whether the message received was the actual message sent. It is vital that the message received be the same as the message sent, particularly in negotiation and bargaining.

Responds openly and appropriately to people

The negotiator, more than the bargainer, needs to be able to express openly and appropriately the responses generated by the other's communication. This allows for a better understanding between the parties. The bargainer may choose to hold back responses as part of a strategy. When the other's comments trigger an angry feeling, that feeling needs to be expressed so that there is clear understanding of the effects of the other's communication. This is different from message feedback in that it deals with the responses to a message rather than the nature of the message itself.

The appropriateness is also a matter of judgment by the responder. Some more violent emotions, generated by the discourse, may be better stored for awhile until they can be shared without causing reciprocating anger to arise with the result of stopping the interaction. Appropriateness must be determined on the basis of the effect on the other. What is appropriate in one situation may not be in another because of a different set of conditions.

> *A couple who prided themselves on being open with each other on all matters ran into serious difficulty when she told him seriously that the new dress he bought for her was in terrible taste. He responded angrily and told her to "get your own damn dresses." His defensiveness and lack of care in holding back his response led to a quick and rather bitter exchange. He responded openly, but not appropriately.*

Self-disclosures at the proper time, amount ,and manner

Closely related to the process of open responses, our disclosure of our feelings and inner thoughts may sometimes be quite valuable and useful in working out differences, whereas at other times, as in bargaining, they are better retained. This goes for nonemotional matters as well as emotional ones. In bargaining it is not wise to disclose critical positions until the appropriate time because of the more adversarial nature of the interaction. In negotiation the disclosure of positions and interests is much more appropriate.

> *I very much wanted a beautiful emerald and gold pendant that I saw in a jeweler's window. It would be a perfect gift for my wife. So, I entered the store, asked the clerk to show me the pendant, and immediately looked at it carefully through the magnifying glass. When the jeweler approached I asked for the price. It was much more than I could afford. I looked at the pendant again and then told him I wanted it very much. It was a beautiful bit of work he had done but that I simply could not meet his price. As a matter of fact I did not know how much I would be willing to pay for it but I knew, at that moment, that the price was more than I could or would pay. He took his pad, checked his catalogue, wrote figures down on the pad, and added them up. I watched carefully. The total was still much more than I could handle and I told him so. He tried figuring again and came up with a lower figure, but still out of my reach. In the meantime, I was going over in my mind just how much I would be willing to pay for the piece. After doing some jotting on the pad myself I gave him a figure that I would pay right now. He looked at his figures again and as I stood with my heart in my mouth, he looked up and said , "Okay, you've got it."*

Notice that in the above negotiation neither of us held back any disclosure of where we were at any given moment. We were, in fact, working the price out together. I believe that my open disclosure of my pleasure at the beauty and quality of the piece had an effect on the final decision. Had it been more of a bargaining situation I would have known from the beginning just what my upper limit was and would have entered into the discussion with that figure in mind without revealing it. He, likewise, would have known just what his lowest limit was and would have kept that in mind without revealing it as we talked, and we both would have followed the script of the bargainer.

Neither was the case and the process did not fall into the bargaining mode in which our proposals were controlled by our preset base. Of course, I knew that he certainly had a cost base that had been the basis of his original pricing, but I also knew that he would be as fair with me as he could because we had mutual friends.

Perceives others and achieves empathy

Closely tied to the listening process it is also important that we make the time and effort to observe the behavior, the attitudes, the manner of speaking, the kind of language used, the physical appearance and presentation, and so on of our counterparts. The more we know about our counterparts the easier it is for us to either negotiate or bargain with them.

Although perceiving others gives us an idea of what is available for us to see, we need to reach beyond that and try to see the world as the other sees it. The more we can "get behind the eyeballs" of the other the more we are able to anticipate their moves, thoughts, and behaviors. The accuracy of that anticipation affects the outcome of either our negotiations or bargaining with them. The more I reveal of myself the more the other can anticipate what I will do, think, or feel. Also, the more skilled the other is in reading my verbal and nonverbal behavior as an expression of my internal thoughts and feelings, the more effective that person can be in finding mutually agreeable solutions (see Chapter 5 for a further discussion of empathy).

Is able to work with groups of people

Some people are "loners" and are simply not effective in working with people in a group. They prefer to deal one-on-one or not at all. Bargaining, in particular, and negotiation, to a lesser extent, involve more than one-on-one interactions. Usually the bargaining context occurs in a situation in which there are more than two people involved, and the group pressures and group communication processes are important forces with which to contend. Thus, the ability to deal with people in groups as well as one-on-one is important.

Understands and applies problem solving and joint decision making

Both the negotiator and the bargainer need to understand and apply the problem-solving process and the processes of joint decision making. The difference between the two should be clearly understood, and the role that decision making plays in problem solving should be not only understood but part of the functional apparatus of the person. Negotiation is both a decision-making mode and a problem-solving process. The decision-making mode is described as a way in which choices between alternatives are made: mutually, consensually, by majority, or by another combination of choices.

Speaks effectively

Most negotiation and bargaining occur via the spoken word and the nonverbal activity that accompanies the spoken word. The effective negotiator and bargainer must be skilled in speech communication. The basic skills in interpersonal speech communication are very important. Special skills in public speaking may also be useful in situations involving more than just a few people. These skills include the nonverbal systems of communication that are supportive of the speech act.

When you are able to perform these skills you will discover that your ability to handle internal conflict as well as conflict between yourself and others will improve. There are literally hundreds of books, courses, and teachers who are advocating these skills as basic to good human relations. This is not accidental. The following are tested skills, and the knowledge of their usefulness is thousands of years old.

Deals with the others as people with problems, needs, and human reactions

Recognizes that the others involved in the negotiations have different perceptions of the world and that their needs and problems are very much a part of the situation. In effect, the good bargainer-negotiator does not become isolated in social space and unaware of others and their problems.

Is willing and able to face the issues directly and precisely

The negotiator-bargainer must be able to cut through the communication fog of the party across the table and of his or her own constituency and get to the issues and the hidden agendas that may be present.

Separates the relationship problems with the others from the content or substance of the issues and deals with both

Each negotiation deals with content and relationships. These must be dealt with separately so that they do not get mixed together. The skilled negotiator shows concern for relationships during and following the negotiation while dealing with the substance of the issues. Bargainers may choose not to reveal their concern for relationships during the process.

Must be willing to speak plainly and to the point when it becomes necessary to do so

There are times when it is wise to avoid a pointed attack because of its untimeliness and the effect it would have on the total negotiations. However, when the time comes for the "moment of truth," the skilled negotiator can react swiftly and surely. "Plain speaking" is a vital skill for good negotiators and bargainers.

Believes in the proposition or propositions he or she is representing

Particularly when a person assumes negotiating responsibility for some other person or group, he or she will be more effective if he or she is able to speak from the depth of his or her own convictions, and his or her interests are close to those of the constituents.

Is willing and able to make decisions concerning changes in position when it becomes necessary to alter positions in order to reach agreement

Similarly, when the negotiator or bargainer is representing others he or she must maintain a close communication with his or her constituency so that its interests and will can be interpreted accurately. The good negotiator makes decisions to change position knowing that it is consistent with the interests, policy, and will of the constituency.

When representing others is willing to assume responsibility for keeping the principals informed

When others are being represented, and when they must make the final decision, it is vital to keep them informed of the trends, directions, barriers, and other issues involved in the interaction. When representing others it is important to remain consistent with their interests and policy and to interpret their attitudes and opinions accurately at the bargaining table.

Is a person with positive self-perception and self-confidence

He or she must be at least reasonably aware of his or her own strengths and weaknesses. He or she must have a positive self-image and not be egotistical and/or overbearing. The good negotiator-bargainer has great poise under fire.

Operates in terms of "practical possibility" rather than in terms of fantasy, theory, or impossible alternatives

In each situation, the negotiator-bargainer recognizes that under ideal conditions he or she could get the maximum for self or the principals but that no situation is ideal. He or she, therefore, is willing to practice the "art of the possible."

Recently I went to an auto dealer to replace my old pickup. What I had in mind was a new pickup with a heavier chassis, more horsepower, more bed space in the back, a "king cab" type that was like the interior of a sedan, 4-wheel drive, air conditioning, 5 speed on the floor, and a classy grey finish that would not need a lot of attention. All for my old pickup and a figure of less than $10,000.

(continued)

> As I was led through the lot and as I looked at the prices I began to realize that I really was dreaming if I thought I was going to get all the things I wanted for the price I had set as my limit. So, I negotiated for as much as I would get for the price I could afford. I ended up with a newer model of the old pickup that included the same size bed, the king cab but without an interior like a sedan, and a little more horsepower (6 cylinders instead of 4). In negotiating with the dealer I worked on the practical reality of what was possible for me in that situation.

> A new park had recently been built along the riverfront in a small college town. One group of college faculty, aided by a number of "equal rights" advocates and others, wanted to name the part after Martin Luther King. They met with a great deal of opposition from the noncollege segments of the community and business people who wanted the part to be named "The Waterfront Park." The debate when on intensely for months with the King supporters holding firm and doing everything they could to force the city council to agree to their position.
>
> The council would not make a decision in the face of such wide differences over the naming of the park. With the help of a facilitator, the King advocates became aware that they simply could not prevail in the situation. Thereupon, they put forth a series of proposals that would still provide some recognition for King. They soon realized that so long as King's name was included, it would not be accepted. After much community discussion it was agreed to it the Riverfront Memorial Park. The King group had to eventually confront the "art of the possible," and they were able to get the word "memorial" into the name.

Is reasonably skeptical

He or she does not take the opinions and statements of the opposition at face value but seeks to understand the intent behind the communications of his or her counterparts on the other side of the table. On the other hand, he or she must remain open to being convinced of the soundness or stability of the other side's positions.

Inspires trust in his or her constituents and in his or her counterparts

Trust is one of those elusive conditions difficult to describe behaviorally. In this context, the negotiator must inspire trust in that he or she can convince his or her constituents and counterparts that they can anticipate his or her actions accurately. When we trust another person, we feel that we can anticipate his or her actions with considerable accuracy and have confidence that he or she will respond as we anticipate. In this sense, it is possible to trust an enemy; that is, we may be able to anticipate accurately how that enemy will behave under certain conditions. Another dimension of trust is that we can anticipate that the other's actions will be in our interest. The good negotiator is perceived as a person who will seek his or her own goals with vigor, but who will not ignore or unnecessarily deny the goals and interests of the other side. Trust is a condition that can result from insights and perceptions of ourselves and each other. The bargainer, however, may often use strategies that cause the other side to distrust the person. These are not the best strategies even though they often have some success.

Desires respect rather than popularity

The good negotiator is a salesperson in a general sense. He or she is also an advocate. That advocacy should be based on sound positions, carefully developed and clearly presented. The good advocate in this context shows an openness to alternative positions that meet the underlying needs of both parties. He or she does not, however, sacrifice substantive interests or needs for the sake of increasing personal popularity and prestige. It is often the case that popularity with opponents creates doubts. On the other hand, a solid respect by the other side for the negotiator's judgment and integrity is highly valuable.

Can perform his or her role as an advocate and representative with vigor and imagination

The effective negotiator should be able to convey to his or her opponents the emotional implications of the issues being discussed without losing control of his or her own emotions. New ideas, creative suggestions, and a sense of moving forward are important to the negotiation process.

Has a sense of humor

The good negotiator can enjoy the incongruity of some situations, share good jokes, laugh at him- or herself, and be able to apply good humor when things get too tight and intense.

Understands and is skilled in persuasion

The good negotiator knows the nature of persuasion, its personal, logical, and emotional characteristics, and is able to use the tools of persuasion effectively.

Is always prepared when negotiating

The skilled negotiator does the homework necessary to understand the positions, the arguments, the alternatives, the consequences, and the relationships before entering into the negotiations themselves. Even in those spontaneous negotiations that arise when we are bargaining over the price of a product or other situation, the skilled negotiator brings to the situation experience and understanding which allows for the impromptu encounter.

Shows respect for other(s) involved in the interaction

This includes being patient with counterparts, controlling personal vexation at obstinance or vagueness, avoiding being hostile without solid reason, and avoiding making personal attacks, but when the occasion demands attacking the situation or the concept rather than the person.

Maintains common courtesy and makes an effort to extend personal consideration to counterparts

The skilled negotiator-bargainer serves as a host or guest with poise and good will, puts others at ease, avoids false effusiveness, and shows self-assurance throughout.

Is skilled as an interrogator

The skilled negotiator and bargainer can ask questions effectively in order to gather information, direct discussion, facilitate discussion, emphasize a point, confirm information, and so on (see Chapter 5 for a further discussion of interrogation). Good negotiators do not assume the role of a "district attorney" and harass the other side as if it were on the witness stand. The questions asked are carefully formed so as to elicit important information, arouse interest in an idea, provide alternatives, facilitate the thinking and response of the other side, and demonstrate that the questioner is interested and knows what is being said.

Shows persistence

Skilled negotiators stick to their purpose and do not concede issues without compelling reasons. They do not ignore the needs of the other side, but sustain their attempts to solve the problem(s) and advocate their particular solution as long as it is the better alternative available. Their approach to making compromises or concessions is reflective and carefully presented so as to not suggest a weakness.

Does not avoid struggle and dispute

Expression of the positions and interests of both sides are encouraged. The skilled negotiator acknowledges differences of opinions and sees to it that these differences are discussed openly.

PRECONDITIONS TO EFFECTIVE NEGOTIATION AND BARGAINING

Negotiation begins when we seek to work out with our counterparts the conditions under which we will interact with each other. This process of "setting the stage" for negotiation and bargaining involves an understanding of a number of factors that influence our working together. There are situations that lead to negotiation, and there are attitudes and perspectives that serve to facilitate the negotiation process.

Situational Preconditions

What brings you to negotiation? What are the factors that lead you into a negotiating process? If we look at the Struggle Spectrum we can see that negotiation and bargaining are basic processes at the disagreement and dispute stages (Stages 2 and 3). So, the essential precondition is that a difference in needs, perceptions, goals, or interests has not been resolved and, because of its significance to us, has become a matter for action at a more intense level than mild disagreement. Here are some examples.

> *Mild differences between a husband and wife have not been resolved and their continued presence begins to affect the relationship between the two. The wife has decided that she wants to separate.*
>
> *You want a beautiful pin on the street display of the Indian artist. When you ask the cost, the artist gives you a price that is more than you know it is worth.*
>
> *You want a raise in your salary and simply suggesting the matter to your superior had unsatisfactory results. So, in order to get the raise you must initiate some negotiation.*
>
> *You are a salesperson. To meet your needs you must move the potential customer to want your product and then to be willing to pay the price you ask for it. The customer, of course, may want the product, but may not want to pay what you ask.*
>
> *You have been leasing a house and property and the lease is about to expire. You want to continue leasing the property. You have information that others are seeking to lease the property and that the cost may increase. Some negotiation with the owner becomes necessary. There is a similar precondition in labor-management relations when an existing contract is about to expire and a new one must be agreed upon.*
>
> *Two partners in a production enterprise are becoming more and more alienated toward each other to the point where they rarely speak except to deal with the most critical of business matters. A crisis is pending.*

You will note that in all of these examples both sides are involved in the situational pre-condition. However, both sides do not usually have the same interests, goals, perception of the situation, and desire to solve the problem. So, the conditions that may lead you to seek negotiation may not be the factors that bring your counterpart into the interaction.

Some of these preconditions involve incompatible goals, needs, perceptions, and so forth. The wife's desire to separate may be diametrically opposed to the husband's desire and goal to stay together. These incompatible goals, if they persist, may not allow the parties to negotiate and will simply thrust them into a win-lose context which will allow only for bargaining, if that. Usually those kinds of preconditions lead to litigation.

In addition to the kinds of circumstances that precede negotiation and bargaining there are some attitudinal and procedural factors that appear to be necessary for successful negotiation and bargaining.

Desirable Prenegotiation Attitudes and Perspectives of Negotiators

Good Faith

Regardless of the social context of negotiating and bargaining, whether it be in a marital rift, a family struggle, a professional problem, a labor-management problem, or on an international level, both parties must be willing to discuss the situation with each other in "good faith." Although the definition of good faith is elusive, the term is generally accepted to mean that the parties are willing to and intend to meet with each other and that they expect to reach a mutually acceptable solution to the conflict. *Both parties must have a basic willingness to agree and to make the negotiation and bargaining process work; that is, each must be willing to exert maximum effort to reach an accommodation with respect to the issues in conflict.*

> *In the latter months of 1990, President Bush and Saddam Hussein demonstrated the opposite of good faith in their struggle over the Kuwait issue. There was no evidence that either party had any desire to meet with the other or to discuss the situation face-to-face without a multitude of conditions and controls. The polarization was clearly established and every pronouncement from either side thrust the parties further apart.*

Good faith can be achieved when there is a genuine interest in finding a settlement to the dispute and when that interest in settlement transcends the polarized positions of the parties. That is to say, the desire to settle is stronger than the desire to win. In 1993 one of the restraining conditions in the attempts to bring Serbs, Croats, and Muslims together in Geneva for peace negotiations was the lack of good faith among the principals. Good faith is also related to trust. Many unions have accused employers of not bargaining in good faith when the bargaining fails to produce a solution to the dispute. What is actually being said is that the union does not trust the employer to come up with a proposal that the union can accept. The employer may want to settle and actively seeks settlement, but not on the terms proposed by the union, and is not thereby violating good faith. In hearing disputes over this matter a judge or arbitrator will seek evidence showing whether the parties were willing to meet and whether the parties were interested in finding a solution to the problem.

Viability

Further, both parties to the negotiations need to be "viable." That is, they must be willing to make changes in their present conditions and positions in order to achieve maximum growth and development and a resolution of the difficulties. When both parties have taken positions that are "non-negotiable" and apart, no resolution can occur.

Absence of Win-Lose Attitude and Condition

Effective negotiation and bargaining are practically impossible in a situation of intense win-lose polarization in which the goals are clearly incompatible. (There isn't much negotiation on the floor of a basketball game or any game with a zero-sum nature.) Ideally, the parties must be able to seek common goals and deal with common problems without being trapped into feeling that they must "win" over the other side.

This state of being is often difficult to achieve if the win-lose atmosphere has become dominant. It is desirable to get into negotiations before the win-lose pressure has become too great and overwhelming. There is no room for negotiation, for example, when a couple going through a divorce are each deeply committed to having full custody of their children and view anything less as a loss. Before real negotiation can begin they need to be de-escalated from this rigid position and become more willing to look for alternative possibilities.

To accomplish such de-escalation is one of the functions that a mediator can perform. The process usually is to convince the parties that there are other interests than their own at stake, namely the interests of their children. Another technique a mediator may use is to raise questions to each of the parties in such a way that each privately begins to doubt the quality or efficacy of his or her position. There is more about this in Chapter 5 on Mediation.

Willingness to Reveal Interests and Positions

Zartman (1977) argues that "negotiation tends to be a matter of finding a formula encompassing the optimum combination of interests of both parties and then of working out the details that implement these principles" (p. 635). Such a formula cannot be found unless there is sufficient revelation of interests and position that would allow such a formula to emerge. Therefore, in most negotiations it is necessary that each party be willing to reveal its basic interests and maximum position. Because the eventual decision will probably be somewhere between the two maximum positions taken by the two parties, these extreme points of reference should be established as soon as possible. Thus, in a labor-management bargaining session, the maximum demands of the union and the maximum demands and position of the company are usually made explicit as soon as possible.

The underlying interests of each party need to be expressed. Until these interests and maximum conditions are known, it is impossible for either party to effectively accommodate the other.

The timing of the release of information describing these interests and positions is important. There is no neat formula for deciding the time when such information should be made available. In most bargaining cases the maximum positions need to be expressed at the outset. Modified positions then can be revealed when it appears that the other side will accommodate them. The same is true in working out a settlement during a divorce, a land-sale agreement, a purchase-sell agreement, or the like.

Does Not View the Other as "Enemy"

One of the critical conditions of the negotiating and bargaining relationship is the perception of each other. Clearly, if I perceive my counterpart as an enemy who will try to destroy me (as described in Stages 5 and 6 of the Spectrum) my approach and planning will be quite different from what it would be when I see my counterpart as being friendly, cooperative, and interested in our mutual welfare.

Research on international relations has confirmed the hypothesis that the perception of the opponent as one who is not trustworthy or is an "adversary" leads to a devaluation of concessions on issues involved in the negotiations. "If one actor believes that the other side is an enemy, then that actor is likely to believe that the other side's concession is not really worth anything. A concession cannot really be a concession if it is coming from an untrustworthy enemy" (Zisk, 1990, p. 688). Thus, one of the key preconditions to effective negotiation is to gain a perception of the counterpart as a friend or compatriot with a different point of view, but not one that is negative to the other as a person.

Willingness to Set Aside "Self-Interest" and Replace It With "Mutual Interest"

Replacing self-interest with mutual interest may be one of the more difficult preconditions to accomplish. Most of the time when we become involved in negotiation or bargaining we are there because our own goals or needs have been challenged or we perceive them to be in jeopardy. Our self-interest is usually one of the key factors that brings us into a clash with our counterparts. However, the search for factors of mutual interest in the situation can lead us to a better base for negotiation. Actually, a balance between mutual interests and self-interest needs to be found in order to maximize negotiation outcomes. Although there may be differences in the perceptions of how best to realize the mutual interests, the chances of resolving those differences are much greater when the perception of mutual interest is present.

In summary, the above are some of the attitudinal preconditions that will facilitate the negotiations. Not all of them will be equally useful to bargainers. Let us look now at the actual preparation of the negotiators and bargainers for the process. What and how should I get ready to negotiate or bargain ?

PREPARING TO NEGOTIATE OR BARGAIN

Good negotiation requires careful preparation. Although there are certain habits and processes that good negotiators carry with them like a tool kit, these are enhanced and implemented by preparing for the specific confrontation.

You may negotiate for yourself in informal situations that occur daily. For this your preparation is very important. When you are a member of a group and/or *represent* a group or person that is negotiating or bargaining with another group or person the preparation becomes very critical. *It is not wise to enter important negotiations and bargaining for yourself or others without thorough and complete preparation for what is coming.* Whether you are representing yourself, a client in negotiation or bargaining, a friend in a family argument, or a colleague in a professional argument, it is absolutely vital that you be prepared to perform to the best of your ability. All of the preparations that you would use in negotiating for yourself should be used. Additional preparations are also necessary when you are representing a client, a group, a constituency, and so on.

Know Your Time Limitations and Conditions

You should know how long you can maintain a particular position without agreement and without risk to your total goals and objectives. Remember that most changes in position, and therefore concessions, occur near a deadline. You need to know what the deadlines are. If I know that a seller of a house has a deadline at which time he or she will offer it to someone else, then I know I must adjust my planning to that. If a union representative knows that his constituents will not work without a contract, he or she then knows that the contract termination time is an important deadline. You should know the time limits of your counterparts so that you can avoid time crises except when they might be helpful in bringing about agreement.

In some situations, time is a valuable tool that can be used to bring pressure to bear on the decision making. The skipper of a fishing boat knows how long his catch will remain fresh and so does the processor. The processor will use this as a tool to hold the price down. In many labor-management contract negotiations the decisions are not made until hours or even minutes before a midnight expiration of the old contract because until that time the pressure for getting a settlement is not sufficient to motivate the parties to reach a decision. The same is true for many other types of negotiations. A group of terrorists at the 1972 Olympics, for example, tried unsuccessfully to set a time deadline for action. Food suppliers and processors have deadlines set by the perishability of the food and the food source.

Know What Should and What Should Not be Negotiated

Often negotiators get into areas of decision making that are not at issue or that are not their province to settle. For example, it is not the province of negotiators in collective bargaining between labor and management to set the prices of the product or the service of the employer. If there are existing agreements favorable to your constituents, avoid being forced into a position that requires you to renegotiate these agreements. Similarly, it is not the function of divorce lawyers to perform therapy on their clients nor to negotiate such. Many times advocates representing someone in a grievance procedure waste a lot of time trying to negotiate matters that are truly not at issue. Militants often demand the right to negotiate on items that are definitely not their prerogative, yet not within the prerogatives of the opposite side to decide and act on. In the area of public employee collective bargaining the laws providing for the negotiation usually provide for some issues over which management may not bargain (illegal), some over which they may bargain if they choose (permissive), and some over which they must bargain (mandatory). It is the responsibility of the negotiator to know the issues that are subject and not subject to negotiation and bargaining.

Arrange Your Goals and Issues into Several Categories

Identify those things that are:

1. Absolute "musts" and simply have to be in the agreement;
2. Desirable but that could be traded if necessary to get one of your "musts;"
3. Just tolerable and that you could accept only as a last resort in order to bring agreement; and
4. Not possible to agree to under any conditions.

Number 3 represents a point after which negotiating or bargaining stops. It is, in a sense, the "bottom line" beyond which you or your constituents will not go. This position should be most carefully determined because under the pressure of the negotiations and new information you may be swayed to vary from this position and later regret your decision. Consider the situation in which the seller of a business property, under pressure from the buyer, sold his property for less than he felt was the basic appraisal value and later discovered by accident that the buyer was prepared to pay even more than the seller's appraisal value. Or, on the contrary, you may stick to your bottom line and lose what you wanted.

> *A shrimp fishing group negotiating with processors for the price of shrimp decided that they would accept nothing less than $4.00 a pound for their catch. The processor refused to pay this amount under any conditions and because the fishing group had set a minimum from which it would not move, it lost the contract with the processors and the shrimp had to be destroyed.*

Had the fishing group been less adamant in their position they would probably have reached an agreement short of their $4.00 but enough to save the catch and avoid a total loss. "Bottom lines" or "musts" rigidly sustained also often reduce the possibilities of creating solutions that bring together different interests.

Develop Your BATNA

In order to mitigate the difficulties that firm and unvarying "bottom lines" introduce into the negotiations, Fisher and Ury (1981) have suggested the establishment of the "Best Alternative To a Negotiated Agreement" (called BATNA) as the standard against which any proposal can be measured. Your BATNA represents the best you can get without any agreement or "how well I can do for myself if I walk away" (Fisher, 1983, p. 156).

> *A potential customer appears to purchase a parcel of land I have to sell. I ask $30,000 for the lot. That represents what I hope to get for the lot and includes my original cost, improvements, taxes, and a small profit. We negotiate. It becomes apparent that this customer is not willing to meet my asking price. At this point I have several options: break off the negotiations—no deal; lower my asking price closer to what the customer seems willing to pay and continue the negotiations; or accept the customer's offer of $24,000. Before I went into these negotiations I had decided that I would not sell the property for less than I paid for it plus the improvements. That figure is $27,000. If I cannot get that minimum price for the property, I will not sell.*

What is my BATNA in this situation? What is the best alternative in case the buyer and I cannot negotiate an agreement? Notice how I found it. There are several alternatives from which to choose. One is to hold onto the property until the value escalates to meet my figure, but that is not viable because I must turn over the property in order to build elsewhere immediately. Another is to hold on the $27,000, but I must move immediately and need at least $25,000. Another is to build on it myself and then sell it with a residence. There is good evidence that the property values are going to go up but that would take time that I do not have for completing another building I've started. Further, I have already been offered $25,700 for the property. So, if these negotiations fail my "best" alternative to agreeing to the offer of $24,000 is to accept the $25,700. That's my BATNA. Even though it does not cover my $27,000 in costs, it is the best alternative I have available if the current negotiations fail. That position puts me in a strong spot in the current negotiations. It allows me to say "no" to any offer less than $25,700 and to actually negotiate from that base.

Clearly the closer my BATNA is to desired outcome, the more power I have in the negotiations. Fisher and Ury (1981) put it this way: "In fact, the relative negotiating power of two parties depends primarily upon how attractive to each is the option of not reaching agreement" (p. 106).

Also it is important to set priorities for Category 1 and Category 2 matters. Be sure you know what the top and the bottom priorities are. Then, for each issue or goal identify maximum, fallback, and minimum positions for that particular item.

Identify, also, acceptable options based on basic needs, concerns, and expectations. Develop a rationale to support your position as a solution to a problem or concern or need. Keep an open mind to other solutions.

Identify Your Flexibility

Particularly in the bargaining context, AVOID PRESENTING A BARE MINIMUM POSITION IF YOU CAN. Instead:

1. Add "give" factors as concessions.

> *In preparing to negotiate with the union over conditions in the workplace, a company decided to allow longer lunch periods as a "concession" to the demand for paid lunches. This was a planned concession aimed at eliminating the demand for paid lunches.*

2. Give the other party room to change something without affecting what you really must have.

> *Joe and Pete were negotiating over the purchase of access to a river property held by Pete who had no entry-exit road. Joe held the property between the river and the road. Pete had to have some access or the property would be useless. Joe had taken the position that Pete had no right to cross his property for access. He refused to allow Pete to put a small entry road to the river because it would bisect his land and thereby interfere with the cattle access to the other half that would become isolated by the road. So, Pete proposed that if Joe would allow access, he would purchase the property covered by the road and put fences on either side of the entry road and a tunnel under the road to enable Joe's cattle to cross the road.*

3. Look at the elements in a package. Particularly in the bargaining setting, tie "give" elements to "must" elements to obtain greater flexibility. In the case above, Pete was willing to give some protection to Joe in order to get access. Joe, on the other hand, was willing to sell Pete access if there were some protections for his cattle. These flexibilities allowed them to reach an agreement that was beneficial to both.

Test the Fairness and Reasonableness of Your Positions

Make this test from the perspective of BOTH sides. Anticipate opposing views and reactions and prepare your response (whether it be to ignore, refute, give more information, etc.). You must evaluate the possible outcomes of the negotiations REALISTICALLY. Evaluate the actual strengths and weaknesses of your positions and, if you are representing someone, communicate that evaluation to your client(s) or constituency. Make clear your opponents' probable goals, needs, wants, "gives," and so forth in relation to the goals of your side.

Determine What Your Opposition Will Seek and Plan Your Responses

You can get some indication about the position of your counterparts from the pattern of their demands in the past and on other occasions. Use any sources of information available to you. You will benefit from research into the situation and evaluation of its ramifications for your opposition as well as for yourself. In the usual purchasing situation there is a published price or figure quoted. In real estate, for example, the seller usually has a price range attached to the property. Also try to anticipate the tactics the other party will use in order to maintain its position.

Planning your response is vital. For each issue you may have several alternative response possibilities, ranging in order from the maximum benefit you wish to the "tolerable" as I suggested above. It is wise to start with the maximum and move to the tolerable only under extreme pressure.

Plan Your Basic Presentation to the Other Side

Particularly in more formal negotiations or bargaining it is important that you decide on the order of the issues and positions you are going to take and have a good reason for placing them in this order. Determine the amount of detail you are going to develop in support of each of your positions. Plan the timing of your presentation. Are you going to throw the whole package in at once or are you going to spread it out over several sessions? You will have to make these decisions. Identify your strongest points and use them strategically. Sometimes it is wise to hold back on the strong points until later in the negotiations. At other times it may be important to get them out early so that you set a pattern of strength. Some negotiators will carefully arrange the strong points at places in the negotiations when they seem to be in some difficulty with a weaker position. In less formal situations, such as negotiating in a bazaar, your plan should emerge as you initiate the contact with the seller.

Determine Where, When, and the Ground Rules You Prefer for the Negotiations

Again, in more formal and extensive situations you should work out with your counterpart the time and place of meetings and a set of ground rules to be used in the presentations and discussions. Such things as the admission of the press into the negotiations, recording of the sessions, and length of the sessions are important when the negotiations involve significant matters of public interest. In matters of personal interest, such as in divorce and child custody or neighborhood disputes, working out the ground rules are very important. Pete and Joe, in their dispute over access to Pete's property, agreed at the very beginning that they would meet in a neutral place, in this case the local grange hall; would not lose their temper with each other; would be as honest as possible with each other, including sharing any particular problems that they experienced in the negotiations; and would not bring in lawyers to negotiate for them unless they mutually agreed.

Rehearse the Negotiation in Your Mind or in Role-playing

Imagine that the negotiation is in session and run through it as you would like it to be. Be honest with yourself. If you are bound to encounter strong opposition, let your imagination explore the kind of opposition and what you will do with it. If you are working with a team, role play the anticipated negotiations. This part of your preparation is very important.

Arrange All Your Materials, References, and Data

Do not depend entirely on your memory in more complex negotiations. Have the material organized and filed in a quick access manner. If you have a portable computer that has enough storage to include your materials, use it. Similarly, if the negotiation involves figures, have an adding machine or pocket calculator within reach.

Know How to Represent a Group or Client

Know whom you represent

When negotiating for others it is not enough to know the broad general nature of the policy of your constituents. You should know them as people whenever possible. You should know where *their* limits are and where their allegiances lie. If you are representing a company, you should be familiar with the nature of that company, its problems, its plans for the future, and how this negotiation relates to them. If you are representing a single person, you should have a very good insight into where that person is in relation to the situation.

Identify who is to do the negotiating for both sides

If you are to be the prime negotiator, it should be understood by all. You also need to know who is to represent the other side so that you can plan for dealing with that person. When you are working as a team make sure that everyone knows who is to be the spokesperson and who is to do the principal talking. It is often confusing if several people are trying to do the talking from one side of the table. There needs to be clear understanding of the several roles. When the company attorney is constantly being interrupted by the company president and their statements are not consistent with each other, the company position is weakened.

Know your constituent's goals and the points or issues of the interaction

As their representative, it is necessary that you be privy to the ultimate objectives of your principals in this situation and beyond it. From this base, you should then determine the major conflicts or differences between your position and that of your counterparts on the other side.

Identify your authority and the authority of your counterpart

Are you a messenger, a representative, or the principal negotiator-bargainer? If you do not have complete authority to reach agreement, it is best to identify and agree with your clients or constituents as to where you can move and the range of alternatives available to you. When possible you should get as much authority to make decisions as you can. Realizing that in certain areas this authority may be limited, you should know how to get in touch with those who can make the decisions and have it understood that you have a priority for their time and attention when needed. Know what your authority is and what it is not. Do not assume authority you do not have. Some negotiators prefer to work out a general decision with their principals and then work out the details in the negotiations. When the principals trust the representative, this is an excellent procedure. At other times, the principals may have determined the decisions precisely, and there is little room for adjustment. When this happens the negotiator should know of these decisions so that the limits are not reached too soon.

You should also know where your counterpart stands with respect to the ability to make decisions. You should know whether agreements reached between the representatives can be expected to hold up when the principals or constituents have a look at them. If your counterpart cannot guarantee support of the decisions made at the table, you should avoid making key commitments. If he or she is nothing more than a messenger you will need to alter your strategy from the one you would use if he or she had prime decision-making power.

Adequately prepared, a person can enter a series of negotiations knowing that his or her communication effort is going to be received with some respect and significance. One of the first things an opponent can detect is the lack of adequate preparation on the part of a negotiator. This is true whether you are negotiating a labor contract, a grade from a teacher, or a date with a person. Good preparation requires many hours for every hour of actual meeting time with the other side.

IN-SESSION CONDUCT

The procedures of the negotiation and bargaining are a set of ground rules mutually agreed on by the parties to the interaction. Sometimes the procedural agreement is implicit in the working relationship between the parties. For example, in a family I know the manner of negotiation as to who is going to have the car often follows a formula. Similarly, a contractor negotiating with a builder usually can expect certain ground rules for their bargaining. Many union-management contract bargaining sessions follow procedures that have evolved over many such meetings. At other times it becomes necessary to spell out or to work out the conditions under which the negotiations will proceed. In any event, the procedures under which the negotiation is to take place must be understood by both parties. Here are some suggested ways to conduct in-session negotiations.

Be Sure There is an Agreement on Procedures

Whether you are negotiating or bargaining there should be a clear understanding about such things as who is to call meetings, who is to be the contact person for each side, what the meeting times should be, where the meetings should be held, who should speak first, and who is to represent each side.

Begin with Stated Objectives Well Beyond the Limits Set by Your "Must" Items

Keep your overall objectives clearly in mind. Know how much "give" remains on each point or issue and in the total "package." Consider the effect of each change as you compromise or make concessions. In mild negotiations this may not be necessary, but in bargaining your counterpart will assume that your stated objectives or positions are beyond your actual limits and will behave accordingly. That is one of the significant differences between negotiation and bargaining.

Keep a Record of Each Session

It is important to know what was said and who said it. The usual way is for you to keep careful notes of what is offered and the reply. If you are working with a team or group you may have another person on the team who can serve as a recorder. Rarely are negotiations tape recorded or otherwise reported word-for-word because most parties would prefer not to have their exploratory proposals and tactics made a matter of record. It is best that each side keep its own record.

Keep All Your Notes and Records Until You Have the Agreement Signed, Sealed, and Delivered

Keeping records is not a matter of distrust. Many slips can occur in translating an oral agreement to writing. Different perceptions of the same words often indicate that there was really no agreement on substance. There could be an agreement based on words, but each side could have different referents to the same words. Be sure to scrutinize any document for possible misunderstandings and accuracy of language before you sign it even if you or your office typed it up!

Consider the Long-range Relationship between the Parties

If you permit an unfair agreement to be made or knowingly allow a mistake to be finalized, you have done a poor job and discontent, hard feelings, and disputes may remain. Many poorly designed divorce agreements, for example, do not settle the dispute but aggravate it and create future bitter encounters. It happens in other contexts as well.

> *Two local accountants agreed to join forces and merge their accounting business after having discussed the matter over a period of a year or so. As they negotiated out the terms of the agreement they left a lot of areas unexplored. Matters such as the responsibility for managing the office personnel and for taking care of the office facility were left undecided. When, during the heavy period of work at the end of the year, problems arose with some of the temporary personnel and the use of office space, a serious dispute arose as to whose responsibility it was to take care of such matters. This dispute led, eventually, to a termination of the partnership. Had these matters been included in the original negotiations the seeds for the eventual breakup would not have been sown.*

Never Underestimate Your Counterpart Regardless of His or Her Status or Title

Genuine respect and friendly relations with the other side are helpful, if not necessary. Making special efforts to be popular or well liked by the opponent, however, is not conducive to good negotiations. The special efforts are usually pretty obvious and will tend to alienate your counterpart.

Treating your counterpart as an inferior or attacking him or her personally is not conducive to long-range amicable relationships. It is important that you understand the other and the factors that are being faced from that side of the issue(s). Remember the negotiation process is still aimed at solving problems and that means both parties are a part of the problem solving.

If You Bluff, Be Prepared to Have Your Bluff Called

Bluffing usually occurs in the bargaining setting. At the negotiation end of the continuum bluffing is rarely appropriate. But in the more polarized bargaining situations, it is common.

When you bluff, be sure that you can be protected if your bluff is called. If your bluff works, all is fine. If it fails, you should admit your error immediately. Do not try to cover up obvious errors or provide long explanations for the cause of the error. Admit it and get on with it! But, you should have a countermove ready for quick use. To admit error without a countermove leaves you stranded, with a complete loss of face and position.

> *Jerry implied that he represented a very large constituency as he negotiated for a right of way through a series of empty lots. The other party asked him to give a list of the constituents. Jerry replied that he had probably exaggerated the number but that the ones he knew were important landholders in town. The other party had called his bluff, and Jerry knew it.*

Be Prepared to Vary Your Communication Approach to Your Presentation

As a negotiator and bargainer, you should be able to demonstrate firmness when necessary, to be conciliatory when necessary, and even hostile when it is honest and vital to getting your point across. (In bargaining the parties will often "play act" hostility for the sake of satisfying a constituency that it is being well represented or to convince the counterpart that the matter is serious.) You should avoid getting frozen into a single attitude or type of behavior. Your counterparts will try to force you into a stereotype position or a single frozen position because that is much easier to handle than a constantly shifting image. This is not to say that you shift your commitment, except when it's necessary, but that you keep your method of approach flexible.

Negotiate So That Any Concession on Your Flexible Points Brings You Closer to an Agreement on the Less Flexible Points

It is good strategy, particularly in the bargaining context, to avoid giving in on all items that you consider able to be traded for concessions before your have settled the items you consider to be "musts" and for which you have much less flexibility. Keep some of the "give" points to use as bait for the "must" items when the going gets rough. If you have traded away all your "give" positions and very critical items still remain to be settled, you are in a pretty difficult situation.

In the bargaining situation it is useful, when you can, to tie the "give" and "must" points into a package. But at the same time get agreement from the other side point-by-point on your maximum terms if possible.

In the more critical bargaining situations it is wise not to indicate agreement or pleasure to any point of the other side until you know all of their points and have related them to each other and to your overall objectives.

In both negotiation and bargaining the "Quid-Pro-Quo" rule is useful. That is, do not grant concessions without trying to get something in return.

Explore the issues, the differences, and the clashes. Identify the root needs and concerns underlying the proposed solutions. Search for information from your counterpart. LISTEN! LISTEN! LISTEN! and then ask questions. When you phrase questions formulate them so they can be easily answered "yes" in your favor.

> *Joan was negotiating with the sales manager of a hotel about the arrangements for the annual convention of her professional association. Among the "must" items she had to have were the following: guaranteed rooms for at least 150 people, meals on a regular schedule, free transportation from the airport to the hotel (25 minutes),*
> *(continued)*

meeting space for large meetings of all delegates and for five concurrent small meetings of at least 30 persons each, and adequate facilities for meals. Among the items she wanted, but that were all flexible as possible "give" items were: room rates at 10% lower than comparable hotels in the area, recreational facilities including a swimming pool, a hospitality room for the president, a hospitality room for the executive director (herself), notebooks with pens and local information, the services of a secretary for the entire time of the conference, the use of the hotel office for duplications and other offices needs, and a percentage of the income derived from all room reservations. She submitted her full list of requirements (without showing priorities) to the sales director at their first meeting.

When the hotel objected to the two hospitality rooms, Joan offered to allow the base rate for the rooms to meet the "government" service standard that was almost the same as the lowest comparable rate in the city. After some negotiation she got the two hospitality rooms, but in return the room rates were pegged at the average of comparable hotels in the area. As the negotiations continued, the trading continued. When a contract was finally reached it provided for Joan's "must" items except the free transportation from the airport. That was modified to van transportation at half the cost of taxi service for the same trip. She did not get a percentage of the reservation fees but in return did get a special conference room for the meetings of the Executive Committee of her association (which was not on her original list of items). She got a registration table supervised by a hotel secretary during the day, but no notebooks from the hotel.

Obtain and Maintain the Initiative

Psychology and a sense of humor can cause a change of pace in the negotiations which frequently keeps the other side off balance. In the more open negotiations getting and holding initiative is less important than in the more polarized bargaining context. But in both bargaining and negotiation, tactics are used to keep the other party off balance and thereby give the user the upper hand. Prior information about the other side is useful in determining which tactics to use at any point in time. Understanding the type of person with whom you are dealing is important so that you can vary your approach and treatment accordingly. Here are some ways to maintain initiative in the more formal bargaining situation:

- Type proposals. They give more legitimacy and strength to a position.
- Try to stay in joint meetings. The more time that is invested in joint deliberations the more likely an agreement will be reached.
- Caucus when necessary. Caucus or break time can be used to divert/cool off the opponent's momentum.
- Silence can be used as a reply to an unacceptable offer.
- If the opponent brings out a position on a key point first, you may be on the defensive trying to beat it down. You may wish, then, to defer the discussion of key issues so that you can learn more facts and further evaluate the situation. Lay the issue aside for later consideration and then you decide when to bring it up.
- Settle easy issues early to create an environment of agreement.
- End each session on a positive note.
- Do not leave a session without an agreement on the start of the next session.
- Keep your objectives in mind and the session on the subject.
- Do not confront over trivia. To do so would jeopardize the overall success of the negotiations.
- Be organized and keep it that way!
- Discuss matters in person. Face-to-face discussion of the issues is vital. Seeing the others' reactions is important in adjusting your strategy and tactics. The phone is a better place for discussion than the mail if face-to-face discussion is not possible (see Calero & Oskam, 1983, for some interesting ideas on phone negotiation).
- Once you get an agreement, leave. This reduces the chance that the other party will change position or remember something which might be added or extracted.
- When you find yourself in a position of defending a proposal, you are allowing your counterpart time to prepare counter attacks and other strategies. On the other hand, if you offer no support for your proposals it is difficult to find agreement on them. Make a distinction

between defending yourself against the attack of the other and supporting your proposals. When you are under attack, keep cool and sustain the support of your position. Do not counterattack for that will drive you further apart.

Change of Pace Can be Useful

Discussions away from the table can be helpful. These discussions may be with the opposing spokespersons, with an authority higher than the spokespersons, between authorities who are higher, and so forth. But be careful in using this process. Do not let the information that your opponent went over *your* head to a higher authority in an attempt to influence the outcome of the negotiations surprise or unbalance you. It is a reasonable thing to do when the situation needs some outside pressure.

Keep Your Temper

There may be times in hard bargaining situations when tactics call for a show of irritation or anger in order to pressure opponents; but any display of temper should be only for effect. If you do feel anger, make every effort to avoid revealing it. This is quite different in the bargaining situation in which revealing anger may be more important than it is in the softer negotiation context. A high school boxing coach once said, "The first guy to lose his temper will lose the fight;" and that statement generally holds true for adversary situations. Angry and hostile statements and attitudes do not weaken or harm your opponent, but they do give him or her the advantage over you. If you find that the pressure is getting so great that your feelings are beginning to get in the way of your reason, you should call a halt to the bargaining and recess to cool off.

Treat as Completely Confidential What Goes on in Negotiation and Bargaining Meetings

It is particularly important to maintain the highest secrecy concerning the positions and attitudes of the opposition. Too many times leaks have destroyed possible agreements that were beginning to develop.

> *During the negotiations concerning the confirmation of Judge Thomas to the U.S. Supreme Court, confidential information about Judge Thomas was given to the Senate Judiciary Committee by Anita Hill. When this information was leaked to the press the controversy became a national (even international) event. The efforts to deal with the issues became extended and complex as well as embarrassing to the Judiciary Committee, Judge Thomas, and Anita Hill.*

Always Be Ready to Meet to Negotiate or Bargain

If you are not prepared for some items that come up during a meeting, move for a recess. As soon as you have evaluated your position on these items, make it known that you are ready to meet again. Failure can often be attributed to discouragement and refusal to meet on the part of one or both of the parties.

Of course, if a genuine stalemate or impasse exists and neither party can make any more moves, there is no point in meeting. But, a negotiator or bargainer should rarely veto a meeting if the other side gives any indication that it is willing and has a reason to meet. Many stalemates have been broken by simply meeting for long periods of time and going over the frozen positions until a crack begins to show. On the other hand, the most obvious settlements are often *prevented* by refusals to meet.

Some bargainers use refusal to meet as a tactic to infuriate or put the opponent under pressure. Although this may be useful in some situations, it is not a valuable tactic in the long run when there is room for discussion and positions are not rigidly frozen. In these conditions, refusal to meet tends to make useful dialogue impossible. No joint settlement can be reached in the absence of discussion.

Always Treat Your Counterparts Across the Table with Respect

Your counterparts are persons with responsibilities, interests, and needs similar to yours who are trying to maximize their position against your effort to maximize yours. Efforts to understand them as persons and as communicators will help you get closer to them and to be more aware of the things that are putting pressure on them.

There is a difference between honest respect and apparent respect for the purpose of deceit and manipulation. Phony respect is so often glaring and demeaning. In my early days as a mediator some of the parties felt they would gain a few points by calling me "Doctor." Because I knew that in those particular circles the academic title of Ph.D. really meant nothing I quickly tagged these people as trying to manipulate me. The effective negotiator and bargainer find good reason to respect their counterparts.

Be Sure That Any Interim Agreement Reached through Bargaining is Understood to be Tentative and Conditional on the Acceptance of the Final and Total "Package"

It is common practice and of general understanding that an agreement is not complete until all matters have been agreed on and ratified by the principles and/or constituents. In normal bargaining procedures, each matter of the agenda is discussed and tentatively agreed on. This strategy is of considerable importance. By making tentative agreements, subject to agreement on the total package, you avoid having your position chopped away bit by bit until you suddenly end up with a total agreement that just does not make any sense for you.

WORKING WITH A TEAM

Maintain Control of Your Team

When you are working with a team it must present a unified position. Your group should present a solid and well-coordinated image to the opposition. Signs of real defection are immediately used as evidence that your position is weak. This is a kind of nonverbal communication that is watched most carefully in all negotiations by all the participants. In the labor-management field some teams play a game of "bad guy-good guy" wherein they have different members of the team take hard and soft positions. This is usually a tactic to draw the opponent in toward the "good guy" and through that person to gain concessions that the hard bargainer could not gain.

Be Sure That it is Clear Who the Spokesperson is for Your Team

It is usually appropriate for only the spokesperson to talk for the team. In some situations, the chairman or chief of a negotiating team serves as a gatekeeper for participation by other members of the team. Some teams often divide the responsibility for various arguments and problems. But whatever the division of duties, the chief spokesperson should be clearly identified.

Someone Must Coordinate the Effort

No sign of individual differences of opinion or internal strife within your team should ever be allowed to appear during bargaining unless you have planned this carefully as a tactic. Be sure each team member understands the strategy before the meeting. Do not include anyone on the team who is not needed. Do not include anyone who might violate the ground rules. If you are the spokesperson you must control the discussion with the other side. You are the gatekeeper and the coach for your team as well as the star player.

Use Your Team Members as Resources

Do not try to know all the answers. Your team is there to provide information and support. If you have not anticipated a question that you desire to answer, tell the other side you do not have that information and you will get back to them at a later time. Someone else on your team may be better to present critical information. If so, just be sure that it is well prepared and that you know what will be said.

Do Not Discuss Your Points and Positions with Anyone Who Does Not Need to Know Them

If an impasse is reached, either because good faith or flexibility have expired, a public discussion of your positions and reasons for the impasse *may* be useful. But be careful with this. Media relations should be handled very carefully.

> *In a recent dispute on the West Coast involving the union and country commissioners, the differences over wages and benefits was preventing the parties from reaching agreement. The union called in the local press and released a prepared statement alleging that the county was spending more on the negotiations than the added wages and benefits would cost. After the area media carried the story, intense pressure was put on the commissioners to change their position, which is what the union apparently wanted. But instead of changing positions, the commissioners became more adamant and fired back with another media release accusing the union of falsehoods and attempts to manipulate the public. Bringing the matter to public attention in this fashion prolonged the negotiations, and the accompanying costs to both sides negated the eventual resolution.*
>
> *In another instance in the southwest some years ago involving chemical companies and miners, the company representatives at the bargaining table kept the local press informed of what was going on at the bargaining meetings with emphasis on the rightness of the company position. The media, pretty much under the control of one powerful editor, ran scare stories in actual red ink headlines depicting the union as criminals. The local citizens became so aroused that violence emerged within the town and on the properties of the chemical companies.*

The rights of free speech for the press often collide with the necessity to contain negotiations so that they do not escalate into campaigns. It is difficult to draw the line generally. However, when media involvement actually escalates a struggle instead of facilitates a resolution, it should be carefully conducted.

Keep the Key Negotiators or Bargainers for Your Team Fully Supplied with Information for Bargaining

To support your positions, there should be at least twice as much material as you will ever use. All materials should be as accurate as they can be, as up to date as possible, and when feasible, attested to by responsible persons.

Share Negotiation and Bargaining Information Only with Those Who Have a Legitimate and Direct Interest

When you are working with a team you need to be careful about outside discussions that do not include the members of the team.

When representing someone else the spokesperson should provide reports to the constituencies regarding the progress of the negotiations.

Do Not Expect Your Counterparts to be Consistent in their Goals and Proposals

On a person-to-person basis it is often possible for two people to trust each other sufficiently to accept what each other says at face value. This is not necessarily so when you have the responsibility of representing others. Often, in labor-management relations, the negotiators for each side are professionals who have a high degree of respect and trust for each other. But, as spokespersons for a constituency that is dynamic and changing, the motives and statements of such counterparts are usually subject to change. This is not because they, as individuals, are not to be trusted, but because the pressures of a constituency are dynamic and constantly changing and thus the representative of a constituency will not always behave with the same goals and conditions.

Develop and Maintain Your Own Trustworthiness as a Negotiator-Bargainer

Some of the toughest and at the same time most skilled negotiators I have experienced are people I trust highly. They are the ones who negotiate heartily, enjoy the process, and are willing to seek settlements of mutual interest. They are the ones who, when they have made a commitment, can be counted on to abide by that agreement. I have discovered that without that trustworthiness the effectiveness of the negotiator is limited.

In the presence of skilled bargainers, unskilled counterparts may feel they have been treated deceitfully or have been manipulated. The skilled bargainer perceives the strategies and methods of getting an agreement as part of the accepted processes of bargaining and is prepared to deal with them.

Even so, purposeful, substantial deceit and the use of lies will eventually destroy a relationship or increase the difficulty of continuing the relationship. Effective negotiation cannot take place when the parties cannot trust each other (see the discussion of trust under preventive processes in Chapter 2). We have all played bridge, poker, or other kinds of games in which there is an advantage to be gained by finesse, diversion, or hidden power. Negotiation-bargaining has some of the same characteristics. The use of such strategies should not create distrust but rather increase the respect for the person who uses them effectively and with good will.

> REMEMBER, THAT ALTHOUGH THESE GUIDELINES APPLY IN ANY SITUATION
> IN WHICH YOU ARE INVOLVED IN THE NEGOTIATION AND BARGAINING
> LEVELS OF DECISION MAKING AND DISPUTE RESOLUTION,
> THEY MUST BE DIRECTED TOWARD THE RESOLUTION OF DIFFERENCES

All of the guidelines we have listed should assist in successful negotiations or bargaining. Let's now look at some of the things to avoid as negotiators.

HOW TO FAIL AT NEGOTIATIONS AND BARGAINING

- Assume that everything is okay and that the other side is willing to give you what you want.
- Be so concerned with "looking good" in the eyes of the other that you lose track of your goals and needs (assuming that "looking good" is not the critical need you have at that moment).
- Show no skill or understanding of the negotiation or bargaining process.
- Take initial positions from which you will not move.
- Pay no attention to the interests, needs, and behavior of the others.
- Try to negotiate non-negotiable matters.
- Try to negotiate at stages in a struggle that do not allow for negotiation or bargaining (campaign, litigation, fight, or war).
- Look at your counterpart as an "enemy" who must be defeated.
- Deal in personalities and attack your counterpart personally.
- Be defensive, assume that you are going to be defeated if you do not fight.
- Ignore the ego needs of your opposite.
- Be nasty, aggressive, and combative.
- Do not listen to the other side, do all the talking yourself.
- Use deception throughout.
- Do not honor any procedural agreements you make.
- Make your questions similar to a criminal lawyer interrogating a witness.
- Be "hard nosed" and uncompromising in the search for your goals.
- Keep everything to yourself, divulge an absolute minimum of information to the other side.
- Criticize the other side on every point you can.
- Refuse to allow any silence in the negotiations.
- Pretend that you have many counter positions and other alternatives when you actually do not (a dangerous bluff).
- Threaten your opposite frequently when you cannot carry out the threats you make.
- Try bluffing when you are not prepared to have your bluff called.
- Make promises you do not keep.
- Assume that your opposite sees the world in the same way you do, has the same information as you, responds to the same pressures, wants to listen to everything you have to say, and uses language in the same way as you.

- Use as many tricks and pressure tactics as you can.
- Debate instead of negotiate.
- Avoid compromise.
- Deny any common interests.
- Do not define the issues in the situation, just argue.
- Negotiate or bargain about positions not issues, interests, needs, or problems.
- Engage in frequent emotional and irrational outbursts.
- Make no attempt to get in touch with your own needs, perceptions, stress factors, abilities, expectations, and goals.
- Assume that you are going to lose before you start negotiating or bargaining.
- Avoid making decisions when they are called for.
- Make big concessions too early in the interaction.
- Do nothing to satisfy the opponent.

There are other behaviors that will lead to failure. Some of these as listed, if used as part of stronger bargaining styles, may not result in failure. But, for the most part, these behaviors are not likely to facilitate successful negotiations or bargaining.

SUMMARY

Negotiation and bargaining are processes of struggle management aimed at fulfilling needs and interests when in opposition to each other. Negotiation and bargaining can be developed in systems in which there is freedom from conformity and room for dissent and difference of opinions. When the system demands conformity there is not much opportunity for negotiation or joint decision making.

Negotiation and bargaining involve mutual communication, joint decision making, the coordination of interests, and the influencing of decisions. Most negotiations move through stages involving contact, the setting of objectives and rules of procedure, specific definition of the issues and establishing an agenda, focus on demands and differing perspectives, fallback and re-exploration of the issues needed for a settlement, and working out the details of an agreement.

Bargaining and negotiation are viewed here as separate but related processes. Negotiation is at the "soft" end of a behavioral continuum in which the emphasis is on interests, open communication, and mutual decision making. Bargaining is at the "hard" end of the continuum and is used when polarization between the parties is stronger, when there is more attention to positions, when communication is less open, and when compromise is the more frequent form of resolution. The skills and techniques required for both overlap.

There are several types of negotiation and bargaining: distributive, integrative, attitudinal, and intraorganizational. All of them require communication and cooperation between the parties. Negotiation-bargaining is viewed as part of a system of joint problem solving and cooperative decision making short of arbitrary and unilateral decision making.

Power plays a significant function in the process. Those who have a stake in the process are more powerful than those who have nothing to gain. The dependence on each other in the bargaining process provides a power base from which the process may develop. Several types of power discussed in Chapter 3 are particularly involved in negotiation-bargaining. The understanding of the BATNA is an element in the power of the negotiators as well as in their ability as negotiators. The balance of power between negotiators-bargainers may facilitate the process.

Skilled negotiators and bargainers use interpersonal communication, are self-aware, listen, provide message feedback, respond appropriately to others, self-disclose appropriately, perceive others and achieve empathy, are able to work with groups of people, understand and apply problem solving and joint decision making, speak effectively, deal with others as people with problems, are willing to face issues directly, separate relationship problems from content, speak plainly, believe in what they are representing, are willing to make decisions involving change, keep principals informed, have positive self-perception, operate on a level of practical possibility, are reasonably skeptical, inspire trust, desire respect rather than popularity, perform their role with vigor, have a sense of humor, are skilled in persuasion, are prepared, show respect for others, maintain common courtesy, are skilled as interrogators, show persistence, and do not avoid dispute and struggle.

The preconditions to effective negotiation and bargaining include good faith, absence of a win-lose attitude, willingness to reveal interests and positions, absence of viewing the other as an enemy, and willingness to set aside self-interest for mutual interest.

In preparing to negotiate and bargain, good negotiators know their time limitations, know what should and should not be negotiated, arrange goals into categories of must and tradable, develop the BATNA, know their flexible points, test the fairness of positions, determine what the opposition will seek, plan their presentation, set ground rules, rehearse the approach, arrange data material so it is usable, know whom they represent, know who is to negotiate for both sides, know the goals and the potential issues, and identify their own authority and that of the counterpart.

The in-session conduct of negotiators and bargainers includes agreement on procedures, beginning with objectives beyond basic limits, keeping records, consideration of long-range relationships between the parties, never underestimating the counterpart, being prepared to have bluffs called, varying communication approaches, making concessions when they bring things closer to agreement, getting and maintaining the initiative, changing the pace of the negotiations, keeping tempers under control, maintaining confidentiality, being ready to meet, treating counterparts with respect, and making interim agreements conditional on the final package.

When working with a team the principal negotiator maintains control over the team, makes sure it is clear who is the spokesperson, coordinates the team effort, uses the team members as resources does not discuss positions with those who do not need to know, keeps fully in touch with information for bargaining, does not expect counterparts to be consistent, and develops and maintains his or her own trustworthiness.

There are also a number of behaviors that lead to failure in negotiations. These are listed earlier in the chapter.

Negotiation and bargaining are processes for which we all need skills. They are basic to our whole system: personal, interpersonal, intragroup, intergroup, and international. They are part of our social, religious, business, and professional world. We cannot get along without them. We therefore need to develop high skills in these processes.

CHAPTER 5

//

Mediation

DEFINITIONS, PERCEPTIONS AND CHARACTERISTICS

The Struggle Spectrum shows two main stages in which the impartial third party as a mediator may be used most effectively: Stage 2, Disagreement, and Stage 3, Dispute. This is not to say that mediation is not attempted at more polarized stages. But when mediation is attempted during litigation, for example, the situation needs to be de-escalated before mediation can function. A divorcing couple, for example, in court with their lawyers struggling over the custody of their children are hardly ready or able to mediate. The judge may suggest that the parties mediate but *until each party is willing to lay aside the litigation stance and become more involved in a mutual discussion of the problem no fruitful mediation can take place.*

As we witnessed in the Persian Gulf War, attempts at mediation failed when the parties became so polarized that they were unable to sit down together and negotiate the problems.

What Is Mediation?

The word mediation comes from a Latin root, "mediare," to be in the middle or to halve. In different cultures it has somewhat different meanings. Wall and Lynn (1993) report that whereas in Chinese it means to "step between two parties and solve their problem . . . in Arabic it indicates manipulation." Whereas in Eastern cultures the terms may have a different meaning, in Western culture it has come to mean a procedure for conflict resolution (p. 160).

Mediation in Western culture has been defined in several ways. Kressel and Pruitt (1985) define mediation as "third-party assistance to two or more disputing parties who are trying to reach agreement" (p. 1). Moore (1986) says it is "an intervention into a dispute or negotiation by an acceptable, impartial, and neutral third party who has no authoritative decision-making power to assist disputing parties in voluntarily reaching their own mutually acceptable settlement of issues in dispute" (p. 14). Coulson (1983) says it is "a process by which an impartial third person (sometimes more than one person) helps parties to resolve disputes through mutual concessions and face-to-face bargaining (p. 9). Folberg and Taylor (1984) define it

> as the process by which participants, together with the assistance of a neutral person or persons, systematically isolate disputed issues in order to develop options, consider alternatives, and reach a consensual settlement that will accommodate their needs . . . [it] emphasizes the participants own responsibility for making decisions that affect their lives . . . a self-empowering process. (pp. 7-8)

Putting these together with what we have already discussed leads to the following definition which I use throughout this book:

Mediation is an intervention by an impartial third person(s) into an already existing process of negotiation in order to facilitate the joint decision-making process between people who are becoming polarized and are colliding unproductively over differences in goals, methods, values, perceptions, and interests. The mediator makes no decisions for the parties, has no authority to direct or control the action of the parties, and can only work effectively when both parties are willing to use the process.

Contrary to some current practice and thought, mediation as we view it cannot be imposed on people by an outside authority against their will without seriously abridging its quality and potential. *It is essential that the parties to the dispute want to settle their differences and want the assistance of the mediator in accomplishing this goal.*

Mediation is Not the Practice of Law As We Have Known It

A number of law schools, the American Bar Association, and other law-based agencies have recently been encouraging attorneys to become mediators. A number of lawyers do mediate disputes of various kinds. It is important to emphasize that mediation is not the practice of law as we have traditionally viewed that function for a mediator should not give legal advice, advise, represent the clients, prescribe courses of action, or champion the cause of one side at the expense of the other. The ethics of the Bar have traditionally been strongly based on the adversarial relationship between people. The lawyer has been expected to press the advantage of the client being represented and to protect that client's right to due process. Although this is a very important and necessary function in our system of justice, it is not the function of mediation.

The growing interest of the legal profession in alternative dispute resolution suggests that it is trying to alter its image. In doing so a number of lawyers-in-training are being exposed to mediation, arbitration, and other dispute resolution procedures. These are not, however, taking the place of the essential adversarial model of the lawyer's function. They represent an added function that some lawyers are now trying to include as part of their arsenal of services to their clients. But a change in posture toward their clients when they try to mediate is significant and often difficult for lawyers to accomplish. Cobb (1991) suggests that the influence of lawyers trained in formal legal practice going into mediation practice is that more formal mediation practice emerges. This, however, is not necessarily a blessing, for as Cobb says, "rather than clarify standards for informal practice, this formalization process makes the inadequacies of informal standards for ethical practice more and more visible" (p. 99).

Mediation is Not the Practice of Therapy

Mediation is not a form of therapy. Although a number of therapists have assumed the role of mediator in certain circumstances that does not make the process a therapeutic one. Rosanova (1983) says:

> the mediator has no right to find individual behavior healthy or pathological, or to convince clients to amend general patterns of behavior, or to undertake searches for unconscious motives . . . the mediator's clients are not sick people; they are normal people facing many exceptionally distressing problems. (p. 64)

Kelly (1983) states strongly that:

> the role of the therapist is to encourage exploration of the meanings and levels of dysfunctional psychological reactions. In contrast, the role of the mediator is to manage and contain emotional expression so that the process of reaching settlement can proceed . . . the practice of family and divorce mediation is clearly distinct from the practice of psychotherapy (p. 44).

Haynes and Haynes (1989) believe that the therapist reorganizes interpersonal conflicts, whereas the mediator negotiates agreement over issues. Forlenza (1991) argues that mediation and psychotherapy are parallel processes with distinctly different goals although certain common elements occur.

The same concern is true for those who call themselves counselors as opposed to therapists. The essential criteria for counselor certification leads to a "treatment" process for the patient or client. This makes the counselor and therapist role essentially the same. In spite of the debate among professional therapists about their role in family mediation, the basic differences of the functions cannot be overlooked or ignored. Mediation demands a different posture and attitude toward the client than must be taken in performing the counseling-therapy function. Those counselor-therapists who can bridge that difference and are also trained as mediators will be generally effective. This, however, does not make what they do as mediators a therapeutic process as it has long been recognized.

ORIGINS AND DEVELOPMENT OF MEDIATION

Mediation has a long history and tradition in many different cultures. "[It] must surely be one of the oldest and most common forms of conflict resolution" (Kressel & Pruitt, 1985, p. 1). The Chinese culture used mediation for centuries. Wall and Blum (1991) identify in the teachings of Confucius (551-497 BC) one of the roots of Chinese community mediation—that harmony was the desirable state and that once disturbed it should be restored by compromise (p. 4). In Japan there is a rich history of the use of conciliation and mediation in community disputes, personal disputes, and other less formal situations (Folberg & Taylor, 1984). In Africa respected notables are often called to mediate disputes between neighbors (Gibbs, 1963). In Hawaii, resolving interpersonal conflict is referred to as *ho'oponopono*. The term is drawn from the practice of "disentangling" or of putting things rights (Wall & Callister, 1993, p. 9). In Western culture the churches, since their inception, have used mediation among members. In the Christian church the role of the "peacemaker" has been glorified: "Blessed are the peacemakers: for they shall be called the children of God" (Matthew, V:9). The Jewish Beth Din for many generations has existed as a dispute resolution body (Folberg & Taylor, 1984). The Quakers in the United States have for generations dealt with disputes among their members through mediation.

Anthropological research indicates that in different cultures mediation operates differently. Such things as cultural values, beliefs, self-concepts, functions of the state, relationships between the parties, and other matters affect the processes used. However, the basic methods have a certain universality that appears to transcend cultures. The addition of the impartial third party to negotiation is one of these. The processes of review, exploration, and resolution are common to all. In all cultures the mediators' standing in the community is contingent to mediation's success. Finally the mediator "gives meaning" to the dispute by narrowing, expanding, replenishing, and rephrasing, and by other communication processes (Kolb & Rubin, 1989).

The Management-Labor Context of Mediation

Probably the most developed and efficient model of mediation in this country and Britain up to now has been the handling of labor-management disputes. In the United States, beginning in 1898 with the Erdman Act, the role of mediation has been a respected and substantial part of public policy in coping with such disputes. During World War II, mediation was a principal function of the War Labor Board and the U.S. Conciliation Service. The Taft-Hartley Act of 1947 formed the Federal Mediation and Conciliation Service (FMCS) to provide mediation for interstate labor-management disputes. The FMCS pioneered a number of innovations in the mediation process, developed standards and ethics of procedures, and provided training for persons who were willing to undergo the strenuous discipline necessary to become mediators. A number of states have developed their own state mediation services more or less patterned on the FMCS.

The Revolution of Mediation Services

Since the 1960s in the United States there has been a growing interest in alternative dispute resolution forms in many other contexts. The civil rights struggles, the Vietnam war protests, the women's rights movement, consumer protection concern, the increasing incidence of divorce in family affairs, public sector collective bargaining, environmental struggles, the threat of nuclear war, and other stresses have focused attention on alternative methods of resolving disputes. A literal explosion of attempts at mediation services in almost all of these areas has followed. Cobb (1991) notes:

> mediation has developed . . . in a rather asymmetrical fashion, with practice far ahead of theory's ability to account for that practice. Managing a conversation in ways that promote participation of all parties is still more of an art than a science because we lack adequate tools to describe, prescribe or predict the course of that process. (pp. 87-88)

Public sector mediation agencies now intervene in thousands of community disputes. The Community Relations Service founded by Congress in 1964 to help resolve community disputes employs mediators stationed across the U.S. Over 180 neighborhood justice centers have arisen employing mediation as an alternative dispute resolution process. The American Bar Association has established a special committee on Alternative Means of Dispute Resolution that includes mediation.

Community mediation programs grew out of attempts around 1960 in Philadelphia and Columbus, OH to speed up the process of handling minor criminal issues in the courts. It was not until the 1980s that these programs surged. By the mid-1980s it was estimated that there were some 400 programs in 40 states. These programs fall into three types: justice-system-based, community-based, and composite (Duffy, Grosch, & Olczak, 1991).

Family and divorce mediation has exploded since the early 1970s into a national movement. In many states, such as California, "mediation" is a mandated process in custody and visitation disputes. (I put the term mediation in quotes because I have doubts about true mediation being possible in mandated situations.) Private practitioners are increasing in number and offering their services in many issues.

Student vs. student and student vs. teacher disputes are now being mediated in many schools. Araki (1990) reports high success rates in a 3-year project by the Hawaii State Department of Education. Many of these programs involve training students to mediate struggles themselves between their peers.

Environmental issues related to public and private resources are now being referred to mediation.

The severe economic hardships of the 1980s in rural areas of the United States and Canada led to the Agricultural Credit Act of 1987 which provided financial support for the NSDA to develop farmer credit dispute programs. Mediation services are now emerging in several states to deal with many of the struggles between farmers and creditors (Van Hook, 1990).

Disputes between landlords and tenants, neighbors, governmental agencies, individuals, and many others are now being mediated through community mediation agencies and services. Many of the issues that arise in small claims courts are being referred to mediation. It is apparent that mediation has become a process whose time has come. Along with the explosion of interest in the use of the process has come a demand for skilled mediators. The preparation of mediators is discussed in further detail later in this chapter.

In the face of the growing millions of civil legal cases overloading the courts Chief Justice Warren Burger urged "increased use of alternative methods such as mediation . . . in divorce, child custody, adoptions, personal injury, landlord and tenant cases and probate of estates" (Kressel & Pruitt, 1985, pp. 2-4).

Professional Organizations

Parallel to the increasing use of mediation in different contexts, there is an emerging number of professional societies that provide an opportunity for dialogue and study to those interested in the practice. The Society for Professionals in Dispute Resolution (SPIDR) started in 1973 and is probably the oldest national group. Family and divorce mediators have two major professional organizations, the Family Mediation Association and the Academy of Family Mediators. Private granting agencies such as the National Institute for Dispute Resolution that support research and development have appeared. In addition, academic training programs are being developed. Oregon State University, Department of Speech Communication, for example, has conducted graduate courses in conflict management and in mediation for over a decade. A number of alternative dispute resolution centers have been formed in law schools and in other academic settings (Kressel & Pruitt, 1985).

In the face of all these developments, there are increasing efforts being made to understand the processes related to mediation. Even so, few of the recent agencies and centers claiming to prepare mediators have the depth of experience and understanding, the mastery of the basic skills, and the cadre of trained mediators that are found in the FMCS and the various state agencies. Realistically, at the present time the best source of information, experience, and skill are those who have practiced mediation in the labor-management field.

Some concern has been expressed concerning the use of mediators who are skilled in one area but are used in another content field. For example, can we expect a skilled labor-management mediator to be able to handle divorce, family, environmental, community, and other types of disputes successfully? In my experience *the nature of the process is such that the concepts and skills developed in the labor-management context are applicable to almost any other context.* My own experience as a labor-management mediator has been invaluable in mediating other types of disputes. The process and the procedures are the same in spite of differences in content and minor variations in application. Honeyman (1990) identified seven mediation skill areas: investigation, empathy, inventiveness and problem solving, persuasion and presentation, distraction (reducing tension by diverting attention), managing the interaction, and substantive knowledge. None of these is exclusive to any given field. Honeyman reports:

> if a mediator's personal balance of skills is compatible with the balance of needs perceived to exist in the . . . field and that field is one in which high levels of substantive knowledge are typically embedded in the groundwork of the dispute or provided by someone else present there should be little problem with the transfer. (p. 78)

MISUSES OF MEDIATION

We have already touched on some of the misuses of mediation when we talked about "meddlers" in Chapter 2 on managing struggle. Kriesberg (1993) points to the problem:

> We are dealing with deep-rooted, seemingly intractable conflicts. They entail great tragedies as people seek and sometimes kill each other in order to fulfill their heart-felt desires. But we should not rush in to fix other people. Distressing as are the bloody fights and wronged peoples, we need to be careful not to exacerbate their problems by meddling, whether we are U.S. government, or church groups, or private individuals. (p. 27)

However, there are more specific areas in which opportunities for misuse arise. Mediation, as can be seen in the Struggle Spectrum, *does not fit in all dispute situations.* Also, there are many situations in which the intervention process being practiced does not actually fit the standard of neutrality or impartiality. An example is when court-appointed "mediators" are charged with representing the childrens' interests in custody disputes. These people are not actually mediators but not very subtle advocates in the negotiation process. Another example is a program in which offenders are "invited" by the court or community to confront their victims and to work out some recompense to them. The persons appointed by the court or agency as "mediators" are not functioning impartially as much as they are representing the interests of the victim, the community, the court, or the agency. Thus, they are truly advocates. Although this victim-offender type of program is a valuable one, it is an error to identify the process as a true mediation process. It is more like a facilitative process aimed at gaining some kind of recompense for the victim and providing an opportunity for the offender to understand the victim's situation, and thus to make some kind of restitution.

According to Erickson and Erickson (1988), "many things that are called mediation these days are little more than competitive negotiations in disguise" (p. xii). This kind of confusion gives clients and the public a false impression of the actual or basic nature of mediation and, in many cases, may result in a rejection of the process because under these conditions it is not perceived as unbiased and impartial even though the facilitators themselves may be reasonably neutral.

In some states, in labor-management disputes, mediation must be attempted before a union can go on strike. In a way this forces the parties to go through the process. Therefore, it is often simply used as a stepping stone to the ultimate strike. When this happens, the parties are not concerned with using the mediation process in the pursuit of settling the dispute, but instead are using it as a tool with which to fight. Such is often the case with court-mandated mediation when one or both of the parties goes through the process because of the effect it will have on the court and subsequent references to the court. This defeats the purpose of mediation.

Even so, many groups, once they get involved in the process, discover that mediation allows them to get back to negotiating in a productive way, which may lead to a settlement. When this happens you can bet that there is a skilled mediator involved.

In many family and divorce situations, counselors who are primarily concerned with their client's mental health and adjustment attempt to mediate disputes. Because, by definition, these counselor-therapists are not impartial, they have great difficulty when they try to function as mediators without special training and preparation. They must adopt a significantly different role from that for which they were trained and certified. Many of them are taking short courses in mediation, weekend seminars, and other "quick-fix" training programs. Although these may be helpful, they do not take the place of the kind of training that the labor-management mediators have to complete before they are allowed to operate in the profession. This problem is one with which the profession must cope before the practice of professional mediation becomes truly stable and significant.

As I have noted above, many lawyers are trying to include mediation in their practice. When they undergo substantial training and supervised experience they usually make good mediators. The lawyer has, traditionally, been trained as an advocate in the adversarial process. Law schools are now beginning to provide training in alternative dispute methods, but usually this is not a part of the basic curriculum. There is still the danger that many lawyers who claim that they mediate are actually representing the interest of a single client. They are surely misusing the process and, perhaps, misleading the client.

Several fears about mediation have emerged as it has moved rapidly from the early labor-management and intergroup context to more interpersonal disputes of divorce, family, and community affairs in this country. One of these is that mediation may cause exploitation of less powerful persons, provide for more governmental control of private life, and deny due process (Roehe & Cook, 1989). These fears are being addressed through increasing emphasis in the training of mediators on issues of power balance, freedom to choose mediation, and other issues. Also, the professional organizations of mediators and other neutrals are addressing these problems.

However, "fears that mediation expands state control and subsequently denies due process appear to stem from individuals' political philosophy rather than empirical evidence" (Roehe & Cook, 1989, pp. 46-47). As long as mediation can be sustained as a *voluntary* process, minus coercion, and parties are allowed to drop out at will, these fears can be countered. In those cases in which courts mandate mediation (as in child custody and divorce, some small claims, and others), the quality of mediation is probably adequate but even then a freedom to exit the process without prejudice must always be available.

Serious threats to the mediation process arise from the effects of mediators who structure the process, advocate their own ideas, and manipulate the process to serve their own ends or the ends of agencies, philosophies, or entities that are not in the primary interest of the disputants and are not impartial in the dispute.

I recently heard of a training program advertising "Mediation for Managers." This is an example of many training programs that want to profit from the mediation bandwagon that is sweeping the country and are willing to stretch the definition of mediation to cover almost any kind of interventive behavior. That program proposed to teach managers how to mediate work disputes among their employees. Although many mediator skills are applicable to the management process, we can hardly assume that managers meet the criteria of impartiality when they have a significant stake in the outcome of a dispute among employees. Kolb and Sheppard (1985) examined whether managers can impartially mediate. They point out that, "managers are not in any sense disinterested in the substance and outcome of disputes. Indeed, they have considerable interests to preserve and to protect" (p. 383). They emphasize the many areas of difference between the third party mediator, who is not a part of the managerial structure, and the manager whose concern is the nature of the decisions made and who cannot, by the nature of the institution, cede control of those decisions. They report:

> managers are more likely to act as inquisitors rather than either arbitrators or mediators in specific conflict situations. . . . Managers neither consider the same sorts of disputes nor do they have the same role expectations as mediators or arbitrators. (p. 385)

THE MEDIATOR: CHARACTER, QUALIFICATIONS, TRAINING, STANDARDS OF PERFORMANCE

As the mediation movement grows and expands there is an increasing need for qualified and capable mediators. People from many backgrounds are asking, "How can I become a mediator?" Davis (1993) says that mediation is becoming the "hot career" of the 1990s. She calls it the "field of dreams." We are being besieged by many people who see it as such, including social workers, lawyers, school teachers, former activists from the 1960s, dentists, doctors, therapists, seniors from many professions and avocations, judges, women who see it as closely related to the feminine experience, many who see it as a way to fulfill an "inner personal" need, some who want to master their fear of conflict, and many many others. Many of them have no perception of the fundamental nature of mediation, the qualifications for effective performance, or the standards of performance.

What is needed is greater competence by the volunteers and professionals in the business. The "field of dreams" image needs to be supplanted with the solid professional respectability that comes only from thorough and careful selection, training, and performance. Zack (1985) points out that those mediators with years of experience and training are getting old. In spite of the desire to replace them with new mediators with similar skills and experience, such persons are not available.

> The number of *competent* ad hoc mediators is small compared to the number who would like to do the work or who hold themselves out as mediators. Indeed, in the general absence of training or certification programs, anyone can proclaim himself a mediator (p. 21, emphasis added).

> In the last few years, however, increasing pressure has emerged to set standards of training and qualifications.

Mediator Competence and Qualities

Competence is critical in the growing demand for mediators. Unless there are ways to identify and develop competent people the profession may be overcome with the burden and discouraging consequences of unqualified persons meddling in disputes. Many people want to be peacemakers and to thereby "enter the kingdom of God" but few are willing to undergo the rigors of the training experience and personal sacrifice necessary to become effective in the profession. Self-interest is not a good prerequisite for a mediator.

Folberg and Taylor (1984) report the concepts, skills, and techniques that an experienced group of family mediators selected. Among them were the following:

Understanding of such things as stages of negotiation, nature and role of power, accepting failure and defining success, parameters of professional ethics, budgeting, standards of reasonableness, responsibility to unrepresented parties, bargaining, timing, influence of constituencies, nature of agreements, distributive versus integrative bargaining, post-mediation processes, rituals of agreement, and effective communication.

Skills in such behaviors as listening, trust and rapport building, interests and needs assessment, option inventory, dealing with anger, empowerment, sensitivity, refocusing and reframing, reality-testing, paraphrasing, negotiating, information sharing, techniques for breaking deadlocks, remaining neutral, self-awareness techniques, pattern and stereotype breaking, techniques to include other parties, rumor, goal setting, interview techniques, identifying agenda items and ordering, strategic planning, designing temporary plans, rewarding and affirmation techniques, techniques of building momentum, caucusing techniques, techniques of balancing power, conflict identification and analysis, agreement writing, credibility building, techniques for developing ground rules, and referral techniques.

The late William Simkin, former Director of the Federal Mediation and Conciliation Service, in a "semifacetious" moment, listed the following qualities sought in a mediator:

1. the patience of Job
2. the sincerity and bulldog characteristics of the English
3. the wit of the Irish
4. the physical endurance of the marathon runner
5. the broken-field dodging abilities of a halfback
6. the guile of Machiavelli
7. the personality-probing skills of a good psychiatrist
8. the confidence-retaining characteristics of a mute
9. the hide of a rhinoceros
10. the wisdom of Solomon

In a more reflective mood, one could extend the list to include:

11. demonstrated integrity and impartiality
12. basic knowledge of and belief in the collective bargaining process
13. firm faith in voluntarism in contrast to dictation
14. fundamental belief in human values and potentials, tempered by ability to assess personal weaknesses as well as strengths
15. hard-nosed ability to analyze what is available in contrast to what might be desirable
16. sufficient personal drive and ego, qualified by willingness to be self-effacing. (1971, p. 53)

Zack (1985) thinks the qualities one should look for in a mediator are humility, patience, sensitivity, sense of timing, tolerance, humor, ability to innovate, bargaining or negotiation experience, analytical ability, conceptualizing ability, and impartiality.

Both Simkin and Zack admit that these criteria are wide-ranging and somewhat diverse, that most humans are not likely to even approach having all of them, and that this scheme is perhaps an idealized version of what clients hope for in their mediators. Both agree that if mediation is to merit support and be endorsed by the clients these high standards must be insisted upon. Zack (1985) puts it this way: "Only through such critical expectations can the true craftsman be nurtured and encouraged until one day there will no longer be any question of whether mediation is an art or a trade" (p. 31).

In 1989, the Society of Professionals in Dispute Resolution adopted a report, with the assistance of the National Institute for Dispute Resolution's Commission on Qualifications, on the principles of qualifying neutrals (Singer, 1989b). That report recommended criteria for neutrals in dispute resolution, including mediators. They are summarized below:

a. Skills necessary for competent performance as a neutral include:
   (1) General
       (a) ability to listen actively;
       (b) ability to analyze problems, identify and separate the issues involved, and frame these issues for resolution or decision making;
       (c) ability to use clear, neutral language in speaking and (if written opinions are required) in writing;
       (d) sensitivity to strongly felt values of the disputants, including gender, ethnic, and cultural differences;
       (e) ability to deal with complex factual materials;
       (f) presence and persistence, i.e., an overt commitment to honesty, dignified behavior, respect for the parties, and an ability to create and maintain control of a diverse group of disputants;
       (g) ability to identify and to separate the neutral's personal values from issues under consideration; and
       (h) ability to understand power imbalances.
   (2) For mediation
       (a) ability to understand the negotiating process and the role of advocacy;
       (b) ability to earn trust and maintain acceptability;
       (c) ability to convert parties' positions into needs and interests;
       (d) ability to screen out non-mediable issues;
       (e) ability to help parties to invent creative options;
       (f) ability to help parties identify principles and criteria that will guide their decision making;
       (g) ability to help the parties make their own informed choices; and
       (h) ability to help parties assess whether their agreement can be implemented.
   (3) For arbitration
       (a) ability to make decisions;
       (b) ability to run a hearing;
       (c) ability to distinguish facts from opinions; and
       (d) ability to write reasoned opinions.

 b. Knowledge of the particular dispute resolution process being used includes:
  (1) familiarity with existing standards of practice covering the dispute resolution process; and
  (2) familiarity with commonly encountered ethical dilemmas.
  c. Knowledge of the range of available dispute resolution processes, so that, where appropriate, cases can be referred to a more suitable process;
  d. Knowledge of the institutional context in which the dispute arose and will be settled.
  e. In mediation, knowledge of the process that will be used to resolve the dispute if no agreement is reached, such as judicial or administrative adjudication or arbitration;
  f. Where parties' legal rights and remedies are involved, awareness of the legal standards that would be applicable if the case were taken to a court or other legal forum; and
  g. Adherence to ethical standards. (pp. 17-19)

Carnevale, Putnam, Conlon, and O'Connor (1991) studied mediator effectiveness in community mediation. They found that "success in mediation is more complex than simply whether or not agreement is achieved" (p. 133). They found that certain mediator behaviors appear to be more closely related to successful mediation than others. They did not, however, ascribe the success to these behaviors. Those behaviors that showed a positive association with success in mediation included developing rapport with the parties, keeping the process focused on the issues, expressing pleasure when the parties were making progress, avoiding taking sides, and discussing the interests of all parties in the dispute.

Training Mediators

"Mediation skills are not intuitive and must therefore be initially acquired by training and honed by experience" (McKay, 1990, p. 23).

How much and what kind of training does it take to make a good mediator? There are wide differences of opinion on this. Much depends, as in the case of any professional training, on the natural abilities and prior experience and training of the would-be mediator. However, mediation requires a different approach to disputes from that found in any other line of endeavor. The lawyer, the counselor, the preacher, the teacher, the politician, the manager, and the interested citizen all must adapt their own particular substantive and procedural knowledge to the particular requirements of the mediation process. This may be more difficult for some than for others depending on the individuals' personality. The range and variety of training that is developing in this country is remarkable when we consider the amount of common systems and principles that underlie the process.

The Federal Mediation and Conciliation Service probably had at that time the most extensive training program for mediators. After careful screening and selection of the trainee by the Service, the training program began with a concentrated 2-week orientation on the principles and practices of mediation. Simulation and extensive discussion were used in this program. Experienced mediators and trainers conducted the sessions. Upon completion of this basic program the trainee was assigned to a regional office of the agency where the training was continued under the direction of the regional director and experienced mediators. The trainee first sat with and watched mediators at work. The processes were discussed at length with the experienced mediators. As time went on and the trainee got more experience with the trainers, he or she would begin to take part in the actual processes along with the experienced mediator. This continued with the trainee taking a more and more active part in the sessions. The experienced mediators who were supervising reported on the progress and problems of the trainee on a regular basis to the regional director. When the trainee was perceived to be ready by the trainers and the regional director, a case was assigned. There was no set period from the time of the orientation to the assignment of the first case. In practice it has taken from a minimum of five or six weeks to a whole year. Those who take the least amount of time are usually persons who have had negotiation experience and have actually been involved in mediation as clients and as mediators in an informal setting. (Union business agents and company labor relations personnel are good examples of this group.) However, the actual probationary period for the mediator trainee was one year at full time.

The FMCS had another category of mediator trainees comprised of those who did not have the same depth of qualifying experience as the regular trainees. These trainees were usually given more than one basic orientation session in the national office and were sent temporarily to two or three different regions for field experience before they were sent to their assigned region for regular training (Simkin, 1971). In recent years the emphasis has been on selecting new mediators with approximately seven years of experience in negotiation and bargaining.

State labor-management mediation agencies have more limited training programs. Again, the selection process is very important and applicants are screened carefully before they are hired. Because of the size of these agencies, mediators usually come on duty one at a time and are trained on a one-on-one basis by seasoned mediators, in much the same way as the federal mediators are trained after they move out from the initial orientation.

Outside the labor-management field, the nonacademic training programs for potential mediators are usually much less rigorous and take much less time. These other programs range from one-day "quick fixes" to more intensive 2-day to 1-week programs. Nicolau (1986) reports that the first volunteer training program of the Institute for Mediation and Conflict Resolution ran for 55 hours. Davis (1991) reports that the training of Community Mediation volunteers is brief. The average number of hours ranges from 25 to 55 hours of training plus internships. It was his opinion that 30 hours of training is not enough, but that 40-50 hours plus supervised experience makes more sense and should be accompanied by careful evaluation of the trainee.

Folberg and Taylor (1984) point out that these short programs "should not be oversold. The time restrictions imposed on a training format of one week or less limit their role to mediation orientation, an introduction to substantive knowledge, and skill refinement. They should not be regarded as comprehensive professional curricula" (p. 234). There is also some question as to whether these short programs produce the quality of mediator that is found in the labor-management field. I believe that basic mediation training (not including internships or supervised experience in the field) should never be less than 80 contact hours (40 hours of basic training, 15 hours of role play mediation exercises, and 25 hours of supervised observation of another mediator).

In the past several years minimum training standards have developed for community dispute resolution programs. Typical of this is the Oregon program which provides the following:

(2) Training; Mediators in a community dispute resolution program shall complete a basic mediation curriculum and an apprenticeship.
    (a) The basic mediation curriculum of at least 30 hours shall include participation by each trainee in a minimum of three supervised role plays, trainee self-assessment, and assessment of the trainee by the trainer identifying for the trainee areas for improvement. The mediation curriculum shall address the following elements:
    (A) Knowledge of the stages and value of conflict in empowering change;
    (B) Understanding of the principles of dispute resolution;
    (C) Listening skills;
    (D) Empathy and validation skills;
    (E) Sensitivity and awareness of cross-cultural issues;
    (F) Ability to maintain neutrality;
    (G) Ability to identify and reframe issues;
    (H) Ability to establish trust and respect;
    (I) Ability to use techniques for achieving agreement and settlement, including creating a climate conducive to resolution, identifying options, reaching consensus, and working toward agreement;
    (J) Ability to shape and write agreements; and
    (K) an understanding of the ethical standards for mediator conduct.
    (b) The apprenticeship shall include participation in a minimum of two mediations under the supervision of an experienced mediator or trainer.
(3) Any individual who has participated in substantial similar training or completed 100 hours as a mediator prior to the adoption of these rules shall be deemed to have met the training requirement established by these rules.
(4) Any individual who has completed a substantially similar training in another jurisdiction subsequent to adoption of these rules shall be deemed to have met the training requirements established by these rules.

(5) Each Grantee shall insure that its mediators have received their basic curriculum training from trainers who have:
(a) At least two years active dispute resolution experience as a mediator; and
(b) Previous mediation training experience as a trainer or an assistant.
(6) A Grantee may establish additional training requirements beyond these minimum training requirements. There shall be no formal academic requirement in community dispute resolution programs. (Community Dispute Resolution Program Rules: Working Draft for Public Comment. State of Oregon Dispute Resolution Commission, 1990, p. 2)

These rules are in the process of being revised upward as the recognition of the importance of training become more apparent.

There are a growing number of academic programs on mediation. Some universities and law schools are now offering curricula in dispute management, including work in mediation. These range from the offering of a single course in conflict management to a series of courses ranging through conflict, conflict management, arbitration, mediation, negotiation and bargaining, and related subjects. As these academic training programs grow, they are beginning to develop a set of basic areas of study required for preparing mediator trainees for the "real world" of mediation. These areas of study include the understanding of struggle and conflict, alternative dispute resolution, negotiation, collective bargaining (for those in the labor-management relations field), arbitration, and mediation. Prerequisites to these courses often include such subjects as interpersonal communication, leadership, persuasion, small group processes, and public speaking.

Persons with special training in counseling and therapy, law, environmental sciences, business management, education, and other content areas add dispute management studies to their content specialty as an application of their basic content field. The combination of these make an excellent background of training. More and more academic programs in mediation and related dispute management are interdisciplinary in nature. However, even though the academic training may be experiential in many aspects of mediation study, nothing is going to take the place of actual supervised experience on the firing line.

Qualifications of Trainers

Those who organize, design, and present training programs for mediators and mediators-to-be need to have some special qualifications. What these qualifications should be has been a matter of concern in all of the professional societies and to others concerned with providing a corps of trained professionals (note the Oregon standards above). Assuredly, the standards should be much higher than required for the minimum practice of mediation. The tendency in too many situations in the past decade has been for people with a minimum of training, understanding, and experience in mediation to assume the role of trainers. The results are problematical. What has resulted, also, is a mass of programs led by trainers with limited experience but advertised as providing the participant with skills sufficient to perform professionally. This kind of questionable endeavor does not help the profession.

The results of high-quality professional training suggest that there are some standards that, when met, facilitate high-quality mediator training. Among them are the following:

- Experience as a professional mediator in at least one content area for three years.
- On-the-job training in mediation of no less than one-year under the supervision of professional mediators and mediator-trainers (may be part of the above).
- Professional or academic training in mediation and dispute resolution of no less than 60 contact hours (the equivalent of two one-quarter 3-hour credit courses).
- Special training in communication skills.
- Special training in group process facilitation skills.
- Special studies in learning and training processes.

In 1991, the Academy of Family Mediators increased its basic training from 40 to 60 hours, including training in a specialty area. Twenty hours of continuing education every two years is also required (Zumeta, 1991).

It should be clear from the above that the holding of an academic degree does not suffice for the preparation of trainers. Nor does professional and/or volunteer mediation experience alone prepare one to become a trainer. The academic training that does occur must be directed toward those subjects and skills that have direct bearing on the mediation process. This would include such subjects as persuasion, listening, consultation, group processes, conflict management, and so on.

Standards of Professional Practice

Some years ago the state mediation agencies and the FMCS joined forces in formulating a code of professional conduct for mediators. This code was adopted by the FMCS and most state agencies and has served as the cornerstone of professional ethics in the mediation profession (Simkin, 1971). Its principles and standards reveal the underlying qualifications of a mediator. One mediator likened his role to that of an obstetrician—he served to assist in the delivery of a baby that could have been done without his services. The effective mediator makes the "delivery" easier and safer. This implies that the mediator is fully trained and prepared to do the job required of mediation.

Subsequently, sets of standards and ethics have been formulated by the American Academy of Family Mediators, the American Bar Association, the Colorado Council of Mediation, and other agencies. All of these combine similar elements (see Lemmon, 1984a, 1985a, 1985b; Moore, 1986).

Ethics and Ground Rules for Mediators

Underlying any set of principles and standards for mediation is the basic assumption that the process must be voluntary. That is, the parties must voluntarily choose to seek the assistance of mediation and must be free to exit the process at will. When parties are mandated or coerced into mediation they have already had their freedom of choice violated. Mediation cannot operate most effectively under conditions in which the parties are forced into the process against their will. The parties must have a desire to settle their dispute and a willingness to do it through the mediation process. When they are forced to mediate, the consequences may often result in half-hearted negotiation and in less than reasonable resolutions in order to get out from under the coercion.

> *A divorcing couple went to court to settle their dispute over custody of their children. They had negotiated, argued, and fussed over the matter for many months and were unable to work things out together. In desperation they agreed to let the court make the decision for them. The court ordered them to go to mediation before it would hear their case further. Neither of them wanted to negotiate with each other any more. They did not cooperate with the mediator, made half-hearted efforts to talk the thing over again, and finally agreed on an arrangement that neither intended to follow. Afterwards they were queried as to whether mediation was helpful. Both agreed that it was something they did not want to do and that they were unhappy with the results.*

The following comments and principles represent a set of basic ground rules for mediation that are applicable in any mediation situation:

1. *The primary responsibility for the resolution of a dispute lies with the parties themselves.* They must voluntarily reach agreement. Although the mediator may make suggestions of alternatives, the decisions must be made jointly by the parties to the dispute.

2. *The mediator is to assist the parties in reaching agreement.* This assistance can be helping them to communicate, to explore alternatives, to gather information, and other processes facilitating such an agreement.

3. *Intervention should be determined primarily by the desires and initiation of the parties to the dispute.* Ideally, the resolution of disputes should occur without the assistance of the mediator. However, in some cases required by public policy, mediators may appropriately intervene. Unsolicited intervention by the mediator should be limited to exceptional circumstances. When mediators intervene at their own option or by mandate, they have an added and very important responsibility to orient the parties to the process and to lead them to make the decision to become involved in mediation.

> *John and Mary Smith were divorcing and had been referred to mediation by the judge hearing their case. Neither felt that mediation would be of any use to them, but they agreed to attend the orientation session. At that session the mediator explained and demonstrated the process and in so doing developed sufficient acceptance on the part of the couple that they were willing to proceed into mediation. Had they refused the matter would have been heard in court. Unlike the couple above, John and Mary were satisfied with their experience. A significant difference seemed to be the degree of freedom they had to make the decision to go to mediation and the quality of the mediator's orientation.*

4. *The mediator should be able to provide the parties with procedural and substantive suggestions and alternatives which will assist them in forging a solution to their mutual problems.* This means that the mediator has done the "homework" necessary to understand the issues at point. Although the mediator is primarily a process specialist, a knowledge of the content is helpful. Skilled mediators, however, grasp the content of the issues rapidly no matter what their prior experience with the material.

5. *Acceptability of the mediator by the parties is essential.* No mediation can take place unless both parties accept the mediator. When a friend of Mary's offered to mediate the dispute with John, John refused because he felt that Mary's friend would be biased in her favor.

6. *The mediator should demonstrate integrity, objectivity, fairness, intelligence, knowledge of the areas in dispute, emotional balance, social perceptiveness, and skill in spoken and written communication.* All of these can become apparent to the parties by reputation, through an orientation session, or by prior experience.

7. *A mediator should not enter any dispute being mediated by other mediators without their approval* and without fully conferring with them about the matter.

8. *Mediators should avoid any appearance of disagreement or criticism of fellow mediators in a given case situation.* Discussion between the mediators concerning positions and actions should be carried on solely in private. It is unwise to discuss pending cases in a public place, such as a restaurant or on public transportation. Furthermore, public criticism of other mediators, no matter how justified, is not considered ethical. Private criticism and evaluation with appropriate persons, including the subject mediators who are legitimately seeking such information, is acceptable.

9. *Failure to function ethically and professionally does harm to the perception of the process itself, as well as the agency for whom the mediator may work.* The effect of such behavior spreads rapidly and the process and the sponsoring agency is harmed.

> *Two lawyers in a Western city advertised themselves as mediators. Neither was well trained or skilled in mediation. At the first session with the clients they spent most of the time discussing their fee. During the mediation periods they made unsolicited proposals and tried to force the parties to accept them. Afterward both parties described the experience as a frustrating argument with the lawyers who posed as mediators and tried to force a decision neither wanted. Both of the clients averred that if that was mediation they wanted no more of it.*

10. *Mediators should not use their position for private gain or advantage, nor should they engage in any employment or enterprise that conflicts with their function as mediator in relation to any given case.* A counselor or lawyer, for example, who has been working for a client is not in a position to serve as a mediator between that client and another person. A so-called mediator told his clients that if he helped them settle their dispute he would expect a big steak and champagne dinner for him and his girlfriend. He did not last long.

11. *Mediators should not accept money or things of value other than previously agreed-upon fees, expenses, and/or salary.* They should not incur obligations to any party that would interfere with the impartial performance of mediation functions. Fees should be set and published beforehand and made a part of the orientation session. Special fees to some clients and not others should be avoided. A mediator who has a sliding scale of fees depending on the ability of the client to pay must be very careful to be consistent in the application of the sliding scale.

   The "pro bono" work of some volunteers may often undercut the efforts of professionals who depend on the work for their income. This creates a problem that has not yet been resolved in the profession.

12. *The mediator should not regulate nor control the content of an agreement or settlement between the parties.* As we have said frequently, the decision must be made by the parties. The areas of agreement and their content are not the responsibility of the mediator. This does not deny the mediator the opportunity to make suggestions for possible changes or additions in the content, but those suggestions should be made only as suggestions and not directions. For example, Ed, the mediator, helped the union and the management work out their contract agreement. In his opinion, they left out a part of the contract he considered very important. He could have raised a question as to whether they wanted to address this area without violating this concept. But if he tried to insist that they include a clause covering that matter, or if he even suggested such a clause, he would be violating this principle.

13. *When the mediator is a representative of a public agency and the parties are moving toward an agreement that is contrary to public policy or in violation of the law, it may be necessary to withdraw from the negotiations.* The mediator has no right to impose standards of behavior on the parties. At the same time, if the mediator is clearly aware that there is a violation in the agreement he or she has a responsibility to bring the matter to the attention of the parties, but not to insist that it be changed or to threaten to report the violation to officials. If the parties continue to insist that the known violation remain in the agreement, the mediator should withdraw from the case.

14. *Publicity in a given dispute situation shall not be used by a mediator to enhance his or her position or that of the agency.* Public information should only be released consistent with (a) the desire of the parties, (b) the value of the information in assisting the settlement of the dispute, and (c) the public's need to be informed.

> *I once was involved as a mediator in a very difficult dispute that involved several unions and several companies. The industry involved was the predominant support of the small community. Everyone in town depended on the industry in one way or another and were therefore vitally interested in the negotiations that were taking place. During the negotiations prior to my entrance as mediator, both sides had been using the press and media to advance their cause with the result that there was a high degree of animosity within the town toward one side or the other. People were fighting with each other, shots were fired, malicious property damage was evident, and the local newspaper was running special editions almost twice a day with scare headlines in red ink about the violence. The local paper was selling out every edition.*
>
> *When I got into the case as mediator I discovered immediately that any report I gave to a reporter was not accurately reported and was slanted toward the newspaper's interest. After talking with one of the key reporters and his editor I realized how the parties were misusing the media. With the approval of the management and union representatives, I put a lid on the information about the negotiations. The representatives of the unions and the companies agreed to release no information concerning negotiations except in joint meeting with the mediator and a representative of each party present. The effect on the community was almost immediately noticed as the anger and violence subsided while, at the same time, information that kept the community aware that the parties were working toward a solution was released on a practical schedule.*

15. *Mediators are not to bring pressures to bear that jeopardize voluntary decision making by the parties to the dispute.* Threats, rewards, promises of special treatment, and special incentives that bring the parties to make decisions they would not otherwise have made if they were thinking independently are not to be used.

> *A so-called "mediator" in a delicate case between two community agencies informed both of them in a joint meeting that she would be very angry with each of them if they did not accept the proposal she was about to make. She then threatened to bring in a superior agency officer if they didn't reach an agreement satisfactory to her. The parties responded by removing her from the case, and they filed a complaint with her supervisor.*
>
> *Another "mediator" informed an offender that unless he made some contribution to the victim his probation officer would be informed. The offender then "froze-up" and refused any further attempts to meet with the party to provide restitution.*

16. *Suggestions and recommendations for settlement made by the mediator should be evaluated carefully for their effect on the parties* and he or she should accept full responsibility for their honesty and merit.

17. *Mediators have full and continuing responsibility to study the areas involved in the disputes which they mediate and to improve their skills and upgrade their abilities.*

18. *Suggestions to the parties that imply that they should transfer from one mediation "forum" or person to another mediation person or forum in order to produce better results are unprofessional and are to be condemned.*

19. *Negotiating positions, proposals, suggestions, and other information given to the mediator in confidence during the course of negotiations must not be disclosed to the other party without first securing permission from the person or persons initiating the information.*

20. *Confidential information acquired by the mediator shall not be disclosed for any purpose nor be used directly or indirectly for the personal benefit or profit of the mediator, or in a legal proceeding.* This confidentiality is a significant part of the process. Protection of it has been the subject of a number of laws. Most of the regulations provide that the parties must agree to keep the information confidential. Once this is done the confidentiality protection exists. The State of Oregon statute on mediation and arbitration provides the following:

36.205 Confidentiality; disclosure of materials and communications.

(1) If there is a written agreement between any parties to a dispute that mediation communications will be confidential, then all memoranda, work products and other materials contained in the case files of a mediator or mediation program are confidential. Any communication made in or in connection with such mediation which relates to the controversy being mediated, whether made to the mediator or a party, or to any other person if made at a mediation session, is confidential. However, a mediated agreement shall not be confidential unless the parties otherwise agree in writing.

(2) Confidential materials and communications are not subject to disclosure in any judicial or administrative proceeding except:
   (a) When all parties to the mediation agree in writing to waive the confidentiality;
   (b) In a subsequent action between the mediator and a party to the mediation for damages arising out of the mediation; or
   (c) Statements, memoranda, materials and other tangible evidence, otherwise subject to discovery, that were not prepared specifically for use in and actually used in the mediation.

(3) When there is a written agreement as described in this section, the mediator may not be compelled to testify in any proceeding, unless all parties to the mediation and the mediator agree in writing (1989 c. 718 P 231).

21. *The mediator has no power to enforce law nor to act in any way as an agent of law enforcement or investigative agencies.*

THE MEDIATOR IN ACTION

We have looked at the background of struggle and conflict, the nature of mediation in general, the arenas in which it is used, its role in the Struggle Spectrum, its misuses, the qualifications and training of the mediator, and have summarized the ethics and standards of practice. Now we examine some of the tools and techniques that a mediator uses. These are not prescriptive in nature although, in most instances, they represent tried and true procedures that most professional mediators perform with great skill no matter what the arena of engagement.

First, remember that the mediator does not make decisions for the parties but is serving as a *facilitator* for the clients' own decision making. The mediator's primary concern is that a *settlement* be forthcoming from the parties themselves. In facilitating this process the mediator uses persuasion, deals with the issues of control and power necessary to empower the parties to do their own decision making, and provides consulting services when the parties need assistance in thinking through their substantive and procedural processes.

COMMUNICATION AND MEDIATION

Our social world is constituted through the process of communication (Cobb, 1991). Mediator competence in communication means a "sophisticated sense of control" (Donohue, 1989). Kolb and Rubin (1989) found that "those mediators who are most successful in securing agreements . . . are the ones who use their communication competence to control the interaction . . . " (p. 4).

Because communication is the heart of the mediation process mediators must be skilled in many communication elements. There are some communication tools that are of particular importance. These come from the area of interpersonal communication. They are not significantly different from what we seek in basic interpersonal communication courses and training. Briefly, they include the following.

Credibility

The most basic and continuing tool is the credibility and integrity of the mediator (Keltner, 1965). At the very outset of the relationship with the clients the mediator must be accepted as a person who can be trusted, who thoroughly knows the process involved, who relates well to the parties, is respected, and who demonstrates good will by setting aside his or her self-interest in the situation. For example, if mediators show undue concern about who is going to pay the fees, or what fees are to be paid, or if they attempt to perform "surveillance" type acts, clients quickly lose confidence in the actual concern of the mediator for helping them deal with their problems.

> *A "would-be-mediator" in a dispute between a landlord and renter appeared at the door of the apartment of the renter one day and insisted that she be allowed to inspect the property. Neither the landlord nor the renter had asked for this. The resulting misconception of the process of mediation spread and lingered long after this event.*

Empathy

Empathy is a state of being. It is a condition we experience when we are able to see things as if we were behind another person's eyes, hear things as if we were between another person's ears, and experience things as if we were in another person's shoes. Bruneau, a communication research scholar studying the nature of empathy, points out that "one may not be able to be fully empathetic . . . unless he or she can view the world imaginatively from the perspective of another" (1989, p. 12). When we are in a state of empathy we are able to switch between our own and the "as if I were the other" perspective. In an empathic state we share the same "here and now" as the person with whom we are empathizing. Time, space, processes, feelings, intent, and content of the other is perceived by the empathic one.

Just taking the position of the other person is not empathy. In an empathic state one becomes involved in a "dynamic biopsychic entrainment" (DBE) that allows one to discover the feelings and content of another. Empathy is not sympathy. When we are sympathetic with a person we are "feeling for" that person. When we are in an empathic state we are "feeling with" that person.

Empathy is not something we can communicate to another person because it is functionally an inner sense of awareness that allows us to see the world as if we were someone else. What we do communicate to others is the information and insight that we gain while we are in an empathic state. When I sense that another person is angry, feel that anger as if it were mine, and then report to that person some of my perceptions of what he or she is likely feeling, I am communicating what I discovered from my empathic frame of reference. When the other person recognizes that the things I am communicating back match what he or she is thinking and/or feeling, a sense of rapport emerges that usually allows the receiver to feel more confidence in the ability of the transmitter to understand his or her point of view.

Many people seeking rapport and acceptance will feign empathy by using phrases such as, "I really understand your feeling," or "I've felt the same way," or "That's what I think, too." When a person really does not have a perception of the world from the other person's point of view attempts to feign empathy are superficial and potentially dangerous.

Our ability to become empathetic, that is, to be able to see the world as another sees it, depends a great deal on a number of our perceptual skills, including such things as high awareness of ourselves and our surroundings; openness to different images and messages; control of our attention;

mental and physical focusing processes; and our ability to see and hear the many subtle messages that sur-round the central message that another may be sending. In order to become empathic we must be willing to lose our own "egocentric identity." That is, our personal goals and perceptions of the other must be laid aside, and the ego of the other must be experienced.

Those persons who appear to be most empathic are those who have a better than average understanding of themselves. It is vital to the empathic condition that the person be able to separate his or her inner goals, expectations, predispositions, and so on from the information that is gathered about the other person while at the same time recognizing conditions that are both similar to and different from their own view of the world. Developing skills of empathy is not easy. Some people have a natural ability to be empathic. Others need a great deal of assistance. Solid work in self-awareness and practice, under supervision, in "getting behind the other's eyeballs" is a basic for all who wish to be mediators.

Being empathetic can be a very important process for the mediator. The mediator can establish rapport by being empathetic with the clients in their respective situations. It is important that the mediator not have a predetermined outcome for the situation in mind. The more the mediator can experience, through empathy, the ideas and feelings of both clients, the more effective he or she can be in performing as a mediator.

Listening

A basic skill for any mediator is the ability to listen, and listening is a basic prerequisite to the empathic condition. Listening calls for many of the perception skills, such as hearing, seeing, kinetic awareness, space awareness, and so on. Listening itself functions to accomplish various purposes, such as the ability to discriminate, to be critical, to evaluate, to appreciate and enjoy, and to assimilate. Listening is a dynamic process of gathering information through the specialized use of the perception skills listed above.

Most people are pretty poor listeners. We listen at about 25% efficiency, retain only 50% of the information immediately after hearing it, and retain only 25% within 48 hours. Good listening can be learned. The good listener is able to focus attention where it needs to be focused in order to maximize his or her understanding of the situation. Many people confuse the process of listening with the things that good listening can make possible. For example, good listening may allow me to clarify differences in the points of view expressed by the clients. The clarification of these differences is not good listening, but a process that good listening can facilitate. Skills other than listening are required to clarify what people are saying and believing. Empathy, for example, is often listed as a listening skill. Actually, listening is separate from empathy but is a skill that accompanies and is prerequisite to empathy.

The good listener finds areas of interest in what the speaker is saying, judges the content of what is said rather than the delivery, withholds judgment about what is said, tries to identify the central themes of what is said, takes few notes and accommodates them to what is being said, works at listening well, avoids distractions by concentrating on what is being said, is able to avoid reacting to colored language, keeps mentally summarizing what is being said, anticipates what is coming, listens for information between the lines, and weighs evidence carefully.

Many things operate to block our listening processes. All of us tend to see and hear what we want, what satisfies our needs, what confirms our prior assumptions, what is consistent with our values, what we expect to see and hear, what we have been taught or conditioned to see and hear, and so on. These predispositions are major blocks to our listening processes. We tend to block out information that would run contrary to our predisposed expectations.

One of the huge barriers to good listening is the speech-thought differential. The fastest talkers may be able to speak in the vicinity of 175 words per minute and average talkers at 125 wpm or less. But the mind processes words at over 400 words per minute. Notice how much faster reading a message is from listening to it aurally. So, when people are speaking, what is going on inside the heads of the listeners? What is being done in the gap between the 125 wpm and the 400-500 wpm capacity? Here is where the listener goes astray. Our minds take off ahead of the speaker and we miss the actual messages being transmitted. The listener may take off on another trip and reflect on what happened last night, a person in the room, some object other than the speaker, or some other unrelated matter, and by becoming involved with the other matter, may lose contact and focus with the speaker.

Certain words or habits the speaker uses may send the listener to another context. A friend of mine reported that every time he tried to listen to a woman with a Southern accent he would get lost in imagining a scenario much like *Gone With The Wind.* Another testified that whenever he tried to listen to a person with a certain voice quality he would think of his father, immediately shut out the speaker, and lose anything that he said. A remedy to these kinds of problems (and there are many) is to develop skill in controlling our attention processes, in listening for marginal messages that support or contradict the central message, and in separating out our predispositions from what is happening here and now.

Some people have trouble listening because immediately on hearing a position by another person they begin to frame an answer. The listener thus becomes so preoccupied with formulating an answer or an intervention that he or she does not hear the full message of the speaker.

The poor listener is usually inattentive, self-centered, defensive, uncaring, impatient, quick to make judgments, interrupts others frequently, easily distracted, disinterested, apathetic, insensitive, overly emotional, and unresponsive. The bad listener tunes out if the subject does not interest him or her and if the delivery is poor, enters into argument with the speaker, listens for facts only and ignores the other information being presented, takes numerous notes without thinking through what is being said, fakes attention, reacts quickly to emotional words, and daydreams while others are talking.

Many other factors are involved in the listening process. You should make some effort to diagnose your own listening skills and needs and embark on a training program that will improve your own listening.

The mediator must be highly efficient in applying all the listening skills and the purposes they serve. This involves nonverbal as well as verbal cues. The nonverbal cues that the clients reveal are important information from which the mediator makes decisions about which procedures to introduce. Tone of voice, physical positions, use of body action, directness of speaking, and language patterns are all important information sources that the mediator must be able to understand. Double messages must be identified quickly. Subtle, almost-hidden qualifiers in language must be quickly perceived. As I have noted above, the processes of listening are directly related to skills in attention and the ability to direct and control our perception processes.

Feedback

The process of using feedback to check the accurate receipt of a message is also important to the mediator. Not all responses are feedback, and the mediator must be able to recognize the difference (Keltner, 1986). Feedback allows the mediator to remind the parties of what has been said, to summarize, to check the accuracy of perceptions, to correct miscommunications or misperceptions, and to keep the communication lines open between all those involved in the interaction. Much of what people call *feedback* is evaluative or judgmental. The best feedback for mediators is *message feedback*, in which the sole purpose is to inform the speaker of what message was received through repetition, paraphrase, or summary.

In a mediation session involving a dispute between an employee and his supervisor arising out a the employee's suspension for being drunk at a local bar while off duty, the grievant stated, "I do my job well while on duty and what I do off the job has nothing to do with my ability to do this job." The mediator replied, "You're saying that as long as you do your job well, what you do off the job is irrelevant?"

A single father and his teenage son were in dispute about the son's recent citation for violating a city curfew. In the mediation session the son said, "That curfew is nuts. Everybody knows that kids my age are not going to close up that early. I don't intend to follow any stupid curfew when I don't have classes the next day." The mediator replied, "I heard you say that you don't like the curfew because its too early and that you will not respect it, particularly if it is on a nonschool night."

Interrogation and the Use of Questions

Properly used questions can be an effective tool in facilitating the mediation process. Poorly used, they can stifle the process and its participants.

The mediator must be skilled in the use of many types of questions: directive, nondirective, and others. Skill in the use and misuse of the rhetorical question (questions that have the answer imbedded such as "You don't like Jim do you?") is also essential. The use of questions for gathering facts and opinions is an important tool.

Effective questioning or interrogation has several characteristics:

1. The language of the question is shared, that is, the question is stated so that the respondent can understand it.
2. The language of the question is economical. Excessive or long questions are very difficult to answer and tend to confuse rather than clarify.
3. The language of the question is suited to the method and the nature of the information that is being sought. When a specific answer is desired the question should be specific. When the respondent is free to select the level of response the question can be more general in nature.
4. The question is relevant to the context of the discussion and to the frame of reference of the respondent. That is, it is related to what is being discussed and fits into what the respondent is doing.
5. The question requires a response. Often we become caught up in a pattern of asking questions that are actually answers and no new information emerges. Any single question may fit several purposes.

There are several types of questions available to the mediator. Each type has advantages and disadvantages.

Open-Ended Questions

These are not answerable with a "yes" or "no." They may require more than a few words for response, and they invite sometimes unrushed and sometimes rambling answers. There is some evidence that suggests that they get to the heart of the matter faster in the long run than closed or directive questions. They leave the respondent free to select the basis of an answer from his or her own alternatives. For example, open-ended questions include "How can we deal with our differences?" "What can I do to help you?" "How do you feel?" and "What's been happening?"

Closed or Directive Questions

These questions seek brief answers, pinpoint specific data, do not require lengthy responses, tend to limit the flexibility and scope of the respondent's answers, and tend to force the respondent to focus on a particular matter or issue. There are several types of closed questions:

Either-or: Gives two alternatives from which the respondent selects one. The purpose is to reduce the alternatives to two and ask the respondent to select one of them. It makes it difficult for the respondent to respond when the choice is neither of the alternatives in the question. These questions eliminate many creative options that may emerge from the dialogue. They often create hostility in the respondent because they limit the possibilities. Examples include: "Which of these did you think happened, A or B?" "Did you mean that she should shut up?" "Do you approve or disapprove of her proposal?" "Do you like the red one or the blue one?" "Which of these do you like best, the red or the blue?"

Yes-No: Similar to the "either-or" in that there are usually only two answers (sometimes a third possibility occurs as a "don't know" or another alternative emerges). However, the basic nature of the question is to get an affirmation or denial. This type is basically different from the "either-or" because the alternatives are only "yes" or "no," affirm or deny, accept or reject, and so on. This form of question is used in many courtroom litigations by the interrogating attorneys. They frequently frustrate the respondent and trigger anger and/or withdrawal. Examples include: "Do you accept this proposal?" "Did you steal the car?" "Were you present when the machine broke down?"

Rhetorical or Leading Questions

These are often called "loaded" questions. The answer is within the question itself. These questions make it easier and more tempting for the respondent to give the answer desired by the questioner, and they reveal the bias of the questioner. They carry messages about what the interrogator desires, values, or seeks. They are used to persuade and amplify the point of view of the questioner. These are manipulative little beasts because they often catch us unaware of their subtle control power. Like the "either-or" questions they can often be answered with a "yes" or "no," but unlike the "either-or" type they do not use a dichotomy of choices because they suggest the desired answer. Really only one choice is given to be affirmed or denied.

Examples include: "You didn't like that incomplete answer, did you?" "Sam interrupted you, didn't he?" "You dislike this process, don't you?" "You dislike that boring bartender, don't you?" "You like challenging compute work, don't you?" "Wouldn't you rather have a reliable Honda?" "How do you feel about that nutty teacher?" "Would you say you were a liberal or a crazy radical?"

The mediator should avoid these kinds of questions when they show bias or partiality.

Command Questions

These questions focus the attention of the respondent on predetermined contexts, sources, or subjects. They are often orders or commands sheathed in an interrogative holder. They can have an open quality when they bring the respondent to follow a given direction of content. They can be "yes-no" when the reply can satisfy the intent of the question. They can also be rhetorical in nature.

A question such as "Will you tell me about your mother?" can be "yes-no" or "open" in its consequences. That is, the respondent can say "no" and that is the end of the response or he or she can begin a response talking about Mother. Other examples include: "Will you talk about your feelings for Mary?" "Are you ready to agree to the proposal now?" "Are there things you can do to help the children?" "Will you give me a quarter?" "You said you would talk about your marriage situation, will you do that now?"

"Why" questions

These questions are often very distracting and can push people away from dealing with the present issues. The "why" question assumes that the cause of what is happening or has happened is of prime importance, and it seeks to engage the respondent in an examination of those causal factors. Their usefulness is limited in the mediation situation (and others) because they usually distract attention away from the problems and issues being considered in the "here and now." The parties do not come together to identify causes but to find solutions to problems that are facing them in the present. Whatever the cause of the current circumstances things have to change and dwelling on the alleged "causes" that emanate from the "why" questions tends to distract from that purpose. Examples include: "Why did you burn the toast?" "Why are the children unhappy?" "Why did you shut the door in my face?"

This is not to say that such questions are of no value at all because they can be helpful in dealing with hidden issues that have bearing on the present, and they may help to discover conditions that may need to be changed. However, the use of "why" questions in stress situations tends to cause the respondent to become defensive and to thereby block effective information gathering. Such questions create an atmosphere of attack. They usually sound like the interrogator is putting the respondent through an inquisition and this results in defensive responses.

Examples include: "Why do you dislike men?" (also a rhetorical question in certain contexts) "Why have you treated your wife that way?" "Why don't you speak up?" "Why did you hit your husband?" and "Why were you late today?"

"What" Questions

These questions are more reliable than "why" questions for getting at problems and the "here and now" issues in a dispute. The nature of the "what" question is to get a focus on what is currently happening, to prevent flight into factors that may not be present in the immediate setting, and to avoid making a person feel that he or she has to defend his or her behavior.

For example, "What are you saying with your silence, Jim?" may bring more information than "Why are you silent, Jim?" "What are you saying to Carol by your shouting?" may get more vital information than "Why are you shouting?"

Some Strategies of Questioning (Conditions for Use)

- Closed questions are usually best used after the parties have become familiar with the situation, the method, and the mediator. If used too early they will limit the amount of information brought to the table.

- Open questions are useful in the early stages of the process. They encourage the respondent to talk and share. They also allow for the emergence of trust between the respondent and the questioner. However, sometimes open questions can be so open that the respondent does not deal with the issues at hand.

- Too many questions at once or a lot of questions crammed into one sentence will tend to confuse the respondent.
- Use simple and clear language that is understood by the respondent.
- During the fact-finding stage of mediation, more closed and either-or questions may be useful.
- In formulating questions several things should be considered: language level and character, relevance, level of information desired, complexity, and ability of the respondent to answer the questions.
- Avoid trying to pinpoint a crime or wring out a confession or force a negative response that the respondent obviously does not want to reveal. Let the matter emerge as a result of the dialogue and the trust that develops.

Alternative to Questions

Although questions are very important there is another way to stimulate the sharing of information: Use information statements that reflect what the interrogator is seeking. Instead of asking a question I often suggest something I would like to know or share something I have observed or experienced. This puts me in a better position than if I were the inquisitor in a trial. It does not make the respondents feel that they are being "grilled." It also gives the respondent more freedom to provide the information desired. Instead of asking, "What brought you to mediation?", try saying, "I would like to know what brought you to mediation." Instead of asking, "Do you approve of the actions of your spouse?", try saying, "I wonder if you approve of the actions of your spouse." Some other examples are: "I am concerned with what is causing you to shout," "You've been silent a long time and I wonder what it means," "I think there may be more to your problem than you have told us."

Timing

Good mediators have a keen sense of timing. "Timing refers to the mediator's ability to discriminate between disputants' constructive and destructive communication patterns. The failure to either interrupt destructive conflict cycles or to reinforce productive patterns deprives disputants of the guidance they need to develop trust and mutuality" (Donohue, 1989, p. 325).

The skilled mediator understands when it is appropriate to make suggestions and when it is not. He or she has a sense of when the parties should be pushed and when they should be allowed to go at their own speed. Good mediators are able to sense when the parties are ready to find a solution or make a decision and when they are not. They are able to assess the outside pressures that are impinging on the decision making of the parties and to intervene when they will most likely get productive responses.

Much of this timing comes from the ability of the mediator to become empathetic with the parties. Some mediators claim that this tool is one of the most important. It comes mainly from experience. Early in my mediator training I was being tutored by a skilled fellow who had mediated thousands of cases. He would seem to be very removed from a situation at times, but suddenly he would make a suggestion, call a caucus, or tell a story, and inevitably his intervention changed the course of the events and moved the parties toward resolution.

Speaking and Presentational Skills

The ability of the mediator to converse informally with the parties in a clear, friendly, and useful fashion is also important. The mediator must be able to get the attention of his clients. The messages must be clear, concise, and stated in a language that is understood. The mediator must also be direct and maintain close eye contact. Finally, the mediator must keep his or her ideas well organized and clearly related to what is actually taking place in the interaction.

Message Carrying

One of the unique functions of a mediator is that of carrying messages from one party to another. This requires careful work. Some messages must be transferred as precisely as possible with no loss or variation in the information. Others must be attenuated or modified in order not to upset the delicate relationships that the mediator is trying to develop or enhance.

> *One time during a caucus, a union representative said to me, "Tell that S.O.B. we'll die in hell before we accept that damned stupid, union busting, stinking proposal." When I met with the company shortly thereafter to report the union position my comment was, "The union rejected your proposal with some vigor and strong feeling."*

Still other messages are to be held in abeyance until the time when they can be conveyed with maximum value and impact. Many times a proposal for a settlement may not be accepted until the pressures are right (timing is important here). In labor-management negotiations, settlement proposals, known in advance by the proposer, are often held until a deadline approaches or pressures increase. A mediator must be able to sense the status of each party and the possible acceptability of a proposal and guide the parties in making their proposals at appropriate times (that is, at a time when they are most likely to be accepted or when they need to be tested). All of this requires that the mediator have a deep sense of the forces that are present.

The mediator's communication style will also affect message carrying. If the mediator tends to deliver all messages in a serious and careful manner, they will be interpreted differently than if they are delivered in a half-jovial manner, suggesting that they might be meaningless. The nonverbal factors of message carrying are important matters to control.

By carrying messages between the parties, the mediator can control the flow of certain kinds of information (Keltner, 1965). Moore suggests that the mediator controls what is communicated, how the message is communicated, by whom it is communicated, to whom it is delivered, when it is delivered, and where it is delivered (Moore, 1986, p. 144).

Nonverbal Communication

All of the nonverbal matters apply in the mediation session. The control of personal and physical space, seating arrangements, and other such elements are important. The ability to perceive the use of gestures and physical behaviors is a vital function of the mediator's communication. The significance of the use of objects such as pencils, glasses, documents, and so on should not be overlooked. Clothing is of great importance in understanding the clients and their attitudes, as well as in reflecting the nature of the mediator (Moore, 1986).

> *The late Cyrus Ching, the first director of the Federal Mediation and Conciliation Service, used to use the deliberate filling and lighting of his pipe as a significant nonverbal tool to calm the parties and set of tone of deliberation.*

Persuasion

Mediators use all the tools of persuasion at one time or another. If the parties are to reach a settlement they must change from the rigid positions that keep them apart at the beginning. This means that some persuasive experiences must take place. The mediator must facilitate the parties in moving closer together through the various means of persuasion. Logical and emotional factors are used in the attempt to reconcile the differences. We have already talked about the credibility of the mediator, which is one of the most persuasive influences. Although the parties must make the final decision themselves, the mediator's persuasion is directed at *changing the conditions so that such decision making can take place.* This does not commit the mediator to a particular position or settlement in favor of one client over the other. Mediators must be very careful not to allow themselves to move in this direction. At the same time, they may add considerable persuasive pressure on one or both clients to move more closely together on a given issue. It is in this context of change that the persuasion of the mediator plays its most significant part.

The persuasion process involves emotional elements that stir up feelings, logical elements that involve facts and reasoning, and credibility factors that bring acceptance and trust. The mediator must be skilled in all these elements. There is a time when the logical aspects are important and effective in bringing change. There are also times when no amount of logic will move a person and some emotion must be aroused. The credibility of the mediator is always a powerful tool of persuasion.

During a landlord-renter dispute, the parties were unable to even explore possible choices because of mutual distrust. Finally, after a long caucus with the tenant, the mediator caucused with the landlord and told her that in her opinion the renter was really trying to do the "right thing" and did not want to violate the relationship or the contract. As a result of the mediator's comments, the landlord listened to the proposal and with some modifications, accepted by the renter, they agreed to a new arrangement.

Communication Skills Check

Check yourself on the communication skills required of a good mediator.

Skill	Low	Medium	High
Credibility	——	——	——
Empathy	——	——	——
Listening	——	——	——
Feedback	——	——	——
Interrogation	——	——	——
Alternative methods	——	——	——
Timing	——	——	——
Speaking	——	——	——
Message carrying	——	——	——
Nonverbal	——	——	——
Persuasion	——	——	——

PHASES IN THE MEDIATION PROCESS

There appear to be differences in the conception of the stages through which mediation progresses. My experience as a mediator and as a student of the process suggests several stages. It is important to remember that, for the most part, although these stages appear to be successive to each other they may not necessarily follow the exact order in which they are presented here. In fact, the process is more cyclical than linear.

Phase 1: Setting the Stage

The time before mediation sessions begin is very important. It is during this period that the basic relationship between the mediator and the clients is established. The first task of the mediator is to develop credibility. Regardless of how he or she gets into the dispute, the mediator must make contact with each of the parties, help them understand what the mediation process can and cannot do, assure them of the protection of their own decision making, assure them of the confidentiality of the process, assure them of his or her background and ability to help them in the situation, and listen to their descriptions of the situation. A time and place for an initial meeting must be decided and suggestions made to the clients about what materials may be needed for that meeting and who is to attend. The clients should understand fully the fee basis under which the mediator is to work. Also, an agenda for the first meeting should be cleared with both parties. It is common, in non-labor-management situations for the agenda to include such things as working out an agreement to mediate, reviewing the fee basis of the mediation, and beginning the review of the general nature of the dispute. (In the labor-management situation the parties are usually familiar with the mediator or with the process and are less anxious about entering into the process than in the other contexts.)

As the mediator takes care of these preliminary matters, either by telephone or face-to-face with the parties, it can be useful to get some idea of how the clients came to mediation, what feelings they may have about the process, and what specific events or situations brought the matter to this point. The mediator should avoid getting into a discussion of any of the issues or the problems. The main thrust of this preliminary phase is to establish a rapport with the clients and to begin to develop their trust in the mediator. The clients should emerge from this phase ready to meet and to get started on the "hard stuff" of negotiating with the help of the mediator.

Phase 2: Opening and Development

Phase 2 begins with the first formal mediation session. At the very outset of this meeting the unique nature of the process of mediation must be explored again so that the clients understand they are the parties responsible for working out the settlement. The ground rules for the process also need to be set and agreed on. Many mediators have a set of ground rules ready that they share with their clients, asking them to agree to follow them or to suggest some of their own. Such things as being open with the mediator and with each other, giving each other a chance to be heard, or trying to restrain emotional tirades are all things that are often included in such ground rules. In some instances these rules are written up and all parties sign them (see the example in the Appendix).

During this opening session the parties should be made comfortable, a positive atmosphere should be created, tensions should be relieved as much as possible, and the general nature of the dispute should be reviewed by the mediator. There should be a review by others who have been a party to the dispute up to this point and a discussion of some of the expectations of the parties regarding how they would like to see the situation resolved. After the opening explanations and ground rules, the mediator encourages both of the parties to participate fully.

Trust building is a very important part of this phase. During all the interactions the mediator should attempt to generate increasing trust and to establish the necessary credibility with which to operate during the remainder of the process. Encouraging the clients to ask questions about the process and the mediator is one way of developing this phase. Answering the questions with forthright and clear statements is another way of building good will and trust into the relationship.

In this phase it is valuable for the mediator to help the parties explore alternatives to the mediation and to the negotiation process that is going on. Both parties need to be aware of what alternatives they have to what may emerge in the mediation. Ury and others have identified this as the BATNA or "Best Alternative to a Negotiated Agreement" (see Chapter 4).

Phase 3: Exploration of the Issues: Isolation of Basic Interests, Needs, and Positions

During this phase the parties tell their story and, with the mediator's guidance, define the issues and determine their relative value or importance. The mediator may also discourage the introduction of new issues once the basic set has been determined. Here is where the mediator's skill in questioning and empathy is needed to discover the hidden assumptions, feelings, expectations, and perceptions of each party.

This is the primary data collection stage of the process. Sometimes this process begins before the first joint meeting of the parties. Some mediators begin to collect key data at the first contact with the parties. Even so, that data needs to be reviewed, updated, and confirmed at the contact level with the clients.

During this phase the mediator helps the clients understand where areas of agreement and differences actually exist. It is here that the mediator can discover the nature of the underlying interests of the parties, the intensity of the differences, their immediacy, how long they have existed, and how rigid the clients are with regard to their particular positions. The principal tools the mediator uses for this are interrogation and discussion. Often a private caucus may be useful when feelings seem to block the full sharing of information.

A very important part of this phase for the mediator is to help the parties assess the priority and significance of the issues and to develop an *issue agenda*. An issue agenda is a list of those issues that separate the parties, and it often may also include priorities. For example, an issue agenda in a dispute over a property line might include such items as the accuracy of the original line, the propriety of subsequent changes, the costs of adjustments, the positions of each party to the dispute, and so on. Frequently the mediator must help the parties see the difference between their interests, their positions, and their solutions to the problem(s).

It is during this phase that the mediator begins to see what strategy might be employed in working with the clients and what personal and interpersonal issues are going to be involved in the interaction. It is also during this period that the mediator begins to discover what is behind the positions held by the parties. The relation of the needs and interests of the parties to their positions is important information and needs to be discovered at this stage.

It is here that the session should be turned over to the clients, and they should be encouraged to state their positions, interests, and needs openly. The mediator must listen carefully throughout and, when necessary, facilitate their communication with each other. Several processes are particularly useful at this stage:

—*Message feedback* is very useful as in, "What I heard you say was . . ."

—*Summarizing* involves a review of the matters expressed as in, "Up to now we've heard the basic position of each of you as . . . and . . ."

—*Elaboration* takes place when the mediator explores an idea at greater depth than was originally discussed. He or she might say, "You mentioned the education of the children. Are you including in that such things as out of school activities, church activities, and the like?"

—*Organizing* takes place when the mediator gathers a number of ideas expressed at random and puts them in some order. This goes beyond message feedback because it assembles the ideas in an order that did not previously exist, as when a mediator has listened to a recital of events that was disconnected and disorganized and intervenes with, "Let's see, first . . . , then second . . . , and finally . . ."

—*Partitioning* the ideas is more complex. Here the mediator takes a theme or an issue and helps the parties break it down into its subparts. For example, a union demands an increase in economic benefits as a key part of a new contract. The mediator then helps them identify these benefits in terms of wages, health and welfare, retirement, and so on.

—*Reframing* an issue is a very important method for the mediator. Watzlawick, Weaklan, and Fisch (1974) wrote that "To reframe . . . means to change the conceptual and/or emotional setting or viewpoint in relation to which a situation is experienced and to place it in another frame which fits the 'facts' of the same concrete situation equally well or even better, and thereby change its entire meaning." (p. 95). In mediation the reframing process includes rephrasing an issue so that is more neutral. For example, one professor demands that her class be given top priority in a curriculum design and another demands the same position. The mediator reframes the issue as "What is the best position for each of these two courses?" Reframing may also involve the identification of the interests of the parties. For example, the concern of one professor is that the subject matter of the course, no matter who teaches it, be a part of the program. The other really wants her work on the subject to be recognized. By reframing the mediator may help the parties realize some commonalty. Positions should be reframed into interests. When people claim a "right," it can be reframed into a need. "Right" or "wrong" can be reframed into "differences." One of the key reframing skills is to help clients move from a recital of mutual past faults to future action.

Part of the strategy during this phase is to move the parties from their highly adversarial and contentious approach to a more cooperative effort at solving their problems. "Positions" inherently stimulate antagonists. "Interests" and "needs" suggest matters that can be seen as collaborative or cooperative. Setting an issue agenda can assist in this process. Also, reframing the issues into those of a more superordinate or jointly held nature can be very helpful at this phase.

Subsequent to the issue agenda, the mediator can begin a very useful process called *criteria-setting*. The clients, before they begin looking at alternative solutions, are encouraged to set some basic standards or conditions that any solution or alternative must meet. If the mediator can get the parties to think along these terms, the subsequent stages can be bridged much more effectively. These criteria can represent areas of agreement on a general scale that can set some patterns of acceptance by the clients.

Phase 4: Identification of Alternatives

Each party usually comes into mediation with a rigid set of choices or positions as to the settlement options available. It is the collision of these choices/positions and their mutual incompatibility that focuses the dispute. The task of the mediator is to help the parties see that other options are available that need to be explored. This is not easy. It is often only after the clients have struggled without success to get their point of view accepted that they are willing to look at alternatives.

The mediator needs to persuade the parties to commit themselves to consider alternatives. It is often useful to separate the parties and work with them individually to attempt to disengage them from their rigid position and free them for more creative efforts to resolve their differences.

Once the parties are convinced that their old rigid positions are not going to work, it is time for the exploration of alternatives. The mediator may then bring several processes into play. On the assumption that each party has started from an extreme position the mediator may, in private sessions, encourage each party to explore interests that allow for less extreme alternatives on which they would settle. These may be kept under cover or confidential by the mediator until there is some evidence that the two parties are coming close together around these new options. Further, the mediator seeks more than one option and encourages the parties to seek as many different alternatives as they can find.

Often, when one client is hesitant about proposing an option to the other, because it might be interpreted as a weakness, the mediator can make the proposal as if it were his or her idea. This, in a way, protects the client who proposed it from being vulnerable.

> *Tom, a neighbor involved in a dispute with Bill over parking, told the mediator during a caucus that "If that old bastard would just apologize and treat us like neighbors instead of enemies we'd let him park his truck on our side of the back fence." The mediator asked Tom if he would be willing to share this with Bill. Tom refused, but told the mediator to "Go ahead . . . you tell 'im. He won't do anything anyway." The mediator met with Bill privately and after a while said to him, "Y'know, Bill, I think Tom and his family would really like to be more neighborly with you." Bill replied, "Ugh, taint hard," to which the mediator replied, "Well if they would let you park on their side of the fence could you be more neighborly?" Bill grunted, "Ats possible." (It was later that the mediator helped Bill decide on what acts constituted "neighborly" acts.)*

During the search for alternatives the mediator can be helpful by suggesting options that the parties have not considered. Using "brainstorming" either in private caucus or with the parties together is another way of getting new ideas to the floor.

The outcome of this phase of the process is the accumulation of a number of possible solutions to the problem(s) identified by the issues. Here, also, the mediator can discover some of the "trades" that the parties are willing to make in order to settle the dispute and that lead to the next phase.

As much as possible, it is useful for the mediator to help the parties explore the principles underlying the options. The mediator can encourage the parties by pointing out interests and shared concerns. The more options that emerge the greater the possibility of the clients finding one on which they will agree.

Phase 5: Evaluation, Negotiation, and Bargaining

Once alternatives (options) are available the parties begin to evaluate them and negotiate over their acceptance. If the criteria setting stage in Phase 3 has been successful, there will be a set of standards that can be used to assist the parties in judging the alternatives. As each client assesses the relative value of each alternative, he or she begins to indicate where there may be trade-offs and where their limits are. These processes usually occur simultaneously. Each party judges an alternative in terms of his or her own goals, needs, interests, and concerns as they are reflected in the criteria and then begins to seek acceptance of the alternative that best fits. Here is where a great deal of guidance from the mediator can be effective.

This phase is conducted in both joint and separate sessions with the clients. The mediator must make the decision when to separate the parties and when to work with them together. We say more about this later.

Here is where compromise, cooperation, and other forms of joint decision making become important to the process and where the "trade-offs" are developed that will lead to a settlement. The mediator plays a vital role in setting the stage for this by suggesting how it can be accomplished and by providing tools for the clients to use to communicate with each other without making themselves vulnerable.

Phase 6: Decision Making and Testing

Sooner or later in a successful mediation Phase 5 moves to Phase 6, and the parties begin to make commitments (decisions) in relation to the issues and problems. In some situations, such as labor-management situations, an upcoming deadline may put pressure on the parties to reach decisions. It is often the case that until there is some external deadline pressure of a financial, personal, or procedural nature, the decision making is delayed. Remember, the mediator does not make the decisions but can, at this phase, encourage the decision making by reminding the parties of deadlines, pressures, and so on that would increase the incentive to get a decision in the situation. At other times the parties may move smoothly into the decision making from their evaluation of the alternatives.

Often the mediator first directs the decision making toward the easier issues so that a pattern of agreement can emerge. This usually encourages the clients to move ahead and tackle the more difficult problems. At this stage the parties may engage in "trading" with each other over the terms of a settlement—"I'll give you X if you'll give me Y."

One of the important functions a mediator can perform at this stage is "reality testing," that is, encouraging the parties to explore the consequences of the available decisions. Sometimes this is part of the evaluation. At other times it is a kind of final stage in the process of affirming that a decision is viable and functional.

Phase 7: Finalizing the Process

When an agreement is reached the mediator makes a clear record of it and reviews it with both parties. Usually this is done by an item-by-item review of the issue and the decision that has been reached. This is done in face-to-face sessions.

A written record is made of the agreement and both parties sign this record. It is not necessary that the mediator be a signatory to the agreement unless a witness is required, as in the case of a divorce and/or custody settlement. The agreements that have the greatest value clarify what is to be done or exchanged, cover all the issues, and hold firm, thereby terminating the dispute. Less valuable agreements are those that are primarily procedural, do not include a solution of all the issues, are temporary or contingent, and do not include sufficient detail to allow them to work.

CHECK YOUR PHASES

For Each Phase Identify What Was Accomplished

Setting the Stage
___ Contact with the parties
___ Established personal credibility
___ Set time and place for initial meeting
___ Set agenda for first meeting
___ Got background of the dispute

Opening and Development
___ Reviewed processes
___ Set ground rules
___ Created comfortable setting
___ Set expectations of outcome
___ Built trust
___ Reviewed alternatives to mediation

Exploration of Issues, Interests, and Positions
___ Parties told their story
___ Issues were defined
___ Issue values determined
___ Issue agenda developed
___ Positions clarified
___ Interests explored
___ Areas of agreement determined
___ Moved parties to more cooperation
___ Set criteria for possible solutions

Identification of Alternatives
___ Reviewed alternatives available
___ Created new options via brainstorming, etc.
___ Explored interests of parties in relation to alternatives

(continued)

Evaluation, Negotiation, and Bargaining

___ Tested and evaluated alternatives
___ Explored limits of each side
___ Worked on cooperative solutions

Decision Making and Testing

___ Explored trade-offs and compromises
___ Reality tested alternatives
___ Joint decisions emerged
___ Reviewed deadlines
___ Resolved easier issues first
___ Final decision agreed on

Finalizing the Process

___ Decisions on issues reviewed jointly
___ Written record of the agreement signed
___ Post-agreement actions clarified
___ Firmness of the decisions reviewed
___ Client satisfaction explored

Special Tools Used

___ Message feedback
___ Summaries
___ Elaborations
___ Organized ideas
___ Partitioned
___ Reframed concepts, interests, and positions

MEDIATOR BEHAVIOR: STRATEGIES AND TACTICS

It has been thoroughly established that "mediators do different things in different situations to achieve success" (Carnevale, Lim, & McLaughlin, 1989b, p. 213). Successful mediators are able to adapt quickly to the different situations they encounter and to use tactics that are most likely to bring success in the situation. However, tactics that lead to success in one situation may not be useful in another. There is no single combination of skills and tactics that make for effective mediation in all situations, but there are some basic skills that are vital to any mediation situation.

Honeyman (1990) identifies what he calls seven "parameters of mediation behavior."

Investigation. Effectiveness in identifying and seeking out relevant information pertinent to the case . . .

Empathy. Conspicuous awareness and consideration of the needs of others . . .

Inventiveness and Problem Solving. Pursuit of collaborative solutions, and generation of ideas and proposals consistent with case facts and workable for opposing parties . . .

Persuasion and Presentation Skills. Effectiveness of verbal expression, gesture, and "body language" (for example, eye contact) in communicating with the parties . . .

Distraction. Effectiveness at reducing tensions at appropriate times by temporarily diverting parties' attention . . .

Managing the Interaction. Effectiveness in developing strategy, managing the process, coping with conflicts between clients and professional representatives . . .

Substantive Knowledge. Expertise in the issues and type of dispute. (pp. 79-82)

We explore these and other factors in greater detail as we continue with the more specific elements of mediator behavior.

Mediators enter into the process with two interrelated systems of behavior. They have an overall scheme or plan whereby they attempt to bring about a settlement. This is their strategy. They bring this plan together through their use of maneuvers, accommodations, and other techniques that serve the overall objective. These are their tactics. Together these make up the mediator behavior system.

As I have observed and experienced, effective mediators alter their intervention behaviors as the situation changes. These behaviors can all be identified as strategies and/or tactics for bringing about a resolution of the dispute. Carnevale, Conlon, Hanisch, and Harris (1989a) identify four mediator strategies: integrating, pressing, compensating, and inaction. They see *integrating* as involving efforts to find a solution satisfying to both parties. *Pressing* involves attempts to reduce the aspirations of either or both of the parties. *Compensating* involves the mediator providing rewards or positive benefits for compromise or agreement. *Inaction* lets the parties deal with matters by themselves.

The compensation strategy is applicable mainly to international negotiations in which the mediator represents a third country that has resources with which to compensate the disputants should a satisfactory resolution occur.

> *In the Persian Gulf War the USSR attempted to mediate the war between Iraq and the Allied Nations. In that instance, the USSR, because of its proximity to Iraq, had many economic and political benefits it could offer Iraq in the event it accepted the cease fire proposals.*

In other areas of mediation this is not a functional strategy except when praise and approval by the mediator can be considered as compensation by the parties. The mediator has little reward and punishment power other than that which the parties confer (see the section on power). The two significant strategies for mediators in most interpersonal and organizational disputes are the integrate and press strategies. Most mediator strategies fit into either or both of these types. Inaction, at certain times, can be a useful strategy when it comes to the point that the parties must make decisions.

In looking at mediator behaviors we mainly examine the tactics that fit into the larger strategies leading to a settlement of the dispute. As the several phases of the mediation evolve, the mediator is engaged in a number of behaviors (strategies and tactics) that may be useful in a particular phase, or that cut across all phases and affect the total process.

Relationship behaviors are those things the mediator does that are primarily aimed at affecting the relationships among the parties, their constituents, and the mediator (this is similar to the reflexive category of Kressel & Pruitt, 1985). *Process* behaviors are things the mediator does that affect the conduct and management of negotiations and the reaching of decisions. *Substance* behaviors are things the mediator does primarily in relation to the content and substance of the negotiations that aim especially to facilitate the reaching of a settlement.

The three categories—relationship, process, and substance—are not mutually exclusive. Some behaviors that seem to be relationship related may also be closely involved with the substantive aspects. For example, one solid trust-building tactic is to discuss the issues knowingly, a substance-oriented behavior. Covering general and easy issues first involves both process and substance.

Carnevale, Lim, and McLaughlin (1989b) asked 255 professionals in dispute resolution to list and rank 43 different tactics (interventions) used in mediation. Recent studies show there are about 100 behaviors or techniques that mediators apply in the process. These have been variously classified and several taxonomies were developed (Wall & Lynn, 1993, pp. 165-166). I have included and integrated their lists with a collection of my own drawn from reports by labor-management mediators and my own experience as a mediator in other contexts.

The following list of behaviors is useful for identifying and understanding many of the things a mediator does.

Relationship-Oriented Behaviors

Develop rapport with parties
Develop trust between parties
Discuss mutual interests
Establish credibility and gain parties' trust
Express pleasure at progress
Reduce hostility
Help parties save face

Process-Oriented Behaviors

Speak their language
Let them blow off steam
Use humor
Avoid taking sides on issues
Maintain order
Make interventions on procedures
Set caucuses and separate meetings
Keep caucus focused on issues
Keep parties at the table
Cover general issues first
Devise framework for negotiation
Settle simple issues first
Focus negotiations on issues
Simplify agenda
Joint meetings
Press parties hard

Substance-Oriented Behaviors

Form clear goals for mediation
Help prioritize the issues
Move them off position by stressing interests and needs
Identify unrealistic ideas and positions
Change their expectations
Warn of consequences of a decision or action
Test for reality
Give examples
Deal with principles vs. facts
Suggest face-saving proposals
Deal with constituent problems
Take responsibility for concessions
Suggest compromises
Suggest trade-offs among issues
Suggest a settlement
Clarify needs of other party

A number of these are self-descriptive. Others may involve more discussion. I next discuss some of the more complicated behaviors.

RELATIONSHIP BEHAVIORS

Developing Rapport With Parties

A prerequisite for developing trust and empathy with the parties is that the mediator have rapport with them. This requires that the mediator find areas where there may be common experiences or mutual interests, or to encourage the parties to talk about their personal interests as well as professional affiliations. The orientation sessions are important times to accomplish this connection. In the absence of any known common ground, the mediator will need to indicate an interest in what the person is doing, likes, enjoys, and so on. This rapport is a very useful tool in developing empathy so that the mediator can begin to "get behind the eyeballs of the parties." This connection is a vital beginning to the development of credibility and trust. Warning: Don't try to dig more out of the party than he or she wants to share. Being too "pushy" can quickly alienate the parties.

Establishing Credibility and Confidence (Trust)

From the very first contact with the parties and throughout the whole process the mediator must generate confidence and trust in the process as well as in him- or herself. The clients need to feel that they can depend on the behavior and the statements of the mediator to be accurate and truthful, that the mediator is not working contrary to their interests, and that the process will lead them to a solution to the problem(s) they face. There are many ways a mediator can build such trust into the relationships. These include the friendliness of the mediator, acceptance of the clients' ideas and feelings, use of nonaggressive questions, a show of concern for the problems the clients face, and accuracy of message feedback,

There is another aspect of trust that is important in the mediation process and is often overlooked. The mediator needs to facilitate the building of trust *between the clients*. Clients are usually in need of intervention because the trust between them is usually not sufficient to allow them to negotiate alone. The mediator, then, needs to encourage the parties toward behavior that will enhance their mutual trust. A mediator can have clients do something together, have them identify areas of agreement, give them compliments for their work on the relationship, talk openly about their perceptions of each other, reflect their positive perceptions of each other, encourage them to level with each other, help them recognize goals that they share, and discourage them from making negative and disparaging remarks about each other.

Reducing Hostility and Tension

At the outset, the parties usually show some tension and often demonstrate some hostility toward each other. Their ego involvement may be such that every suggestion of points of difference is perceived as a personal attack. This hostility needs to be reduced in order for the parties to negotiate with each other in a more open climate. The mediator may help to reduce these tensions by several means. Hostile outbursts may be allowed to occur within limits. However, they should not be permitted to reach the point at which they may disrupt the development of a basis for progress. The mediator must determine how much of the expression is useful as a cathartic and stop it when it begins to deteriorate.

When there is a strong expression of feelings that seems to be blocking progress the mediator may ask the parties to alter their language to less emotional or judgmental terms. Frequently this can be accomplished by restating or paraphrasing the value-loaded phrases of the clients in a more objective, nonemotional form.

Another way of dealing with this is to separate the parties and deal with them individually. In any event, the mediator must stay calm and poised, listen to the angry individuals, and then ask the others if they also have feelings that need to be expressed. This demonstration of the understanding of the feelings of the clients usually helps to calm them down.

When the hostility and tension go beyond usefulness, the mediator must take positive steps to prevent verbal attacks and escalation of the negative feelings. Here is where the mediator operates in a forceful way to prevent interruptions and to take control of the communication and the sharing of time. The expression of feelings is not to be discouraged, but must be controlled. The parties must be brought *to focus on the problems rather than on each other*.

If it appears that the parties are simply unable to attend to anything but their anger at each other, the mediator should refer them to therapy and terminate the mediation. The mediator should not try to provide personal and interpersonal therapy on their relationship.

In one case a couple involved in a child custody dispute spent all of their mediation time, in spite of the mediator's efforts to direct them in other channels, in violent emotionally loaded verbal attacks on each other through accusations, reference to past mistakes and so on. They could not get down to the functional issues of the custody problem. After trying many approaches without success, the mediator finally terminated the mediation and referred them both to psychotherapy to work on their personal relationship.

When all else fails, the mediator may have to remind the parties of their opening agreements to discuss the problems objectively and without rancor and anger.

Use of Humor

Another valuable tool is the use of humor. Humor is a form of distraction and has many uses in relationships, processes, and substance. When the interaction becomes tense and nonproductive, the effective mediator can divert discussion to irrelevant matters for a while, tell jokes or anecdotes at his or her own expense, or discuss matters not at all related to the dispute but that are funny. Some mediators I know are magnificent storytellers. They have a tale for every condition. They have a valuable tool when used judiciously. It becomes a bore when it is overused. Warning: Making jokes about some critical issues having deep personal significance can be highly dysfunctional. Never use humor in a denigrative way.

Helping the Parties Save Face

We all have perceptions of ourselves and perceptions of how others perceive us. In dispute relationships in which mediation is functional, the parties are quite sensitive about how they are perceived by others. People in a dispute engage in many antagonistic behaviors in an attempt to protect or repair the images others have of them. Fear of losing, of being perceived as weak and vulnerable, and of being undervalued will often intensify and dominate the struggle. Ways to remove and counter these perceptions must be provided by the mediator without becoming a therapist. It is very important that the mediator assist the parties in finding ways to save face in any agreement reached.

The mediator has many opportunities to help the negotiators save face. One way is for the mediator to assume the burden of responsibility for proposing unpalatable compromises or other proposals instead of the side initiating the proposal. This allows the onus attached to such compromises to be attached to the mediator. Another useful way is to, jointly and separately, warn the parties to avoid taking fixed positions from which they may be unable to back out gracefully at a later time. Keeping the proposals tentative until the total agreement is in place is a good way to protect the parties' image of each other.

When parties are unable to achieve all they wanted from the negotiations, the mediator can assure them that they are getting all that the circumstances will allow and that their negotiation was well done. Here the mediator must be careful not to overstate reality. When the parties have made significant progress it is easy to compliment them. When they have not been successful, and the results are not good, the mediator should not suggest something that does not exist. The parties can sense the falsity immediately, and the mediator loses the respect of the parties.

Still another technique is to carry proposals back and forth from the caucuses as "possibilities" and "what ifs," thus not revealing the source of any proposal but allowing it to be attached to the mediator instead of to one of the parties. It is prudent for the mediator to inform the parties that the proposals they make (in caucuses) may be delivered directly in face-to-face joint meetings by the mediator as an agent of the party making the proposal, with the mediator protecting the suggestion by assuming the proposal came from the him or her.

Face saving may also be necessary with the constituents of the persons present at the negotiation. This is particularly true in the labor-management sector where a joint decision that is not popular with the constituents on either or both sides can be facilitated by mediator support. However, that support must be within the context of the mediation and not by direct representation to the constituents themselves. That responsibility lies with the parties at the mediation table.

PROCESS BEHAVIORS

Speaking Their Language

I am often astounded at the degree to which some mediators are able to adopt the language style and idiom of the parties to the dispute.

> *A Maine-born friend of mine could sit in the middle of a dispute involving "down-south" Georgians, and you couldn't tell who was the "Southerner" and who was the "Yankee."*

Such behavior may be taking the matter too far because the credibility of the person soon becomes an issue. At the same time it is useful for the mediator to be familiar with the idiom, the special expressions, the technical language, and the style of the parties. It is not necessary for the mediator to replicate their style of speaking, but it is important to use those significant elements of the language that indicate the mediator knows and understands the parties. This does not mean that the mediator should start using profanity because the parties do. Warning: Don't mimic the language of others.

Letting Them Blow Off Steam (Ventilate)

When there is a considerable amount of feeling present either in a joint session or in a caucus, the mediator should allow the feelings to be expressed. In joint sessions the parties will often attack each other verbally with some vigor. Most mediators allow this to take place for a while in order to get a "feel" for the depth of the emotions and the nature of the relations between the parties. It also sometimes helps to reduce the tension when the parties feel that they can speak openly in the mediation session. Such "steam-letting," however, should not be allowed to go on too long or to the extent that it begins to add fuel to the dispute. It should be cut off by the mediator either by a request or by calling a caucus (see section on reducing hostility and tension).

Maintaining Order

Effective mediators keep the negotiations orderly and functioning at all times. When one party is caucusing, the mediator will often have the other party working on another issue problem. During joint sessions the mediator will serve as the meeting chair and stop interruptions and other disorderly behaviors. When the meetings get out of hand the mediator will adjourn with a clear understanding that another meeting will be scheduled when the parties can agree to an orderly procedure.

Procedural Interventions

Throughout the process the mediator must suggest ways of proceeding in order to deal with the issues and the interactions of the parties. This ranges from suggestions regarding personal behavior, such as "Let's try to avoid making personal attacks on each other," to "While we are in a separate session will you review the areas where you feel we still need to make changes." The mediator may also wish to suggest possible shifts in the issue being discussed. When the parties seem to have exhausted their resources on one issue without resolution, the mediator may put that aside and pick up another that is still pending. In the labor-management setting, often the mediator will have the parties working in small subcommittees on particular issues. *The mediator needs to have a clear understanding of the dynamics of groups and group processes and how to facilitate those processes.*

Setting an Example of Behavior

Throughout the whole process, effective mediators are discrete, friendly, and understanding. They try to set an example of sober, careful, and concerned negotiation. Even when the parties are haranguing each other, the mediator retains a firm, concerned, and objective posture. Such behavior usually causes the parties to begin to temper their aggression.

Reality Testing

In the process of seeking solutions to the problem(s) the mediator needs to encourage the parties to test out the ideas in the conditions under which they would be applied. Any proposal that is made should be explored in terms of its actual consequences for both parties immediately and in the future. Mediator questions can be used, such as "Will it work?", "How do you foresee this happening?", "Can you apply that in your situation?", and "Will this be accepted by your constituents?"

Principles vs. Facts

Principles, opinions, and values are always subject to argument because people differ. Facts are not usually subject to such differences. The skilled mediator will keep the parties from unnecessarily repeating their principles and opinions and will encourage and stimulate the use of facts in developing proposals and areas of agreement. Warning: Keep in mind that even facts can be viewed differently. Thus, when there is a dispute over the nature of the facts, take time to get them clear and to get agreement on what they are. In a dispute over what the facts mean you will need to help the parties recognize that differences of perception do not change the facts.

> *A tree on the boundary line between two neighbors had grown to great height and girth. It shaded one man's garden and the other man's backyard patio. These were the basic facts in the matter and could be confirmed by outside observation. One neighbor, however, viewed the tree as an obstruction to his garden and the other viewed the tree as shade for his patio. How each neighbor viewed the tree was also a matter of fact. However, the nature of their perception was based on value systems and represented opinions that could not be considered as immediately verifiable information. The mediator had to help each neighbor see the tree from the other's point of view before a settlement could be developed.*
>
> *It was a fact that the combined net worth of Susan and Tim amounted to $150,000. Susan, however, insisted that it should be divided evenly (principle). Tim argued that because he had generated most of that worth he should have the greater proportion (principle). The mediator had to help them adjust their principles before the agreement could be reached.*

Dealing with Interests Rather Than Positions

The persons on each side of a dispute have needs and interests that lead to the position taken. The positions are the focus of the dispute and are usually mutually exclusive, however, the needs and interests may be less exclusive. The mediator, as soon as possible, must get the parties to explore their needs and interests alone and together. Positions tend to freeze people into their defense. Once the positions have been stated, it is helpful for the mediator to avoid their repetition and to bring the parties to focus on their needs and interests. If possible, the mediator should attempt to help the parties find common interests and needs. These can then lead to a restructuring or reframing of positions.

The discussion of interests rather than positions is particularly useful when hostility and tension seem to be out of control. The mediator can encourage the restatement of positions into interests as a way of depolarizing the hostility. Usually this is best done in separate sessions with the parties.

> *In a dispute between two faculty members, one took the position that the other was harassing her in her work. In a caucus the mediator asked her to restate the matter in terms of what she felt she needed and wanted out of the situation. After some thought she replied that she was really interested in avoiding any contact with the other person.*

Warning: Sometimes interests and needs are deeply hidden either intentionally or unintentionally. The process of helping to get these out in the open is a delicate one and may require skills bordering on those used by a counselor or therapist. Be careful that they don't lead to therapy sessions.

Joint Meeting Behaviors

The joint meeting is the meeting of the parties with the mediator face-to-face. This occurs at the outset and throughout the process, either continually or at intervals between the private caucuses. The mediator must clearly be in charge of these meetings, including opening the session, closing it, stating the issues to be considered, reviewing the status of the matter at that moment, emphasizing the function of mediation and what it can and cannot do, directing the communication of the clients, encouraging the clients to talk and negotiate with each other, calling the recesses, asking for facts, recommending things for the clients to do together, listening and listening and listening, summarizing, providing support for both parties, and dealing with tensions and anger. All are processes or tools that the skilled mediator uses naturally and spontaneously.

It is also important that the mediator allow relatively equal time for each of the parties to present their ideas. A mediator trainee once became so intrigued with the elaboration of one of the parties that he forgot to give the other party a chance to be heard. At the end of the elaboration he then turned to the other side and declared, "You can surely accept that." Needless to say the response was anything but positive, and questions about the trainee's bias were immediately aired forcefully.

In the early phases of the joint meetings, the mediator may suggest that the parties work on items that appear to be easily resolved so that a pattern of agreement and success can be established.

Separate Session Processes: The Caucus

The caucus is one of the highly valuable tools that the mediator has for helping to defuse feelings, to get at underlying issues and agendas that are not forthcoming at the joint sessions, and to assist in a host of other functions necessary in reaching settlements. Research involving disputes in a neighborhood justice center and a community dispute program show that approximately 35% of mediation time is spent in caucus (Kressel, Pruitt et al., 1989). In labor-management mediation the percentage of time spent in caucus is probably much higher.

Even so, there is still some controversy among divorce and community mediators about its use. Some mediators reject caucusing because they believe that joint problem solving must take place in a face-to-face situation, that the mediator invites suspicion by spending private time with the other side, that mediators will be misled in caucus sessions because the opponent is not there to correct them, and that when one side is not in caucus it may be meeting with supporters and thus gaining greater commitment to its positions (Pruitt, McGillicuddy, Welton, & Fry, 1989). Let's look more closely at the process.

When should these caucuses take place? There is no firm and hard rule. Each mediator works from his or her own perception of the situation and makes a decision in terms of the forces that are present. A number of factors are recognized, however, as bearing on the decision. Welton, Pruitt, McGillicuddy, Ippolito, and Zubek (1992) investigated the role of caucusing in 73 cases in two community mediation centers and found that mediators were more likely to caucus when the parties had a history of escalating disputes and were hostile to each other and failed to engage in problem solving in the joint sessions (p. 303). Walter Maggiolo, a professional labor-management mediator with many years of experience, suggests that a separate session should be requested when the joint conference becomes so heated that the parties cannot deal with each other, when there is no progress and the parties are simply repeating themselves, when one of the parties indicates some desire to compromise but obviously cannot do so without endangering a basic position, when both parties seem inflexible, or when one party seems to be moving prematurely toward a final position that will not lead to settlement (Maggiolo, 1971).

Three types of problems may require a caucus: *relationships* between team members or opponents involving intense emotions, misperceptions, negative behavior, and miscommunications; *procedural* matters of clarifying or modifying the process; and *substantive* issues such as defining and clarifying positions, finding new offers, weighing proposals, testing positions, and so on (Moore, 1986). The *timing* of the caucuses is always a critical matter. Again, the mediator's own perception of the situation is the guiding factor. Actually, caucuses can occur at any time. Some situations are such that the parties demonstrate almost immediately that they are unable to deal with each other across the table, and the only way to get movement is to separate them. In some instances in which the parties are able to negotiate with each other and progress continues in the joint session, there is no reason for the caucus. (My practice, for example, is always to start with the parties face-to-face even though preliminary investigation may show that they may not be able to deal with each other on that level. I still like to see them try. The mere presence of a third party creates a different atmosphere, and they often start to negotiate with each other.) At other times the caucus comes as a natural process once the parties have stated their positions face-to-face, let off a little steam, and demonstrated their "frozen" status.

The mediator moves into the caucus by expressing the desire to talk with each side privately about the matters at hand. If the parties are neophytes the mediator must spend time explaining the function of the caucus, how they will work together, discussing confidentiality, how each party can use the mediator to explore ideas and issues, and answering remaining questions. When the parties seem reassured and ready, the mediator then places them in separate rooms where they cannot hear each other and there is a feeling of privacy. The mediator then shuttles back and forth between them.

Moving back into joint sessions after caucusing should not occur until the mediator has had an opportunity to work with both parties alone. It is important to maintain this balance. It is also important, in the early stages, to spend relatively equal time with each party. Later on, as the confidence in the mediator increases, this may change.

The mediator's role in the caucus is considerably different than in the joint meeting. A high level of trust in the mediator is an important prerequisite for the effective use of the caucus. In the caucus the mediator explores positions in greater depth than is possible in the joint session. Welton et al. (1992) report that "many mediators subtly but persuasively introduce each party's viewpoint into caucus sessions with the other. . . . By this approach, they can clear up misunderstandings between the disputants and help the disputants grasp each others' situation" (p. 314). Here is where needs and interests can be revealed and discussed. Also, in most cases, the mediator in the caucus will deal with the party in a more personal fashion. What is said in the caucus is not necessarily intended for both sides and is therefore less inhibited than what is said in the joint conference. In the caucus the mediator is able to admonish a party without embarrassing it in front of the other. Suggestions may be made with the knowledge that they may be rejected with no embarrassment to the mediator or to the parties. A number of techniques can be used that would not be appropriate in the joint conference. The atmosphere and procedure is more informal. In the separate caucus the mediator plays more the role of a "confidant."

The caucus, *unless there is agreement otherwise,* is a confidential conversation. This confidentiality is important in allowing the parties to be open and candid with the mediator. When the mediator feels that some of what is discussed confidentially may be of use if shared with the other party, then the party initiating the information *must approve* that sharing.

This matter of confidentiality can be a problem if a mediator, in private caucus, becomes aware of information that may involve illegal acts or otherwise questionable behavior (such as child abuse, hidden resources not revealed in joint session that affect the settlement, etc.). Here the confidentiality of mediation comes under heavy stress. Should the mediator reveal this information to the other side, or to law enforcement agencies?

My position is that the mediator has a responsibility for maintaining confidential information to the same degree as do lawyers with their clients; ministers and priests with their confessors; and counselors, psychiatrists, and physicians with their patients. The essential confidentiality of the process was fought for with great effort in the labor-management field over the years when government officials attempted to gain information about the issues and processes of negotiations for the purposes of suits or other adversarial functions. Federal mediators are highly protected by their own legal counsel and by the traditions of many years. The same is true of state personnel. In recent years an issue has been raised involving such protection in relation to mediation and spouse-child abuse and other forms of illegal abuse (Lemmon, 1990).

By separating the parties in caucuses the mediator, for a while, becomes the main channel of information between the parties. In that capacity communication between the parties may be controlled in order to suppress some information, initiate other kinds, control some of the negotiating power of the parties with each other, test the acceptability of ideas by assuming authorship of proposals, and, in general, facilitate message giving and receiving both qualitatively and quantitatively.

In that this process puts a great deal of power into the hands of the mediator, it raises a critical ethical issue. This power can be misused against the interests of either or both of the parties. This, again, reinforces the extreme importance of the special training and screening of mediators and the development of high ethical standards of performance. As we all know, the skilled communicator has more power than the unskilled one. The communicator who controls the channels of communication is capable of exerting a great deal of influence over the behavior of the receivers and senders. We deal with these issues constantly in all phases of the communication discipline (Johannesen, 1983). The ethical considerations of the process must be examined carefully by each mediator and by the profession when setting up its training and qualification procedures.

The value of the caucuses to the mediation process is determined by the conditions under which they were called. Among those useful outcomes and procedures are the following:

The mediator can

- share ideas about the situation with the parties alone.
- make alternative solution suggestions with respect to the single party's position that would not be possible in the joint session.
- encourage the party to explore the "what ifs" of the situation with greater depth and candor.
- make appeals to the single party to adopt more realistic and/or superordinate goals.
- within the caucus, discover the limits of each party's position and the needs and interests that underlie it.

- test out proposals that may come from the other side, but that would not be accepted if they were recognized as such.
- provide communication between the parties that focuses on substantial aspects of the negotiation and block out emotional material that is loaded into the messages.
- discover confidential information that does not come forth in the joint session.
- break a tense situation in the joint session that may lead to escalation rather than resolution of the dispute.
- encourage the exploration of other positions that might be useful for raising doubts.
- establish credibility acceptance.
- assess the real possibilities of finding a settlement to the dispute.

The party can

- be helped to understand the process, and the mediator can be provided an opportunity to make suggestions on how to conduct the negotiations in an orderly way.
- be prevented from making a premature concession in a joint session that would eventually destroy an agreement or that would be accepted later but not at the present time.
- express feelings and thoughts it was unable to express in the face-to-face joint session.
- be helped to examine its position in light of the goals and the possibility of reaching a settlement.

The research shows that a variety of similarly positive results emerge from the caucus: problem solving is more likely to occur in caucus than in joint sessions; more information about feelings, values and goals emerge; mediators are more likely to get the parties to generate new ideas; mediators themselves generate more ideas for solutions than in joint sessions; tension is reduced; and it is easier for mediators to persuade the parties to take responsibility for solving their problem. Additionally, in the caucus mediators are more likely to talk positively about the counterpart, argue the other party's position, and explain the interests and needs of the other party. Mediators are also more likely to help the parties by using restatement and to critique the proposals made by the party (Pruitt, McGillicuddy, et al., 1989).

Consistent with our discussion of the ethics of the mediator's behavior in the caucus sessions, there are several "don'ts" for the mediator during the caucus:

DON'T
- denigrate the other side in any way.
- reveal any information that the party does not want revealed.
- pass on false information from or about the other side or from any other alleged source.
- discourage the party in caucus from working toward settlement.
- try to maintain the formality or impersonal attitude that you may have used in the joint session.
- try to force the parties to any position that they clearly and unequivocally oppose.
- assume all that you hear in the caucus is selfless and factual unless the contrary is confirmed by the other party.

When it appears that the parties are close to agreement the mediator should bring them together and encourage them to talk over their areas of agreement and to work out the details. In this final joint session the mediator should summarize the areas of agreement and get the parties to write out and sign a memorandum of agreement.

Session Lengths: Delay and Termination

Tales of round-the-clock negotiation abound in the labor-management field of mediation. When this takes place there is usually some clearly significant deadline facing the parties: the impending expiration of an already existing contract; a financial or professional cut-off-point; an impending strike; and so on. In the presence of such deadlines, which may have negative consequences to one or both of the parties, there is a strong motivation to stay with the problems and try to reach a settlement before the impending "catastrophe" occurs.

But in any field of dispute, the mediator often has to confront the reality that the parties are simply not ready to settle, and no matter how long they are held in session the effort will be fruitless. A basic principle in most mediation sessions in any arena is that when the parties stop making progress it is time to stop, take stock, and if there seems no inclination to go further, to adjourn.

In divorce, family, and neighborhood disputes this can be very important. After a mediator has worked with the parties and the progress seems to be stopped, it is important that the mediation be halted and the parties confronted with their failure to find a solution. The mediator may then either ask them to convene at a later time, allow them to think about it a while, or simply report that nothing can be done and close the negotiations. Sometimes this latter action will startle and shake the parties to a realization that they must make added efforts to reach settlement.

> *After weeks of negotiation, the parties had agreed on all items to settle the dispute. They froze over who would sign the agreement first. The mediator struggled with them for several hours and finally called them together and announced that an agreement had been reached but was being blocked by their inability to resolve an immaterial difference and that he could do no more. He then left. The parties stared at each other a while, then one of them said, "Is he coming back?" Another said, "I guess not." Then another exclaimed heatedly, "Well, let's settle this damn thing, give me that pen!"*

At other times, if they are not really willing to settle, the parties will simply move away from mediation and resort to the more restrictive forms of intervention such as arbitration or the courts. In many court-mandated divorce and child custody mediations the amount of paid time for mediation is limited to 3 or 4 hours. After that, if there is no settlement, the parties must pay the fee themselves. This time limit tends to encourage settlement.

Sometimes the mediator is aware that there may be ideas for a settlement on the table, but the parties simply are not ready to examine them yet. In this case the mediator will usually postpone the continuation of the negotiations until such time as one or both of the parties make contact and request further meetings. This kind of delay is often very useful when there are outside influences affecting the decision making of the parties at the bargaining table.

> *The two loving children of a wealthy landowner who had been killed in an auto accident were involved in a heated dispute over the will and its contents. They came to mediation shortly after their father died and were quite unable to talk coherently or reasonably about the property. The mediator, after spending several hours with them, suggested that they lay aside the matter for a few weeks and try again after they had time to grieve. In about a month they called for an appointment saying that they were ready to try again.*

SUBSTANCE-ORIENTED BEHAVIORS

Probing for Causes and Justifications

There is a reason for every position taken by the parties. When the positions are particularly "frozen" the mediator must probe for causes and precipitating events that will help him or her to understand the force and the intensity of the position.

> *A landlord and a renter came to mediation to help settle a dispute over the return of the cleaning deposit. The positions were firm: return the deposit vs. I won't return the deposit. From the beginning of the negotiations the mediator probed for reasons (including interests and needs) underlying these two positions. After several sessions a whole tapestry of irritations, mutual distrust, code violations, and other issues emerged. Both sides had a full agenda of "wrongs." Only when these came out could the mediator be of any substantive assistance in helping them deal with their differences.*

Sometimes the positions are imposed from a constituency that is adamant. The mediator needs to know and understand this. It is very important to understand the power of the constituency on the negotiations. When the positions are "fond hopes" of negotiators representing a constituency, rather than instructed demands or replies, the mediator has a better chance of developing movement.

The president of a faculty senate and the dean of administration asked for mediation help in trying to settle a dispute over faculty class loads. The members of the faculty senate had instructed their president that they must have a reduction in class load to 9 course hours per term. The dean had been instructed by the board of governors that every teacher must teach 12 course hours. Neither the senate nor the board of governors were present for the mediation. The mediator spent some time alone and together with the dean and senate president going over the history of the situation and the reasons for their respective positions. It was out of this information that she was able to begin to make suggestions, raise doubts, and use other strategies that helped bring a resolution.

In a similar situation the faculty had taken a rigid position that if it didn't get its demand it would strike, and the board had taken the position that if the teachers didn't attend classes they would be fired for cause. These rigid positions made the job of the mediator much more difficult than in the other situation.

Raising Doubts

Parties to a dispute bring to the table a kind of rigidity. In terms of force-field psychology, they tend to be locked into their positions as a result of a number of forces pro and con. The mediator needs to facilitate the alteration of these forces so that a shift can take place. A useful way to deal with this is to cause the parties to have doubts about their position. The mediator may pose questions about the efficacy of the position, ask the party to look carefully at the consequences from the other point of view and to examine its position realistically, suggest that there might be better ways to deal with the problem, or in extreme cases, actually point out the weaknesses in the position. This behavior can be influential in relaxing the rigidity of their positions.

In a child custody dispute the mother's position was firm on her having full custody of the children. She had many reasons for this that had some credibility. The father would simply not allow this to happen, wanted full custody, and he had some good reasons as well. In separate caucuses the mediator asked both of them what they thought the children would prefer and whether either of them could adequately perform the emotional and psychological functions of both mother and father. The doubt that this generated about their respective positions was immediately apparent. From this they developed a sharing scheme that would meet the children's wishes more than either of the other alternatives.

Another way of raising doubts is to play the "devil's advocate" with a party in caucus and try to show as many reasons as possible why the position is not a good one. Explain to them that you are going to take this role in order to help clarify the whole situation. If the mediator does a good job, the confidence of the party in its position will be shaken and it will seek another position on which to stand.

Warning: Be careful that in raising doubts you don't suggest to the party that you favor the other side.

Planting "Seeds"

Ideas dropped into the discussion early will often mature later. The mediator needs to be willing to suggest a lot of ideas and then back off and see what happens. Being too aggressive toward ideas of one kind or another may short circuit the reasoning processes of the parties and cause them to back off from what could be a reasonable solution.

In a dispute over a property line each party had surveyor records, deeds, and other supporting documents. Each claimed his survey was right and done by a reputable surveyor. Early in the negotiations the mediator asked if they had considered mutually agreeing on another surveyor and accepting the result. Both parties, at that time, replied that this would not be of any value. The matter was dropped. As time went on and the parties were unable to find areas of agreement they became more frustrated. Finally, one had a "bright idea" of the two of them agreeing on a qualified surveyor and accepting his research. They did it.

Helping Prioritize the Issues

As soon as the parties state the issues the mediator can begin to help them set those issues into some sort of order. Through caucuses and joint meetings the "must" matters and the "less important" matters can begin to emerge. In the caucuses, particularly, it is helpful for the mediator to query the parties as to their "bottom line." Sometimes the disputants have not really prioritized their demands in the hope that they can obtain the whole package. When the mediator encourages them to rank their demands and the issues according to importance it helps them begin to see areas where they may have to change position.

Getting the Goal of Mediation Clarified

Early in the orientation or first phases of the mediation it is necessary for the mediator to help the parties clarify what they can accomplish through the mediation process. It is important that the mediator make clear that the goal of mediation is to get a settlement. The more the parties can become directed toward this goal the greater the possibilities of finding a settlement. Along with getting a settlement, the parties must also be brought to understand that they are free to chose from the alternatives and to work the problem out themselves. These goals are vital to the success of any mediation effort.

Pressing the Parties

There are several ways in which a mediator can put pressure on the parties to work toward a solution(s): keep them in session as long as some progress is being made; accuse them of being unrealistic and of dealing with impossible ideas and proposals; keep repeating some of the goals they are seeking; put them into a caucus with a specific assignment of issues to resolve; and/or get in touch with people who are involved but are not a party to the mediation and who have some influence over the parties.

> *Two attorneys were representing their clients in a difficult negotiation over the termination of a partnership. The attorneys had frozen on the positions they thought their clients wanted. With their permission the mediator got in touch with the clients and persuaded them to change their instructions to their lawyers.*

In the labor-management field I have seen mediators work as a team to keep the pressure on the parties to settle. In one instance the mediators were holding the parties in session all through the night. One mediator would nap on his office couch a few hours while the other mediator worked with the parties. Then they would change places. In this way they kept the heat on the parties, and early one morning a settlement emerged.

Dealing with Principles vs. Facts

In the section above we talked about separating facts from principles, opinions, and so on. Many disputes emerge because the principles on which people base their thoughts and behavior are in opposition.

> *An owner of a considerable acreage of wetlands wanted to drain the wetlands for cultivation. The state law forbid the reduction of wetlands in the state. The owner claimed that as owner of the land he had a right to do with it as he wished. The state argued that the good of the community as a whole, and the protection of the environment, was at stake. In mediating this case the mediator heard each side express intense and strong arguments in favor of their principles. Few facts about the nature of the particular wetlands, their juxtaposition to other land forms, and the nature of the cultivation were presented. Until the mediator began to ask for the facts of the situation there was little progress toward settlement. Investigation of the facts from experts in land use and development changed the nature of the dispute and allowed a compromise to develop.*

Dealing with Constituent Problems

In many dispute situations the negotiators are representatives of a larger constituency to whom they are responsible. This is particularly true in labor-management negotiations, international negotiations, and other forms of intergroup relations. These negotiators have a different perception of the negotiations than persons involved with disputes—divorce, child custody, and other person-to-person disputes—in which they represent themselves. The representatives of the larger constituencies have a much greater grasp of the issues in the dispute, the alternatives available, the forces present, and other factors affecting the search for resolution. This insight often allows the representatives to see solutions jointly that are not recognized by the constituency. It is the responsibility of the representatives to bring the constituents to accept the solutions hacked out in the negotiations.

One of the things a mediator can do, as the resolutions are emerging, is keep the negotiators aware of their selling task to their constituents. In working with labor-management groups, for example, many mediators keep asking whether the constituents will accept a proposal that is being considered. Another thing a mediator often does is suggest ways and means a given resolution can be presented so as to gain its acceptance. Warning: When the mediator does this for one side, he or she must be available to the other side. Avoid becoming involved in the "selling tactic" before the actual resolution has been reached except when the use of such methods is vital to selling the proposal to the representatives.

Authoring Compromises, Trade-offs, and Concessions

Mediators who are actively involved in working with the parties seek alternatives that may facilitate a solution to the problem. One of the significant values of mediation is the ability of the mediator to instill into the negotiations ideas and suggestions that the parties have been unable to generate themselves. Because of the mediator's unbiased position, a number of alternatives can usually be perceived that the parties cannot see. Thus, as the negotiations proceed, the mediator, usually in caucus, may suggest compromises, settlements, trade-offs, and concessions. Each mediator has an individual style for doing this, but the process itself is very important. In making the suggestions the mediator can also indicate that he or she accepts the responsibility for the suggestion, thus relieving the parties from feeling that the other side is trying to gain some advantage by the proposal.

Translating the Other Party's Needs and Interests

One of the common reasons why minor disagreements escalate to more polarized positions is the failure of the parties to grasp where each other actually stands on an issue. A very significant function that a mediator can perform is to review and clarify the interests and position of each side to the other. Again, this is best done in caucus when such clarifications are not forthcoming in the joint sessions.

> *In a dispute over an access to river property the parties had frozen with each side demanding that the other side give in. The owner of the disputed area would not grant an access easement on his property for a road to the other's property. When they came to mediation that is about all they could identify as the basis of the problem. After some discussion in caucus, the mediator discovered that the owner did not want to split his pasture land in half so that the animals would have to be herded through gates to take advantage of the full forage area. The man seeking the easement had purchased land along the river where he wanted to build, but had no access to that land except by river, which was mostly unnavigable. Each had needs that were not expressed. The mediator talked with the owner of the river property about the rancher's needs as he perceived them. Upon hearing his problem the other man immediately suggested that he would build an overpass so that the animals could pass to both sides without obstruction.*

POWER AND THE MEDIATOR

The Mediator's Use of Power

It is a basic principle that a mediator *cannot avoid being involved with power.* A mediator must have power. From the very outset there must be change in the positions and behaviors of the parties before a settlement can occur. This means that some efforts toward change must take place beyond those that have already been exerted by the parties themselves as they attempted to influence each other to move toward their choices. The mediator, by the very nature of the process, must exert some power to bring about change in the outcome of the negotiations.

The problem that faces the mediator, as an impartial intervener, is that the generation and use of power must not violate the basic wishes and goals of the parties nor force them in directions that they do not wish to go. Because of the prestige, credibility, and trust that the effective mediator has at hand, the potential power to influence the parties can be very great. How does the mediator deal with this condition?

It is the function of the mediator to facilitate the parties to reach an agreement *themselves*. What the mediator is doing is actually *empowering* the participants to work out their own destiny together. The power moves of the mediator should be directed toward the *processes* that will allow the parties to resolve their problems and not toward the substantive aspects of the dispute. Thus, the mediator uses power to improve communications between the parties, to encourage looking at other alternatives, to create a setting in which the parties can feel comfortable, to create doubts about current positions so that the parties will become more flexible in seeking alternatives, to encourage fact finding, to restrain emotions that block thinking, and to affect many other process factors that inhibit the process of negotiations. All the tools that the mediator uses exert power directed at facilitation of the decision-making processes of the parties.

When the initial power relations between the parties are symmetrical or equal there is a tendency for them to be more cooperative and to function more effectively with less manipulation of each other (Rubin & Brown, 1975). Moore (1986) points out, however, that the parties with equal power still have influence problems relating to their perceptions of the balance of that power and also relating to a "negative residue of emotions resulting from past exercise of coercive power within the relationship" (p. 279). One of the functions of the mediator within these settings is to facilitate the parties in shifting from dealing with power relations to focusing on mutual needs and cooperative behaviors.

Dealing With Power Imbalance

Many dispute situations arise in which the parties do not have equal power relations. A student tenant faces eviction by the landlord from an apartment for not following legalities about which he is unfamiliar. A wife, with no independent income, is trying to negotiate a divorce from an attorney husband who controls all the finances. A student is trying to negotiate a higher grade with the professor. A small landowner is trying to negotiate a fair price for his land from a right-of-way association that has set the limit on the price it will pay below the assessed value of the land. A small employer with 10 employees is negotiating over a contract with a union that represents over 5,000 workers in surrounding industries.

Disagreement exists about the role of the mediator in situations in which the power of the parties is unbalanced. Some contend that the mediator has no business trying to accommodate to an imbalance, that the function of balancing power is a matter for the courts and the law. Some argue that in order to deal with imbalances a mediator treads on dangerous ethical ground. Others contend that imbalances are a constant in mediation even though their existence makes mediation more difficult. Still others insist that proper mediation cannot take place unless there is some balance of power between the parties and that it is a function of mediation to balance the power when the imbalance will lead to gross inequity, illegal settlement, or other intolerable action.

The very intervention of an impartial third person as a mediator changes the power structure that precedes the intervention. Thus, the process itself tends to balance power. When a couple with one person holding the dominant decision-making power comes to mediation, the person with the least decision power is immediately empowered unless the mediator does nothing to involve both parties in the decision making.

Moore (1986) points out that in some situations the mediator faces problems of the parties' misperception of each others' power (either inflated or deflated for self and other), whereas in extremely divergent situations the weaker party is known to both sides. In these situations the mediator works to "minimize the negative effects of unequal power" and attempts to balance power by assisting in gathering and organizing data, mobilizing what power the party may have, planning negotiation strategy with it, developing financial resources so it can continue to negotiate, encouraging it in the making of realistic concessions, and making referrals to other resource persons. Moore cautions, however, that the mediator should not assist in the development of new power without the approval of the stronger party. *The essence here is that the mediator assists the weaker party in handling the process but not the content of the negotiation.*

My emphasis on process here is not accidental. If people do not communicate well with each other they are not likely to find substantive grounds for agreement. Thus, the process of communication may effect the availability and use of the substance or content. But the substance or content is not the same as the process. It is like the difference between a car and its occupants. The car provides the process whereby the occupants can move toward their destination (goal), but the persons in the car and their goals are the substance or content. The best car in the world cannot take the occupants to where they want to go if they do not know how to drive that car, that is, to use the process. So the mediator uses his or her power to enable the parties to use the processes of negotiation in order to reach their own decision. That is the essential basis of the approach. As long as the mediators maintain this concept and thrust toward their work, the impartiality of their role has less chance of being abridged or placed at unnecessary risk.

The mediator may do a number of things to handle power imbalances. Many of the things we have been discussing here function to handle power imbalances. Davis and Salem (1984), however, isolate 11 elements that they consider to be most useful:

1. Do not make assumptions about the power balance until there is opportunity to explore the matter in session.
2. Use the mediator's inherent character to empower the parties, including a respect for human dignity, the exploration of alternatives, recognition of the need to express emotions safely, recognition of human intelligence, maintaining the impartial and nonjudgmental forum for settling disputes, equal treatment of the parties, maintaining confidentiality, maintaining the voluntary nature of the entry into mediation and the settlements reached, and establishing and sustaining the open process.
3. Encourage the parties to share knowledge.
4. Use the parties' desire to settle as motivation.
5. Compensate for low-level negotiation skills.
6. Interrupt intimidating negotiation patterns.
7. Make accommodations for differences in language and culture.
8. Respect the needs of the participants.
9. Do not allow one party to settle out of fear of violence or retaliation.
10. Provide information and support for both parties.
11. Do not rush into settlement.

All of these behaviors are possible within the context of the mediation process in joint session as well as in the caucus.

There are conditions in which the imbalance is such that it does not respond to the efforts of the mediator. Folberg and Taylor (1984) indicate several: when there is intimidation through physical abuse; disparate financial knowledge and skills; one party is significantly less intelligent and/or mentally competent; or one party has a physical handicap that diminishes the power to negotiate (such as a speech and hearing disorder). To these I add the conditions in which one party has great coercive power over the other through sources external to the parties themselves (political affiliation, organizational hierarchy, status, etc.). This is often the case when a party is forced into mediation by a court or legal situation that requires that the party mediate and settle with the other party on the other party's terms. (An example of this is when a teenager, convicted of robbery, was told [implied force] by the court that he should "mediate" with the teacher he robbed and provide some kind of restitution to the victim.)

In these and other extreme situations in which the dominance of one party destroys the ability of the other party to make decisions freely, and the imbalance is intolerable, the mediator should consider terminating mediation. When these conditions are known prior to the mediation effort, the mediator should frankly point out the problems and continue the effort only on a contingency that the matters be adjusted. Davis and Salem (1984) suggest that it is appropriate to terminate mediation when a party:

- does not understand the mediation process;
- is unwilling to honor the basic guidelines of mediation;
- lacks the ability to identify and express his or her interests and to weigh the consequences of the terms of the agreement;
- is so seriously deficient in information that any agreement will not be based on informed consent;
- indicates agreement not out of free will but out of fear of the other party; and
- when one or both parties agree that they want to end the session.

When the mediator confronts power imbalances that merit termination of the process there are several steps that can be taken. First, the mediator must be sure that the mediation is incapable of being accomplished and that the available methods of balancing the power have been exhausted. Second, the process should be suspended. Third, the mediator, if there is reason to believe that something worthwhile can still emerge from the situation, should caucus with the weaker party and share that concern, observe the reaction, and ask for suggestions. If a suggestion appears that has merit, try it out. If not, or if it does not work, inform the party of the termination and give the reasons. Fourth, meet with both parties and report the decision to terminate and the reasons. Identify the factors that brought this about, discuss the consequences of termination, and point out alternative resources and options. Demonstrate that both parties are being treated with equal respect.

Warning: When terminating a mediation due to power imbalances do so in a way that does not increase the imbalance.

Settlement of disputes through mediation requires a power balance between the parties that allows for free and open decision making. It is the responsibility of the mediator to facilitate such balancing so that rational, open, and useful settlements can be reached. When the imbalance cannot be reduced and free decision making made available to both parties, the mediator should terminate the process and withdraw.

YOU ARE THE MEDIATOR

Suggestions for Mediating Various Disputes

The ideas we have been describing are best explored by applying them in practice. We have been discussing general guidelines for mediating. Now you are the mediator. The guidelines we have been discussing (and others) are included below as a summary of suggestions. These are not theoretical ideas, but principles drawn from the actual experience of many professional mediators. Not all suggestions will fit in every situation.

Suggestions: A Summary

Your Function as a Mediator

1. You *do not make the decisions* for the parties.
2. Your job is to *facilitate* an agreement by the parties themselves.
3. You must be as *unbiased* as possible.
4. *Both sides* must accept your services as a "third" party without prejudice.
5. Your function is to *persuade* both parties to change positions in order to reach agreement.
6. You must also keep *control of communication* between the parties during the mediation session(s).
7. You should help both parties *find rationalizations* that will justify an agreement.
8. You must know the *right time* to advance suggestions, bring people together, or separate them.
9. You must *call the joint sessions* and arrange for time, place, and facilities.
10. You do not "sit in" on a conference as a spectator when you are the mediator. The parties to the dispute should be *your* invited guests.

Things To Do

Before the initial meeting

1. Confer with each party to make yourself known and to find out the nature of the dispute.
2. Show sincere interest in the problems expressed by both parties in these meetings.
3. Do everything you can to win the confidence of both sides.
4. Obtain as many facts as possible from both parties, and other sources as may be necessary, about the nature of the dispute, its effect on both parties, and the people involved.
5. Arrange for a meeting place that is perceived by the parties as "neutral territory" (a place where neither party is the "host" or has a proprietary interest). In labor-management disputes the offices of the mediation agency are best. Other places include courthouse meeting rooms, hotel or motel suites paid for by the parties jointly, the mediators' offices, community meeting places, and so on.
6. If possible, make yourself familiar with similar kinds of disputes and how they have been resolved.

At the joint sessions

1. Chair the session.
2. Make an opening statement that outlines your functions in an affirmative way. For example, "It is my function to assist you in reaching an agreement or a solution to your problem(s) through your own decision making. You make the decisions. I'm just the facilitator."
3. Outline and get agreement on the rules of conduct, and set the tone you expect the meetings to take (see Appendix for an example of rules).
4. State the purpose of the meeting and get agreement from the parties on the goal of the settlement.
5. Get a statement from each side as to the nature of the issues as they perceive them.
6. Use questions sparingly at this stage, particularly those which put either side "on the spot."
7. As long as the parties are willing to talk about the problem(s) in an open manner, keep them together and encourage their joint deliberation.
8. When it appears that one or both of the parties have run out of ideas, patience with the other side, tolerance of the differences, or is becoming particularly angry or wants a separate meeting, separate the parties and deal with them apart from each other (see Caucuses below). The sessions could be recessed until another day or time if you have met for a while, jointly or separately, and neither party is making progress.

At the separate sessions (Caucuses)

1. Meet first with the party that seems most willing to compromise or change its position. If neither shows this willingness, start with the most inflexible.
2. Make it clear to both parties that all things discussed in separate conferences are confidential unless you are given explicit authorization to reveal information or suggestions to the other side.
3. Do not criticize one party to the other.
4. When one side takes a stand that makes settlement impossible, take a firm position as to the effects of this behavior. Be sure that the possible consequences are understood.
5. Continue the separate conferences as long as you think it is necessary to explore alternative solutions. When a lead is found for agreement, return to joint session.
6. Be sure to confer with *both* parties in separate conferences. Avoid just talking with one side before returning to a joint meeting.
7. At the separate sessions make *suggestions* for resolution, not proposals. Let the parties

make the proposals. For example, try "Have you considered . . .?" rather than, "I propose that . . ."

8. When one party wants to try out a proposal before making it, take it to the other side as a "suggestion" that *you* would like to make. For example, if one party wants to know if proposal X will be accepted without actually proposing it, the mediator can meet with the other side and say something like, "Have you considered X?"

9. When you are meeting with one party, give an assignment to the other party. That is, give it a problem to work on, a task to perform, or something that can help lead to a solution.

10. When a party with which you are meeting in separate session wants to caucus privately, encourage it to do so and get out of the way.

At any time

I have arranged these suggestions into the three categories of *relationship, process,* and *substance* as discussed earlier. You will quickly see that many of them fit into more than one category depending on the nature of the situation.

Dealing with Relationships

1. Assume an active role in the process. Don't be just a note-taker or only a message carrier.

2. Always use tact.

3. Be friendly but impersonal at the meetings. For example, instead of "Your cursing at Maria, Jim, is distasteful to me," try, "Profanity doesn't deal with the issue, Jim. Can you express your feelings another way?"

4. Seek information about the personalities with whom you are dealing and the nature of the issues involved from as many different sources as you can without revealing confidences.

5. Avoid taking sides. Keep your personal feelings out of the matter.

6. Avoid wearing pins, rings, or insignia that could be controversial or will destroy your image of impartiality.

7. Both parties should be able to make contact with you at any time other than when you are in session. Let them know you are available to consult with them on the problems as a mediator, but not as a therapist-counselor or lawyer.

8. Be fair, courteous, and impartial at all times.

9. Demonstrate your impartiality by your actions rather than by your spoken allegations. This is similar to the nonverbal process. Keep your actions balanced; do the same or similar things for both sides. If you offer coffee to one side do the same for the other. If you show one side through the office suite do the same for the other, and so on. If you call one side by its formal or official name do the same for the other.

10. If you feel that you have become unacceptable to the parties, get someone whom both parties will respect to take your place .

11. Always remember, the mediator is not the decision maker. You are only the facilitator. Thus, your own humility must show itself in some measure throughout the negotiations. At the same time, don't give up control of the meetings of which you are a part unless by doing so a settlement will be reached.

12. Keep calm. Don't allow the tensions or the frustrations of the dispute to get into your voice or manner of dealing with either side.

13. When the behavior of the two parties is leading to a significant crisis, make this apparent to both of them.

Handling Procedures

1. Be a good listener at all times. Use message feedback constantly. (Be careful about what you consider feedback. In this context we are talking only about repeating or paraphrasing the message to see if you got it correctly. Avoid showing your responses or feelings to a given message or proposal.)

2. Keep note taking to a minimum. Do not use recorders of any kind.

3. Keep both sides working at all times if possible.

4. Try to get areas of agreement clarified and stipulated as soon as possible.

5. Give the parties every opportunity to resolve the issues when they are face-to-face in joint conference. Intervene and/or caucus only when necessary.

6. Keep the discussions orderly. If the meeting gets out of hand, adjourn.

7. Be discreet in what you say, when you say it, and where you say it.

8. Don't be a doormat or errand person for either side. When you carry messages from one party to the other be sure that they are important to the settlement of the dispute. Don't let yourself become the tool of one party over the other.

9. Don't discuss the personal problems of one side with the other unless it has bearing on the dispute. Even then, do it with great care and tact.

10. Do not discuss the significant details of any case in public or with persons with no legitimate concern with the matter.

11. Avoid giving legal or other forms of "official" advice and direction that would manipulate the decision making of either side.

12. At the same time, be willing to try to persuade either side on a position you feel will settle the dispute. Do this carefully and only when you are sure it will work.

13. Be patient. It sometimes takes a long time for a settlement to develop. Just don't give up!

14. When it looks like there is movement on either or both sides, keep the session going. Avoid adjourning when the parties are finding avenues to agreement.

15. You are expected to be an excellent communicator. Don't forget that. But commu-nication involves a great deal more than sounding off. Watch your nonverbal and other subtle forms of sending messages. Try to sit in a position between the parties and not on one side or the other. Keep your caucus time with each party relatively equal. Show *both* sides that you understand their point of view. Use message feedback frequently. Use rhetorical questions rarely. Don't argue with the parties in joint session and only as a "role" in caucuses.

16. Even after failure to reach agreement, don't be afraid to call another meeting. Be persistent in your search for a settlement.

17. Once you have started working on a dispute, don't stop short of resolution for any reason other than your own loss of acceptance, the parties' decision to abandon the effort, or your discovery of information that makes the process untenable (as in power imbalances, illegal behaviors, need for therapy by the parties, etc.). Mediation limited to a pre-arranged time span is often hurried, the results are often unsatisfactory, and often no actual settlement is reached when the time is too short.

18. When tension gets high and threatens to disrupt the negotiations, be able to relieve the tension with humor or a diversion to irrelevant matters.

19. Remember that you rarely succeed with them all. There are situations that are just not subject to resolution through the mediation process. When it becomes apparent that there will be no solution through your service, stop the process.

Handling the Content and Substance

1. Make suggestions to both parties that may help settle the problem(s).

2. Make a recommendation for settlement *only* when you are sure that both sides will accept it.

3. Encourage both sides to bring out the deeper issues that may be under the surface of the dispute.

4. Always get the facts from both parties. Don't depend on one side for all the facts.

5. Keep demonstrating by your suggestions that there are many ways to resolve the dispute.

6. Watch carefully for hints of compromise positions that could lead to an agreement. If, during a caucus, one side indicates that it would make an obviously inequitable trade, be aware that the idea of a "quid pro quo" is there, thus there may be room for changing the trade points.

> *In a difficult custody dispute that seemed stalemated, the husband, in private caucus with the mediator, said, "The children do have some rights, you know." The mediator pressed the idea of children's rights to both sides, which led to both husband and wife compromising on the custody arrangements.*

7. Be willing to suggest settlements reached in similar situations. No two situations are the same, but there are often similar issues that have been resolved. In the review of the alternative possibilities it is useful to call attention to these.

8. Get the facts. Avoid hearsay!

9. When an agreement-settlement is reached, be sure that both sides understand the terms. This is best done in a joint session after you have thoroughly checked it out in separate sessions. One way is to review the factors of agreement and have each side in the joint meeting confirm its agreement with that factor by initialing or "signing off" on it.

10. The final agreement should be made a matter of record and signed by both parties.

11. Don't be protective of your own ideas. Suggestions you make to either side should become *their* ideas if they choose to take them.

12. Don't be afraid to defend your suggestions to either party. When you make them be sure they are practical and possible under the circumstances and then be willing to convince either or both parties of their value. But don't make a fight of it. Remember, you are trying to help them resolve a dispute, not to create another.

13. It is not your responsibility to determine the legality, the ethics, or the justice of any solution jointly reached. The parties are responsible for the decisions they reach. This does not prevent you, however, from speaking out when you feel a possible decision may be in violation of some law. But you have no right to enforce this on the parties.

14. Always help one side to see and understand the position of the other side. In caucus you may ask the party to outline the position of the other side as it sees that position. In joint session you may review the two positions after hearing both.

15. Don't give suggestions until each party is likely to accept them and realizes the disutility of their own maneuvers.

16. Under no conditions are you an interpreter or enforcer of the law. Any matters involving such problems should be called to the attention of the parties, and they should be guided to the proper and qualified authorities. You may, if it seems necessary, call attention to existing laws or conditions that lie outside the jurisdiction of the parties but affect their relationships in relation to the dispute.

17. If you become privy to information that would put the source in legal jeopardy, you are to retain as confidential the source of the information. You must honor the confidence of the parties. This does not prevent you from calling their attention to the consequences and encouraging them to pursue that matter in another arena of proper jurisdiction.

HELPING THE PARTIES USE MEDIATION

Preparing to Work with a Mediator

So far we have emphasized the function of the mediator. Now our concern is with those of you who are not mediators, but who want to use the process and maximize the experience and the outcomes. Usually, when clients who have not experienced good professional mediation approach it for the first time, there are many doubts and misconceptions. Some think that it is like arbitration, some think it is counseling, some figure it is the intervention of an official who does not know the situation, and some may feel that it is a court or legally mandated process and are afraid to raise any questions about it for fear of jeopardizing any possible gain they might acquire.

Most mediators spend time with uninitiated clients in order to instruct them on how mediation works and the kinds of things that they, as participants, can do to facilitate the process. In interpersonal, family and divorce settings, small claims, and other circumstances, the mediator will conduct an "entry" meeting at which the rules and processes are explained and agreed on. This premediation review is vital in those situations in which the clients have had no opportunity to experience the process. In the labor-management field there is less use of this because of the general knowledge of the process and how best to use it.

IN SESSION WITH THE MEDIATOR: USING THE MEDIATOR TO RESOLVE DISPUTES

Once the parties are with the mediator there are a number of things they can do to facilitate the process and guarantee a resolution to the disputes. If you are one of the parties, the following things will help:

1. Seek areas of agreement. Avoid emphasizing what will prevent it. Too much emphasis on technicalities and legalities can often stifle the process. The mediator wants you to seek positive directions and will tend to push aside obstacles to agreement.

2. The facts and evidence need to be on the table. All the important information relating to the dispute needs to be brought to the mediator's attention either in a joint meeting or in a private caucus. The mediator cannot work effectively if you hold back vital information or if you edit your information so carefully that it is not clear.

3. The mediator needs to understand your position and the reasons for it. It must be supported with sound reasoning. Clear and concise justification of it is necessary. Without this information there is no way to determine what you need to do to reach a settlement.

4. When you agree to something, be sure that you mean it. Avoid leaving the implication that you agree when you have no intention of doing so. Don't give "tentative" indications of agreement if you don't mean to keep them.

5. Keep moving along. Do not delay the process. Any delay tends to interfere with the development of an agreement. Let the mediator suggest time tables and limits and try to follow them.

6. Be honest with the mediator. Let the mediator know what your actual position is and how you view the position of the other side. Don't hold back. The mediator needs to know just where you stand.

7. Be practical with your assessment of the situation. Keep in mind that the other side also has reasons and feelings.

8. Maintain patience and try to be as calm as possible. Stay "cool." Usually a mediator is not influenced by highly emotional "play acting." A calm and rational approach is much more likely to facilitate the resolution of the problems.

9. Maintain straightforward and honest communication with the mediator. Attempts at cleverness or "sharp deal making" usually get in the way of reaching a settlement. The agreement is your agreement and it will affect you and your counterpart. Trying to "cut corners" or using tricks simply defeats attempts at a sound settlement.

10. Avoid freezing into a hard and fast position. If, however, you come to a final position that you feel you cannot abandon, make it clear to both the mediator and your counterpart. Do not expect the mediator to do this for you.

11. Throughout the process, keep your communication channels open to the mediator and to your counterpart. If you refuse to communicate with either or both you are shutting down the lines leading to a settlement.

12. Don't give up. Keep trying to find a settlement. Your constancy in seeking a resolution will facilitate the whole process.

CHAPTER 6

///

Arbitrating Disputes
Arbitrators and Advocates

INTRODUCTION TO THE PROCESS OF ARBITRATION

From Stages 3 through 5 of the Struggle Spectrum (see Chapter 1), dispute resolution processes may emerge from the neutral decision making of an individual (or individuals) other than the parties to the dispute. The extreme legalistic end of this scale takes us into the court where judge and/or jury apply their decision making to the struggle under the constraints of the law. In today's global social economy, litigation is growing by leaps and bounds. Some feel that it is getting out of hand. Justice Warren Burger, speaking before the Minnesota State Bar Association on August 21, 1985, noted that "a large part of all the litigation in the courts is an exercise in futility and frustration. A large proportion of civil disputes in the courts could be disposed of more satisfactorily in some other way" (pp. 3-4). Burger went on to say that "we must move toward taking a large volume of private conflicts out of the courts and into the channels of arbitration, mediation, and conciliation" (p. 5).

Arbitration is a neutral third-party decision-making intervention that is less legalistic and more informal than that of the court. It is a quasi-judicial process whereby a neutral third party makes a decision regarding a dispute when the parties to the conflict are unable to resolve the struggle themselves.

Usually by the time a dispute comes to arbitration it has been negotiated, argued, and debated several times in face-to-face interaction by the advocates on both sides. Elkouri and Elkouri (1985) define it as "a simple proceeding voluntarily chosen by parties who want a dispute determined by an impartial judge of their own mutual selection, whose decision, based on the merits of the case, they agree in advance to accept as final and binding" (p. 2). They point out that laws or rules can make arbitration compulsory. A prior agreement between two parties to arbitrate future disputes, such as in a labor-management contract or in a business contract agreement, will bind those parties to the process. Thus, when one party wants to arbitrate the other party must comply. When no prior contract binds the parties to arbitrate they may, at their own option, choose to arbitrate and abide by the decision of the selected arbiter.

The law and the courts have become highly supportive of the arbitration process. The United States Arbitration Act of 1925 provided for the enforcement of commercial agreements to arbitrate. The Labor Management Relations Act (LMRA) of 1947 established the legal basis of arbitration in the collective bargaining process. The Supreme Court followed in the *Textile Workers v. Lincoln Mills* case (353 U.S. 448, 40 LRRM 21123 [1957]) and subsequent cases to affirm Section 301 of the LMRA as the jurisdictional basis for federal courts over labor contract arbitration clauses and the source of procedural law in labor arbitration. State courts have allowed the general pattern set by the U.S. Supreme Court. In 1960 the U.S. Supreme Court issued decisions in three cases that have been called "The Trilogy of 1960." They involved the United Steelworkers v. American Manufacturing Co. (80 S. Ct. 1343, 34 LA 559); the Steelworkers v. Warrior and Gulf Navigation Co. (80 S. Ct. 1347, 34 LA 561); and the Steelworkers v. Enterprise Wheel & Car Corp. (80 St. Ct. 1358, 24 LA 569). These decisions spelled out the relation of the arbitration processes to the courts. The decisions allowed the arbitrator to determine arbitrability; affirmed that the arbitrator has the right to interpret the agreement between the parties; affirmed that the courts had no business overruling agreements because of differences in interpretation of a contract; and affirmed that the courts could not reject an arbitrator's award unless the evidence was clear that he or she had exceeded the authority given in the contract between the parties. The Supreme Court, in the Trilogy, also affirmed that the courts should not become involved in the merits of grievances to compel arbitration or enforce awards. The courts may assume jurisdiction over appeals of arbitration decisions, and they have, for the most part, under the influence of the Trilogy supported the decisions made by arbitrators.

Origins and Development

Arbitration is a popular practice in many dispute arenas. The origins of arbitration go back to ancient society. Arbitration had been in use many centuries before English common law emerged. Elkouri and Elkouri (1985) note that King Solomon was an arbitrator in the mode of many arbitrators of today. Phillip II of Macedon, around 338 B.C., in his peace treaty with southern Greece, specified arbitration as the method to be used in settling disputes between members over territory.

Nolan (1979) reports that according to ancient mythology:

> Venus, Juno, and Pallas Athene agreed to allow Paris to decide their dispute over which of them was the most beautiful. Primitive societies have long favored resolution of disputes by impartial arbitration, frequently to the exclusion of any formal legal process. The arbitration process appears in the Norse sagas, among American Indian tribes and in the early Christian community . . . arbitration was widely accepted as an adjunct to the formal law of the Romans and was the preferred means of settlement of commercial disputes of the Middle Ages. (pp. 2-3)

Businesses have long used arbitration as a substitute for court action in commercial disputes. International arbitration is a standard tool in trying to cope with disputes between nations that can easily escalate to war. In this country in recent years we have experienced an increased use of arbitration procedures in environmental disputes, community disputes, consumer struggles, banking, health services, athletics, and almost all other areas in which disputes arise.

The arbitration process as it now exists has undergone several changes in form and structure since the 1930s, particularly in the area of labor-management relations and collective bargaining. In the 1940s, the prevailing concept of arbitration was as an extension of the collective bargaining process and a substitute for the strike (Mittenthal, 1991, pp. 24-25). Arbitrators in those years tended to resist formality at the hearing, to ignore any rules of evidence, and they were actually more likely to mediate when it appeared that the parties were willing to accept such assistance. They saw themselves as problem solvers for their clients. In the last 20 years the process in labor-management relations has become more like commercial arbitration. It is perceived more often as a quasi-judicial process and a substitute for formal court litigation. It tends to rely on prior decisions of arbitrators as guidelines and to conduct hearings in a more formal manner with more attention to the formal rules of evidence. The shift has come along concurrent with the increase in the use of mediation in many forums as well as in labor-management. Thus, the informal character of mediation may have pushed arbitration to a more formal level of behavior.

Currently, "arbitrators [in labor-management] today, by and large, see themselves as something akin to administrative law judges in an adversarial system in which they are called upon to interpret and apply contract language" (Mittenthal, 1991, p. 25). The result is a trend toward legalism in the proceedings in all contexts. More and more lawyers are becoming involved in the process both as advocates and as arbitrators, and they tend to bring to the hearings the "trappings" of the courtroom. This has some serious implications for the future of arbitration in that the more courtroom practices are used in arbitration, the more the goals of the arbitration process are defeated (Seitz, 1979, p. 7).

Even so, *the arbitration process is still not a court of law*. One of the key differences is the handling of information about the dispute. In the court, judges have before the trial begins almost all the information they need to make decisions and to manage the trial procedure. They have pleadings, motions, applications for discovery, interrogatories, and other documents providing a quite complete picture of the dispute. The arbitrator, on the other hand, walks into the hearing with no such preliminary information, and he or she must facilitate its development on the spot. (Occasionally an arbitrator will request prehearing briefs, but this is very rare.) The parties themselves have at the outset more understanding of the nature of the dispute and the arguments than the arbitrator.

There is still a greater level of informality in the arbitration hearing than in the courtroom. The arbitrator has much more freedom to encourage the parties to produce information to assist in making the decision. This means that the arbitrator will often interrogate both witnesses and advocates in order to expose the facts and information. The role of the arbitrator is still to get the facts, review them carefully, and make a decision. The arbitrator can still decide what information is pertinent in a given case and has the right to request added information beyond what the advocates present.

The clients, however, can still choose between the less formal or the more formal methods. The arbitrator needs to be able to adjust and to be ready to use a mediatory style when requested. On several occasions I have walked into a scheduled arbitration hearing and been asked by both parties to mediate the dispute.

The advantages of arbitration over court procedures include the following:

- parties can select their own arbiter by agreement (they cannot select their judge)
- arbitrators can be selected on the basis of special experience, training, and subject matter knowledge
- all proceedings can be conducted in private
- there is no comparable wait on crowded courtroom calendars
- there is opportunity to submit a large volume of complex evidence such as contracts, technical matters, financial statements, and so on that are not usually allowed in court
- arbitration provides an alternative to litigation in court that is cheaper on the whole and much less formal and restrictive than the court system. At the same time, the courts uphold the decisions made by arbitration.

One of the most widespread uses of the arbitration process in this country is in labor-management relations. Its use has developed concurrent with the growth of collective bargaining. The arbitration process in the field of labor-management (as well as in international situations) serves as an alternative to violence by providing a way for the parties to reach a resolution. Many labor-management contracts in the public sector provide for arbitration of the terms of a contract itself. A frequent and traditional procedure has been for a union to strike when a contract agreement cannot be reached. Laws have emerged that require employees in systems that seriously affect the public health and welfare to settle their disputes without violence or shutdown of the operation through what is called "interest" arbitration—arbitration that involves decisions that directly affect the terms of the working agreement between the parties (note particularly the firefighters and the police).

In contrast to this "interest" arbitration, a great deal of labor-management arbitration involves "grievance" arbitration whereby contractual agreements require grievances to be heard and processed jointly and if not resolved, to be arbitrated (I have more to say about this in the section on the Hearing).

It is in this grievance context that many sources of difference arise in the collective bargaining process:

- a given action is perceived differently by each side
- there is an actual set of conflicting facts in the case
- the terms of a contract or agreement are not interpreted in the same manner by each side
- one side is opposed to anything the other side may want or suggest (an intense zero-sum context)
- the parties have not communicated with each other and therefore do not understand the other's point of view
- there is distrust between the parties
- rights and restraints under the law and under the contract are not truly understood
- personal animosities between individuals create strife that has not been resolved within the working relationship
- the language of the contract is actually unclear and each party insists its interpretation is correct
- the parties have each taken strong positions from which they cannot deviate without losing face and the support of their constituency
- prior behavior in similar situations has been unsatisfactory to one party or the other.

During the course of attempts to deal with the dispute (through negotiation, mediation, etc.) many of the problems may be revealed. However, as these are revealed, there is often the tendency for one side or the other to become defensive and to polarize or "freeze" into its position. Thus, by the time the parties reach the arbitration point they are locked into a "win-lose" type of conflict. This same type of escalation occurs in interpersonal, commercial, and other dispute arenas.

A very important condition accompanies the move by the parties to arbitrate a dispute. When disputants come to the point at which they seek an arbitrator to make the decision and resolve the struggle, they are *abandoning their independent negotiation and decision making*. Thus, in the Struggle Spectrum, as the parties move to the right on the scale (or toward the violent end) their control over their decisions becomes reduced. Unlike mediation in which the parties retain their power to make the decisions, in arbitration they delegate that power to the arbitrator. That delegation of power comes through an agreement that the disputants make to submit the dispute to the arbitrator and to abide by the decision made by the arbitrator.

The function of the arbitrator is to look at the situation, gather all the available facts and information through a hearing, study the situation and the surrounding implications and interpretations, and make a decision as to which side is correct. Many times both sides are in error, and the arbitrator must construct a decision that deals with these joint mistakes while determining which side will prevail in its contention.

ARBITRATORS AND THEIR QUALIFICATIONS

The selection of arbitrators by the parties brings into play a number of matters that demand considerable attention. Let us first take a look at who arbitrators can be. In seeking arbitrators we look for persons who are impartial, and who have high integrity, special knowledge and expertise of the context in which the dispute exists, and some experience in arbitrating disputes.

There are no certified arbitrators. No formal certification exists. However, the American Arbitration Association, The Federal Mediation and Conciliation Service, and many state and federal agencies provide lists of arbitrators who have been selected by review boards provided by these agencies as being qualified to function as arbitrators. Although these review boards do not certify persons as meeting specific criteria, they do select people for listing on the panels who have demonstrated experience, are not advocates, and who have been favorably reviewed by representatives from both sides.

There is nothing preventing the parties from selecting any person who is known to be honest, impartial, understanding of the area in which the dispute is taking place, skilled in analyzing arguments and making decisions, and skilled in communicating the results. As a matter of fact, that is how some arbitrators get started. However, the skilled arbitrator must have experience in the process. That experience is very important because the stress and strain of conducting the hearing, maintaining the order of procedures, and preparing the final decision go beyond the simple elements of impartiality, honesty, and understanding. It is wise to seek experienced arbitrators because of their skill in handling the procedures.

Several years ago Eric Lawson, Jr. attempted to draw a profile of 30 arbitrators in the Buffalo office of the New York State Mediation Board. He found the following: the average age was 48 years old; over two-thirds had served as arbitrators, mediators, and fact finders; and over half the group had completed more than 50 decisions-awards during their career. The average arbitrator had been a paid arbitrator for less then a decade. Sixty percent of the group filed their first awards since 1973. The route of entry into labor relations arbitration usually involved prior service as an advocate, with 13% having over 20 years of such service. Most members of the panel were well educated, had some academic course work in labor relations, all except one held an undergraduate degree, 90% held a graduate degree, and 43% held a degree in law (Lawson, 1981). A review of the panel lists of the FMCS indicate that this review represents the general arbitrator population in the United States.

SELECTING THE ARBITRATOR

The selection process is one of the unique parts of arbitration. The basic condition is that the parties to the dispute select the person who is to serve as arbitrator in their own case. A mutual agreement is the most desirable way. Thus, when two parties decide that they want to take their dispute to arbitration, the first step is to either mutually agree on the arbitrator or to set in motion a procedure which will provide for the selection. One such procedure is to get a list of acceptable candidates from a reliable source and select from that list. Another way that has developed in several fields is for a qualified agency (such as the AAA or the FMCS) to supply a list of five or seven names of persons who are on its approved arbitrator list. Each party then rejects one of the proposed arbitrators alternately until only one remains, and that one is selected for the job.

In reviewing the factors leading to the selection of arbitrators, Lawson (1981) found some significant trends. Overwhelming evidence showed that name recognition was the most important single factor in the selection of arbitrators. Data from colleagues was used in selecting arbitrators. Evidence indicated that users placed less significance on having won a previous arbitration with a given candidate than on securing an arbitrator they felt was capable of rendering a just decision. Geographic location was a factor also. That is, the relatively close availability of the arbitrator made a difference in selection. "Real world" experience was listed as a significant factor and probably reflects the desire to have a well-educated person with practical experience to back up that theoretical information. Little importance was attached to age. In the order of importance, the selection factors were:

- Name recognition
- Reputation for integrity
- Geographic location of arbitrator to the site
- "Real world" experience
- Extent to which awards have been published
- Arbitrator is an attorney
- Level of formal education
- Size of per diem fee
- Number of professional organizations to which arbitrator belongs
- Sex of the arbitrator
- Ethnic or racial origin of the arbitrator. (Lawson, 1981)

FROM THE ARBITRATOR'S POINT OF VIEW: WHAT HE OR SHE DOES AND EXPECTS TO DO

A look at the arbitration situation from the point of view of the arbitrator may help you to understand the process. Here are just a few things expected of an arbitrator and that an arbitrator expects to do:

1. Confers with the principals, representatives, or advocates prior to the hearing to set the time and place of the meeting and ascertains the general nature of the dispute.

2. Convenes and conducts the proceedings at the hearing so that sufficient evidence and argument is presented to allow a proper decision.

3. Decides what evidence is to be admitted and what evidence is to be rejected. Accepts and records for reference purposes all accepted documentary evidence presented.

4. Asks questions of the parties or their witnesses when the parties have not adequately met their obligation of presenting their cases fully. This is usually done after the advocates have had full opportunity to question their witnesses. They may seek to determine the truth-falsity of certain information alleged to be true, to discover information vital to the issue that has not been revealed, and/or to clarify testimony that is confusing or contradictory. The arbitrator views as his or her main function at the hearing to get at the truth as much as possible. If the advocates do not facilitate that process, the arbitrator must invoke the questioning process.

   On the one hand, the parties have the right to determine what they wish to submit and argue in relation to a given case. On the other hand, the process aims at providing a forum where truth can be revealed.

   If the case that one or both of the parties submits violates the rights of a grievant or a cause and the arbitrator is aware of this, should he or she raise added questions aimed at revealing this additional information? *It is not the arbitrator's responsibility to develop the case for either side.* On the other hand, it is an arbitrator's responsibility to see that the actual case for each side is brought to arbitral attention. In most cases, skilled arbitrators will confer with both parties as to the perceived gaps in information and allow them to choose whether to provide the requested data. Or, in many cases, having done this, the parties will allow the arbitrator to introduce some interrogation aimed at helping to clarify the hidden, missing, or confusing information (see Sacks & Kurlantzick, 1987, for a thorough discussion of these problems).

5. May question the advocates on their arguments at the close of the case after the advocates have summarized. This is done primarily for clarification.

6. May conduct independent investigations of some aspects of the case and request special information from the parties, but does so only with the approval and knowledge of both parties.

7. May discuss special problems with experts or others not at the hearing with the approval of the parties. When this is the case, the parties are usually present so that they also can query the informants.

8. Maintains order and decorum during the hearing and sees to it that each side has full opportunity to present its evidence and argument.

9. Avoids any contact with either party without the presence of the other or the other's permission during the time of the consideration of the matter under dispute.

10. May suggest to the parties, if the situation appears amenable, that they may create a settlement themselves without a formal award. In such cases he or she may attempt to mediate the dispute if the parties are willing. However, it is important to remember that when arbitration has been instituted, the parties are not usually willing to be mediated but simply want a decision from a third party. Further, many arbitrators are not skilled in mediation.

11. Keeps personal notes of the material developed at the hearing even when there is a formal transcript being made.

12. Adjourns the hearing at the appropriate time and gets agreement from the parties as to the filing dates when the parties choose to submit post-hearing briefs.

13. In some cases the parties, due to special circumstances, may want what is called "expedited arbitration." Under these rules the arbitrator will make a decision either on the spot at the close of the hearing or within a few hours thereafter in the form of a memorandum.

14. Receives the post-hearing briefs and studies them in depth along with his or her own notes, transcripts, exhibits, and so on.

15. Analyzes the case carefully and makes a decision on the stated issues.

16. Prepares a review of the case, including a decision and an award. This review is usually written and contains the following:
     a. The names of the parties in dispute.
     b. The issue(s) under dispute.
     c. The time, place, and persons attending the hearing.
     d. The contract language pertaining to the issues when such an agreement exists, as in labor-management relations.
     e. References to all exhibits presented.
     f. A summary of the position of each side.
     g. A discussion of the arguments, the criteria and standards for a decision, the nature of the evidence presented, and so on. This is actually a review of the thinking and reasoning of the arbitrator in working through to the decision. This part of the report is often complex and complicated. It should be concise and clear. One of the best examples of this is a discussion organized around the following: the issues, the criteria for fair resolution of the issues, examination of the evidence and argument from each side on the issues, and a statement of the logical conclusion from this examination.
     h. The decision and the award.
     i. The signature and date of the decision.

17. In preparing the decision-award the arbitrator is concerned with at least the following things:
     a. The quality of the evidence.
     b. Determining the reliability and credibility of conflicting testimony, that is, who is telling the truth?

 c. Weighing the evidence as to its relative importance to the case.
 d. Past practice between the parties in dealing with similar situations.
 e. What the agreement or contract says and how it is to be interpreted.
 f. Relevance of other awards cited by the advocates and of awards they have examined.
 g. Relevance of legislation and court decisions.
 h. The nature, appropriateness, and fairness of a remedy or award.

Often, in the discussion part of a report, arbitrators express opinions somewhat related to the dispute but not really material or directly pertinent to the issues present. Zack (1977) has this to say about such opinions:

> Because any award will normally disappoint the losing party, and may thus reduce the future acceptability of the arbitrator to that party, the arbitrator may seek to include in the award opinions that will assuage the feelings of the losing party, for example by taking a favourable view of the losing party's position or putting some kind of blame on the other party on a related point. For example, in a disciplinary case, the arbitrator may uphold the management's decision, but implicitly or explicitly put into question the adequacy or justness of an existing policy by adding an opinion to the effect that the trouble would not have arisen had the management acted otherwise. The danger is that apart from unnecessarily prolonging the text of the award, such statements can be a source of trouble for the parties. In the example cited, the union (as the losing party) would be encouraged to demand modification of the management policy in question. The management would probably resist, and the result would be a dispute unwittingly instigated by the arbitrator. More often, however, the practical result of such statements is resentment by the winning party, a result which is contrary to the arbitrator's purpose in making them. (p. 61)

THE HEARING

It is at the hearing that the focus of the arbitration process occurs. Here the parties to the dispute bring their witnesses, arguments, cases, causes, and advocates. As I indicated earlier in this chapter, in the labor-management context there are two types of hearings that are most prevalent. One is the grievance hearing, and the other is the interest hearing. The grievance hearing usually deals with an alleged violation of a contract or existing agreement between the parties. Thus, matters such as discharge, alleged violation of company rules, and alleged violation of wage rates are explored. The outcome of the grievance arbitration is a ruling on whether there was or was not a violation of the already existing contract, and a remedy if there was a violation.

The interest hearing deals with the dispute between the parties as they attempt to work out an agreement. Wage rates under a contract, grievance procedures, and so on are often subjects of interest arbitration. The outcome of the interest arbitration is an arbitrator's decision that binds the parties in a contract form. A wage rate is established, a grievance procedure outlined, and so forth.

The parties may have a hand in adjusting the rules of procedure to fit the particular nature of the issues. Arbitrators must check this out beforehand, if possible, so that they can be prepared to deal with the style used. The process is flexible and more varieties of hearing style are likely to occur than in a formal court.

Advocates representing a client in an arbitration should prepare both themselves and their witnesses to respond to the arbitrator's interrogations. Then, if the questions are not forthcoming, the information will be what they develop in their presentations. Of course, when the information has been developed thoroughly and clearly, there may be little need for arbitral interrogation.

PREPARING FOR THE ARBITRATION HEARING AS AN ADVOCATE

Advocates must prepare carefully for their presentation to the arbitrator. The nature of that preparation is much the same for the various arenas of dispute: labor-management, commercial, landlord-tenant, environmental, interpersonal, international, and so on. The following are the stages of that preparation:

1. *Review the history of the dispute.*

   If the matter is a grievance, the original grievance statement as well as the original data surrounding the preparation of the statement must be thoroughly understood. Then the events that followed the original initiation of the grievance must be carefully reviewed. What has happened at each step in the grievance procedure? What was the response of either party to the position taken by the other?

   If the matter is an interest matter or an issue not involving grievances, it is important that the background of the struggle be thoroughly understood. For example, a landlord-tenant dispute should be explored from the beginning of the relationship and the conditions which surrounded that beginning and the continuation.

2. *Study any agreements between the parties.*

   There is nothing that will take the place of a full understanding of what any agreement between the parties contains and *does not contain.* Clauses that may have relation to the grievance or dispute must be identified. This includes both direct and indirect relationships to the dispute. In labor-management grievance disputes, an understanding of the nature of the agreement (contract) in relation to the specific grievance is absolutely necessary.

3. *Interview all of the parties to your side of the dispute.*

   Find out the facts of the case as well as you can. What happened? Who did what? Can you rely on the testimony of your witnesses? Do the witnesses understand the principle thrust of your side of the dispute (the theory of your case)? Then you must select those witnesses who are going to be most useful in testifying regarding the situation. Check the testimony several times and run through it with the witnesses. If necessary role play a probable cross examination. Make a written summary of the testimony that each witness produces and use this as a check at the hearing to be sure that nothing is overlooked. Coach the witnesses on how to deal with the questions you raise. Advise them on how to present their testimony so that it is understood and useful.

4. *Gather all the documents, papers, and reports that you will need at the hearing.*

   If some of the documents are in the possession of the other side ask that they be brought to the arbitration. If there is resistance to the submission of these documents by the other party, bring the matter to the attention of the arbitrator. The arbitrator usually has the authority to subpoena documents and witnesses if they are not available in any other way.

   Prepare your documents in a careful order in relation to the presentation you plan to make at the hearing. Make copies of these documents for the other side and for the arbitrator. If you are having a witness explain or discuss a document, it is helpful to have an extra copy for the witness. These documents will become "Exhibits" at the hearing.

5. *Examine the other side's position.*

   It is of great importance that you thoroughly understand the thrust and arguments of the other side. You must know these in order to prepare yourself to deal with the opposing evidence and arguments.

6. *Prepare an outline of your position.*

   Work out as complete an outline as possible of the facts and arguments in support of your position. Have others in your organization review this outline and make suggestions about it. Other points of view will often provide you with additional support and development in your arguments. Make a thorough criticism of your own position and arguments. Do they lead to an absurd result? Do they cause part of the contract to have no meaning? Are they consistent with past practice? Do they hang together logically? Are they based on facts, fantasy, or wishes? Your own critical analysis is very important. Try putting yourself in the role of an impartial third person and evaluate what you have done. If it does not do what you want it to do, then re-do it until it does, or re-evaluate the decision to arbitrate.

7. *Review published decisions on issues similar to those involved in your case.*

   Even though decisions by other arbitrators do not control the decision of the arbitrator in your case they can be very persuasive if they are similar in issue and facts and have sound reasoned opinions that can support your point of view. Have these ready to cite at the hearing and in your post-hearing brief.

PRESENTING YOUR CASE BEFORE THE ARBITRATOR

1. *Opening statement*

   Prepare your opening with great care. You are forming the groundwork and foundation for the development of your case. In your opening statement the following matters should be presented:

   a. *Identify the issues.* The arbitrator will probably ask both parties to identify the issue(s) before the opening statements are made. It is helpful to have the issue(s) available in writing to present to the arbitrator. If you have not discussed the statement of the issue with your counterpart and reached an agreement on it, you will have to justify your statement of the issues in contrast to that taken by the other side. In your opening statement provide a clear and concise statement of the issue(s).

   b. *Summarize what you intend to prove.* Identify the major contentions that you intend to present and sketch in the basic arguments in support of each.

   c. *Identify the remedy or relief* that you seek. State specifically and clearly just what relief you seek from the arbitrator. Be as exact as possible as to what you want and clarify the right of the arbitrator to grant that relief.

   d. *Identify agreements or contract clauses* that are related to the case. Provide the arbitrator with a copy of the contract or agreements and make specific reference to all the clauses and phrases that have a bearing on your position in the dispute.

   e. *Report any stipulated facts* that are uncontested that have to do with the dispute. Frequently the advocates for each side will meet before the hearing and agree on such stipulations. This will expedite the hearing and save time and costs.

2. *Submitting documentary evidence*

   a. Always submit a copy of any related agreement(s).

   b. Provide copies of all documents that have a bearing on the dispute including minutes of contract negotiation meetings (especially when contract language is ambiguous), personnel records, financial records, medical reports, wage records, relevant correspondence, grievance reports, and any other documentary material that can help the arbitrator grasp the facts in the situation.

   c. Provide one set of documents for the arbitrator and one for the other side.

   d. Take time to identify the significance of each document to your position. Whether the document is presented as part of a package or is submitted during the course of the hearing when the matter comes into focus there should be a clear reason for its submission. Often it is helpful to underline key words, phrases, and/or sections of the documents to focus attention on the key matters.

   e. Avoid overwhelming the arbitrator with "tons of paper," but do not refrain from submitting documents that may have bearing on your case. Sometimes it is unnecessary to present a large document when only one paragraph or phrase is key, and the context is clearly understood. On the other hand, don't make the mistake of assuming that the total context of a single paragraph or phrase is understood.

   f. The arbitrator will assign each document an "Exhibit Number." Keep track of these identifications so that you can make proper reference to them later if needed.

3. *Examining witnesses*

   The process of examining witnesses at an arbitration hearing is an art. Properly done it can build the basis for a sound argument. Improperly done it can destroy not only your argument, but your credibility and the credibility of the witnesses. The following are some guidelines:

   a. Review with the witnesses beforehand just what testimony is to be given and the kinds of questions you will ask to bring forth this information.

   b. Have each witness identify him- or herself and provide qualifications as to his or her ability to know or be in possession of critical facts and data about the situation. It is important that you give each witness ample opportunity to establish his or her credibility and integrity in the situation.

c.   Give the witness an opportunity to tell his or her perception of the situation, without interruption if possible. Try to avoid leading questions or questions that include the answer. Testimony is usually more effective when it is stated in the witness's own words and in his or her own manner. When it is necessary to ask a question to bring the witness back to the point at hand, do it carefully and do not confuse the witness.

d.   When you wish to reemphasize some aspect of the testimony, ask the witness to repeat what was said or to state it in another way. A good way to do this is to provide the witness with "feedback," that is, report back to the witness what you thought he or she said and give him or her an opportunity to affirm or deny that information. This is a highly useful process. Be careful when the arbitrator holds a court-type hearing that you don't get called for asking leading questions. To avoid this it is wise to preface a feedback statement with a phrase, such as "You said . . ," or "Let me check to be sure that I got what you said. You said . . ."

e.   When a witness is reticent in the face of the arbitrator and the opposite side, encourage him or her in as many ways as possible to help allay this problem. The best way to prepare for this is to role play the presentation with the witness before the hearing. Also, give the witness some idea of what kinds of questions will be asked in cross examinations.

f.   If the witness is the principal in a grievance be sure that when he or she is finished you give him/her an opportunity to add anything that he or she feels may be pertinent to the situation. It is important for that kind of witness to feel that he or she was given a full opportunity to present his or her case before the arbitrator. At the same time, if you have a "hot head" for a witness who is inclined to "shoot off at the mouth" and antagonize people, be sure to explain to this witness in advance the possible negative consequences of indiscriminate and antagonistic testimony.

4.   *Cross examination of witnesses*
Each witness is subject to being cross examined by the opposite side. The function of such is to disclose facts witnesses may have avoided in the direct testimony, to correct errors in facts and statements, to put facts in a different perspective, to clarify what may appear to be contradictions, and to attack the reliability and credibility of an adverse witness. In performing the cross examination it is well to:

a.   Keep in mind just what you want to achieve by the cross examination.

b.   Waive any cross examination when it would simply reinforce hostile information.

c.   Avoid badgering or attacking a witness even though he or she is a hostile witness. If you wish to show unreliability or implausible testimony do it simply and without apparent rancor. Get the facts out and show inconsistencies with a soft but firm dispassion.

d.   Use message feedback carefully as a way of checking the consistency of the witness. You may want to take several inconsistent statements, put them together, and ask the witness to confirm or deny that they were made.

5.   *Summing up: Tying up the facts and the arguments*
Your opportunity to "put the package together" comes after both sides have presented their witnesses. Here is where you tie up your facts as developed by your witnesses and your documentary material with the principal arguments advanced in your opening statement. In presenting this closing argument you can:

a.   Begin with a restatement of the key issues in the dispute. If they are the same as at the beginning, simply repeat them. If additional data has led to some realignment of the issues, make clear what these changes are and why. Thorough preparation will eliminate the appearance of new data at the arbitration hearing in 99% of the cases. In most instances involving labor-management grievance matters, all of the data has been presented to the other side during the preliminary grievance meetings and discussions. The only person hearing the data for the first time is the arbitrator. The arbitration hearing is usually not the place for the discovery or presentation of new information.

b.   Refute the arguments made by the other side by showing how the facts and testimony presented either fails to confirm or disconfirm their arguments.

    c.   Show how the testimony and facts presented confirm your arguments.

    d.   Close by restating your request for a decision and/or relief.

6.   *General atmosphere of the hearing*

The manner in which the parties conduct themselves at a hearing will often influence the arbitrator. There are several guidelines for handling the procedure:

    a.   Maintain a friendly attitude toward antagonists.

    b.   Conduct yourself in a firm and dignified manner.

    c.   Maintain an orderly presentation.

    d.   Avoid emotional outbursts, personal invective, or caustic remarks. They tend to alienate the arbitrator. If you have a good case, it won't need added emotion to press your point. If your case is lousy, becoming emotional about it will probably make it sound worse to the arbitrator and raise doubts about the real strength of your case.

    e.   Keep to the issue. Avoid bringing in other disputes that do not have any application to the matter at hand.

    f.   Avoid long and irrelevant speeches. Keep to the issues at hand.

    g.   Avoid over-legalistic approaches. Arbitrators are not usually inclined to look with favor on the legalistic maneuverings of advocates. Their job is to get the facts of the situation as completely as possible. When objections to questions seem to be in the direction of suppression or elimination of information, arbitrators will usually overrule them. Or, when objections seem personal or unnecessarily technical, they will not be persuasive with an arbitrator. The arbitrator is a professional and is not likely to be influenced by demonstrations of legal precociousness or courtroom histrionics of the type often used by attorneys before a jury.

    h.   Both sides have the right to object to evidence that may be irrelevant. Objections to the questioning by the opposing advocate of your witness are, however, often nothing more than attempts to confuse the issue and blind the arbitrator to some data. Objection for the sake of objection is a waste of time and tends to create an impression that there is an attempt to suppress information that may have bearing on the case. The arbitrator is the judge of the relevance of the material. He or she will often resent an advocate who presumes to tell him or her what is or is not relevant.

    i.   Often the parties to a dispute being arbitrated have to continue their relationship with each other. The more that can be done at the hearing to provide an atmosphere of careful, thoughtful, objective, and concerned examination of differences the better the chances for the long-range stability and quality of that relationship.

DATA, EVIDENCE, AND THE QUANTUM LEVEL OF PROOF

Proof and support of claims and contentions play a vital role in the arbitration process. The advocate must assemble data and evidence and then formulate a logical and persuasive argument to support the position that is taken. The arbitrator must weigh the evidence and argument presented to determine the direction of the decision. It is important, therefore, that both advocate and arbitrator have knowledge and understanding of the processes that go into the structure of argument.

1.   *Rules of evidence*

The rules of evidence is a system of standards by which the proofs in a dispute or trial are regulated. They have emerged over the years to protect undisciplined lay-person jurors from being controlled in their deliberations by prejudiced and unreliable testimony and exhibits. These rules have emerged primarily for use in the formal context of court and trial situations. In arbitration the proceeding is less formal, and the formal, legal rules of evidence are not always useful.

Even though it is widely accepted that arbitrators are not bound by the formal legal rules of evidence, there is a significant basis for the acceptance of some level of rules of evidence in the arbitral setting. According to the National Academy of Arbitrators:

The rules are based on many generations of judicial experience. They have as their primary objective the search for truth and generally the seeking to confine evidence so as to remove confusion, irrelevancy and manufactured facts. The significant consideration to bear in mind in relation to these rules is that they all have an underpinning of reason. They are not whimsical or arbitrary. Their objective is to encourage the process of unemotional and objective reasoning with the sole purpose to get at the truth. (BNA, 1966, p. 89)

What evidence, then, is admissible in arbitration? Most of it is. However, because there is no naive jury making the decision, the need for rigid rules about the introduction and use of that evidence is not pressing. The key concern of the arbitrator is the relevancy of the data presented to the issues that must be decided. Arbitrators are generally more sophisticated in their understanding of the nature and rules of evidence and are usually quite confident of their ability to judge the value of evidence offered in proof. For this reason and others, arbitrators will tend to allow evidence to be submitted that would not meet formal tests in court. "For what it is worth" is a key phrase, and the arbitrator takes the position that in assessing the relative value of the evidence it is his or her responsibility to judge the weight and the quality of the evidence presented.

The hearsay rule, for example, may not be as important in arbitration as it is in court. In spite of the fact that hearsay is usually not reliable and can be discounted, there are often examples of testimony that are of a hearsay nature that lead to more adequate sources of information or that point the way to new directions of investigation of important value in determination of the case. For these reasons many arbitrators will allow most evidence even though it borders on hearsay, but they usually warn the parties about the dangers of hearsay and irrelevant material. The problem with hearsay is, of course, that it is much less reliable than direct and primary testimony. Also of importance is that in hearsay testimony the alleged originator of the information is not available for defense or for answering questions posed by the other side.

> *Certainly the testimony of Fred who saw John hit Jim with a crowbar, is more reliable than the testimony of Sam who heard from Fred or someone else that John hit Jim, but did not actually view the incident. Sam's testimony is hearsay and if Fred is not present to answer questions, the evidence is not very reliable. If it has any value at all it is in the introduction of some indication that evidence might exist to show that John was the person who hit Jim. It is not the substantial evidence itself.*

Even so, when objections to evidence submitted by the opponent are made by one or both of the parties, the main concern is not that the evidence be excluded but that it serve as a guide to the arbitrator to assess the utility of the evidence. That is why most arbitrators will take evidence proffered "for what it is worth."

Arbitrators are also concerned about the distinction between the testimony of so-called "experts" and "lay" witnesses. That matter is not usually understood by the parties. The tests of expert witnesses and of the reliability of lay witnesses are of importance in arbitration.

The logical consistency of evidence if also of great importance. A chain of evidence that goes off in all directions and shows no logical or credible set of relationships is usually discounted and rejected. Even though disparate evidence may be introduced into a hearing, it is up to the advocates to put order to that collection in order to bring proof to bear on the issue.

2. *Evidence submitted to the arbitrator*

All things being equal, arbitrators are more likely to allow proffered evidence than disallow it. In spite of objections by the parties to evidence submitted by the other side, we must remember that arbitration is not a court of law, and the rules are not as strict as in a court of law. The arbitrator is concerned with "getting the truth" of a situation and not with accepting or only understanding the adversarial position of the parties. It is his or her responsibility to explore all possibilities and all sources of information that are available, no matter how he or she may handle the hearing process. The arbitrator's job is to determine what is fair or accurate rather than to just simply choose between two adversarial positions (except in the case of "last offer interest arbitration"). This is why some decisions are "split down the middle" or are not in response to an "either-or" condition, or why some decisions delay action until further data can be gathered.

Furthermore, the arbitrator is likely to allow most proffered evidence because subsequent challenges to a decision are most often made on the basis of a refusal to hear or allow relevant evidence. The arbitrator does not want this condition to exist. It is better to allow the evidence to be presented and then to evaluate it as being relatively useless than to not allow it in the first place.

Sometimes evidence with no probative value is permitted as its presentation allows the witness to release tension and to feel that there is ample opportunity to state his or her case. The so-called "cathartic" value of this to the witness has been identified as an important part of the dispute resolution process.

The arbitrator makes a personal inquiry to him or herself: "Is this evidence, if correct and adequate, essential and necessary to my decision?" Most of the time this cannot be determined until *after* the hearing when the arbitrator sits down and reviews the entire matter in its total context. Therefore, it is to the arbitrator's advantage to allow most evidence proffered in spite of objections unless there are very clear and obvious reasons why such evidence does nothing to get at the nature of the total situation.

3. *Evidence and levels of certainty*
There is usually a struggle between the parties and differences among arbitrators as to how much evidence is needed to establish a given decision as being justified. On the whole, however, the following scale appears to be weighed either explicitly or implicitly by most arbitrators:

Persuasive Result	Form or Extent of Evidence
Uncertain	Limited
More persuaded than not	Preponderance
Pretty certain	Clear and convincing
Completely certain	Beyond a reasonable doubt

In applying these levels of evidence we must recognize that the amount needed for any given situation will shift according to the nature of the offense and the point of view of the arbitrator. However, several standards seem to apply:

a. A preponderance of competent and reliable evidence is usually needed for matters such as absenteeism, falsification, error, and so on.

b. A beyond-a-reasonable-doubt level of competent and reliable evidence is needed to be completely certain of assault, theft, discrimination, rule violations, and similar infractions.

4. *Relevancy*
The arbitrator is the judge of what submitted evidence is relevant to the issues at point. A federal court stated:

> In an arbitration the parties have submitted the matter to persons whose judgment they trust, and it is for the arbitrators to determine the weight and credibility of evidence presented to them without restrictions as to the rules of admissibility which would apply in a court of law. (*Instrument Workers v. Minneapolis-Honeywell Co.*, 54 LRRM 2660, 2661 [USDC, 1963])

The arbitrator, either at the hearing or in the confines of study, must weigh the evidence as to its significance to the arguments being presented. When, during the hearing, one advocate challenges the evidence of the other by objecting to its introduction on the grounds that it is irrelevant, it is the responsibility of the arbitrator to determine whether it is relevant or whether it will be allowed "for what it is worth" and its relevancy assessed later when all the arguments are completed.

BURDEN OF PROOF

The burden of proof means the "obligation of a party to establish by evidence a requisite degree of belief concerning a fact in the mind of the arbitrator" (Jones, 1967, p. 196). This means that the burden of proof rests on that party who must establish the existence or nonexistence of a fact in order to gain acceptance of its contention(s).

In labor-management matters relating to discipline and discharge, the employer is usually the person or party who must establish the prima facie case before the arbitrator (that is, they are the affirmative in support of their action). This means that they usually go first in the presentation of the case. In other matters the grieving or charging party is the one who must establish the prima facie case before the arbitrator.

The party who has the greatest risk of non-persuasion has the greater burden of proof. Thus, in a discharge or discipline case, management stands to lose more by failing to support its position and it, therefore, has the greater burden of proof at the outset. Or, to put it in another way, if management cannot justify its action, that action will be nullified. It thus has the primary burden of proof. On the other hand, when a union charges that management has not proceeded according to the contract in assigning workers, it has the initial burden of proof for if it fails to prove its position, management's behavior will prevail.

The burden of proof may shift. When management, in a discipline case, has completed its basic presentation, and before any counter-argument or presentation has been made, the assumption is that, at that moment, sufficient grounds exist for acceptance of the disciplinary act. Thus, the risk of non-persuasion has shifted, and the union now runs the risk of non-persuasion if an inadequate counter-argument is not produced. It is an error for the union to assume that the full and only burden of proof in a discipline or discharge case always rests with management. Once the management position has been made and supported, it will stand until adequate challenge is produced. But should a challenge take place it must be more powerful than the original position in order to provide a basis for overthrowing the action of management. Similarly, in a general grievance case in which the burden begins on the side of the union as the moving party, it is a mistake for management to assume that it has no burden of argument. For once the union has established a basis for its charges, it will stand until management refutes it by more powerful arguments.

The burden of *evidence* is a different matter. Here we are dealing with the obligation of a party to introduce *sufficient* evidence to avoid an adverse ruling and to support a positive ruling. Thus *both* parties have a burden of evidence or they would not be at issue before an arbitrator.

In preparing and presenting your case be sure that you present as full a body of evidence as you can bring together to support your position. Remember that mere *allegations of fact or of an action are not sufficient.* The facts must be confirmed and proved by adequate testimony and/or other forms of evidence. Don't depend on hearsay evidence.

PREPARATION OF BRIEFS

In about 65% of arbitration cases the parties submit post-hearing briefs (Ray, 1992, p. 58). A brief is a firm record of the arguments in the case, and it may be referred to in subsequent disputes. The brief is also a complete and tightly organized summary of the case, and it is a very important document in arbitration cases. Ray (1992) wrote, "The best brief is one that makes it easy for the arbitrator to decide your way. Such a brief will provide the arbitrator with everything needed to write a clear opinion favoring your position" (p. 58). Briefs should be carefully prepared and tested before submission to the arbitrator. Most briefs include the following:

- Background of the case: A review of the facts and/or events that led to the action before the arbitrator
- Statement of the issue(s)
- Contract terms involved in the issue(s)
- Position of party
- Evidence and arguments in support of that position
- Conclusion and request for decision by the arbitrator

The main parts of the brief are, of course, the position and argument sections. It is best to organize this material in a clear and concise fashion.

In preparing the case from the outset the advocate *must determine what things must be proved if the final position is to be accepted.* Thus, in the hearing and also in the brief, each of these things must be clearly established.

Do not confuse arguments with the evidence or data presented. The argument is the reasoning process leading to a conclusion. The data or evidence is the raw material on which that reasoning is based. A good way to put this together is to state the conclusions you wish to reach, then give the reasons for those conclusions and support each reason with the necessary data and evidence to make it persuasive. For example:

The lift truck operator performed inadequately. (conclusion)
The lift truck was operated improperly. (reason)

1. It was to be constantly lubricated. When tested it was without necessary lubrication. (data)
2. The truck was to be driven at slow speeds. Witnesses report that the operator drove at excessive speeds. (data)
3. The running gauge showed it had been operated past the point when the operator was to have it serviced. (data)
4. The records show that it was used to carry loads beyond its rated capacity. (data)

In the briefs it is also useful to cite similar cases in which decisions have been made that give support to your argument. Although it may not be compelling, it does build some credibility to your arguments when you can show that in similar circumstances decisions of the type you seek were arrived at. Remember, however, that cases are different, and it is almost impossible to contend that any similar case is totally comparable. It is your responsibility to show that the comparability is of sufficient nature to make your use of the case persuasive.

The briefs should be well organized and clear. Use a basic outline form. Don't try to confuse the arbitrator with fancy language and long expositions. Make the material thorough, to the point, and clearly organized. At the end, summarize precisely.

SUMMARY: PREPARING AND PRESENTING YOUR CASE

1. Each party to the case must present a full body of evidence to support its position. In a discipline and discharge case the union must be able to show that management has failed in at least two or more of the criteria of just cause. In other types of grievance the essential issues must be clearly covered by both parties. It is often fatal if either party assumes that it has no burden of proof or responsibility of proof. Although, as I have noted, the burden may not exist at the outset, this may change rapidly if one of the parties provides a substantial argument.

2. Mere allegations of an act or fact are not sufficient. Both parties have to present proof of their contentions.

3. Objecting to the evidence or testimony presented by the other side is rarely useful in the arbitration process, although it is frequently used by less experienced advocates to "put on a show for their clients." Let the arbitrator decide if the information is useful and relevant. You may, however, use an "objection" to call the attention of the arbitrator to the matter of relevancy. You may also, through cross examination or other argument, show that you believe the material submitted to be irrelevant or inconclusive. That is part of *your* rebuttal responsibility. Trying to keep the material from being presented will often do you more harm than good in the eyes of the arbitrator. Remember that this is not a court of law in which rigid standards of information apply and in which the naivete of the jury is protected by rigorous rules of admissibility. The arbitrator has much greater freedom and is seeking to get at the heart of the dispute. He or she will often be somewhat suspicious if certain evidence relating to the case is consistently objected to.

4. In preparing your witnesses be sure that you know what they are going to say, not in the exact words, but in the general content of the testimony. It is very destructive to have your own witness testify to matters that destroy your case.

5. Most arbitrators are primarily concerned with the logic and soundness of the evidence presented in support of a position. Citing other decisions by other arbitrators in similar cases should be reserved for the briefs and should only be used to reinforce what has *already been clearly established.*

6. In questioning witnesses avoid redundancy and needless repetition. If the information is already on the record it need not be repeated. If no record is being kept except by the arbitrator, it may be important to summarize the testimony at some place in the hearing.

7. Be sure to summarize your position in your closing statement. Even if you are to have post-hearing briefs, your summary statement is important to the arbitrator in getting a perspective on your position. Furthermore, many arbitrators leave the hearing with the final summaries in their mind. A good summary can be a powerful influence on the arbitrator.

8. In discipline and discharge cases insist on post-hearing briefs.

9. Be sure that the grievant has an opportunity to testify if the grievant so desires. In cases involving "class action" be sure to have representative testimony that is typical of all grievants.

10. Maintain the informality of the hearing as much as the arbitrator will allow. If the arbitrator gives you the choice as to formality or informality, select the more informal route if possible.

11. Don't depend on hearsay evidence to give you much support. If all you have is hearsay you are in trouble.

12. Be sure that the stipulations to the arbitrator are clear and concise. If the two parties cannot agree on the stipulations, be sure that your statements are as fair as possible.

13. Avoid leading questions. Let the witness tell the story. Use questions that seek answers rather than questions that have answers in them.

14. Organize your case clearly so that you and the arbitrator can see how it fits into your position.

15. In presenting your brief be sure that it is outlined carefully and clearly. Provide each contention with its supporting evidence in a clear and organized fashion. If you confuse the arbitrator with your brief you are less likely to prevail.

16. Remember that when you are taking a matter to arbitration you are dealing with the professional and personal livelihood of your client. Whoever your constituent is he or she deserves the best and most careful consideration you can generate.

WHEN THE ARBITRATOR DECIDES

Robert Coulson, President of the American Arbitration Association, claims that, "it may be naive to think that arbitrators base their decisions entirely upon the objective facts and logical presentations made to them by the advocates" (1990, p. 37).

Each arbitrator experiences some worry or stress in making the decision required. In spite of the amount of his or her experience and skill in the process, the decision does not come without some concern on the part of the arbitrator (Davey, 1972).

The specific decision-making process that is used by arbitrators is not significantly different from any other decision making performed by those same people. No two of us follow the same method in decision making. Each of us has developed our own set of systems by which we arrive at decisions or make choices from the alternatives available to us. However, the following are some conditions in decision making that are consistent throughout the arbitral process.

1. Selection from alternatives
    In probably no decision-making endeavor is the process of selection from available alternatives more pronounced than in arbitral (and judicial) decision making. The arbitrator, from the outset, is faced with making a choice between conflicting points of view that have been forcefully brought into focus.

2. Bias, predisposition, and habit are present
    The process of arbitral decision making calls into play inherent biases, predispositions, and the habitual ways of dealing with choice. The arbitrator is not a person who is without all those very human processes that affect choice making.

3. The arbitrator depends on the quality and appropriateness of the evidence and reasoning that is submitted by the parties. In the absence of sound information the decisions themselves will more likely be flawed.

4. There is always a time factor in arbitrator decision making. In labor-management grievances the basic time span from the close of the hearing to the issuance of the decision is not supposed to exceed 30 days. Some go longer and some come forth in a shorter time.

5. Each arbitrator tries to show, in the written award, the reasons leading to the decisions made in that award. Most arbitrators take special care to make this reasoning clear.

6. Primacy of information plays a heavy role in the decision making of the arbitrator (Coulson, 1990). Thus, first impressions and strong initial arguments are likely to be quite influential in arbitrator decision making.

7. Arbitrators depend on various kinds of records to help them keep track of the data and arguments. Personal note taking is the most common. This is backed up by tape recordings of the hearing, and in some cases, by full transcripts of the proceedings. As the arbitrator ponders the decisions in a case these various records become sources of vital reviews of what took place and what was presented.

8. Arbitrators are subject to the many persuasive approaches or frameworks made by the parties. Metaphors play a strong persuasive role in influencing decision making. Skilled arbitrators are sensitive to the persuasive and emotional impact of metaphor on their own judgments.

9. When post-hearing briefs are filed weeks or months after a hearing, the memory of the arbitrator of the conditions of the hearing may be dulled so that important related information has been lost.

10. Arbitrators depend on post-hearing briefs to review and clarify the positions of the parties.

In all arbitral decision making we are facing a process carried on by trained minds who have developed skills in dealing with the kind of data that emerges in disputes. The more experienced the arbitrator the more likely that a stable and reliable decision making process will emerge. This does not mean that the process is one that will automatically bring agreement with the decisions. Each arbitrator realizes that for every decision there is likely to be at least one party who rejects it.

However, we can identify skilled arbitral decisions by the reasons why the parties to the dispute study the decisions. If the party studies the arbitrator's decision to find out where the arbitrator made a mistake, we can assume that the arbitrator is not perceived as highly as the one whose decision is studied by the parties to find out where they made mistakes.

SOME WAYS TO LOSE AT ARBITRATION

- *Be discourteous and nasty to your opponents.*

- *Do not cooperate with the arbitrator's request for information or other matters.*

- *Get into violent arguments with the other side at the table. (These should have taken place long before you come to the arbitration table. Your job at the hearing is to convince the arbitrator. You have already failed to convince your opponents.)*

- *Use the arbitration procedure to harass and irritate your opponents by arbitrating matters that are sure losers.*

- *Don't prepare thoroughly. Bring only a minimum of facts and evidence but a lot of arguments without supporting data.*

- *Use exaggeration and overemphasis on matters that are not primary or significant.*

- *Bring in witnesses who are not adequately prepared as to how they are to behave and the importance of their testimony to the case.*

- *Try to conceal essential facts and distort the truth.*

- *Refuse to bring documents and records pertinent to the case until required to do so by subpoena or other means.*

• *Mess up the procedures with "legal" technicalities. Raise objections frequently to the testimony of the opposing witnesses. Frequently challenge the questions asked of witnesses by the opposing advocate and the arbitrator.*

• *Tell the arbitrator just what he or she is supposed to do in the situation.*

• *Play games prior to the arbitration by refusing to agree on dates for a hearing.*

• *Harass the opponent's witnesses by accusing them of falsehoods, misrepresentation of the truth, and so on.*

• *Ignore the position of your adversary.*

• *Try to make the arbitration hearing a criminal trial.*

• *Argue with the arbitrator about procedure or a decision he or she has made.*

• *Use foul unprofessional language.*

• *Frequently interrupt your adversary when he or she is speaking to challenge what is being said.*

• *Accuse the other side of poor faith, bad judgment, and so on. (Let the facts speak for themselves.)*

• *Don't prepare for the hearing.*

• *Prepare a brief that is not well organized, without clear arguments, and that assumes the arbitrator will understand everything you think.*

CONCLUSION

The arbitration process is a decision-making process in which the parties to a dispute have turned to another to make the decision. By doing so they have acknowledged that their own decision-making powers are insufficient to resolve the dispute. Their function, therefore, is to present their side of the case as fully and as capably as possible so that fairness and justice can prevail.

Professional arbitrators do not waiver from the responsibility of making the decisions and do not try to salve the loser with "soft soap" or irrelevant references. The professional arbitrator is willing to live with the fact that the nature of the process favors one party over the other in the final determination and that the loser inevitably views the arbitrator in a less favorable light because of losing. Being an arbitrator is not a way to gain popularity. It is a trying and demanding process just as being an advocate is often very trying and demanding. The professional advocate is able to recognize sound and rational judgments made by arbitrators and to respect the decision making involved. Similarly, the professional advocate will look with disfavor on decisions that are shoddily made and reasoned out even though they may be in his or her favor.

CHAPTER 7

//

De-escalation and the Struggle Spectrum

> There are no conflicts that cannot be resolved, only conflicts in which the parties stubbornly resist solutions. Sweet reason, that much overrated human capacity, has however little part to play in resolving conflicts because adversaries enter conflicts with very different initial premises . . . Conflicts can be seen as moving over time along a tractability continuum, evolving toward more or less tractability. The temporal dimension is critical. Social contexts change over time, and the nature of conflicts changes as the contexts change. (Boulding, 1989, p. ix)

When struggle escalates to a point where it seems to become stalemated or when the violence or threat of violence becomes intolerable, a special change in the escalation must occur in order for the dispute to be resolved. In this chapter we look at some of those factors that are associated with such change. Negotiation continues or is restarted but takes on different perspectives. The preventive (problem solving, joint deliberations, cooperation) and interventive (mediation, arbitration, judicial, force) systems may continue, but the efforts to reverse the direction of the struggle require understanding and special attention.

In the normal course of events the negotiation and mediation processes seek to find a resolution to a dispute. The context (setting conditions, participants) in which they occur will have a great deal to do with the actual de-escalation that may emerge. When the parties to a dispute cease violence toward each other and attempt less aggressive means of dealing with their differences, de-escalation is taking place. De-escalation takes place when parties move from any phase of a dispute or struggle toward a less violent or less polarized condition. De-escalation does not always mean that the dispute is resolved, but it represents a movement toward resolution.

It is clear, however, that to de-escalate from a high level of violence or war is much more difficult than from a Stage 2 or Stage 3 dispute (see Chapter 1). Similarly, it is easier to de-escalate when in mediation than when in arbitration, although arbitration itself may result in a decision that de-escalates the dispute. Those struggles that have reached the campaign stage are clearly more difficult to defuse than those at the litigation stage because of the wider constituencies that become involved. In the campaign stage the channels of communication (sender-receiver systems) are increased in number and extent and the difficulties of interaction are increased.

Those struggles that persist and resist resolution are considered to be *intractable*. Intractability may occur at any level of struggle, although it is most frequently recognized when it occurs at the more intense and violent ends of the Spectrum. If we look at the Struggle Spectrum (see Chapter 1) in terms of a tractability-intractability continuum, it is reasonable to hypothesize that as we move from mild disagreement levels to levels of violence the potential for intractability increases. Keep in mind also that when we talk of "resolution" of conflict we are talking about the cessation of the activity related to a struggle. It is possible that once a struggle has escalated to the levels of violence it is never resolved irrevocably or totally (Rangarajan, 1985). What takes place is a change in the situation that reduces the violence, or even stops it. Rarely, however, is the whole spectrum of issues and causes resolved. Many remain and fester and may emerge again in other contexts.

In the following pages I discuss some of the current concepts of the intractability of struggles and of the de-escalation contexts and processes. Keep in mind that the processes and strategies are still very much a part of the Spectrum and most have been referred to in the discussion of the several stages and processes.

INTRACTABLE STRUGGLES

Those struggles that are perceived as unable to be resolved are intractable. That is, they resist attempts at resolution, have become intensified, original issues have been submerged, and the parties may attempt to harm or destroy each other.

Intractability occurs in degrees along the Struggle Spectrum. Actually intractability can occur in almost any phase of the Spectrum. The mild disagreement stage, for example, may become frozen as a couple simply allows a disagreement over which food is most nutritionally desirable for their family to continue without resolution. Or, at the dispute level of the Spectrum, the couple allows the disagreement over how much money to spend on food to continue, and they experience the struggle regularly. These examples represent intractable struggles at mild stages and, in fact, may be so unimportant in the relationship between the parties that de-escalation is not even considered. The intractability of the struggle is simply accepted as a fact of life. At the more adversarial and violent levels of the Spectrum intractability is a common condition.

The intractable situation is often characterized by rigid and unchanging perceptions by the parties of their different interests. Each party believes that its interests are more important than the interests of the other side. The city perceives its interests in a library to be more important than the county's interest in county roads.

Self-identity plays a part in the intractable situation. The dominant sense of self and the relation of the self to the rest of the world may be so rigid and unchanging as to make any change in relationships impossible. A gang leader in a poor neighborhood sees himself as being the best leader in the area and simply will not allow any other person to challenge his leadership without a violent fight.

Incompatible values are sure signs of intractability. The value struggles between the factions in Ireland are quite incompatible at this stage, and the struggle seems very intractable. The values of teenagers are often incompatible with those of their parents, and the struggles between them seem to be continuing and not subject to resolution. The values of the Japanese culture constantly clash with American values in their competing work systems. Attempts to deal with these incompatibilities are frequent but not always successful.

Misunderstandings lead to frozen struggles. The communication between the parties may be poor or even nonexistent. When there is no way for perceptions, interests, and variations of desire to be shared with the other party there can be little opportunity for the struggle to be ameliorated. When city council members do not meet or converse with county commissioners, many misunderstandings of common interests and issues arise.

Usually in the intractable state the positions between the parties are rigid and great hostility exists. Although this may not be true of the frozen struggles at the mild end of the Struggle Spectrum, as the struggle moves on to the other levels the rigidity and hostility increases. Because the parties perceive their situation as a win-lose matter they become unable to move from their initial positions and are able to move only to positions that give them advantage over the other.

The intractable condition does not allow for creative problem solving or joint deliberation over mutual problems and interests. The preoccupation of the parties is with sustaining themselves and their position during the struggle and of overcoming the opposing party.

> *The crisis in the coal industry in the 1970s as described by Ury, Brett, and Goldberg (1988) is an example. From 1978 to 1980 miners at Caney Creek mines in Eastern Kentucky struck the company with wildcat strikes 27 times, miners had been fired, a court case was initiated, over 100 miners went to jail overnight, bomb threats, sabotage and theft occurred, and miners were bringing guns in their cars as they went to work. The mine officials were considering closing the mine and in March 1980 laid off one-third of the workforce. The conflict between the mine union members and the company was considered intractable. I experienced a similar condition in the potash mining area of New Mexico in the early 1960s where violence in the streets and on the mining properties had the area divided into armed camps.*

One of the very interesting characteristics of intractability is the acting out of the conflict in ritual form. We see this in international relations when parties go through ceremonial degradation of their opponents as with Bush's regular depiction of Saddam Hussein as a villain during the Persian Gulf War and its antecedents. Different cultures have developed dances, ceremonies, icons, and art objects that depict the enemy as vicious and destructive and their own leaders as godlike or constructive. Street gangs ritualize their relations with opposing gangs through graffiti, gang names, and clothing. The more the social unit ritualizes its struggle with another unit the more the struggle becomes intractable.

Intractability appears when conflicts have lasted so long that the basic issues have been submerged and many parties on all sides have a stake in the continuance of the struggle. The "Hatfield vs. McCoy" syndrome (the fabled interfamily fight) is characteristic of this condition. The story of Romeo and Juliet is built around just such a situation. The Israel-Palestine struggle has these characteristics. As of this writing many other nations and political units have a stake in the struggle between the Israelis and their antagonists. The increasing complexities and involvement of these outside groups seems to act as a deterrent to efforts of the two principal groups to resolve their difficulties. However, these same conditions are serving as triggers to attempts to de-escalate as powerful marginal parties become fearful of the continuation and find it to their benefit to change the nature of the struggle. Indeed, as of late Summer and early Fall 1993, such attempts appeared to be coming to fruition in the peace conferences and agreements concluded in Washington between Israel and the PLO.

THE BASIC NATURE OF DE-ESCALATION

At any stage in the Struggle Spectrum at least three events may be taking place:

1. The situation may be escalating toward a more antagonistic relationship and/or behavior (i.e., from disagreement and argument to litigation);
2. The situation may be stalemated (i.e., stuck on debate, argument, or continuing violence, which neither increases nor abates); and
3. The situation may be de-escalating toward a less antagonistic relationship and behavior level within the Spectrum (i.e., moving from violence to court litigation or mediation, etc.).

De-escalation has been defined as "a reduction in one or more dimensions of the intensity of the conflict behavior between parties" (Kriesberg, 1991, p. 3). It also is a reduction in the extent of the struggle and in the number of parties involved. De-escalation can be considered a roving stage in the Struggle Spectrum. Hurwitz (1991) says, "De-escalation then is not a retreat, down an up-staircase of hostilities but a climb up the war-to-peace staircase with turning where the character of the relationship between the parties in conflict changes" (p. 123). When the parties turn from violence to campaign, litigation, arbitration, or mediation, the process is taking place. Hurwitz reverses the spectrum when he refers to war-to-peace as an advance in the peace-making process.

Escalation and de-escalation are related to each other and are not opposites. Zartman and Aurik (1991) point out that:

[a] decision not to escalate is not necessarily a decision to de-escalate nor is a decision to de-escalate necessarily a decision to wind down conflict . . . a check on escalation (or intensification) does not necessarily mean that the de-escalation process has begun. A decision not to escalate often means a decision to carry on the conflict at its present level, and a decision to de-escalate (especially in means) may mean the continuation of the conflict more cheaply. Both decisions refer to a choice of continuing stalemate as a condition of conflict not to the beginnings of its end. (pp. 155-156)

Sometimes the de-escalation is directed at moving the intractability from one stage to another—of changing the nature of the struggle from violent methods to nonviolent methods—from armed violence to media-based psychological violence and campaigning. The stages of de-escalation appear to roll from one to the other. Kreisberg (1991) identifies them as "signaling or probing by one party, exploratory discussions about possible agendas for negotiations, conducting negotiations, and concluding and sustaining agreements" (p. 4).

Most attempts at de-escalation are directed at the more cooperative levels of the spectrum. Along with these attempts come a reduction of the intense animosity that emerged as the differences moved into disputes. Many de-escalations deal with marginal issues until there is sufficient experience in joint deliberations to allow for tackling the major issues with a greater chance of success. Probably one of the most significant characteristics of de-escalation is when the win-lose, zero-sum atmosphere changes to a non-zero-sum or shared-result condition.

A reduction in the extent of a struggle can be recognized from a number of events that occur. When a struggle that has involved a number of constituents on each side seems to become focused on the action of only a few parties we can expect some de-escalation efforts to emerge.

> *A community-wide dispute over widening the street in front of the school administration offices had pitted landowners, developers, school officials, the school board, financial officers of the schools and the city, real estate sales personnel, the mayor's office, the city manager's office, the city council, the local newspaper, and others in a dispute that threatened to escalate into courtroom proceedings. The dispute began when the schools had requested the city to widen the street. Landowners immediately refused to become involved in the property evaluations and reductions that would be required. Within a few weeks tempers raised, more and more people in the city got involved, and there seemed to be no resolution to the problem. Landowners would not talk with the school board or school officials and held the developers responsible for intruding on their property rights. The city council refused to talk with the land owners, and so on.*
>
> *The struggle escalated to include paid advertisements in the newspaper and over the radio and TV. Every household in the district became involved in one way or another. Former good friends refused to talk with each other, neighborhood groups passed resolutions opposing one side or the other, and there seemed no effort by anyone to find a solution. So, when an unaligned local mediator assisted the landowners association to select a representative to sit with the president of the school board to work on a resolution, the struggle began to de-escalate. The ensuing negotiations changed the situation into a more viable one from the one that existed before the parties had refused to negotiate.*

Most de-escalation efforts involve attempts by the parties to find a resolution to the differences that separate them.

> *Anwar Sadat's famous visit to Jerusalem in 1977 and the subsequent negotiations through the mediation of President Carter are examples of the beginning of negotiation efforts that had significant importance on de-escalating a long-lasting struggle.*

De-escalation is taking place when the parties to a debate or in courtroom litigation move away from confrontive behavior in both these contexts and attempt to sit down together, discuss their mutual problems, and seek solutions through joint deliberation

Similarly, de-escalation occurs when parties in litigation move to mediation.

> *A divorcing couple in court over custody of their only child were advised by the court to seek mediation. Upon doing so both parties began to work through their problems rather than argue them out before the judge.*
>
> *A struggle over the use of government protected wetlands along a river had escalated from a minor dispute between the owner and the city to a state-wide struggle between environmentalists and developers. The matter was being campaigned in the media and many people were becoming involved. A win-lose attitude surrounded the whole situation. Finally, when a mediator was invited into the situation by the land owner and the city, the campaign seemed to slow down and eventually stopped as the parties got into some creative negotiation over the issues.*

To change intractable struggles to viable ones (tractable) may require creative redescription (reframing) of the perceptions and the nature of the language surrounding the struggle situation. Changing or abandoning the metaphors of the conflict may be highly useful. Metaphors seem to play a significant role in escalation and changing them has relevance.

> *The change of the metaphorical image of the USSR from the "Evil Empire" to a more benign group of confused schoolboys made quite a difference in the perceptions of that political system. Changing the metaphorical image of the city manager from that of a stern dictator to a friendly helper made a lot of difference in his acceptance by many of the citizens.*

Metaphors are substitutes for reality and can be terribly destructive when not used carefully and judiciously. (Many people get so caught up in the fun of creating metaphors that the linguistic and psychological damage they can do is often overlooked.)

Our perceptions play an important role in de-escalation. Each of us has a perception of ourselves and the world around us. Some call this a "frame of reference." Others refer to a "life script" or "tape." It is essentially a structure or "frame" by which we assess the world and the events within it.

> Each of us . . . has a structure of existence within which we live, function, and perceive the world. The types of entities that exist for us and the relationships among these entities constitute this structure and serve to constrain our values, goals, and actions. The structure provides the frame for our interactions with other actors and for the strategies we develop for dealing with problems. (Hunter, 1989, p. 26)

Differences in framing appear to be one of the basic conditions of struggle. The way that one person frames his or her perception of the world will determine the manner in which that person deals with others within that frame. These frames come from many sources: conditioning, heritage, goals, desires, experiences, education, and the many contexts of our lives that affect the way we view the world around us. Our view of our world, then, determines the way we will interact with it.

> *Two old friends and highly qualified consultants who had worked together for several years eventually realized that they were in deep competition with each other. "E" had come to view "D" as an aggressive, dominating, bitch who had to be in control of all people, not only in her professional relationships, but those of her immediate family, and a person who was willing to "use" a friendship to advance her own causes. "D" viewed "E" as an intellectually and professionally able person who could play an important role in her professional growth as a kind of 'big-brother' to her, but who was an "easy touch" and could be manipulated easily to provide her with advantages she could not otherwise accomplish herself. These clearly antagonistic differences in their frame made it increasingly difficult for them to work together. They began to encounter an increasing number of disputes over seemingly trivial issues.*

De-escalation may be facilitated by the parties to a dispute exploring the differences in the framing and reframing of their perceptions of the world in which the struggle takes place. In the case of "D" and "E," an attempt at reframing helped to change the relationship. There were limitations, however, on how far they could go on their own, and eventually a third party neutral was brought in to help in the process.

Often de-escalation will occur when there have been episodes of increasing intensity, hostile interactions, or violence between the parties. The sudden eruption of intense feeling and action often shocks the parties into seeking to subdue the violence.

> *In the Cuban missile crisis the United States and the Soviet Union de-escalated dramatically when faced with the violent possibilities that were emerging in the continuing cold war struggle between the U.S. and Cuba. The engineering of that de-escalation was accomplished by the good offices of U. Thant, then Secretary General of the United Nations.*
>
> *At the Caney Creek mines situation described by Ury, after much violence had taken place and the closing of the mines was threatened, attempts to de-escalate the struggle were initiated by calling in a neutral third party (Ury et al., 1988).*
>
> *Two colleges in the same community exchanged athletic contests regularly. It was traditional that before the annual football game there would be parades by each school extolling their champions and denigrating the opposing team. Because the two schools existed at opposite ends of a long boulevard (some 3 miles in length) it was great "fun" to march toward the other school until met by the opposing parade. As the years passed the intensity of the parade increased and the events that took place when the two columns met became more and more violent. Finally, a clash took place in which a number of students from both schools were seriously hurt. Immediately thereafter the presidents of the two institutions decreed that all contests between the schools were suspended, and no more parades were allowed.*

Often when an escalation has been successful in resolving a difference and further struggle is unnecessary or inappropriate, de-escalation will follow.

> *Two faculty members (formerly friends) were struggling with each other over control of the policy-making processes within their department. In order to gain control each was striving to become the department chair. In the process of escalation they had engaged in some nasty campaigning and vicious allegative attacks on each other. When, in a department election, one was selected as chair, the struggle seemed to be closed. Even so, the two adversaries still maintained a strained relationship, the overt struggle ceased but many of the highly interpersonal issues remained, and eventually the two were advised by the dean to go to mediation.*
>
> *Two partners in a training enterprise suddenly found themselves in an intense confrontation over the failure of one of them to respect the privacy of the other. The confrontation brought both parties to realize what was happening, and they agreed to break up their partnership.*

CONDITIONS FACILITATING DE-ESCALATION

Certain conditions seem more effective than others in moving a dispute toward less intense and destructive levels. The strategies for facilitating de-escalation in reality reflect an appropriate integration with the existing conditions. The conditions most frequently identified are timing, nature of the relationships, interpersonal factors, intragroup factors, intergroup factors, and power.

Ripeness and Timing

When is the best time to attempt de-escalation? The obvious answer is anytime the struggle shows signs of becoming destructive, costly, and leading to conditions that are not desirable by both parties. Even so, there are some conditions that appear to make a situation "ripe" for de-escalation. The nature of de-escalation contains a number of points at which de-escalation can take place. "Ripeness" is determined by the ultimate success of the effort. That is, when the effort works, it is considered to be timely.

Rubin (1991) suggests that the time for de-escalation may be when changes in intensity of the struggle occur. "The life cycle of a conflict—whether this be conflict between individuals, groups, or nations—consists of blips and bulges rather than a straight line. Conflict varies in intensity over time, and such changes in intensity create opportunities for movement" (p. 238).

The introduction of ideas that help to bridge conflicting points of view is also considered by Rubin (1991) as a factor of ripeness. The ripeness factor is often the result of great understanding of the underlying interests of both parties.

Timing is almost impossible to describe. So many factors are involved, and each person has a different perception of the factors that are involved in a dispute setting. We know that in the area of negotiation and mediation many professionals have an almost intuitive sense of when to introduce a change or propose a resolution. In my experience the sense of timing seems to emerge from listening very carefully to all that is taking place both verbally and nonverbally and testing ideas in a very tentative way until they "hit." It is much like fishing—you keep checking the waters and changing the bait until the fish takes it.

There is some evidence to suggest that the introduction of third parties into a situation can bring about the ripe moment for initiating de-escalation moves. One reasonable explanation is that the introduction of a third party in any dispute changes the dynamics of the situation and in the presence of such change the de-escalation can emerge.

Again, however, the ripe moment of intervention depends greatly on the competence of the intervener. Consider the minister who intervened in a marriage dispute with an untimely and inept attempt to mediate at the judicial stage when the parties were deeply involved in court proceedings. Immediately the dispute escalated to violence.

Also, if the interveners have a vested interest in either the disputants or the outcome of the dispute there can be serious problems. In recent years we have discovered a number of programs alleging to train managers to "mediate" and in some cases "arbitrate" the disputes between their employees and between themselves and their employees. This can be very contra-functional in that the manager inevitably has a vested interest in the outcome of the dispute if it involves matters related to the business. The consequences of such an intervention can be very costly in the long run. Even if the matter does not involve or affect the business the manager has no independent authority to intervene unless invited by the parties.

A manager attempted to mediate a dispute between two employees who were struggling over who should be lead worker in the shop. The struggle between the workers had escalated to the point where their behavior was disrupting the rest of the shop personnel and was also leading to some serious production losses. The manager, due to his functional power and authority over the two employees, could hardly mediate their dispute because he had a stake in the outcome and the employees knew it. What actually resulted is that he persuaded the employees to settle their dispute to his benefit with little benefit to their concerns and interests. Although he claimed he mediated the situation, what he actually did was to manipulate the matter to come out the way he wanted it. In the process he used many of the same skills he would have used as a true mediator were he in a situation in which he did not have a stake in the outcome. The bias of his position made his efforts part of his managerial function, but it was hardly a mediatory function in spite of what he and his trainers called it. It also provided very poor "press" for the process of mediation. When the union to which the employees belonged wanted to go to mediation over the contract, the employees opposed it because, as a result of their experience, they perceived it as a management control process.

International disputes frequently are "mediated" by other nations who have undeniable stakes in the outcome of the dispute. The United States, for example, has intervened in a mediatory way in those countries where its supply of some vital product such as oil is threatened by the parties—the United States wants a resolution that favors U.S. interests.

The U.S. intervention in the Middle East has been clearly related to its interests in the oil supply that those countries provide. The mediation efforts in respect to the struggle between Israel and the Palestinians have been closely tied to the United States' economic and social interests in those areas. King Hussein of Jordan, in the latter part of 1990 and in early 1991, attempted to mediate the struggle between Iraq and Kuwait because of, among other things, common boundaries and interests in the oil production system of the area.

The introduction of third parties as arbitrators takes the resolution of the dispute out of the hands of the actors. But when it is essential that the parties own the resolution and have responsibility for its administration, this kind of intervention may not be appropriate. However, if the parties agree to perform as the arbitrator decides, the parties do own the resolution (see Chapter 6).

One of the important conditions of ripeness is the matter of power between the parties. If the balance between two parties is asymmetrical, the more powerful feel less inclination to negotiate and the less powerful are afraid that any negotiation will lock them into an inferior position (Rubin, 1991). Thus, timing is closely related to the power of the parties to respond to a de-escalatory intervention. In most cases we find that when the power balance is more symmetrical the chance of mutual change developing appears to be greater.

Still another factor in timing is the leadership of the parties involved in the dispute. If any of the leaders of the parties are unable to negotiate and reach compromise, either by strength or weakness, the ripeness of the situation for de-escalation may not be present.

Internal Personal Factors in Interpersonal Struggles

No matter how we address the whole spectrum of struggle the development of resolution will eventually come down to the internal personal feelings and perceptions of the individuals involved in the struggle. Whether the disputes are bilaterally interpersonal, as between husband and wife, or involve groups (families, communities, states, nations), the contact point between the parties usually is between individuals. Their intrapersonal perceptions and approaches have a significant affect on the possibilities of de-escalating a dispute.

Among the interpersonal conditions that seem to favor de-escalation are:

- a person feels threatened with destruction or loss if the struggle continues. For example, a divorced father, after several harsh court sessions with his ex-wife over custody of their child, begins to feel that if he continues to fight he may lose what rights he has to be with the child. He is, at this point, in a condition where de-escalation efforts may be functional.

- one of the persons at the focal point of the dispute loses energy or desire to continue the struggle. The fight has been draining and debilitating and the desire to keep struggling simply fades away. This person will welcome de-escalation.

> *A farmer had been struggling with his neighbor for many years over a tiny strip of land that had been improperly surveyed at the time the two properties were homesteaded. Repeated requests to the federal, state, and local governments brought no clear resolution. Appeals to the neighbor fell on deaf ears. Many hours and dollars were spent in trying to get clear title to the land. Nothing seemed to resolve the problem. The farmer was growing old and did not want to struggle with the matter any longer. He was glad to have a mediator enter the situation.*

- the intrapersonal context is responsive to de-escalation when the gains by some mutual resolution or compromise appear to be greater than the gains realized by continuing the struggle.

> *Two brothers, Roy and Tim, had been fighting for years over who should have the family home because there was no will giving it to either one. Both Tim and Roy had strong feelings about the place and wanted it very much. But when Tim offering to pay Roy half the value of the place if he would abandon the struggle, Roy realized that he would be better off with that compromise than if he continued to struggle and eventually lost.*

- the internal tensions and feelings relating to the adversaries become relaxed and reduced, and, for one reason or another, the person becomes open to de-escalation efforts.

> *A father and son had been struggling with each other for many years over the family-owned contracting business. When the father was unwilling to bring the son in as a full partner, the son set up a competing company. The competing business became successful and equalled the father's. Each enjoyed winning over the other on some contract and would not hesitate to "strut" about it. But they each realized that the other was a good contractor, and a mutual respect emerged. When the son's stepmother suggested that they should merge, neither one seemed unwilling to explore the possibility.*

Interpersonal Relationships Allowing for Change

The relationships between people involved in an intractable struggle must change in order for de-escalation to take place. These relationships run across a wide spectrum of conditions. The following are some more common ones that favor de-escalation:

- A sudden rise in violence between persons often creates pressure to de-escalate. This often arises from a fear of things getting out of hand and of hurtful consequences.
- When a stalemate exists that contains violence and threats of violence accompanied by high levels of antagonism between the individual participants, a pressure to de-escalate may emerge. The effects of stalemate and antagonism can be very energy draining on individuals. The existence of the stalemate and growing demands to prevent violence become conditions that arouse interest in abating the struggle.
- When the adversaries, either personal or group, have some history of cooperation in the past the possibilities of de-escalating a particular dispute are present. Neighbors who have cooperated in working out the division of the costs of paving the road in front of their properties are more likely to be able to de-escalate an intense struggle arising over the line between their properties than if they had never had a cooperating experience together.
- When the perceived power balance between the parties is symmetrical there is a greater possibility of attempts at de-escalation than when there is wide discrepancy in the balance. Kriesberg (1991) points out that:

  > Each side seems more ready to undertake de-escalation initiatives when it believes it is stronger than its adversary compared to when it believes that it is relatively weak but expects to gain strength in the future. If one party is much stronger, however, it often raises its demands rather than offering to de-escalate the fight. Consequently, de-escalation moves from intense and stable antagonism are more likely to occur when the adversaries experience parity than when one adversary is much stronger than the other. Parity, however, must be considered relative to the issue about which de-escalation is being considered.

The prospective power balance is as important as the current power balance. The party that believes it will gain relative strength in the future tends to resist making concessions in the present, hoping for better terms of settlement later. An adversary that thinks it is winning may keep raising its demands, frequently overextending itself. (pp. 6-7)

- When one party believes that if it makes an effort to de-escalate the opposing party will reciprocate, there is a possibility of de-escalation taking place.
- De-escalation becomes possible when either, both, or all parties to a dispute anticipate a great deal of pain, loss, or destruction if the matter continues. Such perceptions often lead the parties to make efforts to avoid or reduce the struggle.
- When the parties are willing to seek a non-zero-sum-game situation and to move away from the zero-sum-game contexts, de-escalation is possible. This means letting the other side exist in order to exist yourself.

> *Two brothers were fighting over the extensive property of their deceased parents who had left no will. Each was trying to win it all. Finally they both began to see that this attitude carried considerable risk of losing and they joined forces to work out a mutual solution to the distribution of the estate.*

Intragroup Conditions in Intergroup Struggles

When groups are involved intragroup dynamics play an important role in any dispute between them. There are several conditions of in-group dynamics that have particular significance in making the de-escalation of a dispute possible.

- Changes in the leadership within a group may set the stage for de-escalation of a pre-change fight. Changes in the leadership of any group will tend to change the dynamics of that group. To the extent that those dynamics are important in the continuation of the struggle with other groups the change will bring about opportunities for changing the dynamics of the struggle.

> *A struggle between the marketing and manufacturing divisions in a fairly large company had existed for almost a decade. The struggle seemed focused on the two vice presidents in charge of the respective divisions. When one of the vice presidents left and a new one from outside the company was put in place the struggle de-escalated quickly.*

- Many struggles between groups continue to exist because the constituencies of the groups support the dispute.

> *Two neighborhoods were in intense litigation over the wooded acres that separated them. One group wanted the space made into a park and zoned for recreation only. The other side wanted the space zoned as residential so that more homes could be built in the area. The dispute had continued over a number of years and seemed to be stalemated and intractable. As people moved away from the area and new residents moved in, the character of the constituency changed, and the support for both sides appeared to diminish. This made attempts at de-escalation and resolution possible.*

- Another intragroup factor that affects a struggle is the existence of in-group coalitions that are opposed to the struggle. When these coalitions grow to a size large enough to dominate the decision making of the group the direction of the group can change.

> *A company and a union had been in serious dispute for a number of years over several issues involving the personnel policies of the company. The struggle seemed to be intractable as numerous strikes had taken place during contract negotiations, and wildcat strikes had taken place during the contract years. One year a new bargaining committee gained power in the union and it gathered support from a number of newer employees who were opposed to many of the demands being made by the union. They created a powerful subgroup within the union. This resulted in a condition that allowed for de-escalation efforts at the bargaining table and a resolution of many of the differences.*

> *Two street gangs sought to expand their territories of influence and they violently struggled with each other for control of a small district that had a number of motels, bars, and houses of prostitution. When a new district opened on the other side that promised even better opportunities for one of the gang's interests, that gang lost interest in the district over which it had struggled with the competing gang. The de-escalation of their dispute became a real possibility that later bore fruit. What we have here is the condition in which the goals being sought by a group involved in a struggle are being met by other means than those directly involved in the struggle.*

Intergroup Factors in Intergroup Struggles

Probably one of the most obvious conditions leading to de-escalation in struggles between groups is when one group perceives its adversary as seeking de-escalation. This may not lead to de-escalation if the one group views the group seeking de-escalation as engaging in a strategy aimed at giving them an advantage. Absent any such intent, when one group seeks de-escalation the other group may join in the effort.

Much has been said about the process of "reframing" as a function of dispute resolution (see Moore, 1986, pp. 175-180). Frames are another way of expressing the perceptual context from which each party views the other. The struggle between environmentalists and developmentalists can be partially described and understood in terms of their different perspectives of the same situation. A careful analysis of the frames of each of the parties to a struggle can assist in understanding the dispute.

Reframing is accomplished when changes in how the parties define their relationships occur that soften or ameliorate their perceptions of each other. When the image of the other party becomes more humane and the view of the other as an enemy to destroy is reduced, a reframing has taken place. When reframing has taken place or is taking place the conditions for de-escalation may be present.

When the significance of a dispute to either or both of the parties becomes less in the face of other struggles with other parties a de-escalation may take place. When a third group, for example, attempts to control both of the other antagonists to its own ends, the two antagonists may be ready to back away from their struggle with each other.

Another condition that sometimes facilitates de-escalation is when outsiders with superior strength exert pressure on the antagonists to reduce the struggle.

> *Two secretaries had frequent arguments over who should pick up the incoming mail in the morning and deliver the outgoing mail to the post office at the close of the day. They would spend a great deal of valuable time trying to manipulate each other into the undesirable job. Upon discovering this waste of time the supervisor issued instructions that they were to work out a schedule and she would see that it was followed. Their arguments ceased, and they prepared a schedule for their supervisor's approval.*

A condition that has some value in setting the stage for de-escalation is the availability and readiness of skilled and trusted intermediaries. When the parties to a dispute realize that there are trusted third parties available at critical points there can be an atmosphere conducive to de-escalation.

When the leadership of the antagonistic groups perceive that a satisfactory resolution is possible de-escalation becomes possible. The union and the management in an electrical equipment manufacturing business were stalemated over the terms of a contract and particularly the economic package. The union representative and the company president both believed that there was a middle ground that would resolve the strife. The very presence of this perception made it possible for a mediator to find the point at which the two would agree.

When the interests of the adversaries begin to converge there is opportunity to de-escalate the struggle between them. For example, agreement between the Sandinistas and the contras in Nicaragua in 1987 was possible after it became clear that neither party was going to receive the support it had expected from the United States and the Soviets and that their separate security depended on their mutual security.

The flow of information and products between adversaries sets the stage for de-escalation. The flow of information, ideas, products of vital interest, and services that are exchanged opens up the channels of communication and allows for mutual interests to be explored.

De-escalation is likely when both sides perceive that continued conflict between them can lead to excessive costs and major losses. The cost/benefit ratio seems to set a ceiling on the amount of struggle a group will endure before seeking a resolution.

The Cuban Missile Crisis of 1961 is an example of a dramatic event or crisis that forced the antagonists to seek a solution to many of the conflicts of interest that were coming to a head in that situation. Such dramatic events often seem to cut through the vagueness to interrupt the momentum of a struggle.

Clearly, when trust between the warring groups begins to emerge, the conditions for de-escalation may be present.

> *Again, the Cuban Missile Crisis showed that when the acts of opposite parties are interpreted as demonstrations of good faith and/or a redress for past provocation de-escalation becomes viable. In the Cuban affair the U.S. announced that it would not invade Cuba and this affected Khrushchev, who claimed that his installation of the missiles was to forestall a U.S. invasion of Cuba (Hurwitz, 1991).*

> *In a football game the rules limit the amount and time of physical attack on each other. When, in the heat of the contest, players begin to exchange fisticuffs, the rules require that penalties be assessed and that the continuation of that behavior cease. Both parties are in agreement as to these rules and power is mutually given to the referee to assess penalties. Thus, rules relating to limits may set the stage for de-escalation of a fight.*

POWER AND DE-ESCALATION

In general, the application of power in dispute resolution involves, among other things, the use of negative and positive inducements (carrot and stick) which may be used in moving toward de-escalation. The nature of these inducements has been divided into four categories: gratification through promises and predictions, and deprivations through threats and warnings (Zartman & Aurik, 1991). In the case of the dispute between the secretaries over the office mail the power move of the supervisor was clearly in the manner of threat and warning.

Part of the process of power involves the making of decisions. When one or all of the parties to a dispute recognize that the internal cost of either stalemate or escalation is more than can be tolerated, there is usually a decision to halt the dispute interaction. In the Middle East struggles the move toward a peace conference in 1992-93 partly emerged from the tremendous internal human and collateral costs the continuing struggle demanded. Also, at the same time, the power of the United States to bring the parties to the table was the result of the threats to its supply of oil from the area and its decision to act in the Persian Gulf War of 1990-91.

In many international situations threats have had the effect of closing off the escalation and opening the doors to possible negotiation. The effectiveness of threats in any context, however, is related to the dependency of those threatened on those who are threatening.

The uses of promises of favorable outcomes is effective in some situations in moving parties toward de-escalation.

> *Two neighbors were fighting over a property line separating their suburban properties and had threatened to go to court over the matter. The city promised the disputants that if the line settlement could be reached without going to court the city would proceed with its street beautification plan that both neighbors wanted very much to have. The property owners immediately asked for mediation.*

Zartman and Aurik (1991) point out that "for meaningful de-escalation to occur, promises or positive inducements (and predictions of a better future as well) are necessary. If the sticks are in the stalemate, the carrots are in the contract" (p. 181).

STRATEGIES OF DE-ESCALATION

Nature of Strategies

The strategies of de-escalation are those processes and methods that aim to move an intractable struggle to a tractable stage. As you look at the conditions and factors that facilitate de-escalation, it seems that many of them would be considered strategies. However, they become strategies only when a procedure and a process is initiated to bring them about. The strategies, therefore, involve procedures aimed at three levels of movement:

1. Downward in the Struggle Spectrum to less violent or contentious stages;
2. Movement to stages where negotiation can recur; and
3. Movement from a win-lose context to one in which the struggle becomes a shared problem with possible solutions.

Ury et al. (1988) recognize three basic elements of any dispute: interests, rights, and power. The strategies for de-escalation are techniques that are closely related to dealing with these three issues. Selection of the strategies to use is a critical matter. The wrong strategy may escalate or stalemate, rather than de-escalate, a struggle. Ury et al. (1988) suggest that in selecting a strategy or strategies several criteria need to be considered: possible satisfaction with outcome, costs, relationship results, and recurrence of the struggle.

The degree of mutual satisfaction with the outcome expressed by the parties to the dispute is one criteria of success. In most cases compromise-type resolutions may not satisfy all the elements of both sets of interests in terms of their demands, but there may be sufficient adjustments to allow for an approval or agreement that fulfills some of the interests. The strategy that is most valuable is the one that will maximize mutual satisfaction with the result.

Costs are determined in a number of ways. Losses in time, money, prestige, self-image, and pleasure are all factors relating to the price paid for a behavior. Thus, the parties are going to assess the relative costs of the results of a strategy to de-escalate or resolve a dispute compared with the costs of no such effort or result. This comparison of relative costs is of great importance in selecting a strategy for de-escalation.

The subsequent relationship between the parties is another standard to be used in the selection of strategies. The long-term relationship between two neighbors may be an important consideration in assessing the value of a proposed strategy. If the strategy resolves the immediate dispute but leaves the parties at such odds that other disputes will soon arise, the strategy is of less value than one which allows for a long-term positive relationship.

A strategy has not been a successful one when agreements are not followed, when apparent resolutions are only superficial, when disputes keep recurring at the initial pre-strategy level of intensity or go beyond it, or when the dispute escalates or stalemates rather than de-escalates (Ury et al., 1988).

These criteria are not exclusive to one another. They are linked together. Thus, for example, unhappiness over costs may affect satisfaction with the emerging changes. Recurrence of the disputes increases costs, and so on. Thus, as you look at the several individual strategies, the whole set of criteria will apply.

Each situation also presents a different combination of effects. It is therefore impossible to assign a constant value to any one standard because the specific situation determines what the critical standard is.

The Determination of Strategies by Persons

Strategies to be used are determined by the persons seeking to de-escalate a dispute. The leaders of groups in conflict may be the key influential persons who can devise the approach to de-escalation. This is particularly true in intergroup and international disputes. In interpersonal struggles one or both of the adversaries may introduce the efforts to de-escalate. Sometimes a third party not involved in the dispute may seek to reduce the struggle by intervention strategies.

No matter how or when the actors involved in de-escalation may emerge, there are value issues that are involved. These value issues arise from the nature and direction of the efforts of those seeking to de-escalate. Kreisberg (1991) points out that, "the process of de-escalating is not value free. The efforts to de-escalate a conflict are not morally neutral and do not have the same implications for all the partisans. Deciding whether or not to try to de-escalate a conflict and which strategy to pursue, necessarily involves value preferences regarding an acceptable outcome" (p. 24).

Factors to Be Considered in Selecting Strategies

Persons or groups seeking to de-escalate a struggle are those who apply the strategies in managing disputes. That is, the strategies discussed here represent some of the things people can do to set in motion de-escalation processes as well as to deal with struggle within the spectrum. The people most likely to be instrumental in applying the strategies are usually leaders of either political, social, economic, or religious groups. They may also be non-aligned and unaffiliated persons with no commitment to any party. They may also be an ally of one of the disputing groups or parties, or they may be part of one of the adversarial groups seeking to reduce the effects on the group(s).

Evarts, Greenstone, Kirkpatrick, and Leviton (1983) examined four strategies for managing conflict: deterrence, compellance, avoidance, and accommodation. Deterrence, the use of threats and other communication that promises negative consequences, was identified as a frequent effort, but the least effective approach. Compellance, through coercive force and reward by the use of commands, was also identified as a process frequently used in the family and the workplace. Similarly, compellance was identified as a temporary measure and only achievable with the presence of highly authoritarian procedures. Avoidance of necessary decisions and actions by pretending there is no struggle and making no effort to affect the situation is also considered nonfunctional in managing disputes. Accommodation is the basic strategy, according to these authors, for all conflict management. All of the strategies that we examine here are accommodation-based.

In selecting the particular strategies or combinations to be used the conditions surrounding the struggle, the people involved (i.e., who is going to be involved in the effort), and the context of the situation must be considered. It is important to recognize that conflicts are not usually two-sided affairs. Many pairs and combinations are involved in most conflicts that escalate beyond the interpersonal level, and thus the selection of those to be involved must take into account the various constituencies involved in the struggle.

The following are short summaries of several strategies that can be used in attempts to de-escalate struggles.

Setting Deadlines

A well-worn strategy used by unions in their struggles with management is the setting of strike deadlines. During the course of extended and difficult negotiations over a contract, the union may take a position that at midnight on a certain date the union will strike if there is no agreement. This is a kind of threat and has mixed results depending on the situation and the relationship between the union and the company. Another kind of deadline that is often set is the termination date of the contract. Some unions still take the position, "no contract, no work."

Altering Perceptions of the Struggle: Reframing

Changing the perception of the relationship between the parties may induce de-escalation. The perception of a struggle as a win-lose affair may be changed to it being perceived as having outcomes that will benefit both parties. In the case of the dispute in the potash mining district in New Mexico, the parties were involved in violence directed at each other. The situation was a classic win-lose struggle, and the perceptions of the union and of management was that the opponent had to be destroyed or eliminated. The basic strategy used by the mediators was to bring the leaders of the groups together and convince them that mutual benefits were available if negotiations would resume.

When Sherif (1966), in his study of boys involved in intergroup struggles, introduced situations that provided for superordinate shared goals, the relationship between the groups changed from antagonists to partners. When two tribes at war with each other suddenly realized that a larger and more powerful tribe than either was approaching, the two joined forces to fight the common enemy. The changes in the Soviet Union under the leadership of Gorbachov led to a redefinition of its relationship with the United States which, in turn, allowed for a reduction of the Cold War.

Many times the perception altering is accomplished by bringing competing parties together to discuss their interests rather than their positions. Here the strategies of communication play an important part.

Altering the Communication Conditions of the Struggle

In most struggles that have escalated toward the violent stage, the communication between the adversaries appears restricted to statements denigrating the enemy, hostile reports, restriction of information about interests and needs, and so on. The state of the communication becomes less and less open and more and more closed and singly directed. One of the more significant strategies under these conditions is for individuals to begin to reveal more information about the circumstances surrounding the situation. Mediators, for example, often gather information about the alternatives that both parties will consider but that in face-to-face situations they are unwilling to share. Through the confidence of the mediator critical information concerning possible mutual outcomes can be shared with results that de-escalate the situation. The mediator will often attempt to show the positive elements of the disputing parties to each other in an attempt to facilitate the reframing of their relationship.

Mobilizing Support for Change and De-escalation

Bringing together pressures for change from both inside and outside the constituencies of the parties in the dispute is a significant strategy. Working from the inside, members of a group may seek to counter the direction of the leadership of that group by pressing for alteration of positions and reassessment of the interests of the in-group. The Teamsters Union since 1985 underwent significant changes in its leadership brought about by internal pressures to change. At the same time those internal pressures were being supported, if not generated, by outside pressures from the government and other unions.

Internal pressures also affect international struggles. Frequently, support for a change in the position of a country in dispute will emerge from the mobilization of internal forces and groups that want to abandon the struggle and change the conditions. Here leadership plays a significant role in the developing strategy. The rise of new leaders, new power centers, and new themes will facilitate the de-escalation of old struggles if they are directed at reducing the conflict.

Ambassador John McDonald (1991) and others have identified a special form of diplomacy called "Track Two Diplomacy" in international affairs that has an application to interpersonal and intergroup struggles. He defines it as:

> a form of conflict resolution that is nongovernmental, informal, and unofficial. It is interaction between private citizens or groups of people within a country or between different people or groups from different countries, who are outside the formal governmental power structure. Persons involved in Track Two efforts have as their objective the reduction or de-escalation of conflict within a country or between countries by lowering the anger, tension, or fear that exists, by facilitating improved communication, and by helping to bring about a better understanding of each party's point of view. (pp. 202-203)

McDonald (1991) breaks his concept of Track Two into multitracks. Track One is the official interaction between the governments. Track Two is the "unofficial, nongovernmental, analytical, policy oriented, problem solving efforts by skilled, educated, experienced, and informed private citizens interacting with other private citizens" (p. 204). Track Three is carried on by private sector business and corporate leaders. Track Four is conducted by citizen-to-citizen exchange programs. Track Five involves the media-to-media efforts aimed at educating large population units of the conflicting parties to the characteristics and needs of each other.

This same concept of tract diplomacy can be applied to many intergroup and interpersonal struggles. The essence of the multitrack concept is that persons become involved in changing the attitudes and perceptions of the constituencies so that de-escalation can take place at the Track One-level of official diplomacy. These strategies are significant in contemporary dispute resolution processes.

When interracial strife erupted in a large metropolitan district, local citizens mobilized community groups (including business groups, religious groups, and neighborhood groups) to put pressure on the conflicting racial groups to find a common cause. It was not easy because the conflict had a long and violent history. But without this mobilized community pressure accompanied by tangible acts to bring the interests of the groups together, the struggle could not have been resolved short of violent war on the streets.

A husband and wife were in court fighting over the control of their five children and their property. The children, led by the oldest girl, got together and made an informal and unannounced visit to the judge asking that something be done to reduce the antagonism between the parents and to settle the dispute. The judge, having some insight into the alternative dispute resolution procedures available, ordered the parents to go to mediation. The implication she left was clear that if the parents could not reach a mutual settlement through mediation that satisfied the interests of the children she would decide what was to be done. It was the mobilized efforts of the children that brought about a de-escalation of the struggle from litigation to a form of mediation.

Selecting Critical Issues for De-escalation

The issues around which de-escalation takes place are an important part of the strategy planning. In the early stages of the effort, the issues to which the successful work is addressed are usually peripheral, that is, those which are not as important as the central ones. In mediation, for example, we often begin work on the minor issues early in the process. It is a positive gain when, even though the issues are not the central ones, an agreement or a reframing takes place that leads to de-escalation on those matters. The accomplishment on the smaller issues brings the parties to realize that they can resolve things and that by working at a problem together they can effect changes in the relationship. Although this does not always make the approach to the larger issues any easier, it usually lays a groundwork for better negotiations.

In selecting the issues to address in a negotiation it is important to have a priority schedule of those issues that will be dealt with immediately and those that will take longer and need more complicated deliberation. Further, when one or two issues have links to each other and to other issues, these should be isolated and approached as soon as it is possible to get them into the negotiations.

Determine the Level of the Structure

One of the concepts that McDonald's Track II diplomacy leads us to is the point at which the strategies for de-escalation may be introduced. McDonald makes the point that in international negotiations the Track I diplomacy is between the governments involved, and Track II goes outside the government level. This suggests that the initiation of strategy might well be beyond Track I. Although this has great value in international relations, it may not play quite so clearly in the less comprehensive struggles between groups and people.

In labor-management relations in the United States, for example, there are many instances in which communities have worked behind the scenes of the negotiations to bring both the union and management closer together. But the significant work in the negotiation must be done at the bargaining table. The outside activity is directed more toward bringing pressure to bear on the negotiators than it is to actually working out solutions to problems and then submitting them to the negotiators. This is particularly noticeable in teacher-school board disputes. Here the students, the parents, the community, and the school administrators may be working outside the actual negotiations to try to find ways to loosen up intractable disputes between the board and the teachers' union. However, because most of the decision-making power is located in the board and the teacher membership, the basic work must be directed toward those who are at the bargaining table.

Intervention in interpersonal disputes is less subject to the structural entry problem because there is less structure to work through before the point of issue is reached. We do, however, frequently encounter friends, neighbors, and other family members who work together to bring pressure on the major antagonists to de-escalate.

Change Focus of Attention to New Struggles

One of the age-old strategies for de-escalation is to start or call attention to another fight that pulls energy away from the intractable situation. Thus, two neighbors involved in a long intractable dispute over their trees may cease being involved in that dispute when it appears that the city is moving toward destruction of all the trees involved in the neighborhood dispute. Or, a fight between two local-based trucking companies for control of the hauling in a county may suddenly be brought to a halt when they are both threatened by the coming presence of a powerful national trucking company with major capital and facilities. Or, when a struggle between two forwards on a basketball team for ball possession is overpowered by the confrontation with a competing team that threatens their ability to perform as long as they are fighting each other.

Use of Positive and Negative Sanctions or Inducements (Carrots and Sticks)

In many situations various carrot and stick inducements can bring about de-escalation. One such inducement is for one party to make a conciliatory concession without requesting a concession from the other party. Such concessions should not weaken or otherwise jeopardize the initiator. The aim of such inducements is to encourage reciprocal concessions that then lead to an eventual resolution. Thus, when one country unilaterally announces a reduction in its military hardware it often triggers a similar response by the opposing nation. Note the way the United States and the Soviet Union worked on the reduction of arms in Europe in the 1980s and 1990s. The strategy of gradually developing reciprocal initiatives has been called GRIT (gradual reciprocal initiative in tension reduction).

Encouraging and Facilitating the Discovery and Recognition of Joint Interests and Superordinate Goals

When it is possible to aid both parties in discovering the existence of common interests and needs, the avenue for de-escalation may open. Here communication through the efforts of neutral third parties plays a significant role. But many times that discovery derives from the interaction between the adversaries. When two street gangs discover that they both like basketball and both have good players it may be possible to get them into friendly competition with each other instead of violent street fighting. The essence of this approach is to change the character of the game from a zero-sum situation (win-lose) to a non-zero-sum (cooperative) condition in which the results can be shared. Thus, the boys in Sherif's (1966) Robber's Cave study who were fighting each other in the hot summer sun in Oklahoma changed their approach to each other quickly when the water supply to the whole group was perceived as being in danger. The superordinate goal of getting water back for everyone took precedence over any other matter in the relationship between the groups.

Bringing Constituency to Seek De-escalation

In many situations, as long as the constituency of a group seeks to defeat the opponent the intractability continues. Leaders seem to be powerless in some situations to bring their constituencies along with them, and their constituencies hold them firm toward a given antagonistic attitude toward the enemy. In order to alter the intractability, persuasion and other methods can be brought to bear on the constituencies to seek de-escalation. When the constituency changes position, then the leadership will usually follow. When the union members who had previously insisted that the union strike the company discovered that they could not sustain the strike, they immediately instructed their representatives to find ways to call it off.

Errors and Failures in Strategy

A number of things can go wrong with even the best designed and planned strategies. Foremost among the sources of error is the selection of the wrong strategy for a given situation. For example, a Track II type of approach to a situation would not be appropriate if the principal negotiators were extremely jealous of their respective positions and resisted outside pressure.

Wrong timing is the source of many failed strategies. A settlement proposal by a mediator in a situation in which the parties are still venting their hostilities at each other in the ritual of negotiation is a sure fire loser. (Although it may emerge later when the timing is better.) An attempt to facilitate discovery of joint needs and interests will not usually work until the parties are ready to consider what is happening on the other side. The opposite of this is also true, that is, missing the "ripe" time when the parties are ready to find a common cause and the leaders or interveners make nothing of it.

Using already rejected proposals at inappropriate times will usually fail. Once a proposal for a settlement has been rejected by either or both parties it is not likely that they will reconsider it until the conditions surrounding the rejection have changed and the pressures for settlement have increased beyond what they were at the time the proposal was made.

The selection of the issues can also very easily go wrong. Although it is recognized as being useful to deal with limited issues early in the negotiations, it can also be an error to focus on so limited an issue that the large issues are not addressed. This simply extends the stalemate. Teacher-school board negotiations often deal with peripheral issues early on, but do not deal with ones that have any substantial significance to the dispute. If the resolution of the peripheral issues takes place and nothing is tied to them, the big issues may hang around and the intractability will continue.

Of most importance in seeking to de-escalate struggle is the act of trying to do something about it. Not trying to do something about it leaves us nowhere but in the middle of the intractable struggle. It is better, for the most part, to keep trying to find strategies and conditions that will break the stalemate then to give up and let it continue. This is particularly true when the stalemate is destructive to both sides and to others who exist on the sidelines.

SUMMARY

Struggles may become stalemated and intractable at almost any level of the Struggle Spectrum from interpersonal to international contexts. They may persist and resist resolution. Intractable struggles involve rigid perceptions by the parties, problems in self-identity, incompatible values, and misunderstanding; forms of hostility emerge and the condition blocks creative problem solving or joint deliberation. Rituals appear frequently as part of an intractable situation. The basic issues of a struggle may become lost in the intractable condition.

De-escalation is a process of reducing the intensity, direction, and extent of a struggle and moving it toward more peaceful and cooperative levels of struggle interaction. De-escalation may often be a process of moving intractability from one stage to another and changing the nature of the struggle from violent to nonviolent methods.

De-escalation occurs when parties seek to find resolution of the differences between them. When parties in litigation move to mediation, they are de-escalating their struggle. Processes such as reframing of perceptions and interests are useful.

De-escalation often occurs when there have been episodes of high intensity, hostility, and violence. It is often the case that a rapid escalation to the level at which a difference has been resolved and further struggle becomes unnecessary leads to immediate de-escalation.

Several conditions affect de-escalation: ripeness and timing, internal personal factors, interpersonal relationships, intragroup condition in intergroup struggles, intergroup factors in intergroup struggles, and power relationships.

The strategies of de-escalation are those processes that aim to move struggle from intractability to tractability. Interests, rights, and power play important roles in developing strategies. Criteria for the selection of strategies include costs, subsequent relationships between the parties, prestige, self-image, and pleasure. The determination of strategies are made by persons who seek to de-escalate the dispute. Third parties are often the ones who affect the strategy decisions. Leaders of groups are often the key persons. The constituents in an organization are often influential in pressing for de-escalation.

In selecting strategies for de-escalation several factors must be considered: the context of the situation, the players involved, the constituencies involved, the degree to which deterrence, compellance, avoidance, and accommodation is required, and the conditions surrounding the struggle.

Several strategies that can be used to de-escalate struggles are settings deadlines, reframing, altering the communication conditions, mobilizing support for change, "Track Two Diplomacy," selecting key issues for de-escalation, changing the focus of attention to other struggles, using positive and negative sanctions, facilitating the discovery of joint interests and superordinate goals; and bringing constituents together to seek change.

Ultimately, the de-escalation of intractable struggles as well as of other differences requires that active efforts be made to accomplish the change.

CONCLUSION

Struggle is inherent in our personal and social worlds. It cannot be destroyed. In the process great amounts of energy are generated and dispersed. Some of this energy produces growth and progress, some results in destruction and or retrogression. All of us are involved in struggle. At any given time we may be struggling over many different issues in different contexts and situations. Some of those struggles may be at mild disagreement stages. At the same time, others may be in more intense stages in which win-lose goals are involved and we are engaged in litigations, campaigns, and even fights and wars. Rarely does one struggle command our total attention to the exclusion of all others. Hence we seek to find ways to deal with the struggles that we encounter at every phase of the spectrum.

A peaceful world (from intrapersonal to international) is not a world without struggle. The nature of peace is not a vapid nonadversarial and passive condition. A peaceful world sustains the energy of struggle and that energy is managed so that it facilitates growth and progress instead of destruction.

I need to struggle with my society in order to find myself and to discover how I can enhance it as well as myself. I also need to learn how to manage my struggle so that it does not injure, diminish, or destroy others as well as myself.

When our struggles get out of control and become disputes between ourselves and our counterparts, we have methods available to assist us in resolving differences. Negotiation, mediation, and arbitration are methods we can use to resolve our disputes. Developing skill in these processes is an important task in our society. These processes can facilitate the resolution of disputes and the finding of peace when used properly and in a timely manner.

It seems very clear that the beginning of international peace must be found in intrapersonal and interpersonal conditions. Peace begins within us. Struggle often emerges from within us and our relationships. The seeds of violence remain in each of us. We must learn how to find and use the process of struggle management within ourselves as well as between us. When we help children learn how to manage their disputes, we are laying a groundwork for peace.

The actors at all levels of society are people who struggle with their world as they see it. Peace begins with me and you and then between us. The key to our interaction is found in our communication with each other. Without adequate communication our struggles become destructive, and our interests and needs become buried in the ashes of our violent demise.

And people of all races and perceptions
shall join together to resolve
our manifold struggles without violence!
Let there be joy in the work
and love in the celebration.

APPENDIX

//

Table of Contents

APPENDIX

//

Supplements

SOME KEY TERMS IN DISPUTE RESOLUTION PROCESSES: A GLOSSARY

Advocate and Advocacy

An advocate is one who takes a position and supports it through persuasion and argument and also assists, defends, or pleads for another before a court or tribunal and renders legal advice and aid. An advocate espouses an already determined point of view of his or her own or of his or her constituents and attempts to get this point of view accepted by others. An advocate is not usually interested in compromise or joint decision making but in "winning."

Advocacy is the process whereby a predetermined position is presented, supported, and recommended so that others will accept this point of view rather than a different position.

Arbitration and Arbitrators

A quasi-judiciary process whereby a neutral third party makes a decision regarding a dispute when the parties to the conflict are unable to resolve the struggle themselves. The arbitrator is chosen by mutual agreement of the parties to the dispute and both parties agree to abide by the decision of the arbitrator (except in certain cases called "advisory arbitration" in which the decision of the arbitrator is not binding on the parties). In arbitration the rules of evidence and the procedures are not so stringent as in a court of law.

An arbitrator is: "A private, disinterested person, chosen by the parties to a disputed question, for the purpose of hearing their contention, and giving judgment between them; to whose decision (award) the litigants submit themselves either voluntarily, or, in some cases, compulsorily, by order of a court" (Black, 1968, p. 135).

Bargaining

Argument, persuasion, threats, proposals, counterproposals, and so on between two parties as they seek to win concessions from each other in return for favors granted. Participants see themselves as adversaries and the goal of each is a victory over the other. Distrust of each other in this process is greater than in negotiation. "Bottom lines" are more hidden and protected. A process in which "quid pro quo" is a common condition. Power tactics are more common in this process than in negotiation. Bargaining takes place in a situation in which there is a higher incidence of exclusive goals than in the negotiation process.

Decision Making

The process whereby individuals and groups select from available alternatives those that they prefer. A decision is a commitment to believe or act. Decision making is that process by which those commitments occur. Making a decision is a process of making choices from available alternatives and committing to behavior consistent with those choices. Decisions arise from our reasoning, the influence on us of authorities, social group pressure, tradition and custom, values, environmental needs and conditions, accident, chance, rationalizations, and so on.

A group decision is a collection of common individual commitments. These decisions occur in several ways:

"Onefers:"	One person makes a choice and the rest follow without challenge.
"Twofers:"	Two persons agree and the rest of the group follows.
Consensus:	Everyone in the group agrees to a choice. *It's 100% agreement.*
Majority:	At least 51%, but less than a consensus, agree.
Plurality:	From several alternatives one receives the most choices.
Minority:	Less than 50% of the group swing the balance of power.
"No Objections:"	No one commits openly and a choice is made by default.
"Flipping:"	Flipping a coin, drawing straws, pulling a card—chance prevails
Passing:	Letting someone else make the choice.

Enforcer

One who has special power and influence. He or she intervenes in a dispute or conflict situation and directs and/or controls the outcome of the situation; punishes participants and/or controls the consequences when certain procedures or directions are not followed; imposes constraints on a person or group when they would not otherwise have them; and controls the alternatives available to persons involved in a dispute.

Facilitating and Facilitators

A facilitator is one who brings to a group or a client expertise, insight, special skills in observation, high communication skills, an objective awareness of the situation, and a set of tools for aiding the decision making that are not otherwise present. Facilitators intervene in client and/or group processes. They are usually not regular group members, as are the other participants, but perform a special role in aiding the person or groups to function. The facilitator, by his or her very presence, has more power than the others in the group.

The facilitation process involves interventions by facilitators to assist in problem solving and decision making that are aimed at aiding the persons to perform the necessary functions themselves. The ultimate success of the facilitator is the termination of the relationship between the client or group and the intervenor. The client or group becomes able to function independently.

Fact finding

The process whereby a neutral third party gathers data from both sides to a dispute and prepares a report identifying the facts that exist in the allegations of the parties and their support of those allegations and a proposal for settlement of the dispute. In practice it is very similar to arbitration with the exception that there is no agreement to abide by the report. The fact-finding process may or may not be voluntary by the parties to a dispute. In some cases in labor-management disputes the parties are required by law to go to fact finding if they reach a stage of impasse in their bargaining efforts.

Intervention

An interference in the flow of group or client behavior. It is an interruption of something that is happening in order to insert additional data and influence into the situation. "To intervene is to enter into an ongoing system of relationships, to come between or among persons, groups, or objects for the purpose of helping them . . . the system exists independently of the intervenor" (Argyris, 1970, p. 15).

Litigation

A formal process of carrying on a dispute through legal action. The use of court procedures to find solutions to struggles between people. "Contest in a court of justice for the purpose of enforcing a right . . . a judicial contest, a judicial controversy, a suit at law . . . civil actions" (Black, 1968, p. 1082).

Mediation

"An intervention by a neutral third person into an already existing process of negotiation in order to facilitate the joint decision making process between people who are becoming polarized and are colliding unproductively over differences in goals, methods, values, perceptions, etc. The mediator makes no decisions for the parties, has no authority to direct or control the action of the parties, and can only work effectively when both parties are willing to be mediated" (Keltner, 1987b, p. 11). An essential condition of mediation is its voluntary nature, that is, all parties to a dispute want to settle their differences and independently seek the assistance of the mediator in reaching this goal. Another vital condition is that the mediators do not represent the interests of either of the parties or any outside agency or person. Their primary concern is that the parties reach an agreement through their own efforts. The mediator serves as a facilitator in this process.

Mediation is not useful in all dispute situations. When the parties become involved in litigation, fight, or war, the process of mediation is difficult to accomplish (see "The Struggle Spectrum").

Negotiation

When two or more people with differing opinions or goals interact and seek resolution of their differences. The relatively friendly exchange of ideas for the purpose of changing relationships, finding agreements, and joint decision making. When the goals of two or more persons seem to be in opposition and they agree to try to resolve the dispute through communication with each other. It is a process of managing struggle in a peaceful way. Concessions are made in order to maintain and cultivate the relationship between the people. Trust levels are reasonably high. Changes in position can occur easily. "Bottom lines" are easily disclosed. The goals of the persons involved are more easily shared.

Neutral

A person or persons who have no personal, professional, or organizational interest in the parties or the issues of a dispute. A neutral is an impartial "third party" in a dispute situation. He or she is not involved with nor represents either side or others, nor is an advocate for either side of the dispute or for any other position in relation to the dispute. A neutral has nothing to gain personally, professionally, or ideologically from an advantage of one party over the other. In dispute resolution the neutral intervenor is primarily concerned with the parties reaching a satisfactory settlement of their dispute.

Problem Solving

A process of dealing with goals, obstacles to those goals, and conditions which bring into focus the difficulties when goals are blocked and of finding ways to accomplish the goals. The process involves understanding the problem in terms of goals and obstacles followed by analysis of the conditions and factors accounting for the presence of the disturbing obstacles and the establishment of standards or criteria for any possible solution to the situation. When these factors are accounted for then the process calls for a search for alternative solutions and an evaluation of those alternatives in terms of the standards or criteria established in the analysis. Finally, the process calls for selection of the solution or solutions that best allow for the accomplishment of the goals involved. Throughout the process of problem solving there are many decisions being made. Problem solving is a system of arranging and organizing our decisions so that they will have the greatest usefulness or value (Keltner, 1987a, p. 401).

QUESTIONS AND THEIR USE IN MEDIATION, NEGOTIATION AND ARBITRATION

TYPES OF QUESTIONS

(These types are not mutually exclusive. That is, any given question may have several characteristics.)

Open-ended

Not answerable with yes or no; allows respondent to select own responses. May require more than a few words for response. They invite long, sometimes unrushed, and sometimes rambling answers. There is some evidence that suggests that they get to the heart of matter faster in the long run than closed or directive questions. Examples: "How can we deal with this problem?" "What alternatives do we have in this situation?" "How do you feel?" "What's been happening?" "What are the issues here?" "Who's involved in this situation?"

Closed or directive

Seeks brief answers, pinpoints specific data, does not require lengthy response. Tends to limit the flexibility and scope of the respondent's answers. Tends to force the respondent to focus on a particular matter or issue. Examples: "How did you hit your brother?" "Who gave you the money?"

Either-or (identification)

Gives two alternatives from which the respondent selects one. The purpose is to reduce the alternatives to two and ask the respondent to select one. It makes it difficult for the respondent to respond when the choice is neither of the alternatives in the question. These types eliminate many creative options that may emerge from the dialogue. They often create hostility in the respondent because they limit the possibilities.

Examples: "Do you like the red one or the blue one?" "Which one of these do you like best, the yellow one or the pink one?" "Do you dislike your neighbor on the right or the neighbor on the left?"

Yes-No

Similar to either-or in that there are usually only two answers (sometimes a third possibility occurs as a "don't know" or another alternative emerges). The basic purpose of the question is to get an affirmation or denial. This type is basically different from the "either-or" because the alternatives are only yes or no, affirm or deny, accept or reject. This form is used in many courtroom interrogations. This type frequently frustrates the respondent and triggers anger and/or withdrawal.

Examples: "Do you accept this proposal?" "Did you steal the car?" "Were you present when the machine broke down?"

Rhetorical or leading (often called "loaded" question)

The answer is within the question itself. Makes it easier and more tempting for the respondent to give the answer desired by the questioner. Reveals the bias of the questioner. Carries messages about what the interrogator desires, values, or seeks. Used to persuade and amplify the point of view of the questioner. Can be very manipulative because such questions often catch us unaware. They are often subtle. They may appear as "yes-no," but actually do not give a true choice between the alternatives because they suggest the desired answer. Really only one choice is given to be affirmed or denied.

Examples: "You didn't like that incomplete answer did you?" "Sam interrupted you didn't he?" "You dislike that boring bartender, don't you?" "You like challenging computer work, don't you?" "Wouldn't you rather have a reliable Honda?" "How do you feel about that nutty teacher?" "Would you say you were a liberal or a crazy radical?"

Directive

These questions aim at a particular area of possible answers and focus the attention of the respondent on predetermined contexts or sources of the subject. They are often orders or commands sheathed in an interrogative holder. They can have an open quality when they bring the respondent to follow a given direction of content. They can be "yes-no" when the reply can satisfy the intent of the question. They can also be rhetorical in nature.

Examples: "Will you tell me about your Mother?" (can be "yes-no" or "open" in its consequences, that is, the respondent can say "no" and that's the end of the response or begin a response telling about Mother). "Will you talk about your feelings for Terry?" "Will you give me a quarter?" "You said you would talk about the class situation, will you do that now?"

What and Why

The *why* question assumes that the cause of what is happening is of prime importance and seeks to engage the respondent in an examination of these causal factors. This type is often distracting and can push a person or group away from dealing with the present circumstances of importance or distract them from attending to observable behavior. *Why* questions also create an atmosphere of attack. They usually sound like the questioner is putting the respondent through an inquisition. They often result in defensive behavior on the part of the respondent.

Examples: "Why do you dislike men?" (also a rhetorical question in certain contexts). "Why have you treated your sister that way?" "Why don't you speak up?" "Why did you hit your sister?" "Why were you late today?"

What questions are usually more reliable than *why* questions for getting at problems and in dealing with the "here and now" issues in a struggle-conflict situation. The nature of the *what* question is to get a focus on what is happening and to prevent flight into factors that are not relevant to the situation.

Examples: "What are you saying with your silence Carol?" "What are you saying to Carol by your shouting?" "What brought you to mediation?" (notice that the same content can be dealt with in a *why* question but the *what* is less likely to cause defensive behavior).

SOME STRATEGIES OF QUESTIONING (Conditions for Use)

- Closed questions are usually best used after the parties have become familiar with the situation, the method, and the mediator. If used too early they will limit the amount of information brought to the table.
- Open questions are useful in the early stages of the process. They encourage the respondent to talk and share. They also allow for the emergence of trust between the respondent and the questioner. Sometimes open questions can be so open, however, that the respondent does not deal with the issues at hand.
- Too many questions at once or a lot of questions crammed into one sentence will tend to confuse the respondent.
- Use simple and clear language that is understood by the respondent.
- During the fact finding stage of mediation more closed and either-or questions may be useful.
- In formulating questions several things should be considered:
  the language level and character
  the relevance
  the level of information desired
  the complexity
  the ability of the respondent to answer the questions
- Sometimes it is useful to avoid asking questions but to use information statements that reflect what the interrogator is seeking. Examples:
  Instead of asking "What brought you to Mediation?" try saying " I would like to know what brought you to Mediation."

Instead of asking "Do you approve of the actions of your spouse?" try saying, "I wonder if you approve of the actions of your spouse?"

These have the effect of bringing the interrogator closer to the respondent.

- Avoid trying to pinpoint a crime or wring out a confession or force a negative response that the respondent obviously does not want to reveal. Let the matter emerge as a result of the dialogue and the trust that develops.

APPENDIX

//

Exercises for Mediation Development

"THE MEDIATOR REPLIES"
Special Exercises For Mediators-To-Be

The following are descriptions of several situations in which a mediator is interacting with clients and in which the clients are making statements. You are to examine the situation carefully and write the response you think the mediator should make at that point in the process. Include in the description of the mediator's response suggestions for what the mediator should say, strategies to follow, and nonverbal factors that you think would also be important When you are finished discuss your responses with others who have been doing the same exercises.

Case #1. "I'm Right"

A man and a woman are in a divorce dispute. They have come to the mediator and after the preliminary explanations and agreements regarding the process, the woman begins the discussion with the following statement:

"I suppose I must tell you just what happened. After you hear what I have to say you will see that I'm right in what I'm asking here and that he is absolutely wrong."

What would you, the mediator, say at this point?
How would you say it and what nonverbals would accompany your communication?

Case #2. Faculty Schedules

Two faculty members are in a dispute over scheduling of classes and uses of classrooms. Both want the same classroom at the same time for already scheduled classes. The schedule clerk has refused to make the room assignment until the teachers agree as to whom should have it. The senior faculty member argues that he should have it on the basis of seniority and tenure, and the junior faculty member argues that his class needs the room because it is next to a laboratory where the students in the class work on projects for the class. The two persons have been referred to a faculty mediator and, following the preliminary discussions, the junior faculty member makes the following statement:

"As I've told you, my class needs that room so that the members can move back and forth between the classroom and the laboratory without having to crawl all over the campus. My colleague here is trying to put the seniority rap on me and refuses to consider the actual work situation. What can you do to help me? She is used to getting her way but I feel she is clearly out of line in this instance."

What do you, the mediator, say at this point?
What nonverbal things would be important to support your statement?

Case #3. Will He Listen?

A divorced couple are in a dispute over the custody of their children. During the mediation session a number of alternatives have been discussed but none seem to be acceptable to the ex-wife. The mediator has been able to get the ex-husband to make a proposal that would, on the face of the matter, resolve the dispute and involve the ex-wife making a number of proposals and suggestions for handling the children during the time they were with their father. The father would agree to her making such suggestions. Her response is, "This can't possibly work. He has never listened to anything I have said in the past about how to handle the children and I don't expect he will now."

What do you, the mediator, say at this point?
What nonverbal matters would you include in your behavior?

Case #4. Union Wages

A company and a union have been negotiating for several days over the terms of their new contract. All items have been agreed on except the wage rates. The union originally asked for a 15 cent per hour wage increase. The company offered a 2 cent increase. After much discussion the union moved to a 12 cent request and the company has come up with an offer of 4 cents. In private caucus the mediator has worked on both parties and tried to move them closer toward each other on the issue. At the last session with the union the mediator asked for its final position. The reply was that the union did not want to strike over this and that if necessary it would be willing, as a last resort, to accept a 7 cent increase. The mediator, in private caucus with the company, discovered that the company was very much afraid of a strike and would, in order to prevent one, be willing to pay a 9 cent increase.

As mediator you now have these two sets of confidential facts in your possession. What is your next move?
What will you say to the parties?
What nonverbal conditions will you set up?

Case #5. The Property Line

Two neighbors have been in a dispute over where the line separating their properties should be drawn. Each has a record that supports his claim. The facts show that there were several errors in surveying a couple of generations ago and no one is able to determine where the original line really was. The parties have come to mediation and have just finished reviewing the situation for the mediator. One of the neighbors says, "I'm exhausted from fighting over this mess. I don't really know what I want at this point. I do know that I want this to be over. This constant bickering is messing up my life."

What would you, as mediator, say at this point?
What nonverbals would you include with your comments?

Case #6. Personal Business

A case worker employee of the Family Services division of the state has been suspended for doing personal business with a client of the division. This is in violation of the state code. The employee claims that the "business" was not personal but involved helping the client find a job with a paint company that the employee partially owned. The state claims that this was in violation because it affected the employee's personal business and was therefore wrong.

At the mediation session-employee caucus the employee makes the following statement, "In the first place there are many instances where case workers do personal business with clients. There is one person in our office who is on the board of the bank and he's constantly referring people to his bank. Another owns a restaurant and frequently hires clients to work in his restaurant. The division is discriminating against me unjustly and is obviously out to 'get me' for some reason or other that I can't understand. I'm going to sue the agency for discrimination if we don't get this settled here to my satisfaction."

As the mediator what would you reply?
What nonverbals would you use as you replied?

Case #7. Access to Property

Party A purchased five acres of land along a river for the construction of a country home. When he purchased the land he was assured that there was an agreed-on access through another person's property that joined his and was between his property on the river and the county road. When A approached the owner of the adjoining property he was told that no such agreement for access existed anymore. The original agreement, B claimed, had expired when the property on the river was sold, and B had no intention of renewing it for the new owner. Obviously B resents A having purchased the property for the construction of a home because it has been a favorite fishing ground for all of his life and for his father before him. A purchased the property in good faith from the previous owner but now is quite frustrated with the situation. The parties have agreed to come to mediation. After the preliminary discussions of what mediation can and cannot do Party B says, "Now you fellows can play all the games you want but there is one thing you will not do . . . you will not cut across my land to move equipment and materials and other junk to that property on the river."

A replies, "Look there was an agreement for access to the river property and I bought that agreement. I now have access whether you like it or not. If you don't confirm this I'll take you to court and we'll see who wins."

B responds, "Go ahead, you jerk! You are so stupid that you didn't read that contract right and didn't realize that the agreement expired automatically when the property changed hands. I'm not going to be responsible for your stupidity. Furthermore, there is no way you are going to mess up my land to get to that river property."

What would you, the mediator, do and say at this point?

Case #8. Child Custody

J, 32 years old, a very ambitious and hardworking person, has been unemployed for two months after working for five years for an ad agency where he was successful and known as a workaholic. Two years ago K, his wife, divorced him and left their 7-year-old son for him to raise. J always put his son over his work and lost his job with the ad agency because he was failing to meet appointments and complete assignments on time when he had to take his son to the hospital for emergency treatment. J was very angry with the divorce because he felt that he had never neglected his wife and child. Since the divorce J has raised his son carefully and lovingly and a close relationship has developed between them. J feels that K is not an appropriate mother, that she is unstable, and shows a lack of responsibility and love for her son. J does not want to lose his son nor to drag the matter into court, and he is willing to go to mediation over the matter.

K, 29 years old, has been a CPA for the past nine months and is living alone following her divorce two years ago. During her marriage to J she stayed home and took care of the child. She wanted to work outside the home but J insisted that she take care of the home and child. This led to many arguments between them until she finally decided she had to exit the relationship. After the divorce she went to a psychologist for help with self-identity and self-esteem. She was involved in another relationship after the divorce but is now living alone. She now wants her son back and has threatened to go to court to fight for him. She has come to mediation at J's insistence but still thinks that she'll have to go to court to get the son.

As mediator you have been able to gather the above information from both of the parties during the early stages of the mediation through joint and separate meetings. At a separate meeting with K she told you that unless an agreement could be worked out that would allow her prime custody of the son she would take the matter to court and was sure that she would win.

What kind of a reply or statement would you make to K after she made these threats?
What will you say to J about what K has revealed to you?
What plan or strategy will you now use in mediating the situation?

Case #9. The Loan

G is in the process of restoring a barn into a residential dwelling and is acting as her own contractor. She hired J, a carpenter, after he bid $17,000 for labor and materials. The work has been slow but is nearing completion. J has been paid $15,000 to date and the last $5,000 of that was paid by bank voucher just two weeks ago in order for J allegedly to pay the lumberyard for materials. Since that time he has not returned to the job site. Two days ago G received a mechanics lien from the lumber yard for $7,000. With the help of another carpenter she estimates that there is still $3,000 worth of work to complete the project. She is irate with the bank for advancing the voucher payment without checking the lumberyard, with the lumberyard for not insisting on payment from J because of the long term "friendship" between the proprietor of the yard and J, and she is more than angry at J for not completing the work and for jeopardizing her project and financial stability.

J erroneously underestimated the cost of materials by at least $1,000 and labor time by over 200 hours. Additional labor was necessary because of changes to the plans made by G. J's long time friend at the lumberyard assured him that he would extend his credit for a new job J is now starting even though the barn materials have not been paid. The barn project was his first large job and it turned out to be a disaster. No one wanted the job and he took it because G seemed sincere and concerned about the job. J simply wants to walk away from it. He feels he has no other recourse. He has just been divorced and has a large child support payment. He has a heavy burden of responsibility for his father, an alcoholic who is undergoing special treatment for which J must pay.

As mediator you have determined the above information through joint and separate meetings with both parties. You now have the parties back together again to review the situation. After the general facts have been reviewed, G leans across the table toward J and says, "You had better make this good, young man, or you'll never work in this town again. You cannot bury your mistakes and I'll see to that. I want full restitution for all losses and a penalty of $2,000 for suffering and time loss in completing the work."

As the mediator what would you do and say to the parties at this point?

Case # 10. Who Wants A Divorce?

You are called on the telephone by a man who reports that his lawyer has recommended that he and his wife come to you for mediation of their divorce. The man indicates that there are some serious problems with the relationship and that he wants a divorce but his wife does not.

What would you do and say at this point?

Case 11. Permissive vs. Mandatory

In the course of a dispute between the teacher's union and a school board the issue of mandatory vs. permissive bargaining arises. Mandatory issues are defined as those which the law says must be negotiated between the parties, and permissive issues as those which the law says are to be negotiated only if both parties agree to negotiate on them.

The school board has been firm in its position that the union's proposal to change the method of scheduling classes is a permissive issue, and it will not discuss the matter in negotiations. The union has likewise been firm in its position that the matter is a mandatory issue. You have clear information to the effect that such matters are, as interpreted under the law in this state, permissive and may be negotiated only if both parties agree to work on them.

The union representative says to you in private caucus, "We have pressed this matter again and again and they refuse to discuss it. Clearly this is a factor in our working conditions and thus is a matter that is mandatory under the law. We know we are right on this matter and if they don't come off their high horse and negotiate with us on the matter, our pickets will be up in the morning and we'll bring unfair labor practice charges."

What is your response?
What would you say to the union in caucus?
What would you say to the school board in caucus?
What would you say to both parties in joint session?

Case 12. The Trust Payment

The management of a small company was required, under its contract with the union, to pay into a pension trust a percentage of each hourly wage earned by its employees. The contract under which this agreement was stipulated ran for three years and during that time the employer paid into the trust as proscribed by the contract. At the end of the three years the company refused to sign a contract with the union because of wide differences on many issues, including the pension trust. The old contract expired, but the company continued to pay into the pension trust for another two months, and no settlement on a new contract has been reached. The union claims that management is in violation of the contract by ceasing to pay into the trust even after the contract had expired as long as they were still bargaining. Management claims that once the contract had expired it has no responsibility for abiding by its terms. Neither party seems willing to change its position on the matter.

What would you say to the parties?
What advice or strategy would you present to them?

Case 13. The Family Lands

A family is facing the distribution of property following the demise, over a year ago, of the father. The will of the father left all the property to the mother until her death. The mother is now contemplating remarriage and does not wish to be responsible for the acres of land and improvements. She wants to divide up the property among her three adult children: her oldest son, 43; her only daughter, 35; and her youngest son, 32. The two men have homes on and farm part of the land. The oldest has a home on 200 acres of the land and the youngest has the old homestead on another 200 acres of land. Although the mother has title to these lands it was the intent that the boys would have them after she died. The remaining 300 acres has been rented out. The mother has proposed that the two boys split the 300 acres and add it to their farms because it is adjoining both and share with their sister a portion of the income from the 300 acres.

The mother and daughter are now at great odds over the matter. Because the daughter was left out of the original assignment of lands for a home she feels that she has been pushed away from her rightful share of the property. Her mother feels that providing for her to share in the proceeds of the 300 acres is reasonable for the daughter because she is married, is an attorney, and has a substantial income of her own. Mother and daughter have been alienated from each other since the death of the father. The two boys, realizing that the situation could get bad if their sister took them all to court, have convinced the mother and daughter to go to mediation. You have been selected by the boys and a first meeting has been scheduled.

Should the boys be present at this meeting?
What will you aim to accomplish at this first meeting?
What strategies will you use?

Case 14. The Hanging Tree

Joe and Harry are neighbors. On Joe's property just inside the property line separating his place from Harry's is a large Douglas fir. The lower limbs of that fir tree are now spreading over into Harry's property by some 20 feet. These limbs hang over Harry's garden and cut off the sun for a good part of the day. Harry asked Joe to trim the tree, and Joe has delayed and delayed on the matter. Harry, finally, in desperation, got out his chain saw and started to trim, whereupon Joe appeared on the scene and demanded that Harry stop or he would call the police and have Harry cited for trespassing. Harry stoped but demanded that Joe cut the limbs. The next day there were "No Trespassing" signs on Joe's property around the tree. Harry got mad and threatened court action. Joe, in retaliation, threatened Harry with trespassing if he touched the tree limbs. There is an ordinance that gives Harry some rights to remove offending limbs from a tree that has its roots and stem on another property. However, to bring that ordinance into play would require some police action because of Joe's attitude. Harry does not want to do this. Instead he suggests to Joe that they go to mediation. Joe refuses. Harry asks Joe's neighbor on the other side to try to convince Joe to go to mediation. He tries and Joe reluctantly agrees. You have been referred by the community dispute resolution center.

Who do you contact first?
What do you say?
How will you get the process going?

What rules of procedure will you insist be followed in the case?

What will you do and say if Joe adamantly refuses to do anything about the tree?

RECOMMENDING A MEDIATOR
An Exercise in Assessing Mediator Qualifications

Friends of yours have become embroiled in a serious family dispute that seems to be heading to a divorce. There are three children involved (two subteen girls and one preschool boy). The two parents who are in trouble with each other are both employed. The husband is a basketball coach in the local high school. The wife is a legal secretary for a local attorney. Each of them, at one time or another, has indicated to you that they were in trouble. Finally, the wife approaches you for help in either mediating the matter yourself or in recommending someone who might be qualified to mediate the dispute. You have checked with the husband and he agrees to seek a mediator other than yourself. You have therefore agreed to submit to them names of two or three mediators whom you know from which they may choose the person they want.

The following persons are available in your community to serve in a mediation capacity. Select three of them and rank them for your friends.

The Mediators

Mrs. Aye—A local lawyer who has specialized in family and divorce law. She is a capable lawyer and has won many cases for her clients. She is known for her "go for the jugular" approach to divorce litigation and always brings the opponent to task in strong terms. She has also served in an advisory capacity to the local school board in personnel matters requiring litigation (but has no special connection or concern with your friends). She has had two weekend courses in mediation and is planning to take a course at the local university on dispute resolution. She sees mediation as another legal avenue through which divorce settlements can be reached. Her approach to mediation is likely to be judicial, that is, she will listen to each party separately and then tell them what they should do. Her strengths are her ability to deal with the logic of a situation, to get the facts, to evaluate the evidence and make a reasoned judgment about it, and to persuade others that her position is the proper one.

Mr. Bee—A social worker with a state agency. He has an MS in Social Work from an accredited university. His major area of work is with families. He has led a number of group therapy sessions and is apparently very successful. He is well trained in family group therapy and gestalt therapy. From time to time his clients have been dealing with struggles that could lead to divorce if not handled constructively. He has helped them to overcome these difficulties and avoid divorce. He is partially familiar with the mediation process and feels that it may be useful. He has no direct training, however, in the process and its particular application to family disputes. He does, however, think that his training and background are sufficient to deal with husband-wife disputes that could lead to divorce. His strengths are his confidence in his own ability, skill in facilitating therapy groups, and his ability to diagnose psychological disorders.

Dr. See—An MD with a specialty in Psychiatry. He is on the hospital staff as the resident psychiatrist. His work has centered on individual therapy, with some work with groups. He has also worked with children with behavioral problems. His adult clients are predominantly manic depressives with a sprinkling of the more violent deviations and illnesses. He has been interested in the area of family disputes because of its relation to individual therapy. He recently took a weekend seminar on mediation and has become quite interested in it from a therapeutic viewpoint. He talked with you about that experience with some excitement. Even so, he is a calm, understanding person who is able to assume an empathetic state with his clients very quickly and easily. His other strengths are his high skill as a group therapist-facilitator, his ability to listen, and his enthusiasm about the process of mediation as a facilitative method of settling disputes.

Ms. Dee—Has a bachelor degree in liberal arts with a major in psychology and sociology. Shortly out of college she worked as a counselor in the Outward Bound program for about four years. She is active in her church programs and in the United Way in the community. She is divorced and has custody of her two children. She is independently wealthy and does a great deal of volunteer work in the community. At present, one of her main areas of volunteer activity is with the Victim Offender

Reconciliation Program (VORP). She has gone through the training with that program and serves as one of the so-called "mediators" in this area. Her supervisor reports that she is very good. Ms. Dee feels that her training in VORP qualifies her to "mediate" in other kinds of situations. She has, according to her testimony, actually "mediated" successfully several divorce disputes but you have been unable to talk with the parties to determine their perception of her work. Her strengths are her enthusiasm for her work and for the process that is involved, her ability to encourage people to work things out, her supportive behavior, and her ability to organize programs and people.

Mr. Eee—A lawyer who has been active in encouraging and developing alternative dispute resolution programs throughout the state. He was formerly a trial lawyer and dealt with divorce litigation. He saw opportunities in alternative dispute resolution and mediation as an addition to his legal practice and formed a mediation service center where divorcing couples could receive assistance in working out the terms of their divorce. He has had about 40 hours of instruction in mediation specifically and served as a mediator in approximately 15 cases over the past two years. There are mixed reviews of his work. Some clients dislike him intensely and will not return, and others think that he is a saint. His strengths are his ability to maneuver carefully to get things to come out the way he wants them, to convince his clients that what he wants them to do is the best for them, his persistence in the face of difficult problems, and his ability to advise his clients on the legal aspects of their disputes.

Ms. Eff—A PhD in communication from a major midwestern university. Her major field of study was interpersonal and group communication and conflict resolution. She has had a number of years of experience in teaching conflict management and mediation at the university. For 12 years she was a labor-management mediator with the Federal Mediation and Conciliation Service. Since leaving that agency she has formed her own service and functions as a labor-management arbitrator and mediator of family disputes, divorce and child custody disputes, parent-school board disputes, and community disputes. She has also mediated disputes between faculty members and faculty/students at the university. She has a strong and intense concern for the purity and universality of the mediation process and for the particular value it can bring to dispute resolution in any arena. She has written a book on mediation that is being used widely in mediation training. From time to time she conducts mediation training seminars. Her strengths are her full understanding and experience with the mediation process, her ability to listen, her skill in becoming empathic, her patience in working with clients, and her sense of humor.

Mrs. Gee—The chief mediator of the state labor-management mediation service for six years and a mediator with the state service for a total of 12 years. Before that she was a representative of the school board in contract negotiations with teachers. In addition to functioning as head of the mediation service in the state she also, under the framework of her church, does private mediation for couples, families, and in community disputes. She has participated in a number of mediator training seminars sponsored by various universities in the area. She also conducts an extensive training program for new mediators who are brought into the state service. She has recently published a pamphlet on alternative dispute resolution methods in church affairs. Her case load of agency mediations runs to over 100 cases a year. Her availability for private divorce disputes is limited but not impossible. Her strengths are familiarity with the facilitative function of mediation, ability to encourage disputants to deal with each other, and ability to create alternative solutions to problems.

Mr. Aich—Has an MA in Counseling and a BA in communication and psychology. Shortly after he finished his MA he opened a counseling office with another counselor with an emphasis on family and personal problems. In the past several years he has taken several workshops on mediation of family disputes and has been advertising his services as a family mediator. One of the areas in which he claims some expertise is in prenuptial negotiations. He is attempting to develop a reputation for facilitating couples in working out premarriage agreements regarding property, children, and other items. He claims this is a legitimate mediation process. He is a member of the Academy of Family Mediators and is certified as a family counselor. His strengths are in expressing himself, applying structure to situations that are ambiguous, and in persisting with the client.

Ms. Eye—Has a PhD in communication and counseling with an emphasis on dispute resolution. She has worked in a community mediation center in another state where he clients were mostly welfare families. Her case load in that state was very high. She has recently (within the last six months) moved to your state where she has accepted a newly created position in the local university as a mediator for faculty, student, and staff disputes. The job has some similarity to an ombudsmanship but is more directed toward the mediation functions. Already her client load at the university has started to climb and her services are beginning to be in demand. Her strengths are her ability to communicate with people in trouble, to listen, and to become empathic with her clients.

Rev. Jay—The minister of the First Christian Church in your town. He is well liked and has built a strong and vibrant church. A lot of his good work has been with young and middle-age adults. He has a Doctor of Divinity from the University of Chicago. He has taken a lot of continuing education courses in counseling and group processes. As part of his ministerial duties he frequently counsels husbands and wives who are having difficulty in their marriage. His main concern, of course, is to preserve the marriage, if at all possible, and to retain the partners in the church. He has organized and led several groups of young married adults in encounter groups with a great deal of success. He also serves as a member of a local crisis team who make their services available to persons needing counseling assistance. His strengths are in creating structure and ideas that will stimulate people to deal with their problems. He is a stimulating preacher and well respected.

Mr. Kay—Has a PhD in clinical psychology. Did a residency in psychotherapy at Johns Hopkins Medical school. Has a clinical practice here and is very busy. He does a lot of work in the testing and analysis of children with psychological problems. Also has served as a clinical counselor for people with personal problems and difficulties. Is a member of a state commission on setting standards for clinical practitioners. Has been referred frequently by the medical community in town to people with stress disorders. He has had no specific training in mediation but seems to have a natural ability to mediate disputes between people. His therapeutic style is not Freudian but more interpersonal and behavioral. He happens to be the person to whom you have gone when you needed some counseling during periods of stress on your job. You found him very helpful, nondirective, yet able to facilitate self-examination of your needs and problems.

EM—Write below, if you wish, a brief description of a person you know and who you would recommend to your friends. Rank that person along with the others below.

RANKING OF POTENTIAL MEDIATORS

Rank the potential mediators below. (Include "EM" if you have identified such a person.)

Rank	Name	Reason for Ranking and Comments
1.	_____	
2.	_____	
3.	_____	

APPENDIX

//

Simulations

Negotiation Simulations

1. **The Silver Bracelet.** As you pass down the corridors of the county fair you see a display of silver bracelets. You have wanted one of these for your wife for a long time but have never really looked at them. Here is a beautiful display of some very nice looking pieces. You see one of them that would be just right for your partner. You have $50 to spend. You ask the proprietor the price of the bracelet. The answer is $75. Negotiate with the proprietor for the bracelet.

2. **The Neighbor's Fence.** Your neighbor wants to put up a fence between your property and hers. You do not like the idea of the properties being separated this way because it would mar the beauty of the combined yards. When she proposes the fence to you while you are working in your yard, how do you negotiate with her?

3. **The Apartment Rents.** You recently purchased an apartment house containing 5 two-bedroom apartments. In looking at the cost of maintaining the apartments and meeting the tax obligations, and so on, you decide that the rent on the apartments must be raised. The rent per apartment is now $450 per month. You feel that it will take $550 to break even if you are to maintain the apartments properly. The tenants oppose this move and have formed a tenant group to negotiate with you over the matter. How will you negotiate with the tenant team? Describe your approach, tactics, and so on. Have some others form a tenant team and simulate the negotiations together.

4. **The New Car.** A man and wife are seeking to purchase a new car. They have saved up for this event and now, after looking at several autos, have decided on the one they want. The ticket on the car window shows that it is priced at about $500 beyond what they want to pay. The dealer has priced the cars on her lot at a 10% mark up to cover profit. All other costs, such as transportation, preparation, and so on are included in the base cost. Have two people take the role of the man and wife and one person take the role of the dealer and see what you can negotiate for the automobile.

5. **End of Term Celebration.** Jane and Janet share an apartment. Jane is a graduate student studying electrical engineering, and Janet is an office manager of a local computer store. Both of them have male companions with whom they spend time occasionally. Usually when one is going to entertain in their apartment with a dinner, the other finds a reason to be away from the apartment for the time involved. It is approaching the end of the term and Jane would like to celebrate with a chili supper for her male friend. She wants it on the Friday after the end of examinations.

Janet has been working hard and has planned to invite her man to have dinner at the apartment on the same night. The two are at odds over the matter. Jane feels that Janet takes advantage of her school responsibilities and has used the apartment for tete-a-tetes with her male friend a number of times during the term when Jane was occupied in the library or on campus.

Janet feels that Jane does not realize that Friday nights are when she usually spends time with her man. They usually start off by eating at the apartment and come back after a show or dance for coffee. This has become an important ritual for them, and she resents Jane's attempt to intrude on her relationship with him.

The two are now trying to negotiate the difference.

6. **Your Own Negotiation Situations.** Review the past month and identify situations in which you were negotiating with others over mutual problems. Write at least two of these situations into simulations and select someone to play your role in the situation, while you play the role of your adversary.

7. **The Lousy Paint Job.** Maria had just taken a new job that required her to travel some 70 miles each day. Up to this time she had not needed an automobile. The new job required one. So she went to a used car dealer and looked at the cars.

Finding a 10-year-old Buick she thought might work for her, she asked the price. It was $1500 with a contract for monthly payments plus interest on the unpaid difference. She figured she could barely afford that. She test drove the car, checked the oil, tested the brakes and steering, and it seemed to work fine. However, the paint was in bad condition, the front bumper was bent, and there was one hub cap missing. The additional cost of the painting, hub cap, and bumper repair would take her beyond her budget.

The dealer was not going to make much more than 10% on the deal. The car had been on his lot for over six months and he wanted to get it off. On the other hand, he wasn't going to give it away. After listening to Maria's concern about the paint job and the bumper he agreed to do the painting and get the bumper fixed for another $50. Maria agreed and put $50 down on the car as earnest money.

Two days later she returned to pick up the car. The paint job was finished and it was a mess. There were bubbles in the paint. It was grainy. It had spare spots where the paint hadn't covered the body. Clearly it had not been prepared for the paint and the new paint had been sprayed over the old paint. There was a new hub cap on the wheel but it didn't match the others. The bumper was not straight.

Two persons assume the roles of Maria and the dealer and try to negotiate the matter.

8. **New Job-New Salary.** Jim has a good accounting job paying about $35,000 annually. He likes the work and his employers like what he does. However, the working conditions are not at all satisfactory. He has to commute some 100 miles each day to the job and back, is required to work long hours, and is called frequently to work weekends. He decides that he should look for another position.

Within a short time he learns of a position as director of a small accounting firm. It is closer to home and he would not have the long commute and costs. Upon inquiring from the chairman of the board of directors of the firm, he was told that the salary was "competitive" depending on the qualifications of the applicant. The last director had been paid $32,000 but was let go because of inadequate leadership ability and because of some personnel problems with the accountants that worked under her.

The board of directors is looking for a person with experience who could take over the firm and run it profitably. However, they are not willing to go much above what they had been paying because the income generated by the firm will not support much more.

After an interview, both Jim and the board seemed to have some interest in each other but the salary figure seemed to be a stumbling block.

Try to negotiate a satisfactory salary figure for Jim.

9. **Teacher Salaries.** The teachers in District 1 are negotiating their second contract with the school board. It is just three months until the new school year begins, and the contracts are usually settled by this time. The major issue that blocks a settlement is the matter of teacher salaries.

The teachers are requesting a 10% increase across the board in the salary schedule and an additional step in the top level of the schedule. The latter is important to many of the teachers because over half of them are at the top of the current salary schedule. Furthermore, the teachers in three of the five districts within a 50-mile radius have recently received increases of 7% over their prior contracts. However, these districts have much higher base salaries than District 1. The teachers in District 1 are seeking to become equal to the districts surrounding them. The economic conditions in all the areas in the surrounding territory are comparable to the conditions in District 1.

The school board resists the proposed increases and insists that such a level of raises is simply not possible with the present budget and financial situation in the district. The budget for the coming year pegs the teachers' salaries at an increase of 3% across the board. This level was arrived at after intense discussion within the board. A number of the board members opposed any increase because of the condition of the economy. The District itself is in an economically distressed area. A number of industries in the area have closed down, the value of property in the area has fallen, and it looks like a serious financial crisis is at hand.

Select a team of two persons for the teachers and a team of two persons for the District and see what you can negotiate.

10. **Summer Vacation Plans.** Terry and Alice have been married for 15 years, have two children, and both are working full time. They live in a town of 40,000 on the West Coast of the United States. Terry is an owner-manager of a filling station, and Alice is a teacher in the middle school in town. It has been several years since they had a vacation because Alice has been in school updating her certificate during the summer months. The children, 11 and 13, have usually spent the summers in town in the local parks program.

Alice wants the family to take a vacation this year and visit her folks in Pennsylvania. She wants to drive the family station wagon and take plenty of time (at least a month) going across the country so that they can enjoy the scenery and the historic spots. She wants very much to see her parents and to visit with brothers and sisters in Ohio. Alice does not want to vacation on the West Coast because they have done this a number of times already. She does not like to camp out and would prefer to use motels on the way east and back.

Terry would like to have a vacation also. But the responsibility of managing the station is a heavy one. There are 10 persons working for him at the station, and it's difficult to be away for any length of time. He also has to arrange vacations for the people at the station and most of them want one during the summer when their children are not in school. At the present time there is no one on his staff who would be able to be acting manager for more than a week or so because of the accounting and other financial procedures, including the preparation of the payroll, and so on. In looking forward to the summer Terry had figured that he could maybe take 10 days in late August and that they could go camping at some of the campsites along the California-Oregon-Washington coast.

The children are excited by the possibility of going east to Pennsylvania. They also like to camp out and don't particularly like to go from motel to motel. But, if they get involved in the parks program this year there won't be much time for a trip. Tim, 13, plays in the baseball league and is very much in demand as a first baseman and hitter. Sue is involved in the Girl Scout programs, a church square dance club, and a service group that spends the summer putting together and performing a service program for hospital and nursing homes. This year she has been selected as the junior chairperson of the sub-teen team.

Get the whole family together and negotiate their summer vacation plans.

MEDIATION SIMULATION CASES
(Some may also be used for negotiation simulation)

Additional mediation simulation cases can be found in John W. (Sam) Keltner, 1987, *Mediation: Toward a civilized system of dispute resolution.* Annandale, VA: Speech Communication Association, pp. 41-51.

Suggestions for Using These Cases

1. Use small groups of at least five persons in each group.
2. Assign the following functions:
   a One person to be the mediator.
   b. Two persons to play the roles of the parties to the dispute.
   c. One person to serve as the Activity Identification Specialist (see Activity Identification Analysis form that is to be used by this person in Appendix under Evaluation Instruments).

d. One person to serve as critic-evaluator of the mediator (using the Evaluation forms in Appendix).

3. Give both parties (not the mediator) copies of the "General Information" part of the case.

4. Give each one of the parties the instruction sheet for the role being played. Then give the parties time to study their parts.

5. When everyone is ready, the two parties are asked to leave the room until the mediator brings them into the room again either singly or together.

6. The mediator then proceeds to mediate until a settlement is reached or it is felt that no resolution can be reached.

7. When the mediation session is finished, the Activity Identification Specialist reports on the results of the observation and describes the activities of the mediator.

8. Finally, the critic-evaluator reviews the quality of the performance and opens a group discussion of the whole process.

Variations in this pattern can be adopted depending on the size of the training group. When a single case is being used, the training group can be broken down so that a number of mediators are working at the same time on the same case with different groups. This maximizes the opportunity for practice. In training it is wise not to assign two mediators to a single case. Dual mediation requires special training and should not be attempted until that special training is completed.

Another way to work with these teams is to add a sixth person to be responsible for writing a scenario for the simulation (the "author") and for directing the players in their roles during the simulation.

In a training session running over a period of time, it is important to have everyone on the team function in each of the team assignments. It is advisable to have the "authors" assigned to different areas of dispute. For example, one may write a scenario on divorce, another on labor-management, another on an environmental dispute, and so on. By providing this variety in types of cases, the team experiences a number of different kinds of issues, but also sees the constancy of the mediation process through different content settings.

In addition to participating and/or observing the role play of the situation, each person pays particular attention to the processes used during the course of the simulation and tries to discover and identify the various stages through which the mediation process advanced, the behaviors of both clients and mediator that facilitated and obstructed it, behaviors that might have been used and were not, and the nature of the changes that took place within and between each of the clients as they moved through the experience.

ROMMEL THE BARKER*

*Adapted by Sam Keltner from an original scenario by David Acklin

General Information

Murawski called the police regarding the barking of his neighbor's dog, Rommel. Murawski complained that the dog's barking at night disturbed the family's sleep. Murawski does not want to file a legal action against his neighbor but does want some relief from the disturbance. Murawski claims that he has been unable to talk to his neighbor, Lucas, since the disturbances began. Murawski was told that he might be able to get some help from the Neighborhood Dispute Resolution Program (NDRP). Murawski therefore contacted that group and was told that if both Lucas and Murawski were willing, the agency would attempt to mediate the dispute. Murawski agreed to attempt mediation. The NDRP then called Lucas, appraised him of the complaint, and asked if he would be willing to come to mediation. Lucas, with some irritation that Murawski hadn't approached him directly, agreed to come to mediation. The NDRP then set the time and place for the mediation.

Performance Note. The case detail with respect to pronouns and reference to the characters has been cast so that either male or female participants can function in either role.

Murawski

My next door neighbor, Lucas, owns a German Shepherd dog named Rommel. Lucas keeps Rommel in a run with a kennel in the backyard of his home. Rommel has always been a good dog . . . well trained and quiet . . . until about two weeks ago. Now every night at about 3 or 4 in the morning Rom-mel begins barking and continues for about 15 minutes. The barking is usually stopped by Lucas, who comes outside and locks Rommel in the garage. The barking wakes me in the middle of the night and it is very difficult to go back to sleep. I need all the sleep I can get because my job as a powerline repair person requires that I be alert and aware of what is going on. Something has to be done to shut that dog up!! I hope it won't be necessary to take the law into my own hands.

My neighbors are good neighbors in general but I do not communicate very much with them. The Lucases seems wrapped up in their own world. I leave them alone and they leave me alone. We do not seem to have much in common. Lucas is gone during the day and so are we. (My partner and I have no children at home.) Lucas and I have talked over the back fence once in a while about our gardens and several years ago mutually agreed to trim some trees that are close to the property line separating our lots.

I have wanted to say something to the Lucases but they seem aloof and unapproachable. It was with great hesitation that I talked to the police about it but the annoyance was simply getting out of hand. I was relieved when the police suggested I go to the Neighborhood Dispute Resolution Program (NDRP) because I figured I could then get the matter settled without the cost of a lawsuit or other legal action. I don't know much about this mediation business but I've heard that some good things come of it. I don't know who the mediator is and that worries me a bit. I am a bit afraid I might get someone who is a dog lover and who doesn't sympathize with people who suffer from barking dogs.

Lucas

I have been hauled into Mediation court by the Neighborhood Dispute Resolution Program (NDRP) because Murawski, my neighbor to the south, called the police to complain that my dog, Rommel, barks at night and disturbs them. I see no reason why Murawski should get disturbed about this. When Rommel barks at night I get up and put the dog inside the garage and he stops barking. Why is there a problem? I can't prevent the dog from barking. I don't want the dog to become a house dog. I paid a lot of money for the run and the kennel for Rommel so that he would be outside and could serve as an active companion and watch dog. Barking to warn us of unwelcome intruders is something I want him to do.

There is another thing; the neighbors to the north of me just bought a cat about two weeks ago. I suspect that the cat is tormenting Rommel every night and that this causes the dog to bark. That cat should be not be allowed to roam about the neighborhood at night where there are dogs housed in runs. It's bound to cause a disturbance.

It irritates me that Murawski has never approached me about the situation with Rommel. Shortly after I got Rommel, Murawski saw him in the run and told me what a handsome animal he was. I thought Murawski was a reasonably good neighbor until now. Murawski doesn't bother me and I don't bother Murawski. We talk once in a while when we see each other out in the yard. I know that Murawski is a powerline service person. I do not know what his partner does. So far as I know they have no pets.

I feel that I shouldn't even be here. I've done no harm and I take care of my dog when he gets noisy. But if the Murawskis want a fight I'm just the one to give it to them. What kind of a mealy-mouthed little twerp would not have the guts to face me and tell me the problem so we could work it out together? I don't think they are operating in good faith, as my union business agent would say.

THE MISSING WATER SUPPLY

General Information

Ranchers and farmers in Eastern Oregon work up to 18 hours a day moving sprinkler systems from their various crops to keep them from becoming too dry and eventually dying. Summers are extremely warm and water is very scarce. These ranchers are constantly drilling for new water sources because there is always a chance that one or two of their wells will run dry.

There are 40 farmers and ranchers covering approximately 22 square miles of land all of which are dependent on the water. If, by chance, one of them should happen to tap into one of the main underground streams it would cause most, if not all, the wells to run dry.

Chuck Bartlet, owner of the Circle-Bar Ranch, became concerned about his water supply early this spring and dug several additional wells on his property. He hit into a large underground stream. It is believed that this stream or body of underground water drains into all the other streams that the other ranchers use.

All of this had taken place in the latter part of May and by the time August rolled around there was talk among the farmers and ranchers of how low their wells were getting. Some had even complained that their smaller wells had gone completely dry. Many ranchers began to fear the inevitable complete loss of their crops and eventual bankruptcy.

It wasn't long before the ranchers realized that Chuck seemed to have no water shortage at all. He was watering both day and night. This is as much, if not more, than usual. People began getting curious. Surveys were taken on Chuck's land and it was discovered that he had drained off the main water supply to all the other streams because he built the three wells over the main springs. Thus, while the main springs still had water, the tributaries were being drained dry.

The farmers and ranchers joined together and demanded that Chuck shut down his wells so the water could once again fill their wells. There was still a chance that most of their crops could be saved, but only if action was taken immediately. Chuck refused. The farmer-rancher group intends to take the matter to court but they realize it may take several months to get the matter through the courts and in the meantime their crops will be gone. The group chose one of their members, Phil Taylor, to represent them.

Phil approached Chuck with a request to take the matter to mediation. Chuck reluctantly agreed. The two of them contacted a mediator and the meeting was scheduled.

General Instructions to Disputant Role Players

You will receive two documents: a brief statement of the general problem and a brief description of your role in the dispute.

Your role description is general in nature. Use your own creativity to establish the character you are playing. Once you have laid the groundwork for your position you may then allow yourself to change your position as it seems practical and reasonable as a result of the negotiations with the help of the mediator.

Chuck Bartlet's Position

I am the owner of the Circle-Bar Ranch. Early this year I was worried about my water supply so I decided to dig another well in the hope of finding another spring. Fortunately, I drilled into a large underground body of water that feeds a number of small streams. I found such a great abundance of water I chose to drill two more wells in the same proximity, giving me a total of three wells in the main underground source. I certainly did not tap off all of the water going into the streams.

I didn't do anything wrong. I own the water rights under my land. I needed to increase my water supply because my crop was unusually large this year. So, I drilled for more water on the advice of a farm-ranch engineer. It's not my fault that I tapped into the main spring that feeds all the wells in this area. I didn't know this when the wells came in.

These other ranchers have no right to tell me that I have to quit using these wells so that their wells can fill up again. If I shut mine down I won't have enough water for my needs.

I have a lot of money invested in these wells and in the crops they supply. It would be foolish to turn them off. It would mean some severe financial problems for me.

These people are trying to make a living just like I am. I appreciate that. But they are very "clannish" and resent people like me who operate more or less independently. I don't intend to let them destroy me to save themselves. Neither do I intend to destroy them. But there is a limited supply of water and I happen to be at the main source. I cannot survive without the water. I have no recourse but to hang on to my wells.

I have agreed to go to mediation because I understand that the rancher group intends to take me to court. If we find a settlement in mediation I would not face the long court battle. At the same time, I could outlast them in the court battle because I have control of the water.

Phil Taylor for the Farmers and Ranchers

Chuck Bartlet is "ripping us off." That water does not belong to him. The water is for everyone to use and he cannot claim to own all the water that flows beneath his property. He has, in effect, created an underground dam to stop the flow of water to the other ranchers. He cannot do this. His property rights do not cover natural resources that may go across or even below the surface of his property.

Bartlet has been a bit of a thorn in the side of the ranchers in this area because of his "high-falutin" ways of dealing with them. He rarely works with these people in their joint community efforts. He tends to remain a "loner" in local activities. Most of the ranchers feel that he intends to put them out of business and then grab their land, open up his water, and thrive.

The ranchers have been told that they have a good case against Bartlet but that it will take time for them to press it in court and, in the meantime, they could lose the crop this year. Most of them cannot afford to lose the crop this year. Several of them would be out of business if there is a crop loss this year.

So, in hope of reaching a settlement in good time, the ranchers have agreed to try mediation. They realize, however, that to reach a settlement in mediation they may have to make some concessions. They do not know what these may be but they will not make any concessions that will lead to their complete loss of crops this year.

KAMPF VS. SANCHEZ

General Information

Maria Sanchez and Jurgen Kampf have come to the Neighborhood Dispute Resolution Program for help in resolving a dispute that exists between them. They came as a result of a suggestion by the clerk of the small claims court where Maria had gone to find out how to file against Jurgen for nonpayment of a bill for tree service and yard maintenance. The clerk referred her to the NDRP which got in touch with Kampf concerning the problem and offered their services. Both Kampf and Sanchez have agreed to mediation, the intake data has been collected, and the time set for mediation.

The main issue in the dispute is that Kampf claims that Sanchez had not done what she was instructed to do and that she felled two trees that she was specifically warned not to cut. Sanchez claims that she did what she was told by Kampf's wife and that a number of hours have been used in the yard and tree work for which Kampf is refusing to pay.

Jurgen Kampf

I heard from a neighbor that a M. Sanchez was a good yard maintenance person and was reliable and friendly. When I called Sanchez I noticed first that M. Sanchez was a woman and second that she spoke broken English and seemed to have some difficulty in understanding what I was saying. I had no difficulty in understanding her because she spoke slowly but really didn't say much except "yes," "no, " and that the fee would be figured once she had seen the work.

I told Sanchez to meet me the following Monday at 7:30 a.m. She did not appear until about 7:50. By the time she arrived I was angry because I needed to get to my office before 8 a.m. and it is at least 20 minutes from my home.

She arrived in an old beat up pick-up truck that looked like it had been fished out of the junk yard. She had two men with her who were obviously Mexican. They stayed in the truck while she talked with me. I took Sanchez around the two acres of yard that surrounded my home. There are a number of fir trees, oak trees, and some shore pine on the property. There is a flower garden, a vegetable garden, and a wide expanse of lawn and shrubs in the front and on the side of the house. I showed all these to Sanchez as we walked around the property and instructed her on what was to be done. This included mowing and edging the grass, tilling and hoeing the flower and vegetable gardens, and felling three oak trees that were mixed in with several Douglas firs along the back of the property. I did not want the firs touched. The oak was to be removed in order for the firs to get better growth and because I did not want the leaves piling up on the lawn.

Sanchez said little as I took her around the yard. When we were through she said, "Okay, we will do these things. Do you want us to come back and take care of yard every month?" I replied that it would depend on how well she did the job I had outlined. She said, "Okay."

I then asked her "How much?" She replied, "I will call you later and tell you." I told her I wanted this done immediately and that if she couldn't do it I wanted to know. She said she would call me that evening and left in her rattletrap truck with her two dark skinned companions.

After dinner she called and said they would come the next day and that the price would be around $700 which included felling the trees and cutting them into fireplace chunks. Then she added that they would clean and maintain the yard for an additional $75 a month. I said again that I would wait to see how well she did the job before I would make any agreement for continued work. She said, "Okay," and hung up.

The next day she arrived with her crew after I had left for work. I told my wife to keep watch and to let me know if anything strange took place. When I arrived home that evening I found that two of the oaks had been felled and cut up and two of the firs had been felled and cut. I was mad. The yard and gardens hadn't been touched. I told my wife about it and she said that she hadn't noticed what they were doing, but that Maria had come to her before they started cutting the trees and asked if the four trees were to be cut. My wife said she told them that if that is what I had told them, that is what they are to do.

The next day a bill from Sanchez for $400 was stuck in my front door with a note saying they would be back the following week to do the yard and gardens and finish the cutting. I am refusing to pay the bill because Sanchez did not do what I ordered with the trees and did not do the other garden and yardwork that I ordered. I don't want them back on my property.

Maria Sanchez

I have just gotten this crew together to work and we have had several good contracts with yardwork and tree cutting. Our good reputation is growing.

We talked with Mr. Kampf as we have done for the others and agreed to do what he asked us to do. Usually we charge $100 for each large tree we cut down and $10 an hour for each of the workers. That's cheaper than some of the other groups charge to do the same work. We have to pay insurance for our workers and we don't make very much money for that kind of work. Mr. Kampf did not like that and so I agreed to cut the trees for just $100 each and not charge the $10 an hour for the three of us. Cutting big trees like that is dangerous work and all of us have been hurt once or twice doing it.

When we went to cut the trees we saw that the great big oaks and the firs were mixed up together and that to cut the big oaks would hurt some of the fir trees and so we had to cut some of the firs. Mr. Kampf was not too clear about those particular fir trees. He said he didn't want them hurt if it was possible. When we saw how close they were together we asked Mrs. Kampf if that would be okay and she said it was okay. One oak tree was not cut because it was so big we had to do it another day. After cutting the trees we did some hoeing in the garden but the day was over. We have to go back to do the tilling, mowing, and other yardwork that Mr. Kampf ordered and we agreed to do.

Now Mr. Kampf won't pay us because we did what Mrs. Kampf said we should do and he won't stay with his agreement to keep us on for maintenance on a month-to-month basis. This is not fair. And he won't let us finish our job.

(The following to be revealed only in private caucus if the mediator's behavior indicates you can trust him or her and that he or she is sympathetic with your situation.)

We are from Mexico and have to work or we cannot stay here. We are trying hard to start our work in this country and it seems that we keep having difficulties finding good work that we can do. I have trouble with English and I know that sometimes I don't understand what people are trying to say to me. Mr. Kampf speaks so fast I am not sure that I understand everything he says. Neither of my helpers speaks English. But this time I was very clear to Mrs. Kampf about the problem and she seemed to understand what I was asking her.

Mr. Kampf is not like the others we work for either. He orders me around and doesn't give me a chance to say the things I want to say or ask questions. When he showed me the work in the yard it was like I was his slave. I don't like that either.

I don't like Mr. Kampf and I'm sorry I ever worked for him. But we did the work and we should be paid. What else can I do? My friends say that if I go to court I will have to pay a lawyer. I don't have money to pay a lawyer. Also, to go to court people say I have to pay court fees and I don't have money to pay court fees. I need the money very much.

Will you help me get my money?

SARA'S BARN

General Information

Sara is in the process of restoring a barn on her property into a residential dwelling. She is acting as her own contractor. Jeff, the carpenter, submitted a bid of $17,000 for labor and materials and Sara accepted the bid.

Work has progressed very slowly on the project. It is, however, now nearing completion but some problems have arisen.

To date Jeff has been paid a total of $15,000. The last payment was two weeks ago and consisted of $5000 for him to pay to the lumber yard. Payment is made by a voucher system in which the financial institution from which Sara secured her loan is to check the amount of work done before advancing the payment.

Since that payment Jeff has not appeared on the job and has not replied to telephone calls.

Several days ago Sara received a mechanics lien from the lumber yard from which Jeff purchased the material in the amount of $7,000. Apparently, Jeff has not paid his bill.

Sara is dissatisfied with the quality of some of the work. She has had another carpenter estimate the cost of completing of the project. His estimate was approximately $3,000.

At Sara's suggestion, Jeff is willing to come to mediation. Neither knows too much about it but they have been advised that it is a safe process and that they will make whatever decision is to be made.

Sara's Confidential Information

Sara is irate and very frustrated. She is looking at a potential total cost of $25,000 on a project bid at $17,000. She feels that the financial institution had been remiss in advancing the voucher payment, which had been written for "materials" in Jeff's name. She spoke to the owner of the lumber yard about three weeks ago while at a chance meeting at a restaurant and asked if Jeff was paying his bills. The owner assured her that Jeff was a long-time friend and that there was no problem. When she attempted to pay for her meal she found that the owner had already paid it.

A week later this lumber yard owner filed a lien on her.

Sara feels that Jeff and the owner of the lumber yard are in "cahoots."

She realizes that some of the changes she made in the renovation plans have added costs to the project, but in her opinion these additions and changes have not exceeded $2,000.

A month ago Jeff's father was at the job site to see how Jeff was doing. He had been drinking and while attempting to leave had backed into Sara's car causing $500 in damage. He immediately left the scene. Sara did not see who had done the damage, but a neighbor saw the incident and reported it to Sara.

Sara feels that Jeff is trying to "get back at her for something," perhaps because of the circumstances. She also feels that Jeff, the lumberyard owner, and Jeff's father are trying to take advantage of her because she is a woman.

She contacted her lawyer after receiving the lien and he suggested mediation as a possible means of resolving of the dispute. She finally got hold of Jeff and he agreed to come to mediation.

Jeff's Confidential Information

Jeff made a gross mistake in his estimate of Sara's rebuilding job. The condition of the old building was much worse than he had thought when he inspected the place. He has put in approximately 200 more hours than he estimated and the cost of materials exceeded his estimate by at least $1,000.

The additional labor has been due to changes made by Sara in the original plans. She has said nothing about paying extra for the changes or modifying the original agreement. The original agreement did not have a clause providing for additions to the plans.

Jeff feels bad about not paying his bill at the lumberyard but at this point there is no money to pay such bills. He has just been divorced and has a large child support payment. His father, who had been undergoing treatment for alcoholism, needs further treatment for which Jeff will have to pay.

Jeff's long-time friend who owns the lumberyard understands this situation and has assured him that he will be able to extend credit to Jeff for his next job even though he didn't pay for the barn renovation materials.

Jeff realizes that the present situation is going to hurt his reputation in the community. Even so he has two jobs pending and feels that he must go on to his next job in order to maintain a cash flow.

The barn renovation was a job, Jeff discovered later, that no one else really wanted because of all the hidden costs and labor that Jeff didn't see until after he got into it.

Should there be a legal action Jeff is not worried because he will then file bankruptcy and continue working small jobs as he has in the past. He has little or no equity in his business.

This was Jeff's first large renovation project and it turned out to be a disaster. At this point he simply wants to walk away from it.

At the same time he realizes that Sara is mad and upset. When she suggested mediation he didn't know about it so he asked his lumberyard friend and was told that it was an okay process as long as he didn't give everything away.

ROCK AND ROLL EVICTION*

*Adapted by Sam Keltner from an original scenario by David Acklin

General Information

The owner of a commercial property, Tuss, is attempting to evict the current tenant of the property, Mango. Mango is using the storefront property as a video and audio record store called the Rock and Roll Shop. The owner also claims that there are special reasons why Mango should be out of the property. The owner, Tuss, filed for action in small claims court for the eviction, but on advice of the judge the two parties agreed to go to mediation.

Tuss

I own a small storefront property in the northwest part of town. I acquired that property from my former marriage partner when we divorced. The divorce was finalized just a month ago, but we are still fighting over things that were really not settled in the divorce itself. One of these has to do with the rental of the storefront property.

Before we broke up my partner managed the property. My partner had signed a 2-year lease with Mango for the storefront property. My partner leased it to Mango at $200 per month just a month before our divorce was finalized. The lease also provided that the owner would make alterations and repairs as needed to provide the occupant with a usable store.

This was an absurd rent. By the time I pay the taxes, the various maintenance costs, and other costs associated with the ownership of commercial property, I lose money. The property is easily worth $600 per month. It is quite obvious that my former partner set me up with a lease that I can't break, obviously figuring I would get the storefront property and freezing the income from it at a level that would make me lose money. I think there must have been some hanky panky between her and Mango and they planned to make me pay.

So I talked with Mango about the rent. I said that I would have to raise the rent on the lease but Mango claimed that I could not raise the rent because the lease held for the rest of the two years. We had a heated argument but it got us nowhere.

This left me with only one choice and that was to throw Mango out. So I sent Mango an eviction notice and told Mango to be out of the property in 24 hours. Mango refused to comply so I decided to go to small claims court to see if I couldn't get an eviction on the grounds that the original manager-owner of the property no longer owned the property and that a new owner had taken over. I am hoping the mediator can support me on this.

It doesn't stop there, however. Last month when Mango sent the rent check, included in the envelope was a card that shows a shadow of a creature about to pounce on someone. Obviously this is a death threat of some kind since Mango does not want me to raise the rent. So that's why I filed against Mango. I'm really afraid of what is going on and suspect that my ex-partner is behind this in some way.

Before we were scheduled to go to the hearing, someone from the judge's office called and suggested we could go to mediation rather than go through the court proceedings. And, if we settled in mediation, the small claims costs would be returned. If we didn't settle, then we could go on through the small claims process. It seemed a reasonable thing to me although I don't know much about this mediation business except that the decisions are made by us rather than by the judge. I'm not sure that mediation will work, however, because I've already tried to get the matter settled and it doesn't work. We'll probably have to have someone else make the decision because we can't do it ourselves. Anyway, I'm willing to give it a try.

Mango

Several years ago I started this little record shop. I have had to move several times because the rent is always being increased on me so that I can't make a living from the project. A few months ago a friend of mine, who knew of my difficulties in getting a good place for the business, said she owned a little storefront that was being vacated and asked if I would be interested in using it. I took a look at it and, although it was small and needed a lot of repair and maintenance, I thought I could fit into it with some special shelves and a specially built counter. It also needed some remodeling in order to make it usable. So we worked out a lease agreement for two years. When it came to the monthly rent we negotiated for some time but we finally agreed on $200 per month. That sounded real good to me because I figured I could make a go of it under those conditions particularly if she covered the costs of the remodeling.

Then the owner and marriage partner were divorced. In the separation agreement the ownership of the storefront went to the ex-partner, Tuss. I knew nothing about this until the ex-partner, Tuss, sent me a letter notifying me that the rent was to be raised to $600 and that a new lease would have to be written. I replied that I had a solid lease for two years and that I was not about to pay more rent. Shortly thereafter I received an eviction notice stating that I had to be out of the rental in 24 hours. I did not respond. And then I got a notice from the court that Tuss had filed against me and that I was to appear for a hearing.

I also understand that Tuss is going to press charges against me because I threatened him with some kind of death card. That is preposterous! I haven't sent Tuss any such card or notice. I do remember putting a postcard from the store in the rent envelope as a check block but it was one of those movie memorabilia cards with no threatening implication at all.

I understand that in this state a lease cannot be broken unless the tenant does something extraordinary like making and distributing drugs, harboring a fugitive, or something like that. I'm not involved in anything like that. I'm staying! There is no way I'm going to leave this place with the rent so low.

The other day someone from the court called and said that Tuss was willing to mediate this dispute and that if we got it settled that way we would not have any court costs. Well, I know I'm on safe ground as far as the lease is concerned so I might as well see what Tuss has to say about that threat charge.

My business is beginning to grow but there are some inside repairs to the store that need to be done and some alterations would really be helpful. I would be willing to assume some of the costs of altering the storefront as long as my rent is not be increased.

THE FARM DRIVEWAY*

*Adapted by Sam Keltner from an original scenario by David Acklin

General Information

Kuhl recently bought a 30 acre small farm property, including a barn, which had an access road running some seven miles through timber and marsh. The previous owners had an agreement with the owner of the adjoining property, Hadfield, for access to the barn and surrounding property by a road that ran across a portion of the Hadfield property. This shortened the time of access substantially. Not long after Kuhl had purchased the small farm property Hadfield put a large gate at the entrance of the road traversing their property to the Kuhl's property. Kuhl stormed up to Hadfield's house in anger and Hadfield slammed the door.

The Kuhls sought to get legal access to the road to Kuhl's property but was told by their attorney that the road was on private property and that Kuhl could not force the use of the access road because there was another access road, although longer. Kuhl was advised to seek mediation through the Neighborhood Dispute Resolution Program (NDRP). Kuhl called the NDRP and was told that they could not unilaterally demand mediation and that Hadfield would also have to agree to come to mediation. Kuhl called Hadfield and was met with a cool refusal to discuss the matter. Later, however, Hadfield called the NRDP and informed them that he would be willing to discuss the problem in mediation.

Kuhl

For many years my partner and I wanted a small farm where we could keep some horses and cows. About six months ago just such a place became available and we bought it along with the cows and horses from a family by the name of Mikkelson. Although we live in a city a few miles away we have both been raised on a farm and looked forward to getting back to some of the farm activities, particularly the raising of some horses and having a few cattle.

When we purchased the farm there was access to it by a one mile road off the county highway that went through a small portion of the adjoining property and by the home of the owner. The only other access to our property is via seven miles of county service roads and lowland. We used this short road daily as we went to take care of the animals and haul feed, equipment, and so on to the barn. We really enjoyed working this little plot of our dream. It took us a while to get some fences mended and to get the barn repaired and the feed bins cleaned up.

One day, several weeks ago (after we owned the property for about six months) we went to take care of our animals and found the short access road blocked by a newly erected gate just off the highway. We hiked the mile up to the house to talk with the owner whom we had never met. The owner met us at the door and when I told Hadfield who we were and what we wanted the door was slammed in our face. That made us real mad.

We then went to our attorney, Bob Huber, and he pointed out that the access road is on private property. He told us that we had no recourse against the people owning the property on which the short access road existed. We therefore, according to the attorney, had only one option which was to use the legal access road which runs seven miles through pretty rough roads. He did suggest that we try to negotiate with the owner of the property for use of the short access road. When we told him what had happened when we tried to do that he shook his head and said there wasn't much we could do unless we could get the owner, Hadfield, to negotiate with us. In light of what had happened he suggested that we might try to get Hadfield to come to mediation through the NDRP.

We then went to the NDRP and told them the story. The person who talked with us told us that we could not force Hadfield to come to mediation if he didn't want to and suggested we talk with him and see if he would come to mediation with us. We then called Hadfield. Hadfield was just as abrupt as before and said that he was not about to give away his right to do what he wanted to with his property.

We were stumped and outraged. Hadfield had allowed the previous owners to use this road and we were denied such usage. This was discrimination of some kind even though our attorney said we had no rights. It looks very much like we may have to use the back road, but if we have to do this there will be consequences.

Later when the NDRP called us and reported that Hadfield was willing to come to mediation we were overjoyed. Maybe Hadfield was going to relent.

Hadfield

About six months ago a couple purchased the barn and small acreage behind our home. This acreage used to be part of a larger farm in which our present home was the farm home. This small acreage was separated from the home a long time ago before we bought the home itself. The barn and property are not very large and there are horses and some cows on the acreage. Regular attention to the animals and the property is clearly required. We had not met the new owners until just recently when this matter came to a head. The Mikkelsons, who owned the farm previously, had told us that the name of the new owners was Kuhl. They are too cool for us!

The Mikkelsons were close friends of our family for some time and we had allowed them to use the short road to their property for a long time. They were always courteous about using the road. They helped to pay for the oiling and graveling when it was needed. We have several youngsters and the Mikkelsons would let them ride the horses and play in the field. And, when they had some milk cows, they allowed the kids to milk them on occasion. Whenever the Mikkelsons came to the farm they would take great care in driving on the road, keeping a watchful eye for children, and slowing not to stir unnecessary dust that could blow into our house. During the winter they would be careful not to drive off the graveled ruts so as to avoid the creation of a quagmire at any point in the road. At no time did we ever have a problem with their use of the road. They would usually give us a couple of honks on the horn as they drove past to their barn.

These new owners, the Kuhls, have been quite different and nothing but trouble. Contrary to the Mikkelsons, the Kuhls speed through the road at any time of the day and night kicking up dust and digging in deep ruts. They were not very social and we had never met them personally until the day that Kuhl came to the door to complain about the new gate.

From what we can see, the Kuhls are hobby farmers with little experience. Their use of the road has created dust and mud and left it in a mess that they have made no effort to correct. We fear for the safety of our children and their friends as the Kuhls come tearing through. Not so long ago one of their cows broke through their fence and strayed into our garden, destroying our corn patch and leaving big holes over the soft ground. Enough was enough! We moved the cow off our property, repaired the fence ourselves, and had a contractor install a large gate with a lock on it at the entrance of our property and the road. It was our property and we felt that it was our right to decide who drove on it. It is not like denying them access to the property for they have another access from another direction. I'll admit, however, that this access is closer to town.

The day after we completed the gate Kuhl came pounding on our door demanding that we open the gate so that they could feed the animals. Kuhl was insulting and demanded that we remove the gate or give them a key to the gate. Kuhl made me so angry that I said there was nothing to talk about and shut the door.

A few days later Kuhl called me and requested that we go to mediation over the matter. This didn't make any sense to me because I had nothing to negotiate over. They are not to use the road. It is ours. And that is that! I told Kuhl this on the phone and hung up. My partner overheard the conversation and suggested that I may have been a little harsh and pointed out that these people were neighbors and that if we didn't get along it would be too bad. My partner offered to inquire about this mediation stuff and see if it was worth our while to become involved with it. A couple of days later my partner commented that we might go to mediation because, according to what had been explained, we wouldn't be forced to do anything we didn't want to. And further, my partner argued, it would be a good place to let these Kuhl characters get a good idea of how irritated we were at their behavior. So, I called the NDRP and told them that I would meet with Kuhl and the mediator, but that I was not promising any change in our position.

THE POLLUTED OFFICE

Information for the Mediator

You have been chosen as a mediator to help deal with a dispute that has arisen in a small consulting firm. Your preliminary investigation has led to the discovery of the following facts: The firm has 10 principles, two attorneys, and a support staff of 15 people. It is headquartered in a fairly old building where all the offices are on one floor and the ventilation system is an old unitary one (that is, all offices and work spaces are on the same system).

One of the attorneys, Chris, is a cigar smoker who insists on smoking during the day when he is in the office. The manager and CEO, Hal, is a chain cigarette smoker who claims that he is unable to cease the habit. Karen, the other attorney, is not a smoker and claims she has suffered considerable stress and physical discomfort because the smoke from the cigars and cigarettes flows through the ventilation system into her office. The other employees do not smoke. They either haven't encountered as much physical distress as Karen or are afraid to discuss it. Karen has grieved the matter with Hal, the manager. By mutual agreement they have come to mediation of the issue.

Confidential Information for the Parties

Karen's Perception of the Situation

Karen is an attorney with a specialty in labor-management relations. She has been with the firm for six years. Prior to that she was in private practice, and prior to that she was an attorney for six years with an international union. She graduated from law school in the upper 10% of her class.

As a result of the pollution of the air in the office by cigar and cigarette smoke, Karen has suffered a great deal of lung and nasal congestion as well as pain, difficulty in breathing, and nausea. She has called this to Hall's attention on several occasions. She has had Hal move her office several times in order to try to reduce the problem, but nothing seems to work. The whole system seems contaminated with the smoke and is particularly heavy when Chris is in his office. It is getting to the point at which she is having to do more and more work out of the office because of the distress that being in the office brings. After seeing her physician, Karen filed for workers' compensation to cover her doctor bills and medication, whereupon the insurance company sent in an air specialist to test the air at a time when neither of the smokers, Chris and Hal, had been in the building for at least three days. The report was that the air was not seriously polluted.

Karen's physician has advised her to change her workplace, quit the job, or begin taking a costly medication aimed at covering up the discomfort and pain, thereby giving her some relief. He states unequivocally that the cigar and cigarette smoke in the system is a health hazard. He also filed a report to the insurance company to that effect. The insurance company tried to insist that it could not be the working conditions, but the physician wrote a strong letter to the insurance company to the effect that it was the smoke in the air that caused Karen's problem. The insurance company is now dragging its heels and no action is expected from it on the matter because it is essentially management oriented.

Karen likes and enjoys the work with this firm, but the behavior of Hal and Chris seems to make it very difficult. She has been with the firm for six years and has carried a very heavy load of work with clients and is in great demand as a legal consultant and attorney. Everyone in the firm but Chris seems to like her very much.

She and Chris have not been able to get along since she first came to work with this group. He appears to her as an arrogant, selfish, somewhat stupid, and malicious man who resents her presence. He will not talk directly with Karen about any matter, even those for which they share responsibility. She has tried to engage him in conversation about business, but he responds in meaningless monosyllables. She finally gave up and will not attempt to talk with him about anything. She has had to go to Hal on several occasions when Chris wrote nasty notes or tried to assume authority that he did not have. Hal has listened, but does nothing about it. He now simply assigns them to different cases. He keeps saying that the two of them, Karen and Chris, should work it out together. Karen has tried but Chris is totally unresponsive.

Chris seems totally unwilling to accommodate to any request to reduce smoking. Hal has asked him not to smoke cigars in the building, but when Hal is gone Chris will light up and fill the air with cigar smoke. Hal has been told about this by several employees but does nothing about it. When Hal is gone Chris will strut around the office, cigar in hand, and give orders to secretaries like he is the manager.

Karen has been very loyal to Hal and has been his right hand for several years. He seems to depend on her for legal advice and suggestions for methods of dealing with clients. However, he does not seem to be able to deal with problems among his own employees. He tends to put problems such as this in "deep freeze" hoping that they will work themselves out without his having to do anything about it. Karen, finally, in almost total frustration and with tears in her eyes, told Hal that she could not stay unless the matter was cleared up and the air made livable. She offered to go to mediation, however, if Hal was willing and if Chris were included.

What Karen wants in this situation is relief from the pollution. She is willing to work with Chris and wants to work with Hal, although she is rapidly losing confidence in his ability to manage. She can get jobs elsewhere if she wants them but would prefer to stay here if things could be worked out. She has no desire to be chief counsel of the firm but simply will not stay if Chris is moved to such a position.

Hal's Perception of the Situation

There is no law in this state that requires the management of a private firm to outlaw smoking in a building. This whole smoking issue is a real irritation. Hal has smoked for over 30 years and appears healthy. Why can't other people feel the same? He feels that the increasing pressure to keep smokers out of the workplace is an intrusion on the freedom of the smokers. If people want to smoke they should have the right to do so.

Karen has told Hal of her problem on several occasions. He feels that the problem is hers and that her illness is not the result of the air in the office. He feels that he cannot violate the freedom of his employees to smoke if they choose and that he has tried to accommodate Karen's problem in several ways. He doesn't smoke when he is in her office, for example. He has also had the ventilation system cleaned and he has moved her office.

Hal points to the report of the insurance investigator on the condition of the air as proof that it is Karen's personal problem. He did not direct the insurance investigator as to when to test the office air.

Hal knows that Chris and Karen do not get along. This grieves him but he feels unable to do anything about it. Chris was here before Karen came (by four years). He was a clerk and later became junior associate attorney in the firm. Obviously, Chris expected to be elevated to the position that Karen was hired to fill and this upset him, but he didn't have the qualifications for the job and Karen did.

Hal sees Karen as his key team member and her contribution to the firm is highly valuable and important. She carries a heavy work load, is much in demand by the clients, and bills a substantial amount of time for the firm. He has relied on her in many instances to guide his thinking and work in dealing with difficult clients. Because of her legal background she has a keen insight into many problems that he does not have. Her inability to get along with Chris is a point against her. She should be able, because of her position, background, and training, to get along with people like Chris.

He does not believe that Karen will leave the firm over such a minor issue as smoke in the office. He realizes, however, that Chris can be irritating. On several occasions he has talked with Chris about the smoking of cigars, and they have agreed to try to reduce the amount of smoke in the office. At one time he asked Chris not to smoke cigars. He felt that he could not ask Chris not to smoke because he was a smoker also and he did not intend to quit smoking in the building. He realized that he was addicted, but he simply did not have the time nor energy to do anything about it.

As manager, Hal sees it as his duty to keep the work force on the job and working with each other. Chris was one of his choices to fill an associate position several years ago and he hates to admit he might be wrong. He tries to keep Chris and Karen apart. She has said very bluntly that she wants nothing to do with Chris. This is too bad because we need both of them in this organization.

Hal has just recently been promoted to CEO of the firm. He takes this responsibility with great seriousness and wants to make it work. He has had no previous experience as a CEO. His work has primarily focused on the representation of employers in collective bargaining with unions. He is known as a hard bargainer and one who can "wait 'em out" until the union capitulates. He thinks this may be an important management strategy also. He wants very much to do a good job and to show the board of directors that he can handle this job.

He agreed, reluctantly, to take the matter to a mediator simply because he would rather not have Karen leave. He does not like the idea, however, of someone outside the firm being involved in a problem within the firm.

What Hal wants from this situation is for those two lawyers to cool it and get off his back so he can get on with the terribly difficult job of managing this firm.

Chris's Perception of the Situation

Getting through law school was a real hard job and when he was hired as a law clerk for this firm he liked working in that capacity. It was just natural that after finishing his degree he would move into permanent employment with the firm. He had clerked for the attorney for the firm and they had gotten along well. He pretty well followed her directions after he came on full time and actually continued being a clerk, although not in name. When she left to go to another firm he expected to be made chief attorney for this firm. He had been told by her and by the then CEO of the firm that the staff counsel job would be his. However, when the CEO advertised for another attorney he was shocked. In the interviews Karen seemed quiet, friendly, and unassuming, and she had a very good record. He felt that she would not be a barrier to his being staff counsel. Even though she had more experience than he and her record in law school was better, he felt that she would be a good team member for his legal staff of the firm. At that time (when Karen was hired) things looked good.

Then Karen came on board. At first she was quiet and did not push. She conferred with him frequently on cases and talked with him about the work they were doing. In the meantime he had approached the CEO and asked that he be made chief counsel. He was told that he didn't have the experience to do that job and that now Karen was there he should not think of the firm's having a chief counsel. They were to work as a team. This upset him a great deal and he immediately began to see Karen as a threat to his advancement and security in the firm. Then he realized that Karen was being assigned some of the more significant cases the firm received and this irritated him even more.

Karen seemed like a "Jekyl-Hyde." She was quiet most of the time but when dealing with a case or a problem she was like a harridan and would press and ask questions until he was really irritated. She was highly opinionated and seemed so damned sure of herself. He found it increasingly difficult to talk with her. Her style was to ask questions until she got the answer she wanted. He did not like that style. They just were not on the same wave length. So, when fewer and fewer cases began to come his way he took longer and longer to work on them to be sure he did not make any mistakes. That seemed to make matters worse. After a final attempt to get appointed as chief counsel he was told that Karen had more experience and should really be the chief counsel but because he had been here before she came there would be no chief counsel and they were to work together as a team.

When they both had to work together to hire a clerk, he tried to get the responsibility for directing the work of the clerk, figuring that this would set him up as the chief counsel. Karen blocked that at every turn. That made him even more frustrated and angry. Then he discovered that she had been going to Hal and complaining about his cigar smoking and his handling of the clerk selection and assignment. This made him very angry. All through law school Chris smoked a pipe and cigars. He enjoys cigars very much. The lawyers and judges he admires very much smoke cigars. They do several things for him. Smoking a cigar gives a sense of satisfaction, authority, and control over things. It is a good stress reliever. The more stress that developed around this job the more he smoked cigars. They seemed to relieve some of the stress. Then, too, he discovered that Karen did not smoke and that she definitely did not like cigar smoke. Perhaps, he thought, at the back of his mind, he could "smoke her out" of the job and she would leave. He knew that Hal would not fire or discipline him for smoking because Hal was a chain smoker himself. Chris sees Hal as a relatively incompetent manager. Hal seems unable to make clear decisions regarding personnel issues and doesn't want to "stir the pot" with personnel decisions that someone in the group might not like. So, his style is to put things aside and hope they will solve themselves. That's what he's done with this Karen affair and the more he does it the more opportunity Chris has to have his way in the operation of the legal functions of the firm. He realizes that Hal has depended on Karen for a lot of the legal work and this has bothered him.

Chris has applied for a number of other positions but has not been selected. So, in some frustration he has come to the point that he'll stick with this firm as long as he can. It frustrates him terribly that he cannot get out, but his security depends on his hanging on there. And he realizes that if Karen should leave his future here would be much more secure and pleasant.

In general, Chris feels that he has much to offer the legal profession and this firm particularly. He feels he is a top notch lawyer and deserves to be recognized. What he wants from this situation is to be chief counsel in charge of the legal work of the firm. He would prefer that Karen not be here. He has another person in mind, a former clerk, who would make a good partner in place of Karen. He intends to continue smoking his cigars and pipe unless he is specifically ordered to stop. Even then, he intends to find a way to enjoy his smoking habits.

ARBITRATION SIMULATIONS

Instructions for Using These Simulations

These are simulations of arbitration hearings. Each arbitration hearing should be conducted by a person assigned to act as the "arbitrator." Those of you who are observers may caucus with this person periodically if you wish to raise questions about the manner in which the hearing is being conducted.

Procedure

The arbitrator will call the meeting to order. The two parties and their representatives are usually placed on either side of a long table. The arbitrator makes a quick review of the manner of procedure, sees that the spokespersons for each side understand and are in agreement as to procedure, and then begins the case by requesting such joint stipulations as the parties may wish to submit. Usually these stipulations are joint statements of the issue(s) to be decided by the arbitrator. As such they are then entered as a matter of record as exhibits. (In the usual arbitration, other documents in evidence may be submitted during the hearing and are recorded by the arbitrator.) In this simulation we will not have documentary evidence submitted except for the stipulations.

In a labor-management discharge case the company usually makes the first presentation. When the company has completed its case the union takes its turn.

At the very beginning of the proceedings, once the details have been arranged, it is customary for the spokesperson for each party to present a brief preview of what it intends to prove in the course of the proceedings. Once these "Preliminary Statements" are completed, the company begins its development of the case. (It is traditional and logical for the company to begin the arguments in a discharge case because the burden of proof for supporting the discharge is with the company.)

The case development is usually performed by bringing forth several witnesses who are queried by the spokesperson(s) presenting the case. When the company is presenting its case, the company initiates the questioning of the witnesses (called "direct examination of the witness.") Then the union representative has an opportunity to question the witnesses (called "cross examination of the witnesses"). If the company chooses, thereupon, it may address further questions to the witnesses (called "redirect examination"). If the union then decides it has further questions to ask, this is called "re-cross examination."

When the union is presenting its case the procedure described in the paragraph above is reversed. The union begins with the direct examination and the company follows with the cross examination, and so on.

The company is allowed to call all the witnesses it wishes and to make such statements as it wishes in support of its position. The union then takes its turn in the same manner. When all the witnesses have been heard from both sides, each party is given an opportunity to sum up its position, after which the hearing is terminated.

During the hearing the arbitrator may query the witnesses at any point when she or he needs further clarification or feels additional evidence from that witness is important to an understanding of the case.

Following the close of the hearing, both parties usually submit written briefs in support of their position. In this simulation you will not receive full briefs as is the usual case. You must depend on the evidence submitted during the "hearing" and the summary statements of each spokesperson.

Your Preparation of the Decision-Award

Having heard the case, the summary of the arguments, and having considered the situation, YOU ARE TO WRITE A DECISION-AWARD.

Write this decision in the proper form and substance usually followed in arbitration cases involving labor and management disputes. For examples of form and substance, study the cases in the following two sets of volumes: LABOR ARBITRATION AWARDS, Commerce Clearing House, Chicago, IL; and LABOR ARBITRATION REPORTS: DISPUTE SETTLEMENTS, Bureau of National Affairs, Inc., Washington, DC.

The usual outline of an arbitration and/or fact finding decision is as follows:

- identification of the parties, case number, title, and other designations including the name of the arbitrator.
- the date and place of the hearing.
- a list of the representatives for each side and the witnesses appearing for each side.
- statement of the issues to be resolved.
- contract clauses bearing on the matter
- history and background of the case.
- position of the company.

- position of the union.
- discussion of the arguments by the arbitrator. This is usually an examination of the rationale, the circumstances, comparable cases, the nature of the contract terms, the testimony of the witnesses, and so on.
- the decision and award with the reasons for that decision summarized.

THE DISCHARGE OF JIM SMITH

An Arbitration Simulation

Instructions for Using This Simulation

Personnel for This Case

When this simulation case is presented in a group or class the whole class may be assigned to serve as the "arbitrator." That is, each person in the class will prepare a decision in the matter. One member of the class is to be selected as the performing arbitrator who will conduct the hearing itself.

Unless they are otherwise available to you, select seven people from your group to serve as the witnesses in this case. Each of these persons will be given a specific set of instructions as to the information they are to divulge as witnesses. The simulation directors will either serve as the company and union representatives (spokespersons) or will assign someone to this responsibility.

Prior to the beginning of the hearing each representative (spokesperson) will caucus with the witnesses of the side represented and clarify the arrangements for the presentation. During this time the rest of the group will be briefed on its functions as an arbitrator.

Getting Started

Remember, it is necessary for you to get careful notes of the proceedings: what is said, who says it, the meanings, and issues. There will be no transcript of the proceedings available to you in the preparation of your award. A tape recording can be made of the hearing as a reference point for the situation.

Because each person who serves as a witness will also be asked to write an arbitration decision-award, it would be helpful if each witness had a partner in the group who would make notes and share them with the one who is playing the part of the witness. The witnesses can be a part of the "arbitrator" audience during the time they are not on the witness stand.

Instructions to the Witnesses

Attached to this sheet is a copy of your instructions for this simulation. The essence of these instructions is information that you may reveal at the arbitration hearing. Some conditions under which you are to reveal portions of that information are indicated.

In general, the procedure at the hearing will be for your representative to call you to the witness stand, have you sworn in, and then after properly identifying you and your position begin questioning you concerning the case.

The information on the attached sheet is *the only substantive information you may provide.* You may provide other information with *no bearing on the case* as you care to improvise it.

Special Instructions To Witnesses

Some of the information you have is *not* to be revealed except under cross-examination by the representative of the *other* side. Please be careful that you do not reveal this information unless specifically asked.

Your Testimony: How You Are To Present Yourself

One way in which you can deal with the situation is to paraphrase the essential information in as many ways as you wish, but DO NOT ADD TO THE BASIC INFORMATION! Do not let the actions or questions of the representatives for either party throw you off the essential information you have. Keep your instruction sheet in front of you at all times.

The Materials and Witness Information
JOINT STIPULATIONS IN THE JIM SMITH CASE

JOINT EXHIBIT No. 1.

The Midwest Telephone Company, a subsidiary of International Telephonic, Ltd., terminated the employment of Jim Smith, telephone repairman, on December 31.

This matter has been properly grieved by the union according to contract procedure and is now before the arbitrator according to the grievance procedure of the agreement between the parties.

The issue to be determined by the arbitrator is:
DID THE COMPANY VIOLATE THE LABOR AGREEMENT BETWEEN THE PARTIES WHEN IT DISCHARGED JIM SMITH ON DECEMBER 31? IF SO, WHAT REMEDIES SHOULD BE AWARDED TO SMITH?

The contract clause involved in the termination is as follows:

~Article II. Section 1. The Company will not discharge an employee without proper cause. Any question as to whether an employee has been discharged without proper cause shall be reviewed in accordance with the grievance procedure of this contract.

Jim Smith was a coin telephone station repairman at the time of his discharge. He was assigned to work primarily in the Literberry area where a number of coin operated phones are installed. His termination resulted from the discovery and his admission that he had taken some $4.50 in coins from telephones at the Literberry installation on December 29.

JOINT EXHIBIT Number 2.

Copy
Grievance File

Jim Smith, Grievant
January , 7

I have been unfairly discharged for taking coins to reimburse myself for those I had used in the line of duty for the Company. Others have done this and have not been discharged.

I request that I be given my job back with all back pay plus an extra penalty for unfair discharge.

Signed
Jim Smith

COMPANY PRESENTATION WITNESSES

COMPANY WITNESS No. 1

COMPANY REPAIR FOREMAN

My job at Midwest is Repair Foreman for the company. I am in charge of the repairmen who work in the Literberry area. The Literberry area is a bank of four phones in a shed near a military installation.

The coin telephone is made up of two separate compartments within one housing. The lower compartment contains a till into which the money is dropped. This money is collected later by a coin collecter who has a key to this compartment. Field repair crews do not have keys to this till, nor access to it. The upper compartment has a chute or runway leading to the till or lower compartment. This chute is a source of trouble due to bent coins, slugs, and unauthorized coins. When there is a disfunction, the coins will pile up in the chute and spill over into the upper compartment of the phone and disable the operation of the phone. This is called the overflow condition. The coins do not get into the lower compartment and till but are spilled out in the upper housing where the working mechanism is vulnerable to the contact of metals. The repair men work in the upper housing. The overflow condition can also be created by heavy use of the phone or by the use of slugs that block the chute.

A study of coin shortages from the Literberry phones from June until the end of October showed that there were about 20 shortages amounting to several hundred dollars in loss.

In September, I do not remember the exact date, I read passages from the company documents titled "Conduct Standards of Workers" to several of the repairmen and instructed all repairmen to read the whole document themselves and to discuss it. The essence of that document was:

No employee shall do anything to deceive, defraud, mislead the Company or other employes or those with whom the Company has business; take or misuse Company property, funds, or services; misrepresent the Company; or conduct themselves in a dishonest manner which would reflect discredit to the Company.

Any violation of the basic standards of conduct/or any specific rules therein provided will subject the employee to disciplinary action, including dismissal.

No employee shall be exempt from observation of the basic standards of conduct.

Early in November, because of the continued loss of overflow coins in the Literberry area, I consulted Jim Smith on ways to control or correct the loss. Smith made several suggestions to assist in this matter. I referred him to the special agent for the company who was interested in helping us apprehend or identify the cause of the lost coins.

On November 5 I gave Jim Smith full instructions and directions as to the handling of overflow coins. Again on December 29, just before he went on the repair assignment to Literberry, I again checked Smith out on the handling of overflow coins.

On November 5 I gave the repair employees a written memo on the matter of overflow coins. That memo said, "If the till is empty and will accept the overflow it is then to be deposited into the coin telephone with the desk man or the operator on the line counting the money and logging the amount placed in the coin box of the telephone. In the event the till is full and will not accept any more money, the overflow moneys are to be placed in a brown envelope provided for this purpose. The envelope is to be marked as to the date, the telephone number, the amount of money collected, and the repairman's name who collected the money. This envelope is then to be placed in the upper housing and left there so that the coin collector making the collection of the till can also collect the overflow money."

Past practice with respect to overflow coins has been for the repairmen to present the coins to the supervisor of coin collection along with the data on where, how much, and who had discovered the overflow.

[To be revealed only by cross examination by the opposing side. Do not reveal this information unles it is asked for in one way or another.]

I have worked with Jim Smith many times as a repairman and have always found him to be very knowledgeable about his job and most helpful to others. He has always seemed a reliable and honest person. But this case would seem to prove otherwise. You just never know, do you!

The Company document titled "Conduct Standards of Workers" was not posted on the bulletin board.

We did change the overflow procedure from the one prescribed on November 5 after we fired Jim Smith.

———

COMPANY WITNESS No. 2

COMPANY SERVICE SUPERVISOR

My job at Midwest is Company Service Supervisor. I am the immediate supervisor of the Repair Foreman in this case.

On December 29 I met with Jim Smith just before he went out to work on the telephones at Literberry. Smith told me that he was having coin phone problems at Literberry and mentioned that large amounts of money were being made available by the overflow in the upper housing. Smith also told me that he knew how to handle the overflow money and he produced previous repair tickets to show that the overflow entries had been properly made.

After talking with him about the situation I was convinced that Smith knew exactly what to do with the overflow coins and that he was concerned about the loss of coins we had been talking about for several months.

TO BE REVEALED ONLY BY CROSS EXAMINATION OF THE OPPOSING REPRESENTATIVE.

I did know that the telephones at Literberry were being watched when I talked to Smith on December 29. I did not tell him about this.

There have been a number of losses of coins in the whole system of coin operated phones. We have been trying for several years to get to the heart of the matter. We know about the loss when the office individual phone record tape does not coincide with the actual amounts collected from the telephone itself.

COMPANY WITNESS No. 3

DISTRICT PLANT MANAGER

My job at Midwest is District Plant Manager. As such I am the direct supervisor of the Service Supervisor.

On December 30 I received a call from our Chief Special Agent and was informed that there had been a misappropriation of money at the Literberry station. I called the Service Supervisor and the Repair Foreman to my office. We met and reviewed the evidence presented by the Special Agent. It was clear that there had been an unauthorized taking of funds from one of the phones.

I then checked with my superior officer as to the proper procedure to follow in such a case and after talking the matter over, I then instructed the Service Supervisor and the Foreman to go get Smith and bring him to my office. They did this.

When Smith arrived I asked him to brief me on the way in which he handles overflow coins. His replies were adequate and showed me that he knew how to do it as instructed by the company and that he had done it properly on past occasions. I then asked him if he had ever misappropriated any money found in the coin boxes. He reply was, "I would be lying if I said, no." He claimed, however, that he occasionally kept only a nickel or a dime in order to reimburse himself for calls made to the operator to check out the phone after it had been repaired.

I asked Smith if he had worked on some phones at Literberry on the previous day. He said, "Yes." Then, without any other question, he said, "I took the money. I don't know why." He then took money out of his pocket and put $4.50 on my desk. That was the actual amount found missing in the two phones he had worked on at the Literberry station. The money was four one-dollar bills and a 50 cent coin.

I informed Smith that he had violated the code of conduct and that company regulations were that the penalty was discharge. I thereupon suspended him pending a final decision by my superiors. I told Smith that I would recommend discharge.

[To be revealed only by cross examination by the opposing representative.]

I had heard of another employee involved in a coin larceny situation in August. The other case involved a man who was a repairman under very similar circumstances to Smith. The man's name was Polk. The record shows that Polk took about $25. Polk was suspended for two weeks but not discharged. The reason for the suspension rather than a discharge was that up until that time we had not made specific efforts to warn the men about misappropriation of funds. We did, however, warn employees following that event. We further felt that Polk had not been properly instructed as to the handling of overflow coins. He had only recently been transferred into the coin operation division.

COMPANY WITNESS Number 4.

SPECIAL INVESTIGATIVE AGENT FOR THE COMPANY

I am one of the Special Agents for the telephone company. My job is to handle special investigations as assigned to me by my superiors. Most of these have to do with theft, destruction of property, and personal injury.

In September I approached Smith at the recommendation of his supervisor because he was considered a man who might have some ideas about the coin loss. I wanted to talk with him about possible ways that losses could occur. He (Smith) told me that in his opinion the machines were worn out and had faulty equipment. He said that these faults would have to be changed before the phones would operate properly. He claimed that the company had not taken proper care of these machines so that coin surplusses could be controlled. He seemed to feel that repairmen were not responsible for losses but that there was an error in the record tapes connecting the phones to the central accounting office.

After meeting with Smith I checked with the central office and discovered that there was a general opinion that there was insufficient routine maintenance work on these phones. The accounting office assured me they had found no errors on the tapes. The central office, however, felt that the time of the maintenance crews seemed to be all taken up in answering emergency calls.

Smith was thereafter assigned to work routine maintenance. The coin shortages continued.

On the day of the offense I had carefully placed marked coins in all the phones at the Literberry station and an "out of order" sign on them. I was stationed across the street from the phones when Smith arrived to work on them. He worked on the whole bank for about an hour. I did not see him take any coins from the machines.

———

COMPANY WITNESS Number 5.

COMPANY PERSONNEL VICE PRESIDENT

I am Vice President of Midwest in charge of Personnel. My particular duties include the direction and supervision of all personnel matters.

On December 30 the District Plant Manager called me regarding the Smith situation. We considered the case very carefully and felt that discharge was the only right thing to do under the circumstances.

We were aware of the Polk case, but comparing the two cases showed that Polk did not have sufficient information on how to handle overflow coins.

Prior to the Smith case we had three cases of discharge due to theft of coins from coin operated telephones. Since the Smith case we have had four others. All of these cases are similar in nature. The coins have been overflow coins found in the lower housing.

[To be revealed only by cross examination by the opposing representative.]

None of the cases before and after Smith involved people from the union or even from this bargaining unit. And, although the cases were similar in that the coins were from the lower housing, the persons taking the coins were coin collectors who have access to the lower housing.

UNION PRESENTATION WITNESSES

UNION WITNESS Number 1.

UNION LOCAL PRESIDENT

I am President of the Local Union of the ITTB (International Telephone and Telegraph Brotherhood). I am also a repairman for the company. I had been working in the same crew with Smith before he was discharged.

To my knowledge there was no clear established procedure for being reimbursed for coins used in checking out a repaired phone, particularly at the time of Smith's discharge. As of today there is an established procedure. The Smith case shook everybody up, and the company immediately laid down the law. When men lose money now in working with the coin phones, they are to indicate on a regular reimbursement form how much is used, and they are reimbursed monthly when that form is filed.

The former practice was that if money was lost while testing or working on a phone the repairman would usually reimburse himself from another coin phone in which there was a coin pile up. Many repairmen reimbursed themselves in this fashion. It was not a secret. Everyone in the company knew about this practice.

Smith worked on at least 39 other cases of phone trouble on the day he was accused of taking coins. Most of them were before he got to the Literberry station.

I did know of the Polk case when it arose and was relieved that the company did not discharge him. We were ready to defend him if he had been terminated.

I was aware of the company's coin loss problem and had talked with them several times about it. We had also mentioned it in our union meetings several times. I talked to our International Representative about the matter and along with him cautioned our men in the local about ethical conduct and taking money that did not belong to them.

Never, when I worked with him, did Smith ever take coins not belonging to him at any of the telephone installations. I was shocked when I heard what had happened. I still think there is more to this than meets the eye.

[To be revealed only by cross examination by the company.]

I was contacted by the company after the Polk case and asked to speak to the men about problems with coin loss. I agreed to do this if the International Representative would be with me. My comments to the men did not take place until after the Smith discharge.

———

UNION WITNESS Number 2.

JIM SMITH

I have been with the company 19 years. On several occasions I have acted in the capacity of a supervisor for the company. My main functions have been in relation to the maintenance and repair of coin operated telephones. I consider myself a journeyman repair person and one of the best in the business according to the reports of my employers over the years. I have received commendations in writing from them on several occasions.

I have been married 22 years and have five children, ages 15-20. I am a teacher of a senior high school Sunday school class, and a counselor for 10 merit badges for the Boy Scouts and the Girl Scouts. I am also a junior high school youth fellowship adviser in our church.

Prior to December 30 I lost a lot of money testing coin box signals with the central office operators. For those losses I usually reimbursed myself from the overflow coins in the lower housing of the phones. However, there were many times when there were no overflow coins and I did not reimburse myself, nor did the company reimburse me for the money I spent checking out the phones.

The reason I lost money is that when you work on the coin phones you lose money when you do not have the chance or the time to go to the office and get a voucher to claim reimbursement at the end of the month. Sometimes I forgot to take the phone number down. Over the past five years there was a great amount of money for which I was not reimbursed, nor did I reimburse myself. More money than all of you together have in your pockets right now.

At one time I turned in $25 in overflow coins to the company. That was the most they have ever received in overflow from one phone.

Operators in the central office are often lax and return a customer's money to the customer instead of punching the coin box deposit button.

Further, the machines themselves were not properly wired at installation and the relays burn out rapidly. Thus, the coins would just automatically return to the customer or would be caught in the chute.

Prior to November I did not know of any established procedure for being reimbursed for money lost in testing the coin phones. I did not know that I would be subject to discharge for taking coin box coins to reimburse myself for the money I lost in checking the phones.

A couple of years ago I found a wallet in one of the coin booths containing about $100, and I returned it to the owner and was commended by letter from the company. I have had supervisors tell me that customers and other repairmen have called in and complimented me on my work.

On December 29 I worked on over 30 phones according to my job tickets. The Literberry bank was the last group of phones I worked on that day. Prior to that time I had used a considerable amount of my own money in making check-in calls.

At no time, other than the incident on December 29, did I ever take more than a few nickels or dimes from the coin boxes, and then only to reimburse myself for moneys used for the company. Even with the money I took on December 29, the company is way ahead and still owes me money.

I took the coins that I thought would add up to about what I used that day and changed them into bills. The amount was between $4 and $5. I do not know why I did this.

When I got home after I had been suspended I told my wife and my children exactly what happened and that I would probably be fired. They could not understand why the company would discharge me with all the good years of service I have had. But I told them that sometimes honesty hurts more than lying. My wife and I prayed and I felt better.

I am not sure that the directions that were read to the employees were read to me. I was on the 1 to 9 shift and if they were read in the morning I would have not been there to hear them. I do not remember having them read to me. And, so far as I know, the employees did not discuss any so-called instructions that were given to us to study about methods of reimbursement. The company changes its procedures regarding these overflow coins so often that it is very hard to keep up with just what the procedure is at any given time.

[To be revealed only by company cross examination.]

I am now working for another company as a repair supervisor and dispatcher. My wages there are less than they were here.

I remember talking to the Special Agent sometime in the Fall . I told him that the problem was with the machines and not with the men and that unless the company did something about the machines the losses would continue. Many of the coin losses have no relation to the repairmen. They are caused by operator error in not signalling "deposit" but instead signalling "return" to the customer after a call is completed while the charge amount is recorded on the tape. I have personally called attention to this problem on several occasions. I told the Special Agent about it.

[To be revealed only by redirect examination by the union.]

I was quite shocked by the company decision to discharge me. I knew that Polk had not been discharged and that he had taken much more than I had taken. It just does not seem fair. Even so, I did not take the coins by premeditation or plan. I don't know why I took the coins.

This is a terrible thing to happen to me. It is something I cannot account for. I am not that kind of man and my record shows it. I cannot understand what happened. I was not stealing coins.

THE CASE OF MIKE J.

An Arbitration Simulation
Joint Information

Mike J came to work for the Bay School District #111 in 1963 as an assistant custodian at the Fort Elementary School. In 1966, Mike bid into a vacant position at Beach Junior High School in District #111 as a building custodian. He remained at that position until June 25, 1986, when he was transfered to Bay Senior High beginning July 1, 1986.

In July 1984, a new Supervisor of Buildings and Grounds, Jim Q, came on duty in District #111. Members of the school board had, for a number of years, been dissatisfied with the work of the previous Supervisor and had finally forced him to retire. Great pressure was being put on the administration of the school district to clean up its buildings and to straighten out some personnel problems that had existed for some time. At that time, none of these personnel problems, incidentally, involved Mike directly.

Immediately upon coming on duty, Jim reviewed the custodial personnel of the district and moved a number of employees around. Mike was not moved, but two of the four helpers who were assigned to his building were assigned elsewhere. Mike complained to the Principal.

Jim and Mike did not get along very well. Shortly after coming on duty, Jim surveyed the buildings under his direction and at a meeting of all custodians informed them that the standards of cleanliness were going to be higher than before and asked that everyone assist in meeting this standard. Jim pointed out that there had been serious problems with the cleanliness in the schools in the district and that one of the reasons he was brought in was to clean up the mess. Mike and some others felt that this was a direct attack on them and their work performance when they had never, up to that point, received unsatisfactory ratings on their work. And, even at that point, no specific items were pointed to as needing special attention. In the discussion after the meeting a number of the building custodians bitterly attacked the school administration for the way they had been treated. Mike was one of the most outspoken in this attack. Subsequently, he frequently (both on and off the job) spoke with teachers and others and complained about the administrators and supervisors. His attitude became increasingly negative in relation to his superiors and his job. At union meetings he was particularly aggressive in trying to bring pressure to bear on the school district. On several occasions Mike had spoken with the Superintendent about problems with Jim and Jim's failure to recognize the quality of the work done by the custodians in the district. The Superintendent listened but discounted Mike's criticisms as being overly prejudiced.

The Principal at the Beach Junior High School, Tom Triad, did not concern himself a great deal with the effectiveness of the custodial staff. He left that work up to the supervisor of custodians. From time to time when he discovered an area not cleaned or messy he would ask the custodian to clean it up and it would usually get done in reasonable time. The Principal was not known to have given any custodian in his building a negative evaluation during his term of service. Yet, annually, the Principal was called on to provide an evaluation and a recommendation for future employment. Actually, prior to the time that Jim came on duty as Supervisor, the only evaluation of the building custodians was done by the Principal of that building.

In September 1990 Mike's wife was killed in an accident. His children were all gone and he was left alone. In November he moved from the family home and rented an apartment close to the Beach Junior High School. He also, about that time, began to spend more time at the local tavern and on several occasions had to be escorted home by friendly local police. Several of his custodian friends began to suspect that Mike was an alcoholic and rapidly coming to the point where he needed treatment.

After he grieved, Mike requested that he see his personnel file. In it, with the date of April 16, 1991, was an unsigned inspection report to the effect that his work was unsatisfactory in four rooms that were part of his assignment to clean and maintain. The report showed unacceptable work on door glass, tables, book cases, custodial room, toilet bowls, lights, sinks, floors, and the appearance of dust, cobwebs, and dirt in general in the area for which he was responsible.

Also in the file was another inspection report with duplicate markings and statements to the April 16 document, but the date on the report had clearly been changed to 1992, and it was signed by Jim Q as Supervisor with a listed date of signature of 4/16/92. There was also a note on this document saying that Mike refused to sign this report.

When the faculty at Beach Junior High School found out about the cleaning reports of April 16, 1991 and 1992, tension arose and several teachers signed a letter of protest to the Superintendent of Schools. They defended Mike.

On June 19, 1991, Mike received a performance rating by the Principal of the building showing him to be excellent in cooperation, efficiency, quality of work, dependability, knowledge of job, judgment, attendance, and punctuality, with the recommendation that his employment be continued.

In July 1991 Mike went on his vacation. During his absence, Jim Q brought in a crew to work in the gymnasium floor at Beach. Improper chemicals were used in cleaning the floor and permanent damage resulted. When Mike returned from vacation and found the floor ruined he confronted Jim about the matter and there were harsh words between them. That confrontation was observed by at least one teacher and several students. Jim was quite angry with Mike's attack and apparent challenge to his authority and knowledge. Jim then told the teachers and students who had witnessed the confrontation that the floor was ruined before the special crew came in because of Mike's failure to keep it properly protected.

During the latter part of December 1991, Mike was off on sick leave for two weeks. During Mike's absence his supervisor put on a custodial substitute to clean the rooms and related areas so that he would not have those facing him when he returned. When Mike did return he failed to help the substitute clean some of the areas assigned to be cleaned and made ready for the opening of school in the new year. On January 15, 1992, a cleaning report was made showing that certain areas were still not properly cleaned. It was also reported that at Christmas time seven rooms in Mike's area had to have 24 lights replaced because Mike had not properly handled the replacement procedures for the flourescent lights. Other lights and fixtures were broken when Mike tried to replace the bulbs in the wrong manner.

On March 25, 1992, Mike received an evaluation from his supervisor, Jim, based on an evaluation observation conducted on March 20, 1992, at 10:30 a.m. This report stated that it was quite evident that he had not been mopping or running the automatic scrubber or battery operated high-speed buffer. It was reported that a conversation with Mike indicated the equipment was operating properly and that he would get the building cleaned up immediately. The performance goal stated as a result of this evaluation was that the school was to be kept clean at all times and the floors kept clean and sanitary at all times. Floors were to be polished at all times with the high-speed buffer, and the automatic scrubber was to be used every day in the process of cleaning the floor. The cafeteria area was to be kept especially clean.

On March 26, 1992, at 1 p.m., the situation was again observed and it was reported that the goals set up the previous day had not been achieved.

On March 28, 1992, the custodial cleaning report of the supervisor showed that the work was satisfactory. There was a minor note at the bottom indicating that the floors needed to be cleaned better.

On June 16, 1992, Mike received a performance rating from the custodian supervisor, Jim, citing him as poor or unsatisfactory on cooperation, efficiency, quality of work, and dependability. He was below average on knowledge of job and judgment. Thereupon he was placed on a plan of assistance with the recommendation that, with this plan, Mike be continued in service. A final evaluation of the deficiencies and job performance was to be conducted on September 1, 1992.

On June 25, 1992, Mike was given a letter from his supervisor transferring him to the swing shift at the Bay Senior High School for the following school year beginning on July 1, 1992. At the same time the Principal of Beach Junior High was transferred to another school.

Mike, through his union representative, grieved on October 15, 1992, claiming that District #111 was arbitrary, capricious, discriminatory, without just cause, and without progressive discipline when it placed him on a plan of assistance and transferred him from the position he had bid into 20 years before. He claimed that the plan of assistance was vague and failed to indicate any deficiencies or shortcomings in his work and did not comply with contract requirements. He further argued that the district violated his contractual right to remain where he was and that the transfer was a demotion and therefore improper because it did not follow procedure. He claimed that his Principal was his true evaluator and that he was pleased with Mike's work. Mike also asked that documents in his personnel file that were inaccurate be removed including his most recent evaluations, plan of assistance, and supporting documents.

Position of the Union

The union, in the pre-arbitration attempts to settle the dispute, has claimed that the evaluations of Mike were arbitrary, capricious, and unfounded; that the policy is that the Principal is the evaluator and if that policy has changed it is without the agreement of the union; Mike has lateral transfer rights and therefore has a right to remain where he is unless the district can show cause; the plan of assistance is based on unreliable documents and events that were never brought to Mike's attention; the cleaning report of 3/28/92 shows things were satisfactory; changing lights, and so on are not jobs for custodians but part of the maintenance department's job; unsigned reports were placed in Mike's file and this is in violation of the contract; the action of transfer is a demotion and therefore without just cause; the district refused to follow the proper grievance procedure by forcing the matter directly to arbitration without following the intermediate steps described by the contract; and the district violates Mike's free speech by accusing him of spreading rumors.

Position of the District

The district has taken the position that the union cannot grieve the substantive part of the evaluations because the evaluations are the prerogative of management; management can transfer anyone at anytime for any reason and has done so in the past; evaluation of an employee is a right of management and the union cannot challenge or interfere with this process; the supervisor is in charge of the evaluation procedures and the union has no right to try to force management to assign particular persons to evaluate employees; the grievance is frivolous and does not address substantive issues of contract interpretation in that it involves the substantive content of a performance evaluation; management has a right to change its management procedures as it sees fit; and the grievance is not arbitrable.

UNION WITNESS

Mike J.

Mike sees himself as a good worker and an integral part of the school system. He has a nice working relationship with the teachers at Beach and likes the students. He seems to get along well with both. He is always doing nice things for the teachers such as moving equipment for them, cleaning out project trash, keeping track of students, and in general being a "valuable friend." Mike spends a lot of time with the teachers in the teacher lounge talking about students, parents, the school board, the administration, and the general state of the system. Most of the discussion is negative. Mike and the Principal at Beach have been good friends since Mike first bid into the school. They often go fishing together.

Mike dislikes Jim Q with a hearty antagonism. He feels that Jim came in to axe people like him who are not quiet "rabbits" with respect to oppressive administration policies. He feels that evidence of this is Jim's laying the blame for the gym floor mess on him. Mike had nothing to do with the gym floor mess. In fact it was he who called attention to its needed state of repair. Mike feels that he has done all he can to protect that floor and to use the kind of things that have been given to him for protecting and preserving the surface. Management's failure to take proper maintenance care of the floor over the years caused the mess. On several occasions when Jim has tried to point out where Mike is not doing his job, Mike has tried to show Jim that in those cases there was someone else responsible. Mike feels that if he could Jim would fire him.

The instances in which he was cited for not keeping his building clean are clearly the result of poor work by some of the assistant custodians who he assigned to do those tasks. Mike feels that he can't cover the whole building alone and has to assign tasks to the assistants. It is the work of these assistants that is being criticized and he is having to take the responsibility for the criticism. That is not fair. The plan of assistance was a joke. It is obviously an attempt to put the heat on and force him to leave.

Since his wife's death Mike has been at loose ends. He is beginning to feel that he spends too much time at the tavern but there seems to be nothing else to do. There has been some trouble there but not of any serious nature. He does not believe that he is an alchoholic. Several of the police are former students at Beach and from time to time they will come by the tavern near closing time and drop Mike off at home.

The transfer to the high school is really a demotion. It takes him farther away from his home so that he cannot walk to work. This adds transportation costs. It puts him on a shift that is very inconvenient for him. He will be working at a time when he is not in contact with students or teachers and this removes him from one of the major interests in his job.

The district is doing a lot of things that are unfair, in violation of the contract, and not conducive to good relations with the employees. The teachers are planning to strike if they don't get their contract through this spring and Mike hopes that the other school employees will do the same.

Mike wants to go back to Beach and to have the assistance plan removed.

EMPLOYER WITNESS

Jim Q.

Jim Q is a skilled Building and Grounds manager. He has managed several school system buildings and grounds matters and has also managed the custodial teams in several major commercial buildings in a nearby large city. He welcomed coming to this town because it was smaller and had a more agrarian atmosphere about it. Jim did not seek this job but was contacted by a school board member who asked him to apply. When he did apply he was told that the district buildings were in very poor condition both in their physical condition and in their custodial maintenance. He was taken around to several of the schools and was astonished at the dirt and uncleanliness in the halls, classrooms, rest rooms, and so on. It was apparent that things were not in control and that the custodial staff was not doing its job. Also it was apparent that there were some very old buildings that would either have to be replaced or have major repairs made to them soon. Beach was one of these buildings although it was not the worst.

As soon after he was hired as possible, Jim reviewed the whole custodial staff and made a study of the custodial tasks. His first impression was that they were understaffed and that the absence of sufficient help was the cause of the dirt. Closer examination and analysis in comparison with other systems with which he had worked convinced him that there were more than enough custodians. What was needed was better supervision of their work and more insistence on top quality performance. So, he shuffled the custodial staff around and let attrition reduce the total number. He did this after making a study of the tasks and the performance requirements in each building. This was done with the help of the Superintendent and the director of maintenance for the district.

Soon after coming on board Jim became aware that Mike's building was particularly dirty. He tried to be subtle about it but Mike would just get angry and nothing would come of it. In March 1992 a couple of surprise inspections were made of Beach School and it was evident that Mike and his assistants had not been using the scrubber or buffer on the floors. In the latter part of March, an inspection showed that Mike had used the machines and the inspection was satisfactory.

In April things came to a head. Finally, he had to take strong steps to get Mike's attention and to make clear that he (Jim) intended to have things clean. An unsatisfactory cleaning report was made on April 16 and Mike refused to sign it. (The original copy of the report was erroneously dated. The copy shown to Mike had been changed to read 4-16-92 by marking over the 1.) There were strong words between Mike and Jim over this report. Mike threatened to go to the Superintendent with the matter. Jim, however, felt sure that Mike wasn't doing the job and that if Mike couldn't get the message he must be terminated for cause and insubordination. Finally, at the time of the annual performance ratings, Jim gave Mike a generally unsatisfactory rating and on the same day delivered to Mike a Notice of Deficiency and Plan of Assistance which they discussed. Mike signed the notice but insisted that a note be attached saying that signing did not mean agreement. The records are now quite clear and if the assistance program is not fulfilled Mike will have to go. He has had sufficient notice.

UNION WITNESS

Sara Smith, A Teacher

Sara has been a teacher of English at Beach for 10 years. During that time she has had many occasions to call on Mike for help in keeping her rooms clean and in handling the many matters that custodians can handle. Mike has always been a willing and friendly person. He goes beyond the call of duty to see that things are cared for and that her room is kept clean and orderly. The building itself is a mess. It is an old building, the floors are old and loaded with varnish, the walls are dingy and rarely get a coat of new paint. It is not a place you would be proud to keep clean. Nevertheless Mike does an admirable job in trying to keep things as clean as possible considering the condition of the building.

When Mike showed her the negative report he got she became very angry and showed it to some of the other teachers. They agreed that they should do something about it and wrote a letter to the Superintendent in support of Mike reporting that he was a valuable employee of the district. Mike did not know of this until later.

UNION WITNESS

Tom Triad, former Principal of Beach

Tom has been recently transferred to the Principal's job in a new elementary school in the district. He feels that he has done a good job at Beach and that he is well liked by students, faculty, and employees. The building at Beach is in bad repair and should be either torn down and replaced or completely remodeled. For years he has tried to get the administration to consider building a new junior high school. However, the elementary school seemed to take preference. Things at Beach are, consequently, not as clean and immaculate as he would like them to be. But that is not the result of poor custodial service. With what they have to work with the custodians do a fine job. He has never found it necessary to make negative evaluations of the custodial staff. When there are problems he will speak directly with the person involved and the matter is usually cleared up immediately. For example, after a basketball game one evening, the men's toilets were left in a mess. He called Mike at home later and asked him to see if something couldn't be done about it before school started the next day. Mike came over that night and spent several hours cleaning out the facility and putting it in order. That's the kind of service he got from his custodians.

There have been complaints from the administration and from the custodian supervisor about the lack of cleanliness in the building. Usually, however, these inspections come at a time before the custodial staff has had an opportunity to clean up for the day or after some affair, like a sports event, that causes extra accumulation of dirt and trash. If they would check before school started they would see the clean (as well as this old building can be) halls and rooms ready for the children and faculty.

EMPLOYER WITNESS

Milton Cucumber, Superintendent

I have been Superintendent of this district for 15 years. Mike J was here when I first came on the job. One of the problems the district has is the condition of several of its classroom buildings. At least three of them are in such condition that they must be either substantially rebuilt or torn down and new buildings erected. This last year one new elementary school was built to replace an old one that was simply a shambles. The next buildings in line are another elementary school and the junior high school (Beach).

The particular problems of these buildings were brought to my attention by Jim Q soon after Q came on duty. We knew that the buildings were in trouble but we did not know the extent of it until Q showed us the dry rot and deterioration of the support structure and of the floors, and so on of these buildings. We recognize that they are hard to clean and keep clean. However, under Q's direction we think we are doing a great job with what we have.

I did receive a letter from a few of the teachers at Beach concerning some treatment of Mike J. It did not seem important but I did reply to them that I would look into the matter. I discussed the matter with Jim Q and decided that he had the thing under control and did not need any help from me. He seems to be handling things in a proper manner.

I know Mike J. He seems to have something against those who administer our schools in this town. I don't understand what is wrong. He seems to be in the center of numerous attempts to organize employees or to petition the school board for action against various administrators. He's just a rebel, I guess, and won't be happy no matter what we do.

APPENDIX

//

Analysis and Evaluation Instruments

MEDIATOR SKILL AND PROCESS EVALUATION

An evaluation system for use in judging the quality of mediator performance.

Name of mediator(s): _____

Date of mediation session evaluated:_____

Identification of dispute case by type (check one):
___Labor-Management   ___Family   ___Divorce
___Interpersonal   ___Community   ___Organizational
___Neighborhood   ___Environmental   ___Other _____

Names and affiliations of the parties involved in the dispute:

Brief description of the issues in the dispute:

Name of the evaluator:_____

Date of evaluation:_____

Rate the performance of the mediator(s) you have observed according to the following criteria for each of the items

5= Outstanding. Mature, extremely effective, typical of a top-level professional mediator.

4= Effective. Generally good quality work, seemed to know what to do and how to do it. Typical of "journey-person" mediators.

3= Partly Effective. Some good and some not-so-good work, seemed to have an idea of what to do but did not seem to be able to bring it off at times. Typical of mediators in early training phases and prior to much experience.

2= Weak. Work not very effective, confused, lacked strength and clarity, did not seem to know what to do or how to do it. Let things get out of hand frequently.

1= Inadequate. Simply unable to handle the situation, showed no skill or understanding of the mediation process, lacked insight and process tools to handle the situation.

I. Skills and Techniques

Rate the mediator according to the above criteria on the following specific skills. When there is insufficient performance to allow you to judge leave the blank empty.

Rate at least 25 items in this section including all starred items

*___Listening	*___Trust Building	___Humor
___Identifying Conflicts	___Self-Awareness Skills	*___Poise
*___Needs Assessment	___Offering Alternatives	___Sensitivity
___Dealing with Anger	___Empowerment of Client	*___Reframing
*___Reality Testing	*___Paraphrasing	___Negotiating
*___Message Feedback	___Information Sharing	*___Goal Setting
___Breaking Deadlocks	*___Neutrality	___Inclusion
*___Questioning	___Rewarding	*___Caucusing
___Balancing Power	*___Agenda Building	___Planning
___Support	___Momentum Building	*___Timing
*___Setting Ground Rules	*___Credibility Building	*___Attention
*___Agreement Formation	*___Communication	___Warmth

Total of Rating Scores for Skills and Techniques_____
Average Rating for Skills and Techniques _____

II. Handling The Process

Apply the above criteria to rating the following areas of the mediation process. Refer to the "Mediation Activity Analysis" as the basis of description for the following areas.

Rate at least 10 items in this section including the starred items

General Behaviors During Mediation
*___ Personal and interpersonal behaviors during the mediation process.
*___ Managerial and procedural behaviors during the mediation process.
*___ Persuasive and tactical behaviors during the mediation process.

Joint Session Behaviors
___ Managerial and procedural
___ Persuasive and tactical

Separate or Caucus Session Behaviors
___ Personal and interpersonal
___ Managerial and procedural
___ Persuasive and tactical

Specific Accomplishments with Clients
*___ Elicited trust from the clients.
*___ Clarified role of mediation and mediator for the clients.
___ Stimulated the parties to discuss difficulties freely.
*___ Facilitated discussion and clarification of the issues.
___ Handled differences in power appropriately.
*___ Helped clients to explore alternatives cooperatively.
___ Provided new alternatives the parties had not thought of but accepted.
*___ Clarified the final decision.
*___ Obtained an agreement satisfactory to both parties.

Total Score for Areas of Process _____
Average Score for Areas of Process_____

Total Score for Processes *and* Skills _____
Average Score for Processes *and* Skills_____

Interpretation of the Evaluation Scores

* When all the items are scored the totals listed below apply. When some items have not been scored the average will apply. *To provide a creditable average there must be at least 25 items in Section I: Skills and Techniques and 25 items in Section II: Handling the Process.*

Above 245 total or an average of 4.6 on 40 or more items = Outstanding Mediation Performance of Professional Quality.

Above 217 total or an average of 4.01 on 35 or more items = Good Mediation.

Above 191 total or an average of 3.6 = Fair Mediation.

Above 164 total or an average of 3.09 = Poor Mediation.

Below 164 total or less than an average of 3.09 = Inadequate Mediation.

MEDIATION ACTIVITY IDENTIFICATION ANALYSIS

The following analysis form provides a method for describing and analyzing the nature of a mediation session and the behaviors of the mediators conducting the session(s).

Name of mediator(s):_____

Date of mediation session:_____

Identify the dispute case by type: (Circle type): Labor-Management, Family; Divorce, Community; Neighborhood, Commercial, Interpersonal, Organizational, Environmental

Other:_____

Identify the parties involved in the dispute:

1._____   2._____

3._____   4._____

Number of sessions required to handle the dispute:_____

Name of critic-evaluator:_____

INSTRUCTIONS FOR USING THIS FORM

Identify those items that best describe the activities the mediator performed in this situation. Use the following code for identifying these things:

C=Did this constantly	**F**=Did this frequently	**O**=Did this occasionally
L=Did this once only		**N**= Never did this

The following items are divided into several categories for convenience in checking. Mark in the space in front of each item the frequency with which the mediator performed this behavior in terms of the above codes.

Prior Meeting Behaviors
(Behaviors that took place before the first joint meeting of the parties with the mediator.)
1. ___Made telephone contacts with both parties.
2. ___Made personal face-to-face contact with each party separately before any joint meeting was held.
3. ___Made personal face-to-face contact with only one party before any joint meeting was held.
4. ___Made personal face-to-face contact with one party separately before any contact at all was made with the other party.
5. ___Set the time and place of the joint meeting.

General Behaviors During Mediation Efforts
(Refers to the behaviors that took place in both joint and separate sessions and in other contacts with the parties.)

Personal and Interpersonal
6. ___Showed an actual preference for the position of one party over the position of the other party.
7. ___Wore no insignia or clothing that would be controversial or destroy image of impartiality.
8. ___Did not take sides in any way at any time.

9. ___Gave personal advice to either or both parties
10. ___Showed patience and persistence with both parties.
11. ___Criticized the ethics of one or both parties.
12. ___Used humor.
13. ___Maintained a calm or even tone.
14. ___Allowed either or both parties to "blow off steam" and express emotions about the situation.

Managerial and Procedural
15. ___Recorded all sessions both joint and separate.
16. ___Recorded only joint sessions.
17. ___When areas of agreement occurred, made a formal record of these.
18. ___Asked the parties to separate fact from hearsay.
19. ___Wrote down the terms of the agreement and had both parties sign it.
20. ___Terminated the session when it became clear there would be no settlement possible.
21. ___Kept the session going so long as there appeared to be movement on either side.
22. ___Reminded either or both parties of their legal responsibilities.

Persuasive and Tactical
22. ___Indicated to both parties that their positions were unnecessarily rigid.
23. ___Reminded either or both parties of the consequences of nonsettlement.
24. ___Made a recommendation for settlement only when it appeared that both sides would accept it.
25. ___Restated the issues by paraphrasing them.
26. ___Proposed a number of alternative solutions.
27. ___Warned the parties of the consequences of legal violations.
28. ___Suggested that the parties trade off issues or demands.
29. ___Used hypothetical situations to help parties explore the consequences of the proposals being considered (reality testing).
30. ___Pointed out faulty reasoning on the part of either party.
31. ___Raised doubts in the minds of the parties about the soundness of their positions.
32. ___Got people outside the negotiations to put pressure on the parties involved.
33. ___Helped either or both parties save face in the presence of an impending agreement that would be somewhat contrary to their original positions.
34. ___Warned either or both parties about an impending deadline.
35. ___Made suggestions that were not immediately accepted but that later came through as proposals by the parties.
36. ___Started parties working on areas in which agreements could be easily reached.

Joint Session Behaviors of the Mediator
(Refers to meetings at which both parties were present with the mediator in face-to-face sessions.)

Managerial and Procedural
38. ___Convened the joint session of the parties as the chair.
39. ___Made an opening statement that outlined the functions of the mediator.
40. ___Outlined the rules of conduct for the meeting and the procedures to follow.
41. ___Had the parties sign these rules.
42. ___Maintained control of the meeting.
43. ___Restated, in the joint session, the position of each party through paraphrase or replication.
44. ___Listened actively as each side presented its case and argument.
45. ___Requested either or both parties to clarify statements made to each other.
46. ___Asked one or both of the parties to maintain order and/or courtesy during the presentation of cases.
47. ___Summarized the status of the dispute.
48. ___Brought both parties together after an agreement had been reached and reviewed the terms of the agreement.
49. ___Gave each party relatively equal time to be heard.

Persuasive and Tactical

50. ___Used probing questions to gather information about the problem(s).
51. ___Allowed the parties to talk to each other without interruption by the mediator.
52. ___Gave the parties every opportunity to resolve the issues themselves in a joint conference.
53. ___Broke the main issue down into subissues.

Mediator Behavior in Separate Session or Caucuses

(Refers to meetings when the mediator met alone with one of the parties while the other waited in another room or was working separately on an assignment given by the mediator.)

Personal and Interpersonal

54. ___Expressed sympathy with one of the parties only.
55. ___Expressed sympathy with both of the parties.
56. ___Discussed the personal problems of one side with the other side.
57. ___Shared personal experience in similar cases.
58. ___Gave advice on what should be done to solve the problem(s).

Management and Procedural

59. ___Held separate conferences with each party.
60. ___Made suggestions to one of the parties concerning the manner in which demands were made of the other.
61. ___Assisted either or both parties in wording proposals.
62. ___Helped describe the position of one side to the other.
63. ___Kept the parties separated by space so they could not hear or see each other.
64. ___Before leaving one party to talk with the other, gave suggestions for tasks to be performed by the party left alone.

Persuasive and Tactical

65. ___Carried ideas suggested by one party to the other as an "unofficial," unsolicited, "off-the-record" communication.
66. ___Made suggestions to one of the parties concerning the content of the proposals to be made to the other party.
67. ___Argued in favor of a position of party "A" to party "B" in a separate caucus with party "A".
68. ___Argued in favor of a position of party "B" to party "A" in a separate caucus with party "A".
69. ___Encouraged either or both of the parties to bring other principals or representatives into the negotiation sessions.
70. ___Encouraged either or both sides to make a final proposal.
71. ___Asked one or both of the parties to withhold making a proposal until the other side had given signals that it would be accepted.
72. ___Asked one or both to refrain from taking further legal or physical action until this matter could be settled.
73. ___Indicated to one party that its position was unnecessarily rigid.
74. ___Knew what one party would agree to and held it in confidence until that party gave authorization to present it to the other party.
75. ___Used rhetorical questions to persuade one of both of the parties to accept an idea.
76. ___Used questions to "put down" or "deflate" one or both of the parties.
77. ___Encouraged both sides to bring out the deeper issues that might have been under the surface of the dispute.
78. ___Tried to persuade either or both parties to change their position.
79. ___Ridiculed a proposal of one of the parties without reason.
80. ___Acted angrily.
81. ___Complimented or otherwise commended a party for what it was doing or saying.
82. ___Gave a party a number of alternatives from which to choose.
83. ___Pointed out faulty reasoning, bad data, or faulty assumptions.
84. ___Reassured either or both parties.
85. ___Confronted either or both parties on the necessity for action.

86.   ___Highlighted an alternative solution by repetition or emphasis.
87.   ___Encouraged the parties to look at the facts.

Other Behaviors Noted

88.   _____

89.   _____

90.   _____

91.   _____

92.   _____

93.   _____

94.   _____

95.   _____

General Summary

A.   Was there an agreement reached by the parties?   Yes___ No___

B.   If there was an agreement or settlement, was it primarily
     the result of the parties' negotiation with each other?   Yes___ No___

C.   If there was a settlement, was it primarily the result of
     the persuasion of the mediator?   Yes___ No___

D.   If there was a settlement, was it the result of both the
     persuasion of the mediator and the efforts of the parties
     to find a solution?   Yes___ No___

E.   If there was no settlement, what were the prime reasons?

F.   What skills or procedures should the mediator have used that were not used in this case? Be
     specific.

MEDIATION EVALUATION : SHORT FORM
by
John (Sam) Keltner

Please evaluate the mediation in the case according to the following ratings:

5=Outstanding: Mature, extremely effective, typical of a top-level professional mediator.
4=Effective: Generally good quality work, seemed to know what to do and how to do it.
3=Partially Effective: Some good and some not-so-good work. Seemed to have an idea of what to do but did not seem to be able to bring it off at times.
2=Weak: Not very effective. Confused. Lacked strength and clarity. Did not seem to know what to do or how to do it. Let things get out of hand frequently.
1=Inadequate: Simply unable to handle the situation. Showed no skill or understanding of the mediation process. Lacked insight and process tools to handle mediation.

___1.   Personal and interpersonal behaviors.
___2.   Managerial and procedural behaviors.
___3.   Persuasive and tactical behaviors.
___4.   Joint session performance.
___5.   Separate session performance.
___6.   Evidence of neutrality in the total performance.
___7.   Clients developed trust in the mediator.
___8.   Clarified the role of mediation and the mediator for the clients.
___9.   Stimulated parties to discuss difficulties freely.
___10.   Facilitated discussion.
___11.   Aided in clarifying the issues.
___12.   Handled differences in power appropriately.
___13.   Helped clients to explore alternatives.
___14.   Was a good listener.
___15.   Provided good message feedback.
___16.   Helped the parties deal with anger.
___17.   Used questions effectively.
___18.   Communicated effectively with both parties.
___19.   Showed warmth, humor, and poise.
___20.   Showed good sense of timing.
___21.   Developed own credibility.
___22.   Empowered parties to solve their own problem(s).
___23.   Showed patience with the parties as they struggled.
___24.   Facilitated the negotiation process.
___25.   Supportive of both clients.

Total Rating Score————————————— (_____)

110-125= Outstanding mediation of professional quality
90-109 = Good Mediation
70-89 = Fair Mediation
45-69 = Poor Mediation
Below 45 = Inadequate Mediation

INTERESTS VS. POSITIONS

Interests are rooted in the needs and conditions that bring people into disputes. They emerge from the contexts in which people exist and represent the underlying motives that bring pressure on them to act in certain ways, to demand certain things, and to struggle for achievement. A hungry teenager in a depressed area in the city may request that her more affluent escort take her to a fast food place for a "burger" instead of going to a movie. Behind this demand may be several conditions that drive her to make such a request, including: that she had not eaten for a long time (basic nutritional needs), that she likes to be seen around food places with this particular fellow (ego needs), and that she wants to get away from the dangerous territory where they are now (safety needs).

In many disputes the interests, needs, and motivational forces are not explicit to the struggle until someone voices them. Instead of saying, "I'm hungry and would like to see my friends at the fast food shop," she says, "I want to go to the Burger Shop."

The following are several statements. See if you can identify those that are positions and those that are statements of interest, need, and so on.

(If it is a position mark it "P", if an interest-need mark it "I")

1. ___I really like dogs.
2. ___My garden needs sun.
3. ___That tree must be cut down.
4. ___Pay the rent now.
5. ___I want my salary increased by 10%
6. ___Keep that dog out of my yard.
7. ___I'd like to be recognized for the work I do.
8. ___I enjoy fishing.
9. ___I must have employees who can do the work well.
10. ___I oppose building a convenience store on that lot.
11. ___I want that person fired.
12. ___You must clean this apartment at once.
13. ___That car is no good.
14. ___I have to have more income to feed my kids.
15. ___I want peace and quiet in my neighborhood.
16. ___I want "Chinese" for supper.
17. ___You should buy that house.
18. ___I like to keep my property clean and attractive.
19. ___I want my child on weekends.
20. ___That property was part of my father's gift to me.

In the following situations identify the interests that *could* be underlying the positions taken.

1. Joe wants a new car and his wife does not.

2. Terry wants his neighbor to fence in his back yard. His neighbor refuses.

3. Susan wants her ticket for parking in a handicapped space excused.

4.   Mae wants a promotion in her job. Her boss won't consider it even though there is adequate money available.

5.   Jim demands that the repairs on his car be taken care of immediately, and the mechanic refuses because there are several people ahead of Jim.

6.   Sara demands that her daughter stay away from the Burger Shop, and her daughter says she will not.

7.   John wants his money back from the purchase of a computer that did not work, and the dealer refuses.

8.   A newly retired steelworker tells his neighbors they are not to allow their children to play in his yard even though they have played there before.

HOW EMPATHIC ARE YOU?

(A quick and dirty quiz on responses that reflect an empathic condition)

by Sam Keltner

For each of the items below, indicate whether or not the mediator's (M) response to the client's (C) statement shows that the mediator has experienced some empathy in respect to what the client has been saying. If you feel that the interviewer's response shows that empathy was experienced place an X in the "Empathic" space. If you feel the response does not show the presence of empathy place an X in the "Not Empathic" space and then write a more appropriate response in the space provided.

1. **C:** I know that my neighbor doesn't care whether my yard looks clean and that upsets me.
    M: You should try to listen to what he says.

    Empathic___   Not Empathic___

2. **C:** I had to take two very important days off last week because my wife contracted a bad case of flu.
    M: I'm sorry to hear that. The flu is sure spreading around this year.

    Empathic___   Not Empathic___

3. **C:** You obviously don't understand how it feels to be told by a person you have loved for 30 years that it's all over.
    M: It's a real shock to have someone leave like that. You must feel a real loss. How can I help you deal with the situation?

    Empathic___   Not Empathic___

4. **C:** Why is it that I always have to wait to get in here to see you? It seems that everyone and everything else has priority. It's not fair for me to have to wait like that.
    M: We take the clients in the order of their appointments and those that don't have appointments have to take their turn.

    Empathic___   Not Empathic___

5. **C:** The things you ask me about don't seem to be very important. Why don't you ask about the things that are important to me?
    M: I'm sorry they don't seem important to you. I really want you to see that they are important to both of us. Maybe you can share some of the things you think are important.

    Empathic___   Not Empathic___

6, **C:** That dirty landlord raised the rent on me again. This is the second increase in a year. I won't pay any more.
    M: That would upset me too. Yet, I suspect that the cost of maintaining the building in that area must be rising rapidly.

    Empathic___   Not Empathic___

7. **C:** I told him I wanted two copies of the invoice . . . both originals. I didn't get them and I'm beginning to wonder whether he really wants my business.
    M: I can understand why you were annoyed when you didn't get the invoices you ordered. Let's see what we can do about it.

    Empathic___   Not Empathic___

8. **C:** My ex-wife is a mean little bitch. She does everything she can to make me look bad and I hate it.
    M: That's not good. Are you doing anything about it?

    Empathic___   Not Empathic___

9.   **C:** I don't know about you. It seems you are trying to give support to my neighbor rather than to me. You keep trying to get me to accept his argument.

        M: As you see it, I'm not concerned with your needs or position and you seem to be getting angry about it. Go on, tell me more.

                                            Empathic____   Not Empathic____

10.   **C:** I'm angry! You tell that low down skunk that if he doesn't give me a the same discount as others, I'll see to it that he will be very sorry.

        M: I'm sorry, he doesn't seem to want to do what you ask.

                                            Empathic____   Not Empathic____

Items 3, 5, 6, 7, and 9 reflect the experience of empathy on the part of the mediator. Give yourself 2 points for each correct item.

Items 1, 2, 4, 8, and 10 do not show an empathy experience. Score 2 for each one of these you marked "not empathic."

If your written response to a "not empathic" statement addressed both the customer's feeling and content give yourself 2 points. If your written response dealt only with feeling or only with content give yourself 1 point. Give yourself 0 if you responded by writing such statements as "that's too bad," and so on.

Total score for items selected = _____

Total score for written responses = _____

Total score for items and written responses = _____

Interpretation of Your Score

25-30= High Empathy
19-24= Good Empathy
13-18= Moderate Empathy
0-12= Low Empathy

MEDIATOR-TRAINEE EVALUATION

(For use after mediator trainees have completed 60 or more hours of active training)

Instructions for the Use of Mediator-Trainee Evaluation

Write in the names of the trainees being evaluated at the bottom of the Mediator-Trainee Evaluation sheet, assigning each a capital letter.

Carefully review the criteria statement at the top of the page.

Score each trainee on ALL items. If your records do not show sufficient evidence to indicate performance on an item, score it 1.

Discriminate among trainees. Do not score all of them at the same level on every item or even on a bank of items. You may find it useful to score each category for each trainee across the page so that contrasts and differences appear as you look at each of the items. For example:

	A	B	C	D	E	F
Listening	3	2	3	4	1	4

Attach the *Mediator Process and Skill Evaluation* sheets for each trainee to this evaluation sheet.

If there are special comments or observations (not included in the *Mediator Process and Skill Evaluation* sheets) regarding the trainees, write them on the back of the Mediator-Trainee Evaluation. Include in these comments such things as:

a. If, in your judgment, a trainee will need further training beyond Phase 2 before he or she can be allowed to "solo" as a mediator.
b. General attitude of the trainee toward the training and learning about mediation.
c. If, in your judgment, the trainee should be discouraged from continuing the effort to function as a mediator in this program.
d. Other information you consider important in evaluating these persons.

Return this sheet with the attached materials to the trainer as soon as possible.

THIS INFORMATION IS CONFIDENTIAL! PLEASE DO NOT SHARE IT WITH ANYONE OTHER THAN THE TRAINER.

THANKS VERY MUCH FOR YOUR HELP AND OBJECTIVITY IN THIS EVALUATION.

MEDIATOR EVALUATION

Rate each mediator trainee on the following criteria: **5= Outstanding:** Mature, extremely effective, typical of a top level professional mediator. **4= Effective:** Generally good quality work, seemed to know what to do and how to do it. **3=Partially Effective:** Some good and some not so good work. Seemed to have an idea of what to do but did not seem to be able to bring it off at times. **2= Weak:** Not very effective. Confused. Lacked strength and clarity. Did not seem to know what to do or how to do it. Let things get out of hand frequently. **1=Inadequate:** Simply unable to handle the situation. Showed no skill nor understanding of the mediation process. Lacked insight and process tools to handle mediation.

		Trainees					
		A	B	C	D	E	F
1.	Personal and interpersonal behaviors	___	___	___	___	___	___
2.	Managerial and procedural behaviors	___	___	___	___	___	___
3.	Persuasive and tactical behaviors	___	___	___	___	___	___
4.	Joint session performance	___	___	___	___	___	___
5.	Separate session performance	___	___	___	___	___	___
6.	Neutrality in whole performance	___	___	___	___	___	___
7.	Client trust in mediator	___	___	___	___	___	___
8.	Clarified role to clients`	___	___	___	___	___	___
9.	Stimulated free discussion	___	___	___	___	___	___
10.	Facilitated discussion	___	___	___	___	___	___
11.	Aided in clarifying issues	___	___	___	___	___	___
12.	Handled differences in power	___	___	___	___	___	___
13.	Helped to explore alternatives	___	___	___	___	___	___
14.	Listening	___	___	___	___	___	___
15.	Message feedback	___	___	___	___	___	___
16.	Helped clients deal with anger	___	___	___	___	___	___
17.	Use of questions	___	___	___	___	___	___
18.	Communication	___	___	___	___	___	___
19.	Warmth, humor and poise	___	___	___	___	___	___
20.	Timing	___	___	___	___	___	___
21.	Personal credibility	___	___	___	___	___	___
22.	Empowered parties	___	___	___	___	___	___
23.	Patience	___	___	___	___	___	___
24.	Facilitated negotiation	___	___	___	___	___	___
25.	Supportive of both clients	___	___	___	___	___	___
	Total Rating	___	___	___	___	___	___

**List names of trainees below on the lines corresponding to the letters at the top of each of the above trainee columns.

A_____   B_____   C_____

D_____   E_____   F_____

Signed:_____, Monitor

WHAT DO YOU KNOW ABOUT MEDIATION?

Directions: Please mark each statement either true (T) or false (F) on the line preceding the statement.

____ 1.   Mediation is an intervention by a neutral third person into a dispute in order to facilitate the parties in resolving the dispute.

____ 2.   Conciliation and mediation are the same process.

____ 3.   Currently, the most highly developed form of mediation is in the labor-management sector.

____ 4.   The best national organization for mediators in general is the Association of Marriage and Family Therapists.

____ 5.   Mediation and counseling are the same process.

____ 6.   A mediator has the responsibility to advise the parties in a dispute about their rights under the law.

____ 7.   Mediation as an institutional process is less than 25 years old.

____ 8.   Couples who use the court to settle their divorce are more likely to engage in post-decree litigation than couples who have settled their disputes themselves.

____ 9.   Mediation and arbitration require the professional to assume different roles.

____10.   Mediation can be used effectively at any stage in the Spectrum of Struggle.

____11.   When mediators are mandated by the court to represent the interests of the children in a custody dispute they cannot function as neutrals in the situation.

____12.   Lawyers generally have difficulty becoming mediators because of their training as advocates and their ethical responsibility to represent a client's interests.

____13.   Counselors have difficulty becoming mediators because of their training as therapists and focus of their concern for the personal wellness of their clients.

____14.   In mediation the primary responsibility for the resolution lies with the parties themselves.

____15.   The most effective training for mediators is in short courses of a week or less in which trainees are confronted with the skill needs.

____16.   A skilled and effective mediator can successfully mediate someone who is totally unwilling to resolve a conflict via mediation.

____17.   The mediator does not regulate or control any of the content of an agreement or settlement between the parties.

____18.   The mediator has no right to impose standards of behavior on the parties.

____19.   The mediator has no power to enforce law or act in any way as an agent of law enforcement or investigative agencies.

____20.   A mediator's most basic tool is his or her credibility and integrity.

____21.   The process of feedback for a mediator involves giving the parties responses and reactions to their ideas.

____22.   Negotiation and bargaining between the parties has no place in the mediation process.

____23.   In order to help the parties save face a mediator may often assume the burden of responsibility for proposing unpalatable compromises.

____24.   The mediator should not use separate sessions or caucuses except as a last resort when the parties simply refuse to talk to each other.

____25.   A mediator cannot avoid being involved with power in the mediation situation.

Suggested Readings

Angel, R.C. (1990). The sociology of human conflict. In E. B. McNeill (Ed.), *The nature of human conflict* (pp. 91-115). Englewood Cliffs, NJ: Prentice-Hall.

Archibald, K. (Ed). (1966). *Strategic interaction and conflict.* Berkeley: University of California, Institute of International Studies.

Ball, G., Sutton, M., & Brubaker, L. (1980). Early community consultation in the EIR process: New opportunities for environmental professionals. *The Environmental Professional, 2*, 41-52.

Barrett, J. (1985). *The psychology of a mediator: A third party's psychic balance sheet.* Unpublished manuscript.

Bazerman, M.H., & Lewicki, R. J. (Eds). (1983). *Negotiating in organizations.* Beverly Hills, CA: Sage.

Beer, J. (Ed.). (1984). *Mediator's handbook: Peacemaking in your neighborhood.* Concordville, PA: Friends Suburban Project.

Bercovitch, J. (1989). International dispute mediation: A comparative empirical analysis. In K. Kressel, D. G. Pruitt et al. (Eds.), *Mediation research* (pp. 284-299). San Francisco: Jossey-Bass.

Berlyn, D.E. (1960). *Conflict, arousal, and curiosity.* New York: McGraw-Hill.

Bethel, C.A. (1986). The use of separate sessions in family mediation. *Negotiation Journal, 2*(3), 257-271.

Bienenfeld, F. (1983). *Child custody mediation.* New York: Science and Behavior Books,

Bingham, G. (1986). *Resolving environmental disputes: A decade of experience.* Washington, DC: The Conservation Foundation.

Bingham, G., Vaughn, B., & Gleason, W. (1981). *Environmental conflict resolution: Annotated bibliography.* Palo Alto, CA: Resolve Center for Environmental Conflict Resolution,

Brett, J.M., Drieghe, R., & Shapiro, D. L. (1986). Mediator style and mediation effectiveness. *Negotiation Journal, 2*(3), 277-285.

Cartwright, D. (Ed.). *Studies in social power.* Ann Arbor: University of Michigan Press.

Coffin, R.A. (1973). *The negotiator: A manual for winners.* New York: Barnes and Noble Books.

Cohen, R. (Ed.). *Mediation . . . An alternative that works.* Salem, MA: Trial Court of Massachusetts,

Colosi, T. (1983). Negotiation in the public and private sectors: A core model. *American Behavioral Scientist, 27*(2), 229-253.

Cormick, G.W. (1977, October). *The ethics of mediation: Some unexplored territory.* Paper presented to the Society of Professionals in Dispute Resolusion, New York.

Cormick, G.W. (1980). The 'theory' and practice of environmental mediation. *The Environmental Professional, 2*, 24-33.

Coulson, R. (1973). *Labor arbitration—What you need to know.* New York: American Arbitration Association.

Dahl, R.A. (1957). The concept of power. *Behavioral Science, 2*, 201-218.

Davey, H. (1972). *Arbitration as a substitute for other legal remedies.* Ames, IA: Industrial Relations Center, Iowa State University.

Deutsch, M. (1966). Bargaining, threat and communication: Some experimental studies. In K. Archibald (Ed.), *Strategic interaction and conflict.* Berkeley: University of California, Institute of International Studies.

Dyer, W.G. (1976). *Insight to impact: Strategies for interpersonal and organizational change.* Provo, UT: Brigham Young University Press.

Elkouri, F., & Elkouri, E.A. (1960). How arbitrations works (rev. ed.). Washington, DC: Bureau of National Affairs.

Emerson, R.M. (1962). Power-dependence relations. *American Sociological Review, 27,* 31-41.

Fairweather, O. (1983). *Practice and procedure in labor arbitration* (2nd ed.). Washington, DC: Bureau of National Affairs.

Fisher, R. (1986). The structure of negotiation: An alternative model. *Negotiation Journal, 2*(3), 233-235.

Fisher, R.J., & Ury, W. (1983). *Getting to yes.* New York: Penguin Books.

Frost, J.H., & Wilmot, W.W. (1978). *Interpersonal conflict.* Dubuque, IA: Wm. C. Brown.

Fuller, L. (1971). Mediation—Its forms and functions. *Southern California Law Review, 44,* 305-309

Gibb, J. R. (1961). Defensive communication. *Journal of Communication, 11*(3),141-148.

Ginsberg, R.B. (1978). American Bar Association delegation visits the People's Republic of China. *American Bar Association Journal, 64,* 1516-1525.

Gore, P.B. (1976). *Webster's third new international dictionary of the English language* (unabridged). Springfield, MA: Merriman

Gulliver, P.H. (1979). *Disputes and negotiations: A cross-cultural perspective.* New York: Academic Press.

Hall, J. (1969). *Conflict management survey.* Houston, TX: Teleometrics.

Haman, D.C., Brief, A.P., & Pegnetter, R. (1978). Studies in mediation and the training of public sector mediators. *Journal of Collective Negotiations, 7*(4), 347-360.

Haynes, J.M. (1983). The process of negotiations. *Mediation Quarterly, 1,* 75-92.

Hiltrop, J.M. (1969). Factors associated with successful labor mediation. In K. Kressel, D.G. Pruitt et al. (Eds.), *Mediation research* (pp. 241-262). San Francisco: Jossey-Bass.

Hutschnecker, A. (1974). *The drive for power.* New York: M. Evans & Co.

Ilich, J. (1980). *Power negotiating.* New York: Addison Wesley.

Jackson, E. (1962). *Meeting of minds.* New York: McGraw-Hill.

Jandt, F.E. (Ed.). (1973). *Conflict resolution through communication.* New York: Harper and Row.

Janis, I.L., & Mann, L. (1977). *Decision making: A psychological analysis of conflict, choice, and committment.* New York: Free Press.

Janis, I. (1971). Groupthink. *Psychology Today, 5*(6), 43-46.

Johnson, C. E. (1987). An introduction to powerful and powerless talk in the classroom. *Communication Education, 36*(2), 167-177.

Kagel, S. (1961) *Anatomy of a labor arbitration* Washington, DC: Bureau of National Affairs.

Katz, D. (1964) Approaches to managing conflict. In R.L. Kahn & E. Boulding (Eds.), *Power and conflict in organzations* (pp. 105-114). New York: Basic Books.

Kelley, H.H. (1971). *Attribution in social interaction.* New York: General Learning Press.

Keltner, J W. (1963). The United States federal mediation and conciliation service: Catalyst to collective bargaining. *International Labour Review, 88*(5), 3-16.

Keltner, J.W. (1970). *Interpersonal speech communication.* Belmont, CA: Wadsworth.

Keltner, J.W. (1976, May). *Therapy and relationship counseling.* Paper delivered at the conference of the International Communication Association, Portland, OR.

Keltner, J.W. (1983, November). *Can everybody win? Third party intervention.* Paper presented at the annual meeting of the Speech Communication Association, Washington, DC.

Kessler, S. (1978). *Creative conflict resolution: Mediation. Leaders and participants guides.* Fountain Valley, CA: National Institute for Professional Training.

Kolb, D.M. (1983). *The mediators.* Cambridge, MA: MIT Press.

Kreisberg, L., Northrup, T.A., & Thorson, S.J. (Eds.). (1989). *Intractable conflicts and their transformation.* Syracuse, NY: Syracuse University Press.

Kreisberg, L., & Thorson, S.J. (Eds.). (1991). *Timing the de-escalation of international conflicts.* Syracuse, NY: Syracuse University Press.

Laborde, G. Z. (1984). *Influencing with integrity: Management skills for communication and negotiation.* Palo Alto, CA: Science & Behavior Books.

Lemmon, J.A. (Ed.). (1983a). Dimensions and practice of divorce mediation. *Mediation Quarterly, 1.*

Lemmon, J.A. (Ed.). (1983b). Successful techniques for mediating family breakup. *Mediation Quarterly, 2,* 71-92

Leritz, L. (1987). *No-fault bargaining.* Portland, OR: Pacifica Press.

Lewis, D.V. (1981). *Power negotiating, tactics and techniques.* Englewood Cliffs, NJ: Prentice-Hall.

Lindzey, G., & Aronson E. (Eds.). (1968). *The handbook of social psychology* (vol. 1). Reading, MA: Addison Wesley.

Loeb, L.L. (1984). Standards of practice for family mediators. *Family Law Quarterly, 27*(4), 455-460.

Machiavelli, N. (1952) *The prince* (trans. L. Ricci). New York: New American Library.

Mack, R.W., & Snyder, R. C. (1973). The analysis of social conflict. In F.E. Jandt (Ed.), *Conflict resolution through communication* (pp. 25-87). New York: Harper & Row.

Magoun, F.A. (1960). *Cooperation and conflict in industry.* New York: Harper & Bros.

Marshall, T.F. (1990). The power of mediation. *Mediation Quarterly, 8*(2), 115-124.

McCarthy, J., with Shorett, A. (1984). *Negotiating settlements: A guide to environmental mediation.* New York: American Arbitration Association.

McNeill, E.B. (1965). *The nature of human conflict.* Englewood Cliffs, NJ: Prentice-Hall.

Mendonsa, E.L. (1987). *Negotiating for profit: What you should know about it.* Red Bluff, CA: International & Domestic Negotiating Institute.

Mernitz, S. (1980). *Mediation of environmental disputes : A sourcebook.* New York: Praeger.

Miller, G.R., & Simons, H.W. (Eds.). *Perspectives on communication in social conflict.* Englewood Cliffs, NJ: Prentice-Hall.

Mortensen, C.D. (1974). A transactional paradigm of verbalized social conflict. In G.R. Miller & H. W. Simons (Eds.), *Perspectives on communication in social conflict* (pp. 90-124). Englewood Cliffs, NJ: Prentice-Hall.

Nierenberg, G.I. (1973). *The fundamentals of negotiating.* New York: Hawthorn Books.

Oskamp, S., & Spacapan, S. (Eds.). *Interpersonal processes.* Beverly Hills, CA: Sage.

Phear, W.P. (1984). Family mediation: A choice of options. *The Arbitration Journal, 39*(1), 23-30.

Poole, J.P., & Poole, M.S. (1984). *Working through conflict: A theory of bargaining and negotiation.* Glenview, IL: Scott, Foresman.

Poppleton, A. (1981). The arbitrator's role in expediting the large and complex commercial case. *The Arbitration Journal, 36*(4), 6-10.

Prasow, P., & Peters, E. (1970). *Arbitration and collective bargaining: Conflict resolution in labor relations.* New York: McGraw-Hill.

Pruitt, D.G. (1983). Strategic choice in negotiation. *American Behavioral Scientist, 27*(2), 167-194.

Pruitt, D.G. (1986). Trends in the scientific study of negotiation and mediation. *Negotiation Journal, 2*(3), 237-244.

Raiffa, H. (1982). *The art and science of negotiation.* Cambridge, MA: The Belnap Press.

Raiffa, H. (1983). Mediation of conflicts. *American Behavioral Scientist, 27*(2), 195-210.

Roark, A.E. (1978, March). Interpersonal conflict management. *Personnel and Guidance Journal,* pp. 400-402.

Rose, A.M. (1952). Hypotheses concerning mediation. *Personnel Psychology, 5*(3), 187-199.

Rubin, J.Z. (1983). Negotiation: An introduction to some issues and themes. *American Behavioral Scientist, 27*(2), 145-147.

Sanford, R.N. (1964). Individual conflict and organizational interactions. In R. Kahn & E. Boulding (Eds.), *Power and conflict in organizations* (pp. 95-104). New York: Basic Books.

Saposnek, D.T. (1983). *Mediating child custody disputes.* San Francisco: Jossey-Bass.

Sarbin, T.R., & Alalen, V.L. (1968). Role theory. In G. Lindzey & E. Aronson (Eds.), *The handbook of social psychology* (pp. 223-258). Reading, MA: Addison-Wesley Press.

Satir, V. (1972). *Peoplemaking.* Palo Alto, CA: Science and Behavior Books.

Scheinman, M. F. (1977). *Evidence and proof in arbitration.* Ithaca, NY: School of Industrial and Labor Relations, Cornell University.

Sherif, M., & Sherif, C.W. (1953). *Groups in harmony and tension.* New York: Harper & Bros.

Sherif, M. et al. (1954). *Experimental study of positive and negative intergroup attitudes between experimentally produced groups: Robbers' Cave study.* Norman: University of Oklahoma, Intergroup Relations Project.

Simmel, G. (1955). *Conflict and the web of group-affiliations* (trans. K. H. Wolff & R. Bendix). New York: Free Press.

Society of Professionals in Dispute Resolution. (1984). *The elements of good practice in dispute resolution.* Proceedings of the Twelfth Annual Conference, Washington, DC.

Stevens, C.M. (1966). *The analytics of mediation: The role of the neutral.* Unpublished essay, Reed College, Portland, OR.

Susskind, L. & Ozawa, C. (1983). Mediated negotiation in the public sector. *American Behavioral Scientist, 27*(2), 255-279.

Swingle, P. (Ed.). (1970). *The structure of conflict.* New York: Academic Press.

Thibaut, J., & Kelley, H.H. (1959). *The social psychology of groups.* New York: Wiley.

Touval, S., & Zartman, I.W. (1989). Mediation in international conflicts. In K. Kressell, D.G. Pruitt et al. (Eds.), *Mediation research* (pp. 115-137). San Francisco: Jossey-Bass.

Updegraff, C.M. (1970). *Arbitration and labor relations* (3rd ed.). Washington, DC: Bureau of National Affairs.

Vale, J. W. (1975). *What a mediator expects of the parties and how to use a mediator.* Unpublished paper, Oregon State Conciliation Service.

Wall, J.A., Jr. & Rude, D.E. (1989). Judicial mediation of settlement negotiations. In K. Kressel, D.G. Pruitt et al. (Eds.), *Mediation research* (pp. 190-212). San Francisco: Jossey-Bass.

Warschaw, T.A. (1980). *Winning by negotiation.* New York: McGraw-Hill.

Yates, A.J. (1965). *Frustration and conflict.* New York: Van Nostrand Reinhold.

References

Araki, C. T. (1990). Dispute management in the schools. *Mediation Quarterly, 8*(1), 51-62.

Argyris, C. (1970). *Intervention theory and method: A behavioral science view.* Menlo Park, CA: Addison-Wesley.

Aronson, E. (1972). *The social animal.* New York: Viking Press.

Bacharach, S.B., & Lawler, E.J. (1981). *Bargaining: Power, tactics, and outcomes.* San Francisco: Jossey Bass.

Black, H.C. (1968). *Black's Law Dictionary* (rev. 4th ed.). St. Paul, MN: West Publishing Co.

Blake, R.R., & Mouton, J.S. (1962). The intergroup dynamics of win-lose: Conflict and problem-solving collaboration in union-management relations. In M. Sherif (Ed.), *Intergroup relations and leadership* (pp.161-175). New York: Wiley.

Blake, R.R., & Mouton, J.S. (1984). *Solving costly organizational conflicts.* San Francisco: Jossey-Bass

Boulding, E. (1989). Foreword. In L. Kreisberg, T.A. Northrup, & S.J. Thorson (Eds.), *Intractable conflicts and their transformation.* Syracuse, NY: Syracuse University Press.

Bruneau, T. (1989). Empathy and listening: A conceptual review and theoretical directions. *Journal of the International Listening Association, 3,* 1-21.

Budd, R.W., & Ruben, B.D. (1972). *Approaches to human communication.* New York: Spartan Books.

Burger, W. (1985). Using arbitration to achieve justice. *American Arbitration Journal, 40*(4), 3-4.

Calero, H.H., & Oskam, B. (1983). *Negotiating the deal you want: Talking your way to success in business, community affairs, and personal encounters.* New York: Dodd, Mead.

Canetti, E. (1963). *Crowds and power.* (trans. Carol Stewart from German). New York: Viking Press.

Carnevale, P.J.D., Conlon, D.E., Hanisch, K.A., & Harris, K.L. (1989a). Experimental research on the strategic-choice model of mediation. In K. Kressell, D.G. Pruitt et al. (Eds.), *Mediation research* (pp. 344-367). San Francisco: Jossey-Bass.

Carnevale, P.J.D., Lim, R.G., & McLaughlin, M.E. (1989b). Contingent mediator behavior and its effectiveness. In K. Kressel, D.G. Pruitt et al. (Eds.), *Mediation research* (pp. 213-240). San Francisco: Jossey Bass.

Carnevale, P.J., Putnam, L., Conlon, D.E., & O'Connor, J.M. (1991). Mediator behavior and effectiveness in community mediation. In K.G. Duffy, J.W. Grosch, & P.V. Olczak (Eds.), *Community mediation: A handbook for practitioners and reasearchers* (pp. 119-136). New York: Guilford.

Cobb, S. (1991). Einsteinian practice and Newtonian discouse: An ethical crisis in mediation. *Negotiation Journal, 7*(1), 87-102.

Cohen, H. (1980). *You can negotiate anything: How to get what you want.* Secaucus, NJ: Lyle Stuart.

Coser, L.A. (1956). *The functions of social conflict* Glencoe, IL: Free Press.

Coulson, R. (1983). *Fighting fair: Family mediation will work for you.* New York: Free Press.

Coulson, R. (1990).The decision making process in arbitration. *The Arbitration Journal, 45*(3), 37-41.

Craig, J.H., & Craig, M. (1974). *Synergic power: Beyond domination and permissiveness.* Berkeley, CA: Proactive Press.

Davey, H. (1972). How arbitrators decide cases. *The Arbitration Journal, 27*(4), 274-287.

Davis, A.M. (1991). How to ensure high-quality mediation services: The issue of credentialing. In K. G. Duffy, J.W. Grosch, & P.V. Olczak (Eds.), *Community mediation: A handbook for practitioners and researchers* (pp. 209-225). New York: Guilford.

Davis, A.M. (1993). Mediation: The field of dreams? If we build it, they will come! *Negotiation Journal, 9*(1), 5-12.

Davis, A.M., & Salem, R.A. (1984). Dealing with power imbalances in the mediation of interpersonal disputes. *Mediation Quarterly, 6,* 17-26.

Deutsch, M. (1971). Conflict and its resolution. In C.G. Smith (Ed.), *Conflict resolution: Contributions of the behavioral sciences* (pp. 36-57). Notre Dame, IN: University of Notre Dame Press.

Deutsch, M. (1977). *The resolution of conflict: Constructive and destructive processes.* New Haven, CT: Yale University Press.

Deutsch, M. (1985). *Distributive justice: A social psychological perspective.* New Haven, CT: Yale University Press.

Dobson, T., & Miller, V. (1978). *Giving in to get your way.* New York: Delacorte Press.

Donohue, W.A. (1989). Communication competence in mediation. In K. Kressel, D.G. Pruitt et al. (Eds.), *Mediation research* (pp. 322-343). San Francisco: Jossey Bass.

Duffy, K.G., Grosch, J.W., & Olczak, P.V. (Eds.). (1991). *Community mediation: A handbook for practitioners and researchers.* New York: Guilford.

Duke, J.T. (1976). *Conflict and power in social life.* Provo, UT: Brigham Young University Press.

Erickson, S.K., & Erickson, M.S. (1988). *Family mediation casebook.* New York: Brunner/Mazel.

Evarts, W.R., Greenstone, J.L., Kirkpatrick, G.J., & Leviton, S.C. (1983). *Winning through accommodation: The mediator's handbook.* Dubuque, IA: Kendall Hunt.

Festinger, L. (1957). *A theory of cognitive dissonance.* Evanston, IL: Row Peterson.

Filley, A.C. (1975). *Interpersonal conflict resolution.* Glenview, IL: Scott, Foresman.

Fisher, R. (1983). Negotiating power: Getting and using influence. *American Behavioral Scientist, 27*(2), 149-166.

Fisher, R., & Ury, W. (1981). *Getting to yes: Negotiating agreement without giving in.* Boston: Houghton Mifflin.

Folberg, J., & Taylor, A. (1984). *Mediation: A comprehensive guide to resolving conflicts without litigation.* San Francisco: Jossey Bass.

Folger, J.P., & Poole, M.S. (1984). *Working through conflict. A communication perspective.* Dallas, TX: Scott, Foresman and Company.

Forlenza, S.G. (1991). Mediation and psychotherapy: Parallel processes. In K.G. Duffy, J.W. Grosch, & P.V. Olczak (Eds.), *Community mediation: A handbook for practitioners and researchers* (pp. 227-239). New York: Guilford.

Funkhouser, G.R. (1986). *The power of persuasion: A guide to moving ahead in business and life.* New York: Times Books (Random House).

Gibbs, W. (1963). The Kpelle moot: A therapeutic model for informal justice settlement. *Africa, 33,* 1-11.

Giffin, K., & Patton, B.R. (1971). Personal trust in human interaction. In K. Giffin & B.R. Patton (Eds.), *Readings in interpersonal communication* (pp. 375-391). New York: Harper & Bros.

Gould, J., & Kolb, W.L. (Eds.). (1964). *Dictionary of the social sciences.* New York: Free Press.

Greenhalgh, L. (1987). The case against winning in negotiations. *The Negotiation Journal, 3*(2), 167-174.

Haley, J. (1969). *The power tactics of Jesus Christ and other essays.* New York: Avon Books.

Haynes, J., & Haynes, C. (1989). *Mediating divorce: Casebook of strategies for successful family negotiations.* San Francisco: Jossey Bass.

Hemingway, E. (1933). *Winner take nothing.* New York: Macmillan.

Hocker, J.L., & Wilmot, W.W. (1985). *Interpersonal conflict* (2nd ed.). Dubuque, IA: Wm. C. Brown Publishers.

Honeyman, C. (1990). The common core of mediation. *Mediation Quarterly, 8*(1), op. 78.

Hunter, S. (1989). The roots of environmental conflict in the Taho Basin. In L. Kreisberg, T.A. Northrup, & S.J. Thorson (Eds.), *Intractable conflicts and their transformation* (pp. 25-40). Syracuse, NY: Syracuse University Press.

Hurwitz, R. (1991). "Up the down staircase? A practical theory of de-escalation. In L. Kreisberg & S.J. Thorson (Eds.), *Timing the de-escalation of international conflicts* (pp. 123-151). Syracuse, NY: Syracuse University Press.

Ilich, J. (1973). *The art and skill of successful negotiation.* Englewood Cliffs, NJ: Prentice-Hall.

Instrument Workers Local 116 v. Minneapolis-Honeywell Regulator Company. 59 LRRM 2660, 2661 [United States District Court, Eastern District, PA]. No. 31714, November 26, 1963.

Jacobson, W.D. (1972). *Power and interpersonal relations.* Belmont, CA: Wadsworth Publishing Co.

Janis, I., & Mann, L. (1977). *Decision making: A psychological analysis of conflict, choice, and commitment.* New York: Free Press.

Johannesen, R.L. (1983). *Ethics in human communication* (2nd ed.). Prospect Heights, IL: Waveland Press.

Johnson, C.E. (1987). An introduction to powerful and powerless talk in the classroom. *Communication Education, 36*(2), 167-177.

Jones, D.L. (Ed.) (1967). *Problems in proof in arbitration.* Washington, DC: Bureau of National Affairs.

Kahn, R.L., & Boulding, E. (Eds.). (1964). *Power and conflict in organizations.* New York: Basic Books.

Katz, D., & Kahn, R.L. (1966). *The social psychology of organizations.* New York: Wiley.

Kelley, H.H. (1971). *Attribution in social interaction.* New York: General Learning Press.

Kelley, H.H. (1987). Toward A taxonomy of interpersonal conflict processes. In S. Oskamp & S. Spacapan (Eds.), *Interpersonal processes* (pp. 122-147). Beverly Hills, CA: Sage.

Kelly, J.B. (1983). Mediation and psychotherapy: Distinguishing the differences. *Mediation Quarterly, 1*, 33-44.

Keltner, J.W. (1957). *Group discussion processes.* New York: Longmans Green.

Keltner, J.W. (1965). Communication and the labor-management mediation process: Some aspects and hypotheses. *Journal of Communication, 15*, 64-75.

Keltner, J.W. (1973). *Elements of interpersonal communication* Belmont, CA: Wadsworth.

Keltner, J.W. (1986). Controlling and correcting our messages: Feedback and response. In *Successful communication techniques reading and resource book* (6th ed.). Corvallis, OR: SAIC.

Keltner, J.W. (1987a). When we make decisions. In K.A. McCarthy (Ed.), *Successful communication techniques: Reading and resource book* (7th ed.). Corvallis, OR: SAIC.

Keltner, J.W. (1987b). *Mediation: Toward a civilized system of dispute resolution.* Annandale, VA: Speech Communication Association.

Keltner, J.W. (1990). Foundations and structures of the powerful communication workshops: The origins and development of self and interpersonal communication training. In R. House (Ed.), *Reading and resource book* (10th ed., pp. 1-24). Corvallis, OR: SAIC.

Kennedy, M. M. (1984). *Powerbase: How to build it, how to keep it.* New York: Ballantine Books.

Kiersey, D., & Bates, M. (1978). *Please understand me.* Del Mar, CA: Prometheus Nemesis Books.

King, A. (1987). *Power and communication.* Prospect Heights, IL: Waveland Press.

Kohn, A. (1986). *No contest: The case against competition.* Boston, MA: Houghton-Mifflin.

Kolb, D.M., & Rubin, J.Z. (1989). *Research into mediation: What we know now. What's left to learn.* Washington, DC: Dispute Resolution Forum of National Institute for Dispute Resolution.

Kolb, D., & Sheppard, B.H. (1985). Do managers mediate, or even arbitrate? *Negotiation Journal, 1*(4), 379-400.

Korda, M. (1975). *Power! How to get it, how to use it.* New York: Random House.

Kreisberg, L. (1991). Introduction: Timing, conditions, strategies, and errors. In L. Kreisberg & S.J. Thorson (Eds.), *Timing the de-escalation of international conflicts.* (pp. 1-27). Syracuse, NY: Syracuse University Press.

Kreisberg, L. (1993). Ethnicity, nationalism and violent conflict in the 1990s. *The Peace Studies Bulletin, 2*(1-2), 24-28.

Kressel, K., & Pruitt, D.G. (1985). The mediation of social conflict. *Journal of Social Issues, 41*(2).

Kressel, K., Pruitt, D.G. et al. (Eds.). (1989). *Mediation research.* San Francisco: Jossey Bass.

Lawson, E.W., Jr. (1981). Arbitrator acceptability: Factors affecting selection. *The Arbitration Journal, 36*(4), 22-29.

Lax, D.A., & Sebenius, J.K. (1986). *The Manager as negotiator: Bargaining for cooperation and competitive gain.* New York: Free Press.

Lemmon, J.A. (Ed.). (1984a). Reaching effective agreements. *Mediation Quarterly, 3.*

Lemmon, J.A. (Ed.). (1984b). Ethics, standards, and professional challenges. *Mediation Quarterly, 4.*

Lemmon, J.A. (Ed.). (1984c). Procedures for guiding the divorce mediation process. *Mediation Quarterly, 5.*

Lemmon, J.A. (1985a). *Family mediation practice.* New York: Free Press.

Lemmon, J.A. (1985b). Evaluative criteria and outcomes. *Mediation Quarterly, 10.*

Lewicki, R.J., & Litterer, J.A. (1985). *Negotiation.* Homewood, IL: Irwin.

Likert, R., & Likert, J.G. (1976). *New ways of managing conflict.* New York: McGraw-Hill.

Loomis, J.L. (1959). Communication and the development of trust. *Human Relations, 12*, 305-315.

Maggiolo, W.A. (1971). *Techniques of mediation in labor disputes.* Dobbs Ferry, NY: Oceana Publications.

Mannix, E.A., & Neale, M.A. (1993). Power imbalance and the pattern of negotiation in dyadic negotiation. *Group Decision and Negotiation,* 2(2), 119-134.

May, R. (1972). *Power and innocence: A search for the sources of violence.* New York: W. W. Norton.

McClelland, D.C. (1980). The two faces of power. In P.P. Dawson & S.C. Iman (Eds.), *Introducing organizational behavior: A book of readings* (pp. 215-227). Lexington, MA: Ginn Custom Publishing.

McDonald, J. (1991). Further exploration of track two diplomacy. In L. Kreisberg & S.J. Thorson (Eds.), *Timing the de-escalation of international conflicts* (pp. 201-220). Syracuse, NY: Syracuse University Press.

McKay, R. (1990). Ethical considerations in alternative dispute resolution. *The Arbitration Journal,* 45(1), 15-28.

Mittenthal, R. (1991). Whither arbitration? Major changes in the last half century. *The Arbitration Journal,* 46(4), 24-32.

Moore, C.W. (1986). *The mediation process: Practical strategies for resolving conflict.* San Francisco: Jossey Bass.

Most, B., & Starr, H. (1983). Conceptualizing "war." *The Journal of Conflict Resolution,* 27(1), 137-159.

Myers, I.B. (1987). *Introduction to type: A description of the theory and appplications of the Myers-Briggs type indicator.* Palo Alto, CA: Consulting Psychologists Press.

Nicolau, G. (1986). Community mediation: Progress and problems. *Viewpoint on Mediation, 1*(3), 3-10.

Nierenberg, G.I. (1968). *The art of negotiating.* New York: Hawthorn Books.

Nolan, D.R. (1979). *Labor arbitration law and practice.* St. Paul, MN: West Publishing.

Nye, R.D. (1973). *Conflict among humans: Some basic psychological and social psychological considerations.* New York: Springer.

Peabody, G., & Dietterich, P. (1973). *Powerplay: A simulation dealing with collaboration, negotiation, and coercion.* Naperville, IL: Powerplay.

Pendergast, W.R. (1990). Managing the negotiation agenda. *Negotation Journal,* 6(2), 135-146.

Pruitt, D.G. (1981). *Negotiation behavior.* New York: Academic Press.

Pruitt, D.G., McGillicuddy, N.B., Welton, G.L., & Fry, W.R. (1989). Process of mediation in dispute settlement centers. In K. Kressel, D.G. Pruitt et al. (Eds.), *Mediation research* (pp. 368-393). San Francisco: Jossey Bass.

Rangarajan, L.N. (1985). *The limitation of conflict: A theory of bargaining and negotiation.* New York: St. Martin's Press.

Rapaport, A. (1960). *Fights, games, and debates.* Ann Arbor: The University of Michigan Press.

Ray, D.E. (1992). On writing the post-hearing arbitration brief. *The Arbitration Journal,* 47(4), 58-60.

Raven, B.M., & Rubin, J.Z. (1976). *Social psychology: People in groups.* New York: Wiley.

Robbins, A. (1986). *Unlimited power: The new science of personal achievement.* New York: Simon and Schuster.

Robert, M. (1928). *Managing conflict from the inside out.* Austin, TX: Learning Concepts.

Roehe, J.A., & Cook, F. (1989). Mediation in interpersonal disputes: Effectiveness and limitations In K. Kressel, D.G. Pruitt et al. (Eds.), *Mediation research* (pp. 31-52). San Francisco: Jossey-Bass.

Rosanova, M.J. (1983). Mediation: Professional dynamics. *Mediation Quarterly, 1,* 63-74.

Ruben, H.L. (1980). *Competing: Understanding and winning the strategic games we all play.* New York: Lippincott & Crowell.

Ruben, J., & Brown, B. (1975). *Social psychology of bargaining and negotiation.* New York: Acacemic Press.

Rubin, J.Z. (1991). The timing of ripeness and the ripeness of timing. In L. Kreisberg & S.J. Thorson (Eds.), *Timing the de-escalation of international conflicts.* (pp. 237-246). Syracuse, NY: Syracuse University Press.

Rule, G.W. (1962). *The art of negotiation.* Author.

Sacks, H. R., & Kurlantzick, L. S. (1987). *Missing witnesses, missing testimony, and missing theories. How much initiative by labor arbitrators.* Stoneham, ME: Butterworth Legal Publishers.

Schatzki, M. (1981). *Negotiation: The art of getting what you want.* Bergenfield, NJ: New American Library.

Seitz, P. (1979). Some observations on the role of an arbitrator. *The Arbitration Journal,* 34(3), 3-8.

Shepard, H.A. (1964). Responses to situations of composition and conflict. In R.L. Kahn & E. Boulding (Eds.), *Power and conflict in organizations* (pp.127-135). New York: Basic Books.

Sherif, M. (Ed). (1962). *Intergroup relations and leadership.* New York: Wiley.

Sherif, M. (1966). *In common predicament. Social psychology of intergroup conflict and cooperation.* Boston: Houghton Mifflin.

Sherif, M. et al. (1954). *Experimental study of positive and negative intergroup attitudes between experimentally produced groups: Robbers' Cave study.* Norman: University of Oklahoma Intergroup Relations Project.

Shimanoff, S.B. (1980). *Communication rules: Theory and research.* Beverly Hills, CA: Sage.

Simkin, W.E. (1971). *Mediation and the dynamics of collective bargaining.* Washington, DC: Bureau of National Affairs.

Singer, L. et. al. (1989a). *Principles concerning qualifications.* Washington, DC: SPIDR.

Singer, L. et al. (1989b). *Qualifying neutrals: The basic principles. Report of the SPIDR Commission on Qualifications.* Washington, DC: SPIDR.

Siu, R.G.H. (1979). *The craft of power.* New York: Wiley.

Smith, C.G. (Ed.). (1971). *Conflict resolution: Contributions of the behavioral sciences.* Notre Dame, IN: University of Notre Dame Press.

Stagner, R., & Rosen, H. (1965). *Psychology of union-management relations.* Belmont, CA: Wadsworth.

Terhune, K.W. (1970). The effect of personality on cooperation and conflict. In P. Swingle (Ed.), *The structure of conflict* (pp. 193-234). New York: Academic Press.

Tjosvold, D., & Johnson, D.W. (1983). *Productive conflict management: Perspectives for organizations.* Edina, MN: Interaction Book Company.

Ury, W.L., Brett, J.M., & Goldberg, S.B. (1988). *Getting disputes resolved: Designing systems to cut the costs of conflict.* San Francisco: Jossey Bass.

Van Hook, M.P. (1990). Resolving conflict between farmers and creditors: An analysis of the farmer-creditor mediation process. *Mediation Quarterly, 8*(1), 63-72.

Wall, J.A., Jr., & Blum, M. (1991). Community mediation in the People's Republic of China. *Journal of Conflict Resolution, 35*(1), 3-20.

Wall, J.A., Jr., & Callister, R.R. (1993, June). *Ho'oponopono: Mediation in Hawaii.* Paper delivered at the annual convention of the Interntional Society of Conflict Management, Hengelhoff, Belgium.

Wall, J.A., Jr., & Lynn, A. (1993). Mediation: A current review. *Journal of Conflict Resolution, 37*(1), 160-194.

Walton, R.E., & McKersie, R. B. (1965). *A behavioral theory of labor negotiations.* New York: McGraw-Hill Book Co.

Walton, R.E. & McKersie, R.B. (1969). *Interpersonal peacemaking: Confrontations and third party consultation.* Reading, MA: Addison-Wesley.

Watzlawick, P., Weakland, J.H., & Fisch, R. (1974). Change: Principles of problem formulation and problem resolution. New York: W.W. Norton.

Welton, G.L., Pruitt, D.G., McGillicuddy, C.A., Ippolito, C.A., & Zubek, J.M. (1992). Antecedents and characteristics of caucusing in community mediation. *The International Journal of Conflict Managment, 3*(4), 303-317.

Zack, A.M. (1977). *Grievance arbitration: A practical guide.* Geneva: International Labour Organization.

Zack, A.M. (1985). *Public sector mediation.* Washington, DC: Bureau of National Affairs.

Zartman, I.W. (1977). Negotiation as a joint decision-making process. *Journal of Conflict Resolution, XXI*(4), 619-638.

Zartman, IW., & Aurik, J. (1991). Power strategies in de-escalation. In L. Kreisberg & S.J. Thorson (Ed.), *Timing the de-escalation of international conflicts* (pp. 152-181). Syracuse, NY: Syracuse University Press.

Zimbardo, P.G. (1972). Pathology of imprisonment. *Society, 9*(6), 36-51.

Zisk, K.M. (1990). Soviet academic theories on international conflict and negotiation. *Journal of Conflict Resolution, 34*(4), 678-693.

Zumeta, Z.D. (1991). *Current issues in family mediation.* Paper presented at the conference of the Society of Professionals in Dispute Resolution, San Diego, CA.

Subject Index